MISSION

East Anglia, United Kingdom

Cromer
Splasher 5
Buncher 5
Gallant Lady
Crash Site ✖
Norwich
• Hethel (389th BG)
Old Buckenham
(453rd BG) •
• Tibenham (445th BG)
• Hardwick (93rd BG)

Western Europe

North Sea
England
Cromer
Old Buckenham
Tibenham
Zuiderzee
Wilhelmshaven
Kiel
• Hamburg
• Bremen
Amsterdam
Hardenberg
Achmer
Berlin
London
Holland
• Gilze-Rijen
• Halle
• Brunswick
Beachy Head
Pas-de-Calais
Siracourt
• Antwerp
Germany
English Channel
Bonnières
Belgium
• Gotha
Saint-Aubin-sur-Mer
Eppstein
Frankfurt
• Paris
Russelsheim
Mannheim
• Troyes
• Ludwigshafen
• Homburg
• Tonnerre
France
Munich
Switzerland
Austria

MISSION

Jimmy Stewart and the Fight for Europe

Robert Matzen

GoodKnight Books
Pittsburgh, Pennsylvania

GoodKnight Books

© 2016 by Robert Matzen

Foreword © 2016 by Leonard Maltin

Published by GoodKnight Books, an imprint of Paladin Communications, Pittsburgh, Pennsylvania

Printed in the United States of America

Library of Congress Control Number: 2016946209

ISBN 978-0-9962740-5-0

To Jim Stewart, Clem Leone, Bill Minor, Barry Shillito, and all the other fliers of the 445th Bomb Group (H), and to the men on the ground who worked all night to get the Liberators ready for another mission.

CONTENTS

Foreword ix
Prologue: Unreality 1
1. High-Strung 6
2. Soaring 24
3. Factory Work 27
4 Silver Birds 34
5. Reliable Girls 36
6. A Storybook Life 43
7. Mr. Smith Goes Hollywood 45
8. Seeing History 62
9. Restless Spirit 64
10. The Eagle 71
11. Alias James Smith 73
12. Overachiever 88
13. Static Personnel 90
14. A Game of Chess 97
15. Destination: Meat Grinder 99
16. Boy Scout 116
17. Daft 119
18. Shakedown 121
19. Pushed by Angels 134
20. Mission Today 137

CONTENTS

21. A Late Breakfast 156
22. Topaz Blue 160
23. Bailout 170
24. Roman Candle 176
25. January on the Rhine 185
26. The Dungeon of Eppstein 197
27. Iceman 199
28. Baptism 205
29. Boys Will Be Boys 211
30. Mother Nature's a Bitch 218
31. Fat Dogs 222
32. Argument, Part One 224
33. Argument, Part Two 234
34. Bloodbath 239
35. Physics Lesson 251
36. The Big B 255
37. No-Nonsense Men 260
38. The Sumatran 269
39. Invasionitis 272
40. They Are Coming! 281
41. Germany Burning 284
42. The Great Aviation 290
43. Grounded 293
44. Marching to Death 297
45. Aged in East Anglia 300
46. Gold Light 311
Epilogue: Reaching Beyond 318
Acknowledgments 329
Chapter Notes 335
Glossary 357
Selected Bibliography 359
Index 363

FOREWORD

Ask anyone to describe James Stewart and they're likely to re-call a genial man with an "aw, shucks" manner. This is the pub-lic persona he cultivated and, being a canny showman, he seldom broke character, whether being interviewed by Johnny Carson on *The Tonight Show* or promoting one of his older films' release on home video, as he did for *Harvey* and *The Glenn Miller Story*, among others. He seemed so down-to-earth that fans who had never met him referred to him as Jimmy, not James.

No one I've ever spoken to cites the hard-bitten Stewart that audiences of the 1950s came to know in such films as *Winchester '73*, *The Naked Spur*, and *Bend of the River*. Even Alfred Hitchcock's *Vertigo* isn't thought of as a typical or emblematic Stewart role, although the film is widely revered. It was the darkest character the actor ever played. Moviegoers accepted him in all these guis-es, yet in the public consciousness they were eclipsed by Stewart's winning personality—and the memory of such enduring movies as *Mr. Smith Goes to Washington* and *Destry Rides Again*.

Yet, as we learn in Robert Matzen's compelling narrative, those intense characters he essayed speak not only to the actor's versatili-ty but to the aftermath of his sobering, often shattering, experienc-es during World War II.

Nowhere is this clearer than in the first movie he made following his years of service overseas. *It's a Wonderful Life* was a challenging project for him and his director, Frank Capra. Both of them had been reshaped by the war and were understandably nervous about resuming their careers. It is fitting that Matzen bookends his story by describing Stewart's return to the world of make-believe that this job represented in 1946.

This is not to say that he was a one-trick pony in the 1930s and early '40s. His earnestness was his stock-in-trade, but he reveals a comedic cynicism in *The Shop Around the Corner* and an unexpected sophistication in *The Philadelphia Story*, which earned him his only Academy Award.

But *It's a Wonderful Life* calls on him to express a range of emotions he had never tapped into before. After all, here is a man so overcome by despair and the feeling of failure that he tries to commit suicide. The scene in which he breaks down while sitting at Nick's Bar was so draining that the actor begged his director not to make him do it a second time. After the first take, Capra wanted to do another and have his camera push in toward Stewart; he accomplished the effect with a laboratory blowup instead.

Capra understood that in order to reach a genuinely happy ending he had to bring his hero—and us in the audience—to the lowest depths first. Only then could we share in his ultimate triumph at the finale.

James Stewart's public face wasn't artifice: he was a decent, hard-working man who was well-liked by his colleagues. What the public didn't see was the effort he put into every performance. Like any great artist, he made it look easy…and that made it easy to take his work for granted.

He also had a strong code of ethics and refused to discuss his service during the war, but for a selective anecdote or two. That is why Robert Matzen's groundbreaking book is so valuable. He does something that usually makes me wary, getting inside his subject's head and recreating specific moments in the heat of preparation for combat...but his work is rooted in such extensive research that it has the ring of truth in every case. That's what won me over.

We've read a great many tributes to the men who fought this war and remained silent afterward, blending back into the fabric of American society. They've been called the greatest generation and depicted as a band of brothers. Both appellations are appropriate, and James Stewart's story bears them out. The fact that he had to overcome so many obstacles—in Hollywood and Washington—in order to leave his movie-star life behind and fight for his country on the front lines makes his saga all the more interesting.

Here was a man who would not capitalize on his true-life heroism and went on to play a number of antiheroes in his post-war career. He never lost the humility and relatability that made him a star in the first place, but there is no question that his experiences during World War II deepened and enriched his acting. With this book, we can appreciate James Stewart and his career with a perspective we have never had before.

Leonard Maltin

Leonard Maltin is a film critic and historian with many books to his credit, including his long-running Leonard Maltin's Movie Guide *and its companion,* Leonard Maltin's Classic Movie Guide. *He teaches at the USC School for Cinematic Arts, hosts a weekly podcast, and can be seen regularly on ReelzChannel and Turner Classic Movies. He holds court at leonardmaltin.com.*

Prologue
UNREALITY

The tall man stepped out into a San Fernando evening on one of the longest days of the year, and a hot one, one of the hottest. He had dressed for work in a heavy gray jacket and gray trousers and held a black scarf in his hand; he couldn't bear to place the scarf about his neck until he was asked to do so because, oh, it was hot. He stood there chomping his gum—he had been a big gum chewer since he was a boy.

As if conjured from thought, a nervous-looking kid ran out an umbrella and held it high over the tall man to offer a little relief because, even at 7:30 in the evening, that low, slanting sun produced sweat. It was beautiful light, gold light they called it, and it made the best Technicolor footage anyone could imagine. Too bad they weren't shooting on color stock and rolling right this moment to capture that light.

Off to the north, through the haze, he could see the San Gabriel Mountains gleaming high and brown. The mountains served as a constant reminder that this was desert, no question about it. There were orchards about, and some farms, so there was green here and there. The Hollywood people had discovered the San Fernando Valley some years back. Raoul Walsh was among the first and sold his ranch—just a mile or so to the south—to Clark Gable and Carole Lombard. It was so sad what had happened to

1

Carole, and of course to Clark, who had ended up in the Army Air Corps and tried his best, but a movie star living it up in the Air Corps just couldn't work for long.

The young fella continued to angle the umbrella so it shielded the tall man from the setting sun. The boy was eighteen maybe, fresh faced, with adolescent pimples and abundant energy. Imagine, to be a young American male untouched by war. Not so long ago, the tall man had commanded young men like this one. Why, this kid had probably never said good-bye to a friend in the morning and then learned of his death by evening or, worse, watched him die. Or been at a crash scene and confronted pieces of bodies. But harder than the blood and guts was the endless strain of *being* at war. It was easy to spot the ones who had been over there and understood—one look in the eyes separated those who'd served in harm's way from those who hadn't.

The tall man stood looking up a long main street in a booming town, a long, thriving avenue with an island in the middle that separated the flow of traffic. The island featured an endless row of gnarled oaks, and parked cars lined the street on both sides. Strange how there was no traffic in a town this busy, but then no one had yet cued the cars.

From silence and stillness came a stirring, and in mere moments people were scurrying all about, thirty, forty, fifty people, some he recognized, most he didn't, running this way and that, orders shouted, tense shapes zipping by, heavy equipment roaring past, meters produced and checked, and all the while the tall man stood there, under the shade of the umbrella. He could feel his heart hammering and the sweat flowing under his coat, drenching his underarms and his undershirt, front and back. Thank God this was a night shoot so they wouldn't see. Thank God it didn't matter.

It was all a person could do not to laugh at snow in June in the San Fernando Valley. The tall man had seen snow all right, snow in the Dutch lowlands, snow all across Europe. He had seen

2

it near Denmark and in the distant Alps. He had lived for months in a world that subsisted at forty below zero, where all that he knew was physical pain and living, breathing ice. Now, he beheld a snowstorm in the desert, the creation of special effects men who used several hundred tons of gypsum to literally plaster a town with snow—on the gnarled oaks, on the cars, on the streets, on the storefronts, fire hydrants, mailboxes, fences, and homes. It was a town covered in snow that would never melt and would have to be bulldozed and removed on trucks with the buildings and trees.

The sun had finally decided to set, which only increased the tall man's agitation. Performance level, that's what he would need in a few more moments. Performance level. But what did that mean? And where was he exactly? He couldn't believe he was here; really, was he back here? Or was he still cracked up? Was he still flak happy, on a flak farm? Who could tell what was real after all that had happened over five long years. But he felt he was here, and this seemed to be reality, so he would go with it and see what happened. He wasn't sleeping well, and that added to his disorientation. He worried about his career and if this job would pan out, or whether he'd be just one more guy back in the States who didn't know where his next paycheck would come from. Oh hell, who was he kidding? He had it better than any of them because he had a name and a face and a resumé while headlines screamed about the lack of everything faced by returning servicemen—lack of work, housing, food, even clothes. In every newspaper, in every magazine were stories about families who didn't recognize the boys who had come home. This isn't my son. This isn't my husband; this isn't my brother. He's so cold, so distant, and the rages, the nightmares!

Oh yes, the nightmares came every night. There he was on oxygen at 20,000 feet with 190s zipping past, spraying lead and firing rockets, flak bursting about the cockpit. B-24s hit, burning, spinning out of formation. Bail out! Bail out! Do you see any chutes? How many chutes? Whose ship was it? Oh no, not him!

Not them! Bodies, pieces of bodies smacking off the windshield. And the most frequent dream, an explosion under him and the plane lifted by it and the feeling that this was the end. There he was, straddling a hole at his feet big enough to fall through, feeling the thin air at thirty below biting at his skin and swirling as he choked on the stench of gunpowder, looking four miles straight down at Germany. No wonder he had the shakes sometimes. No wonder he couldn't hear so well after all the flights surrounded by the drone of four big engines, missions seven or eight or nine hours at a stretch.

The boss appeared, and he was as nervous as the tall man. His eyes said, yes, I was over there. What a pair they made, the little boss and the stilted giant. Neither liked to let on he was anxious but both were—the stakes were so high; two war jockeys trying to make their way in a world of peace and recovery, and what if it didn't work out for them and they ended up on the outs? What if they *were* has-beens after all, like it was whispered? What if it all fell apart for them and nobody paid for tickets and nobody came to see them in the dark? What then? The hardware business? Maybe that's what destiny had in store all along.

The light had faded now, and it could almost be called night. The tall man breathed deeply, a sigh of relief that the sun no longer pounded. Umbrella boy had folded up shop and run off. The globes of the streetlights started to illuminate all along the way, and then the town Christmas lights strung on the thoroughfare in jangling ribbons of color began to glow. He could almost imagine Christmases back home. Almost. He asked himself again, what's real? Is the snow real? Is the desert real? Is it really Christmas? Who am I and where am I?

These were very good questions for a man who had seen what he had seen and done what he had done. Thousands of men had been captains in the Army Air Forces. Hundreds had been majors and colonels. But only one had seen those years through his eyes

4

and lived them inside his brain. Only he could know what it all meant to him, to his family, all of it, the years and places and peo-ple. All those wonderful guys he had met, trained with, flown with. Many still living, but so many, so very many, dead. They had died so young, after sharing breakfast with him and climbing into those ships with him. He had briefed them, said happy landings, given them thumbs up, a smile and a wave, and how many never made it back? How many had gone to meet their fate too soon? How many letters home had he written? He saw their faces sometimes in the night, or he saw people on the street in Hollywood who looked like those kids now gone.

The shakes? Oh yes, he had the shakes. Many nights he woke in a drenching sweat with his parachute snapped in place, ready to bail out. Ready to hit that sounder because the plane had been shot to pieces by enemy fighters and was limping home.

This man stood there, sweating under his heavy winter clothes in the thinnest light of June, ready to take on the make-believe of Hollywood. He knew his mission this night, and he knew his dialogue. He had eaten extra, all he was able, because it would be a long session and a hard one, with all that running and shouting and jubilation.

Places! It was time. Motivation? Ha! He was motivated all right. His head swam as he stood there, this tall man stuck in the past, and the present, thinking back to the men who made him who he was, those guys who had given him the mission in the first place. It was all he could do to keep standing there for all the memories.

1
HIGH-STRUNG

James Maitland Stewart had to fly. His earliest memories of flight involved colorful covers of *Literary Digest* depicting the Great War, then in progress, and the incredible use of air power by both sides. Jim tacked up each magazine cover on the wall in his bedroom. "Airplanes were the last thing I thought of every night and the first thing I thought of every morning," he would say as an adult.

Jim had entered the world on May 20, 1908, in the quiet, hilly western Pennsylvania town of Indiana, the county seat with a population of 7,000. He was the first child of Spanish-American War veteran Alexander Mead Stewart and his wife of less than two years, Elizabeth Ruth Jackson Stewart. There was nothing special about Indiana, since America was full of towns roughly that size and that population. King coal ruled the area, with mines boring into the hard earth, undercutting the landscape, which also featured lush and rolling farm fields. An educational facility for teachers, the Indiana Normal School, sat a few blocks south of the Stewart home on Philadelphia Street.

Normal was the word for Indiana, and Jim experienced a normal childhood rooted in faith. "Religion was an important part of our lives," said Jim. "We used to go to church a lot. The Presbyterian Church. My mother played the organ and my father sang in the choir." Jim's friends visiting to dinner would watch the family hold hands as Mr. Stewart said grace.

Jim's father was a favorite son in Indiana, and among his community involvements was service on the volunteer fire department. Some described Alex Stewart as "the town character," a tall, loud, extroverted, opinionated, often-flighty man who required a fair amount of attention and pampering, which made it handy that the family hardware store served as the crossroads of the town of Indiana. He greeted his customers loudly, remembered their names, and always had a story to tell. Earlier in life, he drank to excess and drinking made him grow wild. Later, he would cut down on the booze but not by much.

"Alex should have been an actor. He was a born actor. He made it a business to be a character," said D. Hall Blair, one of Jim's childhood friends. Only one human could wrangle Alex Stewart and that was his wife, Bessie, a stable, strong, commonsense, salt-of-the-earth woman whom her son Jim would describe as "cultured, elegant, and refined."

Young Jim—known as Jimbo to his father and Jimsey to his mother—grew up seeing Dad as his role model every day, and walking in his father's long shadow made it necessary that Jim become something of a performer as well. It was expected. At the same time, Jim possessed none of his father's high volume or blunt extroversion; quite the contrary, Jim grew up quiet like his mother and high-strung, with a nervous stomach that made it difficult to eat a full meal. His whole life, nobody would know what Jim was thinking.

The Stewart boy played ball and caught tadpoles in Two Lick Creek. When a customer offered an accordion as payment in lieu of cash at the hardware store, Jim picked it up and started playing, and liked it well enough to take lessons from the Italian barber up the street. Jim lived a normal childhood with friends Hall Blair and Bill Neff until war in Europe broke out for the United States in 1917 when Jim was nine. At that point, life changed because his father went back into military service as a captain of artillery.

A profound memory in Jim's life involved traveling to New York City, where the Stewarts had trudged up the steps of the Statue of Liberty and Jim had attempted to climb out on her nose, despite his fear of the great height, because he had wanted to prove to his father how brave he was. Alex had always set such high standards and demanded such perfection that Jim felt motivated to take extreme measures to prove himself.

The trip also was memorable because Jim and his parents had watched President Woodrow Wilson deliver a speech at Carnegie Hall. Days later, on October 17, 1917, Capt. Alexander Stewart shipped out for Europe and the Great War.

Jim had grown up on war, beginning when Fergus Moorhead, his great-great-great grandfather on his father's side, served in the Cumberland County Militia in the American Revolution. A counterpart on his mother's side also fought in the Revolution.

Jim's grandfather, James Maitland Stewart, youngest of ten children, followed older brother Archibald into the Union Army; J.M. enlisted in the U.S. Army Signal Corps in 1864 at the advanced age of twenty-four, whereas Archie had joined up at the beginning of the war in 1861. Why J.M. waited until the South was on the ropes is anybody's guess, but he saw a great deal of action in the Shenandoah Valley of western Virginia under Union Maj. Gen. Philip Sheridan and Brig. Gen. George Armstrong Custer, among others. At about the time J.M. Stewart was participating in the battle of New Market, older brother Archie was cut down by mortal wounds at the battle of Spotsylvania Court House. J.M. would continue to see action in engagements at Berryville, Winchester, and Fisher's Hill, which began the scorched-earth march by Sheridan down through the valley, torching farms, factories, and railroads. Virginians called it "The Burning," and Sgt. James Maitland Stewart was there to see it all. Gen. William T. Sherman

8

would soon emulate Sheridan's practice in Georgia on his march to the sea.

Sergeant Stewart kept a colorful diary that detailed much of the fighting in Virginia in the last year of the war, like this entry about the battle of Cedar Creek, fought October 19, 1864, when the army of Confederate Lt. Gen. Jubal Early launched a pre-dawn attack on General Sheridan in the Shenandoah Valley:

"We then went out on station on the banks of Cedar Creek where we remained until Oct. the 19th, when the Johnnies charged our works about an hour before daylight. They carried the works on our left and came in on our left flank and in less then [sic] an hour they had the 8th and 19th Corps on a skedaddle. The 6th Corps was then drawn up in line of battle & held them there till they were ordered to fall back. They fell back in good order till they got a good position then drew up in line of battle & held their position. A heavy fire was kept up all day till about four o'clock PM when the 6th were ordered to charge. The Johnnies broke and skedaddled like [a] flock of sheep without a Sheppard. We encamped for the night near our old camping ground on the Cooly Farm. We took about 4,000 prisoners, 50 pieces of artillery, and about 60 ambulances. Our loss in killed and wounded was pretty heavy. The next morning Thurs. the 20th I rode all out over the battle field, saw some hard sights. That evening went out on station at the breast works. Came off station to reserve camp the next morning."

J.M. would go on to see more action at Dinwiddie Court House, Five Forks, and, finally, Sailor's Creek. He served under Custer when Lee surrendered to Grant at Appomattox Court House in April 1865. In fact, Sgt. Stewart witnessed the ceremony, and fifty years later when he owned J.M. Stewart & Company, the family hardware business, he told young Jim about the time the dignified Lee met the sober Grant, about seeing President Lincoln, and about the flamboyant "boy general" Custer. This wasn't history in a book; this was eyewitness history from a man who had been there to see the hard sights, brother of the late Lt. Archibald Stewart, who became another hero to young Jim. J.M. had lived American history and served as a direct link between Jim and the American Civil War, between Jim and a family's military heritage and a strongly held belief that each generation of Stewart men had a mission, and that mission was to serve their country.

There was a third heavy military shadow hanging over Jim. In addition to Archie and J.M. Stewart, there was Jim's mother's father, Samuel McCartney Jackson, colonel of the Eleventh Pennsylvania Reserves. Whereas Sergeant Stewart was a tough-as-nails workingman remnant of the Civil War, Colonel Jackson—who would become General Jackson by war's end—was J.M.'s officer corps counterpart. Jackson had seen the butchering of Union troops at the stone wall at Fredericksburg and seven months later participated in a successful charge across the hotly contested Wheatfield at Gettysburg as part of Col. Joseph Fisher's brigade. That charge proved just as important to holding the federal left flank and preserving victory for the Union as Joshua Lawrence Chamberlain's stand at Little Round Top the same day, at about the same time. Young Jim would never lay eyes on Sam Jackson, who died May 8, 1906, two years before Jim's birth, but General Jackson remained heavy in the air as a guiding influence in Jim's youth.

The rambunctious Alex Stewart was known throughout his lifetime to Princeton University classmates as "Eck," probably because he insisted on his name being pronounced Alec instead of Alex, causing bemused Princetonians to grant half his request. Eck had run off to fight in the Spanish-American War at age twenty-six, two weeks shy of his college graduation, but he spent only thirty-six days in Puerto Rico, grew ill, and saw no action; it was all over too soon. J.M. must have been displeased with his son's performance in round one of his service, because at age forty-five, by then a father of three and yet under the close scrutiny of J.M., Alex went off to serve again in 1917, this time in the Ordnance Repair

Department, which was close enough to frontline combat in the Great War that Alex had been forced to look into the eye of the beast, just as his father, uncle, and father-in-law had half a century earlier. At one point Alex, referring to the combat death of an Indiana man, wrote home that "the Germans must be exterminated; that is what is coming to them."

With his father away at war, Jim turned ten, and passion for military life burned within him in all its preadolescent glory. He expressed his enthrallment with war by staging plays in his basement and the basements of his friends, plays that depicted the war in progress in Europe as imagined in the minds of schoolchildren. The young troupe of players used as props German trench helmets and other mementos sent home from the European lowlands by Captain Stewart.

The world war ended with the capitulation of the German empire and harsh terms by the victors, who divided up German territory, demanded war reparations, and dictated severe restrictions on Kaiser Wilhelm's military to make sure Germany would never again pose a problem for the world.

J.M. had imparted to Alex, and Alex would now impart to his son: "This is your destiny; this is what the Stewart men do. We serve our country without hesitation whenever there is a need." Jim responded by asking his mother to fashion a uniform for him, so he would be ready when the bugle sounded.

J.M. had hardly been a perfect parent to Alex and his younger brother, Ernest, who had been born with a deformed leg. At one point J.M., frustrated with his unruly eldest child, remarked, "I have one son with a crippled leg and another [Alex] with a crippled head." This remark may have been in response to a questionable incident at Princeton when Alex accidentally (or on purpose) left a Bunsen burner running in the science lab, with a fire resulting. Or was it the incident when Alex and his pals griped to the Chinese laundryman about the quality of his ironing and then, according to

Jim, ganged up and "ironed the laundryman." There was a cruel streak in the Stewart men. J.M. had it and Alex had it, and Jim never did, although perhaps some of his introversion resulted from being too close to hurtful times at home.

Alex's father was a hard-liner, with a view of women that was typical of the times—a view that would prove unhelpful to Jim down the road. J.M. was on his third wife by the time Jim knew him; the two earlier women had up and died on the old man—Alex's mother had died when he was just nine—and J.M. every so often needed to recruit a replacement caregiver. Alex learned from his father just what the role of a good woman was, and this was how Jim grew up, with the notion that a man found a lucky little lady to quietly pamper him and always be there with a kind word or a firm hand, depending on whether he was sober or drunk. Since the Stewart men were quite successful at business, they always found willing candidates to be the next Mrs. Stewart.

Still ten, Jim began helping out at the hardware store and earning wages; just about then the family moved from the house on Philadelphia Street to a larger home on a cliff known as Vinegar Hill, overlooking the center of town. This larger home made Alex a focal point of Indiana since anyone passing by on the streets below could look up and see the Stewarts' front porch and potentially the big man himself. The new place accommodated a growing family that included Jim's two little sisters, Mary, known to all as Doddie, born in 1912, and Virginia, or Ginny, in 1914. Jim's new address meant a change in schools; he began sixth grade at the Model School, a laboratory school for new teaching techniques within the Indiana Normal School. There he earned average grades because he possessed a short attention span and was easily bored—traits he would retain all his life. He perked up some when appearing in school plays, and around that time he joined the Boy Scouts.

Soon after the conclusion of the Great War, a pilot named Jack Law advertised that he would be barnstorming through Pennsylvania, including a stop in Indiana. "I knew a long time in advance that he was coming," said Jim, "and I saved every cent I could. I made up my mind I was going to have an airplane ride. My folks said I wasn't. They said flying wasn't safe."

Jim had convinced his parents to at least go and watch, and he stuffed all the money he had saved, fifteen dollars, in his pocket. "The Bennetts had a farm right south of town," said Stewart, "and a nice big [flat] field where they could land." Down came the Curtiss Jenny onto the field, and the pilot began taking townspeople up for rides, many of them friends of Alex Stewart. "They came back intact, raving about the thrill," said Jim. "They helped me break him down, and he finally said I could go up. So I went up on my ride and from then on, I was stuck on flying."

Like many boys who went on to become pilots, Jim was bowled over by his first taste of being airborne. "It was more than liberation. It was the ultimate experience of being in control…and being alone. I've always been a loner. I don't enjoy being lonely, but I enjoy being on my own."

He went up on at least four barnstorming rides growing up and built model airplanes "by the gross," many of them decorating odd flat surfaces in the hardware store. By now, he was growing into a gangling and shy teenager who had once been to New York City and that's about it. He was a nervous kid on the inside, high-strung and unsure of himself, still a musician who delighted in playing the accordion and an adolescent male interested in girls, although no one knew it because he kept quiet and spoke and moved at a leisurely pace.

In 1921 J.M. Stewart, Civil War veteran and hardware store owner, retired, giving ownership to Alex. But J.M. remained a daily visitor to the enterprise and was there for Jim as a comforting companion and font of wisdom. Questions the self-critical Jim couldn't ask Dad could be directed to Granddad, about life in general and girls in particular. "It's not a crime to be human," said the elder

J.M. at one point. "Make allowances for yourself." This was not advice that demanding perfectionist Alex—and hard-on-himself Jim—would ever allow.

Jim got a job as weekend projectionist at the Ritz Theater in Indiana. Between the plays he produced in basements and participated in at the Model School and the celluloid flickers he unspooled night after night, Jim got an inkling that acting might be an interesting vocation.

In 1923 Jim's stable small-town life saw interruption; Alex had engineered his average-student son into Mercersburg Academy in lieu of Indiana High School so that Jim might boost his grades and follow in his father's footsteps to the hallowed halls of Princeton University in New Jersey.

Mercersburg Academy was a private school located in south-central Pennsylvania that had been founded in 1893 "to prepare young men for college," and not just any colleges, but Ivy League schools. The course of study was five years, not the traditional three of high school. Off went Jim to Mercersburg, 121 twisting, hard miles from Indiana. Jim had never been an A student and barely gained acceptance to the academy, then worked like hell his first year to remain there. His second year was marred by an attack of scarlet fever and then a kidney infection that kept him bedridden for months. When finally on his feet again but too weak to hold a regular job for the summer, Jim teamed up with his Indiana friend Bill Neff on Neff's Magic Show. Neff had found puberty a dark experience; he had become obsessed with magic and the occult, making him an unlikely companion for Jim, who kept Neff's darker stuff from his parents so he could continue to hang out with his friend. Neff's skill at magic and drive to perform earned him local and regional play dates, all precursors to a soaring national career in magic. Jim was in on the ground floor, serving as Neff's on-stage assistant and playing audiences in and out with the accordion. In one summer Jim Stewart became a seasoned performer used to public scrutiny and the spotlight. But he remained quiet and aloof with a mystery about him that attracted the opposite sex.

Jim had always liked girls—his first crush was on silent actress Ruth Roland—and gained a little experience at Mercersburg. "Sex was a sin," he said. "I never could quite believe that…but that was the rule." His lifelong disbelief began here and led him to necking sessions with girls at school dances. "I had fun," he said. "I was a young man, a regular Joe, and a regular Joe likes to smooch with a girl."

When Charles Lindbergh crossed the Atlantic to Paris in May 1927, Jim was home from school and tracked Lindy's progress on a map in his bedroom, listening in on the radio and reading newspaper reports. Lindy became Stewart's hero.

In his final year at Mercersburg, after summers spent working manual labor jobs at his father's insistence or hitting the road with Neff, Jim tried out for a school play—Neff put him up to it—and landed a lead role. He did well enough to please himself, and then he graduated from Mercersburg Academy. He still didn't know what he wanted to do with his life and anticipated agony if forced to spend four more years in classrooms that threatened to bore him to death. But that's what Dad wanted, that's what Dad had his heart set on, and, truth be told, Jim didn't have any better ideas.

In fact, he almost became a Navy man at age twenty after Mercersburg. The military life had been his family mission, and he found the lure of the Navy fascinating. "Snappy uniforms, adventures on the high seas, that sort of thing," he explained. But Alex didn't want that for Jim; not yet. Alex wanted Jim to attend Princeton, and so that's what Jim did after becoming infatuated with the beauty of the campus during a visit by the two of them. Jim majored first in electrical engineering (too difficult), then in political science (too boring), and finally in architecture, which had enough of a mix of disciplines to keep his mind engaged. He was smart, nervous, quiet, and full of self-doubt in his first years at Princeton, surrounded by the sons of the rich and famous, all seemingly handsome, square shouldered, well proportioned, coordinated, immaculately dressed, and sure of themselves. All the things he was not—never had been and never would be.

In his freshman year he went out for track and made the team but didn't do well enough to repeat the experience as a sophomore. Instead he joined the Charter Club and the Glee Club, and through this exercise in the arts learned of a musical play entitled *The Golden Dog* to be staged by Princeton's elite Triangle Club, a respected academic theatrical company that staged well-funded shows on campus and then took them on the road to major U.S. cities. Thinking back to his childhood productions in the basement at home, Jim decided to audition for a speaking part in *The Golden Dog*, making the cut not because of his reading (which was unskilled), but because he played the accordion and with another undergraduate accordionist earned a spot on the bill performing a specialty duet.

The Golden Dog introduced Jim to the co-author of the play and its lyrics, Joshua Logan of Texas, as much a misfit as Jim, aged twenty-one like Jim, and a junior. While Stewart was tall, rail-thin, nervous, stable, and introverted, Logan was tall, husky, high-strung, capricious, and extroverted—the first stage-bound histrionic personality Jim had encountered. Jim also became friends with Myron McCormick, a Phi Beta Kappa and serious, good-looking actor who experienced stage fright before any performance of anything.

Stewart, Logan, McCormick, and the other Triangle Players hit the road, and Jim's accordion playing on stages across the nation made him, suddenly and unexpectedly, a hit as an entertainer. The next year he vaulted to stardom singing and dancing in Josh Logan's latest production, which went on the road to cities as far west as Chicago and Milwaukee. Then, in March 1932 Granddad J.M. died at ninety-two, and Jim took the train home for the funeral, where he was reminded again of his military heritage through

J.M.'s burial with honors in Greenwood Cemetery.

Musicals and dramas followed for Jim up to graduation in spring of 1932, his academic career ending so strongly that he had earned a graduate scholarship in architecture, which thrilled Alex.

That summer Josh Logan wanted Jim to join the University Players, a Cape Cod summer stock company founded by Princeton alums who wanted to hone their craft, and because Jim loved the theater and his Princeton acting troupe, he went. There he met another key personality in his life, red-headed Harvard grad John Swope, son of the president of General Electric. Swope looked more like a prizefighter than an actor but had the sharpest sense of humor in the bunch.

After a hard summer working at everything from set construction to vending to acting for a wealthy, vacationing clientele, Jim—known to all by now as "Slats" or "Slim"—knew he wanted to be an actor. It didn't hurt that successive productions involving Jim, *Carry Nation* and *Goodbye Again*, ended up on Broadway, the latter with a long run. It also didn't hurt that Jim had become close friends with two other professional actors, Nebraska-born Henry Fonda, three years Jim's senior, and Margaret Sullavan of Virginia, soon to be a Broadway star.

Nobody represented the girl next door less than petite, five-foot-two, blue-eyed Margaret Sullavan, but that's what she looked like in still photographs: the pretty—not beautiful; pretty—girl next door. Maggie, as she was known to others in the troupe, sashayed into Jim Stewart's life, turned it upside down, shook it with effortless ease, and changed his molecular structure. He wasn't the first man she had done this to, and she hadn't set out to do it, but some women fire the imagination, captivate, seduce, and ensnare just by walking into a room, and Southern belle Maggie Sullavan was one of them.

"There was nobody like her before or since," said Henry Fonda. "In every way. In talent, in looks, in character, in temperament."

Fonda had become an expert on Margaret Sullavan by marrying her on Christmas Day 1931, in what would become a four-month exercise that ended when she began sleeping with a Broadway producer. To Fonda, Maggie was the original "ballbuster," charming one moment, shrill the next, and given to violent tantrums, but also sexy and flirtatious. She had a great head of hair and knew how to use it, tossing it this way and that as she employed her husky bedroom voice to hint at untold pleasures if she let you get close.

Slats was doing well with women, driven by a compulsion to have those he met not see him as repulsive because of his emaciated frame and gangling extremities. "You could easily believe he was shy with girls and innocent," said Josh Logan. "That was his style in getting women. Any Princeton student had to watch out for him at parties. Didn't matter how handsome you were…, you'd find your girl dancing with Jimmy or disappearing into the moonlight on his arm."

Sullavan intrigued him and the feeling was mutual. Stewart biographer Michael Munn quoted Logan as saying of Jim and Maggie: "When they first met, they did have an affair. And it was a passionate one."

Jim became convinced that the stage would be his career path, despite his father's joy at the prospect that his only son would continue on at Princeton and earn a graduate degree. It would be a decision Jim had to defend face-to-face with Alex and Bessie—but where Jimbo was concerned, Alex would sometimes prove to be a paper tiger. On this occasion, he would back down and support his son, and both parents could only hope that Jim would come to his senses before he met his doom in New York City with that band of bohemian loafers who had led him astray.

But Jim fit with these people; Fonda in particular reminded Jim of himself. Tall, painfully thin, brimming with self-doubt, "Hank," as most called him, had a dark intensity about him. He didn't like himself and it showed. He had a sharp, self-deprecating tongue and an earthiness symbolized by sudden streams of four-letter invective. But he was also a funny, self-aware guy who needed a friend after his failure at marriage with Maggie, and Jim was there to lend counsel at a critical time. As a boy, Fonda had seen a black man lynched; when somebody saw that, it tended to stick, and behind Fonda's eyes was that memory, always there, near or far, but always in sight. It made him an interesting guy, a hard guy, and a sad guy, all at once.

Then there was Margaret Sullavan herself, a year younger than Jim almost to the day yet worldly wise and experienced, so very experienced. She knew how Jim felt about her and saw in him no challenge at all, and, therefore, she experienced no attraction to him. She needed fireworks, men capable of riding out her storms, dishing it out as well as taking it. Jim wasn't that. Jim was a choirboy version of Hank and look what she had done to poor Hank. She rightly sized up Jim as honest, ingenuous, and fragile. As for Jim, well, he believed she was out of his league. It felt right to worship Maggie from afar.

Now, determined to make a living as a New York actor, Jim went in with Joshua Logan and Myron McCormick on a small, spartan apartment on seedy West 63rd Street one block off Central Park. Fonda soon joined them—four grown men living in an apartment that was New York City-sized, with one small bedroom and one bath. A fifth dweller, Burgess "Buzz" Meredith, came and went. Buzz was known to playwright Maxwell Anderson and had just joined famed actress Eva Le Gallienne's new stage company. Meredith described his roommates on 63rd Street, Stewart, Logan, Fonda, and McCormick, as "a species of young stage animals." Everyone got work, now and then. Nobody starved. And fortune continued to smile on Jim Stewart.

"The notorious New York gangster Legs Diamond made his base of operations in a hotel two doors up the street," said Fonda, who summed up their neighborhood with, "The other tenants of the apartment building were prostitutes." Hank also said that he and Jim got freebies from the girls, while Stewart admitted he took small odd jobs from the mobsters—like delivering parcels—when times were toughest.

One morning they learned that the previous night a gangster had been shot to death on their doorstep just an hour before they returned home from a late night out. "Shit," said Fonda, "we have to get home earlier."

As the new year of 1933 began, Jim was working in *Goodbye Again*, playing a chauffeur with two lines of dialogue—a part he knew well since he had been in an earlier run of the show with the University Players. On the last day of January 1933, a Tuesday, Jim Stewart heard that Adolf Hitler had been appointed by Otto von Bismarck to serve as chancellor of Germany. Hitler had a multi-point plan to fix a broken, vanquished nation, with many of those points, such as rearmament and unification of all German areas of Europe into a "greater Germany," causing headlines to scream that Europe was "scared stiff." A young German student visiting America told newspapers, "The youth of Germany had no future in after-war Germany. The government seemed wrong, corrupt, terrible. There was no work. Suddenly Hitler appeared saying, 'I am for a new Germany!'" Jim read of clashes in the streets between National Socialist Party members, Nazis for short, and Communists. But Jim had work, and Germany was a long way off.

Jim supported himself, first on 200 performances of *Goodbye Again* that got him attention for those two measly lines—lines he had made the most of. Now, with a resumé and some clippings from New York papers, he kept auditioning and applying natural charm that got him more parts in plays. Once he had a part, he realized he could memorize the script, and at that point his curiosity at new situations took over and he proceeded to discover how much he didn't know about theater. Jim closed the gaps by learning from people passionate about acting who tossed off knowledge easily, and there he was to catch it. He found the theater a fascinating life, and those who saw him realized he was good at it. Soon, Jim grew passionate about acting as a craft; in place of formal training he studied the star players, how they approached their work, how they refined their performances night after night.

As 1933 turned into 1934, the Depression deepened and work of all types dried up. Maggie Sullavan signed a contract with Universal Pictures and moved to Hollywood. Buzz Meredith continued honing his craft with Eva Le Gallienne; Logan worked regularly; so did McCormick. Due to attrition, their apartment for four on 63rd grew too expensive, and Stewart and Fonda moved forty blocks south to the Madison Square Hotel, scraping together the money for rent. By now, Jim had done everything he could to support himself, including working as a stage manager in New York and Boston. He also got himself on film in a New York-produced two-reel comedy for Vitaphone Pictures called *Art Trouble*, co-starring funnyman Shemp Howard. It didn't change Jim's life, but at fifty dollars a day it paid the rent with money to spare. And Jim was good with money; one had to be to make it as an actor in New York City.

Broadway brimmed with young talent now, newbies inspired by talking pictures, or by the need to make any money they could in a Depression, or by the oldest reason of all: Theater was in their blood, and they lived and breathed it. Mildred Natwick came to Broadway, as did tall, curly-headed Dick Foran, square-shouldered Kent Smith of the University Players, and young, Brooklyn-born Ross Alexander and his girlfriend from New Jersey, talented actress Aleta Friele. They and others became an unofficial guild providing mutual support, tips on available jobs, and shoulders to cry on, whatever the situation required.

The fortunes of the group began to change. Ross Alexander signed a Fox contract and headed to Hollywood, only to bounce back before Paramount signed him and off he went again, with

Aleta in tow. Hank started working in *The Farmer Takes a Wife*, which led to a New York screen test with Fox Studios.

Around this time, Jim and Hank walked into the toy department at Macy's looking for Christmas presents for their families. Soon they became distracted by the boy stuff, the electric trains and the models. They had in common a fascination with flight and walked out of Macy's some time later with gifts for children and one for themselves: the largest model airplane kit sold by the store, an Army Air Corps twin-engine Martin MB-1 biplane, also known as the Glenn Martin Bomber.

"I've never seen such a complicated model," said Stewart. "It had hundreds of parts, most of them so small we needed tweezers to handle them—and magnifying glasses."

January 1935 saw Stewart and Fonda laboring over the airplane model. "Both of us were working in shows, and every night after the performance we'd rush home and start putting the plane together," said Jim. "First thing we knew it would be six in the morning. We'd go to bed and wake up about one o'clock, grab a bite of breakfast, and work on it until time for dinner." They didn't cement just airplane pieces those weeks building the plane; they cemented their friendship. But then Fox called Fonda, and off he went to the West Coast to sign a motion picture contract. Jim went with Hank to the train station and suddenly the Martin bomber had become an orphan.

Not that Jim was a victim and now alone in New York City. He had been learning the craft of acting all along; getting parts had always been easier for Stewart than for Fonda, which frustrated Hank. The year before, Jim had landed a lead role in the yellow fever story *Yellow Jack*, directed by Guthrie McClintic, who coached Jim through exhaustive rehearsals that Stewart would call "the turning point of my work on the stage." Then, in January 1935 came a strong part in the drama *Divided by Three* that drew the attention of MGM casting director Billy Grady. Grady had been haunting Broadway looking for talent to bring west to MGM in Hollywood's growing picture industry and had seen Jim many times. Thanks to McClintic's tutelage, Stewart had reached a turning point as an actor, and Grady arranged for Jim to take a New York test for MGM. Two plays and a follow-up screen test later, Jim received an offer for a three-month contract with MGM in Culver City, California. He wired Fonda the big news. Fonda sent a return wire true to his character and their friendship. The telegram read simply:

DON'T FORGET TO BRING AIRPLANE STOP GUARD WITH LIFE STOP.

2
SOARING

Adolf Joseph Ferdinand Galland had to fly. He grew up in the Westphalia region of Germany in the wake of the Great War, the second of four sons, and from his earliest conscious memory worshipped the aces of aerial combat. One wouldn't know by Adolf's adulation that Germany had lost the war because to him, the air aces—including Manfred von Richthofen with an astonishing eighty kills, Ernst Udet with sixty-two, and Erich Löwenhardt with fifty-four—were akin to the knights of the Middle Ages.

But Germany and her ally Austria-Hungary had indeed lost the war. The bones of millions littering the Low Countries served as proof that this had indeed been a great war, and losing it had cost Germany dearly—thirteen percent of her land and all her military might under horrible terms, agreeing to pay staggering sums in war reparations to France and England.

Within a year hyperinflation hit Germany to such an extent that soon war reparations couldn't be paid, which led French and Belgian troops to invade the industrial Ruhr Valley for the purpose of taking reparations by force. With a worthless currency and occupation by foreign armies to seize goods, Germany's humiliation was complete.

Beginning in 1924 economic prosperity returned to Europe, even seeping into volatile Germany, which entered a period known as *Goldene Zwanziger*, the Golden Twenties, when a liberal backlash and new post-war cynicism took hold.

Young Adolf Galland—nicknamed Dolfo—spent life as oblivious to the renaissance of German society as he had been to its economic disintegration. He was at that time a teenager and a terrible student in traditional schooling, but one who excelled at sports. His greatest passion was girls, far and away, but among other passions were target shooting, model airplanes, and fast cars and motorcycles. He combined the latter at age fifteen when he discovered sailplaning. The wealth of his father made this possible.

Sailplaning involved sitting inside a light glider launched to altitude by a catapult. The pilot of the glider needed a keen eye and deft touch to find the lift and, under the right atmospheric conditions, sail unencumbered for dozens of kilometers and a half hour or more per flight. Dolfo didn't find the lift his first time out and crashed upon launch from the catapult. His second flight went better, and soon he was staying up for two or three minutes and then five.

Before long, Dolfo had earned his pilot's rating after a one-hour flight in a sailing competition in the Rhön Mountains. A pilot's rating in Germany signified much more skill than a private pilot's license in the United States; it meant that Galland could now instruct and perform in air shows. He had become obsessed and spent all his spare time finding the lift in the silent, solitary world high above the earth, becoming one hell of an aviator.

The Great Depression hit Germany full force and the economy crashed, taking all commercial enterprises with it, including passenger aviation. In such an environment, Galland sought to become a pilot for the airlines, the only problem being that so did seemingly every other young man in Germany, so popular had sailplaning become. No one could afford to fly as a passenger, yet everyone sought to become a commercial pilot.

Against all odds—or maybe not since he was handsome, accomplished, and charming—Dolfo Galland landed one of twenty slots at the German airline pilot school in Braunschweig, Germany, which was, in reality, a training facility for military pilots when no such train-ing was allowed under the Treaty of Versailles. Galland saw himself on track to become a commercial pilot, not a military flier; if any of the other students saw the real intentions of the pilot school, no one said anything. As far as they all knew, there were no military fliers—or planes to put them in.

The elite twenty traveled to a remote facility in the Soviet Union where the curriculum proved demanding in all respects. For the first time in his life, Galland found balance between the physical activity he loved and the mental discipline he lacked. By this time, the shadow aviation department within the German War Ministry knew they had a special talent in young Galland and selected him along with four of the original twenty airline pilot trainees to return from the Soviet Union and report to Berlin and the Central Air Line Pilot School. There they learned the truth: These five had been carefully vetted for a course training military pilots—a top-secret operation. Were they interested in becoming the foundation for a new German air force? Galland said an immediate yes and suddenly found himself in league with the idols of his boyhood, the air aces of the Great War.

3
FACTORY WORK

James Stewart was a natural storyteller all his adult life. One of his favorites concerned hauling the Martin Bomber with its three-foot wingspan 3,000 miles from New York to Hollywood. He took the wings off and managed to hand carry the model on the train as far as his hometown, where he found a black packing case big enough to hold the fuselage and wings. With Fonda continuing to send telegrams of "scornful challenge" about the importance of getting the plane to California, Jim set off clutching the box all the way west on the Super Chief. He claimed that conductors believed the case contained a machine gun, and that a little old lady thought it held "a cut-up cadaver." But he did get the plane all the way to Pasadena, where Fonda picked him up in the fall of 1935 at the train station on South Reynolds Avenue, just as Jim had dropped Hank off at the train station in New York City.

Fonda barked, "Where's the airplane?" before even a hello to Stewart.

Hank drove Jim over Colorado Boulevard across mountain passes westward to Sunset Boulevard, through Hollywood and Beverly Hills. There was a lot to catch up on: Fonda had roomed with Ross and Aleta Alexander and their cat Itchy way up on Woodrow Wilson Drive when he hit town (Ross was starting out gangbusters at Warner Bros., but he and Aleta had been sniping at each other a lot); Fonda had gotten invited to a party where Carole Lombard rented an amusement park for an evening (everyone in Hollywood went); Fonda had made the film version of *The Farmer Takes a Wife* (Victor Fleming coached him on the differences between acting for an audience and acting for the camera); Maggie was dating a Princeton man (who hadn't graduated) named Leland Hayward, who was a talent agent, a private pilot, and a good guy.

Fonda didn't stop talking for thirty-five miles, and Stewart got an earful as he took in an eyeful of blue skies, palm trees, jutting mountains, and fancy automobiles on the long ride to Fonda's rented house at 12731 Evanston Drive in Brentwood. Jim stepped out of the car and beheld a wraparound ranch with shutters at the windows in a style somewhere between country and Spanish. Hank mentioned with a nod that Greta Garbo lived *there*—Jim saw a rooftop, the next rooftop over, above the shrubbery. What the hell kind of place was this where there were palm trees and where Greta Garbo lived next door?

The other thing Jim learned as he settled in on Evanston was that Hank had cats, which was fine since Jim liked cats, but there were many felines about and these weren't lap cats but wild ones with the run of the place, cats that didn't like to be picked up, as Jim learned after one bloody failed attempt.

"We found a cat in the greenhouse out in the back," Hank explained, "a cat that had just had a litter.... So this was a good omen, a ready-made family of pets." Then he discovered they were wild, and their numbers kept increasing.

Stewart and Fonda unpacked the Martin Bomber and picked up their friendship where they had left it in New York, except that now they could spread out over a space that seemed the size of the Schubert stage rather than the size of a prison cell. Jim called Bill Grady, the MGM scout that had discovered him, saying he had arrived and was ready to report to the Metro-Goldwyn-Mayer studios—once he had figured out where they were.

Jim got himself a car and as Jim's jaws worked some chewing gum, Hank showed him the streets of Los Angeles. There wasn't any getting used to palm trees for a Pennsylvania kid; Jim knew he was someplace different because of those trees and because of the heat. The sun was always out and the temperature slid along a scale from warm to very warm, and for weeks on end it didn't rain. A man could count on driving with the windows down on the commute from Brentwood to the studio and on the trip home in the evening.

Metro-Goldwyn-Mayer sprawled across Culver City, a small, incorporated city in Los Angeles County, on several motion picture lots totaling 185 acres, pockets of make-believe of varying sizes with one common goal: turning fantasies into cash. No operation succeeded in this endeavor like MGM; nobody even tried to compete with the studio boasting "more stars than there are in heaven." MGM operated as Hollywood's biggest motion picture operation by far, so big it had its own railroad line to haul in raw materials and ship out finished cans of celluloid.

In 1935 MGM flexed its muscles by releasing one blockbuster after another. *Mutiny on the Bounty* placed heartthrob Clark Gable in exotic South Seas locations. *A Tale of Two Cities* plunked Ronald Colman in the middle of the French Revolution. *Anna Karenina* showcased Greta Garbo amidst the passions of nineteenth century Russia. The onslaught of big pictures was relentless, with *Naughty Marietta* bringing together Nelson Eddy and Jeanette MacDonald and *A Night at the Opera* unleashing the Marx Brothers once again after their exile from Paramount.

Jim Stewart hadn't landed just anywhere in Hollywood; Jim had landed in The Place to Be in Hollywood. The studio pace reminded him of New York, all hustle, bustle, motion, and commotion. People worked hard here. People moved fast. Most seemed nice enough but the fact was, they knew what to do and where to go and he didn't, and that should have given him a lot more pause but for the loose gene inside that sought the unknown beyond his reach, the gene that had landed General Jackson in Gettysburg, and Sergeant Stewart at Appomattox, and Alex in the Lowlands. His ancestors had risked their lives in the name of adventure and sometimes been shot to pieces, which made this current enterprise something foolish and even comical, dressing in costumes and pretending to be a character invented by a man on the second floor of the writers' building banging out dialogue on a Royal just in time to have it run down to the dressing rooms so the players could take it home and learn it before shooting the next morning. Sometimes, the scenes came out of the writer on one try, but often they were rewritten three or five or nine times. But as long as Jim received a paycheck of $350 each week, he was damn well going to be anything they wanted him to be and work damn hard at what he already recognized as a craft. He couldn't believe he had been given this opportunity; he didn't know if he would ever be given another. Whatever the studio wanted, he would do his best to provide.

The MGM factory needed on-camera workers. It had its tough-guy ladies' man in Gable; a more genteel version in Robert Taylor; lighter romantic leads in Franchot Tone and Robert Montgomery. What the studio didn't have was a boy next door. Montgomery was almost that but not quite. The publicity department looked at what they had acquired in a six-foot-four skinny kid with hair down in his eyes, a big Adam's apple, thick lips, and not much to say. Publicity decided to bill him on face value, as "America personified." Because of his unique style and the impression he made, he became known to the front office right away, to Mr. Mayer, Mr. Thalberg, and Mr. Mannix, as in Louis B. Mayer, studio boss, Irving Thalberg, boy-genius producer, and Eddie Mannix, vice president and head of operations. They envisioned James Stewart as a young character actor or maybe a comedian; they didn't know what they would do with him, but they had scooped him up with all the others in their raid on Broadway. At $350 per week he had already vaulted over most of the scurrying performers and legion of technicians on the lot—most of whom Mr. Mayer, Mr. Thalberg, and Mr. Mannix did *not* know.

First up for America Personified was a trip to the gym where the Pennsylvanian was measured and weighed.

"Jesus Christ, Bill!" groused studio fitness man Don Loomis in the beginning of his rant to Bill Grady about the telephone-pole circus freak before him, weighing in at a ridiculous 135 pounds. He declared Stewart "hopeless," only to be told that the ink was already dry on a seven-year contract so something had to be done to build up the freakish physique of the signee. Loomis prescribed milk shakes with raw eggs, banana splits, and anything else the men could think of to infuse fat and protein. Stewart was ordered back four days a week for weight training and told to get as much fresh air and exercise as possible.

Grady pressed ahead finding a part for his discovery. He unearthed such a part in *The Murder Man*, the first picture for Spencer Tracy in his MGM contract after having been hired away from Fox. In the script Tracy *was* the murder man, the killer, and Stewart played his friend Shorty, the kind of part character actor Eddie Quillan was making famous. Jim realized the ridiculousness of portraying a character named Shorty and took the part straight over the top by selling director Tim Whelan on Shorty being a dim-witted all-American hayseed; the MGM novice Whelan had been a disciple of Harold Lloyd and didn't mind the comedic slant to a picture that couldn't help but end up as a downer, with the hero turning himself in for murder prior to fade-out.

Stewart spent his few days on this first feature motion picture learning the roles of director, producer, director of photography, grips, gaffers, script girls, lighting technicians, props, wardrobe, makeup, and everyone else hurrying about on the crew, speaking a secret language he didn't yet understand. Everyone moved so fast because time was money, so what the camera saw had to look just right and be lit just right, and it had to be done in a hurry to stay on an aggressive schedule.

Life in Brentwood for Fonda and Stewart went on as normal with both men working at becoming established contract players. The only variables were the number of cats, which kept increasing, and the number of neighborhood Garbos, which decreased by one thanks to the bachelors and their cats.

Jim embraced new challenges and the mental engagement of complex planning for a complex set of problems, which motion picture production certainly was. His enthusiasm on the set and his pleasant interactions with complicated star Spencer Tracy made a favorable impression in the front office. Naturally, Jim's nerves quaked his first time through the process of filmmaking, as he explained to a reporter. "At first I would blow my lines—and what a humiliation. Me, a stage actor who had memorized whole scripts, forgetting a few sentences. It was nothing more than being scared stiff. When they're ready for the take, you can hear a pin drop on the soundstage. It's that dead silence that gets you."

The front office looked favorably on James Stewart's brief on-screen presence as Shorty—an opinion Jim didn't share. "I'll never forget seeing myself on the screen for the first time. I was all hands and feet and altogether pretty awful."

But it was an MGM picture and a Spencer Tracy picture, both good signs, and Fonda translated messages from the front office and the director alike into: They love you; you've won them over; relax and enjoy yourself!

Jim would not soon be relaxing because on the inside he found nothing to relax about, not with his mind always in motion, always seeking new stimulation. He would become known for that halting cinematic persona, the unhurried thinker, slow to speech and slower to anger, but that character had been bred of a man not at peace who needed to gauge his internal pace so he wouldn't burn out; the guy with the metabolism that consumed calories faster than he could ingest them, a metabolism that consumed his own body mass to keep him constantly rail thin. While on camera, he learned to let a beat go by before delivering his lines or do a little take that bought time and made his characters seem canny. None of his characters were really shrewd; they were overwhelmed and strung way too tight, but the technique worked with directors and audiences alike, and a unique screen personality was born.

4
SILVER BIRDS

Clement Francis Leone had to fly. He knew it the first time he saw the M-130, a beast of an airplane, cruise low in the Saturday morning sky and ease down to the glassy surface of Peach Orchard Cove Inlet in Dundalk, Maryland. When its belly and pontoons kissed the water, a spray shot out like some grand fountain, and the seaplane settled right in. Leone and his two friends stood entranced watching the giant flying boat with its four top-mounted engines taxi up to the pier. That spring of 1937 when he was twelve, Clem knew nothing about Juan Trippe, master of Pan American Airways, who envisioned a flying boat capable of crossing the Pacific Ocean carrying passengers and mail from San Francisco to the Far East. Trippe had ordered three M-130s from Glenn L. Martin Corporation right there in Baltimore, the China Clipper, the Hawaii Clipper, and the Philippine Clipper. After Warner Bros. had released a picture called *China Clipper*, with Pat O'Brien playing a character based on Juan Trippe, America knew all flying boats as China Clippers. That's how Clem knew this one now.

Clem Leone was an easy kid not to notice. He was shorter in stature than many of the other boys. His eyes and hair were dark and he had an ethnic look thanks to his father, also named Clement Leone, an alcoholic who had run out on his family and never returned when Clem the younger was all of three. Because Clem was named after his father and his spitting image, and in spite of it, Stella Leone thought Clem a special boy. She loved her other children, Dick and Irma, and the three acquired in a second marriage to a railroad telegrapher, but Clem had a special place in Stella's heart. Clem didn't mind being a momma's boy; in fact, it suited the quiet and easygoing kid who was, by nature, a loner capable of going off and staring at the airplanes all day long, alone or with his friends. Whatever worked. But he was also so much more—honor-roll student, violinist, and one hell of a worker.

He delivered newspapers every weekday morning before leaving for school; after school he delivered afternoon papers, did his homework, went to bed, and then repeated the process the next day, earning five dollars a week, half of which he handed to his mother to pay board. On Saturday he could relax because he had only one round to make with his papers, first thing in the morning. The rest of the day was his and that's when he would climb on his bike, join up with his friends, and ride ten miles, all the way from South Baltimore around the Inner Harbor, through Little Italy, and down to Dundalk. There sat Logan Field with its runways, two-story terminal, and collection of wooden hangars, where the boys would hover around the Jenny biplanes and the Ford Tri-Motors. Clem studied the DC-2 passenger planes as they appeared in the eastern sky flying in from far-off New York City. He could see the sleek, twin-engined silver birds long before he could hear them, and they would glide in and land, spewing gray exhaust as they taxied up near the terminal building for aluminum steps to be wheeled out and set into place.

Yes, Clem Leone was a guy living a full life, making this Saturday investment in aviation a dear thing indeed.

5
RELIABLE GIRLS

Jim Stewart had always liked girls—their company, the way they looked and sounded and thought and moved—and here he was in the most concentrated acreage of beautiful women in the world. MGM contract in hand, Jim began wielding his natural charm with girls like a deadly weapon.

Dad would never stand for it, Jim knew, but Dad was 3,000 miles away and Jim was living his life, making do the best way he knew how—overcoming the repressions of Indiana and following a powerful urge to sow wild oats, California style, because he didn't believe as a youth, and still didn't, that there was anything wrong with sex. So many people in Hollywood, the ones with the good looks, had lived hard before they got there, and now that they had acquired money and fame, they *played* hard with each other. They were a mature lot, these stars, working six days a week from eight to six, plus the occasional night shoot. When the director called "Cut, print it!" on the last take of the day, off they went to satisfy instincts that came from struggle, money, and egos constantly in need of stroking.

The group on Evanston Drive prospered. John Swope had been working for the Roosevelt administration as a code compliance officer for the National Recovery Act, but the program had been shut down, and Fonda encouraged Swope to head west and move in with his old cronies. The cat population exploded and a flea epidemic broke out. The overrunning of this section of quiet Brentwood by gangs of angry, wailing cats in heat and their fleas, was what had prompted Greta Garbo to flee the neighborhood.

The bachelors hardly noticed. They were young and single in a Hollywood overrun with as many women as cats. Later in 1935, Fonda introduced Jim to twenty-four-year-old Ginger Rogers, one-half of the most popular dance team in pictures, fresh off the nationwide sensation *Flying Down to Rio* and its quick RKO follow-up to cash in on the sensation of Fred Astaire and Ginger Rogers, *The Gay Divorcee*. A third Astaire and Rogers picture, *Roberta*, followed on its dancing heels, while a fourth, *Top Hat*, was now in production.

Ginger had just separated from her husband, *All Quiet on the Western Front* star Lew Ayres, her second marriage after a failed first at age eighteen. Ginger had grown up fast, from her first vaudeville performances at a tender fourteen. In Jim Stewart, Ginger found the perfect tonic for her restless soul, a quiet, thoughtful, optimistic, enthusiastic older man on his way up and not burned out like so many she had known. He wasn't brooding like Ayres, but ambitious, funny, full of life, a dynamic kisser, and physically blessed specimen.

Ginger spent 1935 as perhaps the most popular girl in Hollywood, thanks to the association with Mr. Astaire, and gravitated to this new guy, Stewart, with the wry, self-deprecating sense of humor and more natural charm than ought to have been legal. He had a quiet way about him that led women to want to mother him. This was the quality that melted Ginger's heart, and then the hearts of many others in town. Jim Stewart: shy, wounded soul. Clark Gable might employ the cocky Gable grin and land a secretary or bit player in no time, but Jim oozed vulnerability and soon found himself an A-list bachelor about town.

During their time as a dating couple, Rogers had some fun

with Stewart, from nights out and his gangling but coordinated dancing, to nights in on Evanston Drive with Fonda and the cats— or, if possible, without Fonda or the cats. But before long, Jim's withdrawn, loner nature starved the fun out of the romance.

It was at the surface level that Jim Stewart charmed, and that charm drew one lucky break after another, from signing with Metro in the first place to working with Tracy out of the gate to his latest casting in MGM's *Rose-Marie*, the second picture of the studio's sensational new singing duo, Nelson Eddy and Jeanette MacDonald. Neither Jim nor the picture's director, "One-Take Woody" Van Dyke, seemed to know what to do with the part of Jeanette's brother, who turns out to be a killer, but it represented more screen time and led to other roles as the front office began to see Stewart as a reliable resource that could be used here, there, and everywhere, not to mention charismatic, with an instinctual acting style not quite like that of any other male at the studio. They loved nothing so much as a versatile contract player, so when Jim wasn't plugged into a supporting role, they sent him off for bodybuilding, voice, dance, and equestrian lessons.

Rose-Marie premiered in January 1936, a time when Jim Stewart's charm reached critical mass, and as an actor at Metro-Goldwyn-Mayer, he landed roles in two and three pictures at a time. He played boyfriend to Jean Harlow in *Wife vs. Secretary* and kissed her on-screen, which became one of Jim's favorite stories—how it was to kiss Harlow, with the number of retakes increasing as years passed. Multiple sources reported that Jim and Jean turned their on-screen make-out session to an offscreen fling during the making of the picture.

In his next assignment, *After the Thin Man*, sequel to MGM's matrimonial mystery hit of 1934, *The Thin Man*, Jim played another supporting character who happened to be unmasked as the killer. There he developed a crush on leading lady Myrna Loy, although apparently didn't try to round the bases with her.

In *Small Town Girl* he played a hayseed again, and yet another in *The Gorgeous Hussy* in support of Joan Crawford. He rose to top billing playing an auto manufacturer's test driver in the fast-moving *Speed* opposite Wendy Barrie and a guy who would become a close pal, Ted Healy of Three Stooges fame.

The Pennsylvania kid suddenly found himself at the crossroads of the world, mingling with people who were talked about, written about, and photographed. When a feature going into production called *Born to Dance*, Cole Porter's first full Hollywood adaptation, needed a male lead opposite tap-dancing sensation Eleanor Powell, no less than Porter himself suggested Stewart for the part. Porter knew Jim from Broadway, and word had it that Cole wanted Jim to report to the Porter home for an audition to see if Jim could sing well enough to play in a musical. Jim reported; Jim could barely carry a tune, according to Porter in his diary. But Porter secured for Jim the first starring part in an A-picture of his career.

Right about now MGM studio boss Louis B. Mayer began to worry about Stewart's sexual orientation. Why was he living with men—that Fox player Fonda and that Swope character? Hadn't they lived together in New York City? Why was Stewart visiting the house of that notorious "queer" Cole Porter? What was going on here?

MGM publicity boss Howard Strickling stalled for time by stepping in to concoct a romance between the eligible Eleanor Powell and her new co-star. L.B. then told Jim Stewart's "discoverer" Bill Grady to get Stewart laid for real. The solution: Head directly to the notorious House of Francis brothel on Sunset Boulevard in West Hollywood, halfway down the Sunset Strip, the place where Mayer ran a tab to keep his stars happy "inside the family" with reliable girls, many of them cinema has-beens or near misses who were checked regularly for diseases. Little did Mayer realize that pointing Stewart in this direction was turning a rooster loose in the henhouse.

Fonda claims Jim was already busy with just about every contract actress in town. Even Hank's dates gravitated to Jim. "For Christ's sake, will you stop stealing my girls?" Fonda groused at one point.

"I don't steal them," Jim responded. "They steal me."

Stewart's lucky streak was personal *and* professional, and it continued thanks to Fonda, who was lunching on Sunset at Billy Wilkerson's Vendome restaurant in West Hollywood with Leland Hayward one day. Ex-Princeton man Hayward had become a *de facto* member of the University Players alumni when he popped the question to Margaret Sullavan, whom he also represented. Who should walk into the Vendome at that moment but Maggie, who sidled up to her ex and future husbands sitting at the same table. By now Maggie and Hank knew they made fine friends and co-workers but lousy spouses, and had been talking about making another film together, a romance called *Next Time We Love* at Universal Pictures in the Valley. Unfortunately, Fonda wasn't available and recommended Jim Stewart, and Sullavan liked the idea. Jim was designated by MGM for loan-out to Universal. When word got out, eyebrows raised around town since Maggie could have picked from several A-list leading men. Why not Universal's own John Boles? Why not Bob Taylor or George Brent? Why Jim Stewart? Rumors said the two rehearsed together a lot, and some claimed Stewart's performance benefited from Sullavan's coaching. For enigmatic Jim, love died hard, and he remained in love with Margaret Sullavan. According to MGM contract player Walter Pidgeon, who worked with Stewart and Sullavan in 1938, "It was so obvious he was in love with her. He came alive in his scenes with her, playing with a conviction and a deep sincerity I never knew him to summon away from her."

But Stewart had grown to respect the thirty-four-year-old Leland Hayward in short order and would not betray him. Hayward was a dignified man, sharp, outspoken, perfectly dressed. He had a full head of salt-and-pepper hair styled to an inch in length on top. He radiated importance and had become one of the top talent agents in Hollywood, representing both Sullavan and Fonda.

Where but Hollywood, or maybe Twelve Oaks, could a co-quettish southern belle charm three close friends practically at once? But that was the nature of volatile Margaret Sullavan, who led Jim on and remained just out of reach because she knew she "might break him."

Born to Dance and *Next Time We Love* were all it took; James Stewart had become an MGM star. He appeared in eight pictures in 1936, all but one at MGM, reporting where he was told with his lines memorized, even if he were playing three roles in the same calendar week.

By 1937 he was officially in demand, signed to make *Seventh Heaven*, remake of a successful silent picture, at Fox with French actress Simone Simon, and then *The Last Gangster* with Edward G. Robinson and *Navy Blue and Gold* with another MGM boy next door, Robert Young.

It wasn't all fun and games. In 1937 real life hit Stewart and Fonda right between the eyes in their make-believe paradise. War-ner Bros. contract player Ross Alexander, their good friend from Broadway days, told his new wife, Universal starlet Anne Nagel, "Call me when dinner's ready," and carried a pistol to the barn be-hind their Encino ranch house, where he blew his brains out. Just a year earlier, Alexander's first wife and constant companion Aleta Friele, a friend of both Jim and Hank, had committed suicide with a shotgun in their home high in the Hollywood Hills on Woodrow Wilson Drive—where Fonda had bunked on arrival two years ear-lier. She had become despondent over not finding work in pictures after Ross had come west and secured parts at Warner Bros. in *A Midsummer Night's Dream*, *Captain Blood*, and *China Clipper*. Ross had never recovered, and his marriage to Nagel had been one last desperate attempt to hold onto sanity. He was only twenty-nine.

On Friday, January 8, Stewart and Fonda paid their respects in a service at Forest Lawn Glendale. Five months later Jim returned to Forest Lawn for the funeral of fellow MGM star Jean Harlow, dead at just twenty-six of kidney failure, a shocking death that hit Jim hard because he had been close to the girl. He adored her; everyone did. Then in December, Ted Healy, Jim's friend and advisor on the set of his first starring feature, *Speed*, died under mysterious circumstances after a drunken brawl outside the Trocadero on the Sunset Strip.

What a mixed bag of a year, equal parts professional success and personal loss. He ended 1937 with a showcase role in the run-up-to-Civil War feature, *Of Human Hearts*, portraying the son of a righteous preacher that must have reminded Jim of his life at home under Alex's rule. In the final two reels Jim's character becomes a physician in the Union army and there he was, in a blue uniform and smack-dab in the middle of the war he had learned all about on Granddad's knee, and getting a personal scolding from President Lincoln himself, as portrayed by John Carradine. It was enough to challenge a guy's concept of reality. By now, he was chatting with ex-girlfriend Ginger Rogers about making a picture together at RKO. For Jim Stewart at the dawn of 1938, the compass pointed nowhere but north.

6
A STORYBOOK LIFE

Sachsenhausen, nestled into the southern shore of the Main River in Frankfurt, Germany, dated back to the thirteenth century and was famous for pubs known as cider houses because just outside the city of Frankfurt grew apples in vast orchards.

Gertrud Margarete Siepmann was born in Sachsenhausen on October 14, 1933, the first child of Hans and Riele—short for Mariele or "little Marie"—Siepmann. Hans's father Franz had been in the German Navy in the Great War and rose to the rank of chief engineer of the light cruiser *Cöln*, the admiral's flagship. In the first naval engagement of the war at Heligoland Bight, Chief Engineer Siepmann assumed command of the *Cöln* after both the admiral and the ship's captain were killed in combat. Franz went down with the ship, and suddenly, nine-year-old Hans Siepmann was orphaned.

Gertrud spent her early years in a resurgent Germany, with falling unemployment and a strengthening mark. People had purpose and the purpose was rebuilding a will, rebuilding a country that had been crushed by defeat in the Great War and then by Depression.

In the summer of 1936, before Gertrud had turned three, the Siepmanns moved from an apartment in Sachsenhausen to another in Wilhelmshaven so that Hans could begin his new job as a naval engineer at Germany's only deep-water port. Hans, her Pappi, took Gertrud to work one day, and she got to explore a strange all-enclosed ship at the dock that looked like a long giant gray pipe with a little house on top. This was Pappi's project, something called an *Untersee Boot* or U-boat, and everyone was so nice to her, treating her like a smart little girl. She marveled at how compact everything was in the U-boat, including the tiny *Kombüse*, a kitchen that seemed about the size of something her dolls would use. The cook carefully explained to Gertrud how he served a ship full of hungry sailors from that little room.

Wilhelmshaven was another old city and a lively place with the vibrancy of many cultures coming together. Denmark sat not too far north, and England lay across the North Sea to the west.

The Siepmanns' home sat on the ground floor of an apartment complex with a courtyard at center. Gertrud would visit an old man named Rosenzweig who lived in a small house next to the apartment building. Herr Rosenzweig grew beautiful flowers. He seemed very old to Gertrud, with a long white beard, worn face, and simple long black coat. He moved about slowly and always wore a small cap on the crown of his head. Sometimes he would cut flowers from his garden and present them to her with a gentle smile.

These were thrilling times for children in Germany with so much excitement and color and pageantry. They would be told of a parade, and people would line the streets. Then bands marched past in uniforms, playing grand tunes with lots of brass and drums that seemed to go straight through Gertrud. Soldiers went by carrying guns strapped to their shoulders, their black boots striking the cobblestones all at once so the ground shook. At the head of each column of soldiers was a man carrying a Schellenbaum, a silver staff adorned with a gleaming eagle, its wings spread on top with a red, white, and black flag underneath. The Schellenbaum would pound the street in rhythm to the music, and bells on the crossbar of the staff rang in unison. Gertrud watched the people cheer, wave, and applaud as the soldiers moved on by. It was like something out of a grand, life-sized storybook.

7
MR. SMITH GOES HOLLYWOOD

In personal and career terms 1938 topped 1937 for Jim Stewart. Ginger Rogers had asked for Jim to co-star in a picture at RKO called *Vivacious Lady*. Ginger very much wanted to be seen as more than Fred Astaire's dancing partner, and she decided to hitch her star to former boyfriend Jim in what turned out to be a hit picture. The plot presented Ginger as a nightclub singer who falls in love with a small-town college professor and marries him after a whirlwind courtship. Then he has to take his showgirl back to meet the folks, with comedy hijinks ensuing. It was a plot Jim had run through in his mind a time or two, the idea of taking a girl, this girl in fact, to Pennsylvania to meet Dad and Mother, his own small-town parents.

Jim kept working and working. Next MGM cast him in *The Shopworn Angel* as a soldier from Texas about to go off to the Great War who meets and falls in love with a New York stage actress before shipping out to a fatal encounter with trench warfare. Joan Crawford was supposed to star but didn't like the script; instead MGM cast newly signed Margaret Sullavan to star with Jim in what would prove a success at the box office, if never a believable plot line. But these silver screen love stories with Everyman Stewart romancing vivacious ladies earned him plenty of feature space in the fan magazines.

"Whatever it is that James Stewart has," wrote reporter James Reid in the October 1938 issue of *Modern Screen*, "it's enough to give the feminine population of Hollywood gooseflesh and complexes." Reid interviewed Stewart on location in Burbank during summertime production of *You Can't Take It with You*, a loud comedy adapted from a stage play that reminded Hollywood producer and director Frank Capra of his own boisterous family and would soon earn him Best Director and Best Picture Academy Awards. The heat of late spring in Burbank neared 100 and drove the interviewer and his subject to an air-cooled restaurant, where the topic was, "Why hasn't Jim Stewart married now that he has just passed his thirtieth birthday?" Five years earlier, Jim Stewart had been in New York City and struggled to make the rent; now he was giving the women of Hollywood "gooseflesh"?

"He has to find the right girl," Stewart snapped. "So far he hasn't found her."

It soon became a telling interview as Jim showed his cards. "I don't think I'd mind if she were a sort of duplicate of Margaret Sullavan. She could be the same size, look a little like that, be a little like that." It wasn't easy loving a woman married sequentially to two of your best friends and now living with the second of those husbands, Leland Hayward, just a half a block away from Jim's house on Evanston Drive in Brentwood.

To save his sanity, Jim had become a Hollywood bachelor doing what came naturally to such creatures. He dated, gravitating to the leading ladies he used to watch in pictures during his Mercersburg days and then his New York City starvation period when he managed to scrape together dimes to go to the movie houses. The first in a string of Hollywood conquests was Norma Shearer, whom he had seen in many pictures, including *A Free Soul*, silk robe gaping as she reclined on a chaise longue and said to Clark Gable with outstretched arms, "Come on, put 'em around me."

Norma Shearer was an Academy Award winner and the queen

of MGM, once its most famous actress—she had appeared in the first MGM picture ever, *He Who Gets Slapped*, with Lon Chaney in 1924. Now, at the time of the release of her latest and last big picture, *Marie Antoinette*, Norma had become the studio's most tragic figure, widow for going on two years of MGM's executive producer Irving Thalberg.

Stewart bumped into Norma accidentally on purpose at a William Randolph Hearst costume party, he a cowboy, she Marie Antoinette in a massive, glimmering costume from her picture, which was about to be released. Jim had motive and opportunity for the meeting; he idolized Norma Shearer. Sparks flew between thirty-six-year-old Shearer and thirty-year-old Stewart; Josh Logan would claim to be an eyewitness to Jim's tipsy proclamation to Marie Antoinette, "You're the most gorgeous creature I've ever seen." And that was that.

Jim Stewart hit the sexual heights with Irving Thalberg's widow, not quite Norma Desmond but a woman much closer to silent pictures than was he. Norma had grown accustomed to the highest strata of Hollywood culture, and that's where she took Jim, the Pennsylvania kid motivated to purchase a tux so he could squire her about town. Since she was Norma Shearer, queen of MGM, Howard Strickling shooed the press away from what could quickly become an uncomfortable turn of events for ascending star James Stewart. What could the boy next door possibly be doing with the widow Thalberg, a woman six years his senior, a sexually experienced Hollywood type as proven by any number of pre-Code pictures. A mother of two. Was Jim soon going to be taking on not only the siren but her ready-made family as well?

Said Jim, "I was also having a good time with pals like Hank Fonda and Johnny Swope, and a lot of those good times were spent in the company of…various ladies."

This Jim Stewart was the man who sat sweating in Burbank with reporter James Reid in June 1938, Norma Shearer's lover,

Jim Stewart, speaking passionately of Maggie Sullavan as a means of keeping the reporter away from the awful truth. But, of course, Reid would have known all about Norma because the press corps knew everything and averted gazes discreetly as necessary.

Wendy Barrie, Jim's co-star two years earlier in the MGM picture *Speed*, shed light on what Josh Logan called "Jim's womanizing ways," which was part of the Stewart view of the male approach to the female.

"I think part of his aggressiveness with women," said Barrie, "and he was aggressive, was due to his feeling that he was not handsome—he had this image of himself as a tall, gawky loon."

The loon felt it his obligation to test the reaction of the great Norma Shearer to his advances. In response he got more than he bargained for; he found himself in a relationship. He received from Norma a symbol of entrapment, a gold cigarette case inset with diamond chips, which would be memorialized not only in a Broadway play called *Stars in Your Eyes* but also in the script for the 1950 Paramount Picture *Sunset Boulevard*, written by Billy Wilder and Charles Brackett. The aging Brackett had toiled on the MGM lot at the time of Shearer's love affair with Stewart, working on the screenplay for Greta Garbo's *Ninotchka*. In such a position, Brackett had heard all the gossip about Norma and Jim—and the lot was ablaze with it.

But Jim remained the isolated soul that had confounded Ginger Rogers and now froze out Norma Shearer. He didn't like the way Norma spent her money and expected him to spend his own. Night after night in tuxes wasn't for the frugal Stewart. As he told James Reid that June day, "What really pleases me is to get in an evening at the Palomar, the big dance hall down at Third and Vermont. You can dance all evening for forty cents—or a dollar, if you want to sit in the loges between numbers."

Norma had no interest in forty-cent dances. She dressed to the nines, often styled in one of several perfectly coiffed wigs, and insisted on being seen in the best places. The rift between them grew and finally ripped them apart with, as Jim described it, Norma "giving me my freedom."

"Sure, I'm restless," Stewart grumbled. "That's one of the penalties of being a Hollywood bachelor. It's a tough town to settle down in. You're under constant tension, if you're any good at worrying. And I'm an expert at it."

What did Jim, a rising movie star under long-term contract to the biggest studio in town, have to worry about? Well, plenty. His own studio didn't know how to use him. He was like the rookie ballplayer riding the pine waiting for one of the regulars to twist a knee. That worried him. Yearning for a woman he could never have because she belonged to one of his best friends worried him. The act of dating and risking rejection worried him, as did the threat of some news item about a fast Hollywood woman making it to the attention of Dad back in Indiana. He worried about all of it, all the time, and no one ever would have expected it, judging him by that laid-back veneer.

"Jimmy never lost a certain shyness and nervousness," said John Swope, who labeled the condition "a deterrent to him psychologically." That hot-burning inner furnace would keep his metabolic rate so high that no matter what or how much he ate—and it was never a plateful because he couldn't keep it down—he remained rail thin.

And yet the women kept coming. Norma Shearer was barely gone when Fox star Loretta Young, one of the most ardent heterosexuals in Hollywood, stepped up to declare affection for the restless one. Another frantic coupling ensued, and Loretta fell harder for the Stewart charm than Norma had, and Jim—well, Jim had bagged another of Hollywood's vintage leading ladies without half trying. It was becoming quite an obvious pattern: He found only the A-team attractive.

Unfortunately for the trophy collector, Loretta possessed

something Jim had never before seen: an obsessive streak that soon terrified him. Hollywood writer Adela Rogers St. Johns would say that Loretta "chased him around shamelessly, and made a god damned fool of herself." Jim was just being Jim—charm the girl, prove what he needed to prove to himself, then grow bored with any sort of routine, withdraw, and move on. He liked the sex— who wouldn't? He just wasn't going to marry this type of woman, especially somebody with the baggage of Loretta Young, who had already seen one marriage annulled and had become the talk of the town due to her affair with MGM's Clark Gable that, some whispered, had resulted in a daughter out of wedlock. All this was way too messy for Jim, facing again and again the *Vivacious Lady* small-town-boy-meets-showgirl plot when he imagined taking these women back to Indiana to meet his folks. How in the world would he explain Norma or Loretta or even the sweet but worldly wise Ginger?

Jim remained restless, tense, and ascending as his latest picture, *You Can't Take It with You*, went into general release in September 1938. Frank Capra had emerged as one of the most influential directors of the 1930s, reaching the heights with a run of Academy Awards for *It Happened One Night* followed by *Mr. Deeds Goes to Town* and then *Lost Horizon*, a fantasy picture that did well at the box office but couldn't match Capra's extravagant production costs. The energetic director recognized in Jim Stewart's streak of MGM pictures the raw material for something of a leading man next door with gentility, honesty, and solid comic timing for screwball. Capra signed Jim and figured to take him back to his Broadway roots by filming a hit stage play that would more or less guarantee success for all concerned. And a success it was, representing Stewart's longest home run yet—a wallop struck at Columbia Pictures.

Why did MGM not recognize what Cole Porter, Ginger Rogers, Frank Capra, and David O. Selznick did? Selznick was hard at work on his epic-in-the-making *Gone With the Wind* but also churning out other pictures in the meantime, the latest being *Made for Each Other*, a romance intended to rebrand "Screwball Girl" (so dubbed by *Life* magazine) Carole Lombard away from comedies that were beginning to curdle at the box office. Selznick needed someone to play opposite Lombard in the role of an earnest apprentice attorney, one-half of a young couple struggling their way up the ladder. It was a part made for Jim Stewart in a project that ultimately failed due to script second-guessing and rewrites. Mediocre reviews spelled box-office poison, which was bad news for Carole Lombard, although Stewart proved more resilient and moved on.

MGM continued to fumble around with Stewart in successive bombs, *Ice Follies of 1939* with Joan Crawford and *It's a Wonderful World* with Claudette Colbert, proving that even a plug-and-play talent the caliber of Jim couldn't overcome an indifferent script from the middle of the stack. Frank Capra, however, kept Jim's number handy for a project called *The Gentleman from Montana*, a picture about the essence of American democracy to be set in Washington, D.C. Capra could feel this premise in his heart and his bones: An idealistic young senator handpicked by a political machine because of his naïveté settles into a temporary seat in the U.S. Senate and tries his best to genuinely represent the people of his state. It was a part Capra felt was handcrafted for...Gary Cooper, fresh off the arduous production of the French Foreign Legion epic *Beau Geste* for Paramount. Capra negotiated with Samuel Goldwyn for a Cooper loan-out to Columbia. After all, a picture as big as the U.S. Capitol needed a star as big as Gary Cooper to play in it, and six-foot-four Coop actually hailed from Montana! But Sam Goldwyn had already lined up Coop to star in two Goldwyn productions, *The Real Glory* and *The Westerner*. What could be accomplished by loaning his stud out for somebody else's prestige picture?

Instead, Capra's call went out to MGM for another loan-out of

Jim Stewart. Capra had already been to Washington where he shot 2,500 still photos and exposed thousands of feet of motion picture film so he could get the feel of the seat of democracy. The photos would be used as background for set designers who would recreate the U.S. Senate chamber and other D.C. landmarks.

When Stewart took script in hand from a messenger at the front door of Evanston and started to look through it, the gravity of this "tremendous, wonderful role" hit him. He also knew the production would be hell for a man with a nervous disposition and weak stomach, and he was right. Eighty-nine production days culminated with a five-day shoot in Washington, D.C., at the Capitol, National Press Club, Senate Office Building, and a location that knocked Stewart for a loop, the Lincoln Memorial.

Stewart's most dedicated couple of days involved the application of a tincture of mercury bichloride, a caustic mercury-chlorine compound used to treat syphilis, onto his vocal cords by a physician to produce a wicked sore throat—the hoarseness that would come at the end of the twenty-three-hour filibuster staged for *Mr. Smith*'s climax. Stewart didn't simulate that painful last-minute speech about lost causes; he lived it.

But the road to classic status wasn't easy for *Mr. Smith Goes to Washington*, which earned the label "radical" after a premiere at Constitutional Hall in D.C. that was attended by Capra and an audience of congressmen and their hangers-on. How dare Mr. Capra assert that corruption was standard practice within the hallowed halls of Congress? In retrospect, *Mr. Smith Goes to Washington* continues to resonate specifically because it identifies the conflict of interest of politicians at a national level who could be bought and paid for and so malignantly influence American policy. The screenplay also happened to be written by a card-carrying Communist named Sidney Buchman, and so Capra and Stewart sweated out the first few days of release to see if moral outrage would sink the ship. Then, general release in block-booked movie palaces produced unprecedented word of mouth about Stewart, co-star Jean Arthur, and an American fable chronicling a decent young man fighting the good fight and prevailing against all odds.

Jim had remained sober as a judge in all regards through production of *Mr. Smith*, down to driving well below the speed limit, for fear "that something was going to happen to him," according to Jean Arthur, and spoil this chance he had been given. Now with *Mr. Smith* wrapped, Jim took the month of August 1939 to visit France and England, places he always had wanted to see, places so vital, so peaceful. But just to the east lay a Germany that was growing bolder by the day, grabbing land and rattling sabers.

At the time of his European trip, Jim had already been signed by producer Joe Pasternak at Universal Pictures for a western. Pasternak had been making a name with a string of profitable Deanna Durbin pictures. Now Joe was feeling his oats and had latched onto a script called *Destry*, adapted from a book by popular western writer Max Brand that (claimed Pasternak) had a part that was perfect for Jim Stewart. Early trade ads capitalized on the forthcoming *Mr. Smith Goes to Washington* by pitching a working title of *The Man from Montana*. After Pasternak announced that he had signed Stewart, he began to have the script tailored for Jim and went after the perfect woman to work with Jim: Hollywood exile Marlene Dietrich.

What? The MGM string bean Stewart in a western? Paired with a woman who had been driven clean out of the country after a series of lethal bombs, including Selznick's *The Garden of Allah*? Hadn't Tom Mix already ridden Max Brand's *Destry* dinosaur in a 1932 picture? But Pasternak had a gut feeling and a vision that motivated him to track down Dietrich on the French Riviera. He managed to get her to the phone, where he explained that he wanted her in Hollywood for a western.

"You must be crazy," she moaned in a voice known the world over. "Haven't you heard? I'm box office poison."

In the end Pasternak got his girl, the hottest ticket in Hollywood eight years earlier in the wake of *The Blue Angel* and *Morocco*, but then with each fancy, inaccessible-to-middle-America production thereafter, she had lost her audience.

Jim returned to New York City from his European vacation aboard the French liner *Normandie* on August 28, 1939, after an Atlantic crossing that also transported George Raft, Constance Bennett, Sonja Henie, director Josef von Sternberg, and many other high-profile celebrities across the North Atlantic. Stewart then flew cross-country, arriving in Hollywood August 30 to start memorizing early scenes for his *Destry* picture, even though much of the script hadn't been finalized. Two days later, radios blasted the news of German tanks rolling through Poland, and a few days after that, Pasternak picked up Marlene and her lover and companion, famed German novelist Erich Maria Remarque, at the Pasadena train station, where once Hank had picked up Jim. Then, as now, no reporters or photographers covered the event.

Over at Universal, Pasternak introduced the incomparable Marlene to her star-struck co-star, charming and charmable (if you were a movie queen) Jim. He beheld five-foot-four, blue-eyed, honey-haired Dietrich in the flesh, complete with that cat-ate-the-canary smirk, which came with the package. She had him at hello.

"She liked having sex with big-name male stars and called each one a 'conquest,'" said her friend, Hollywood actor and writer Steve Hayes, who also knew Stewart. "That's an interesting viewpoint. No mention of love or attraction; just one conquest after another." For Joan Crawford, sleeping with and controlling directors and co-stars was business; for Marlene, it was sport. Conquests.

Tight-lipped Jim would admit later that his association with Dietrich was "fairly romantic" and that he was "taken off guard by her adult concept of life." That's saying something for a man who had dated Norma Shearer. His relationship with Dietrich grew plenty adult and, according to Remarque, the thirty-eight-year-old

Marlene became pregnant as a consequence of the passionate affair with Stewart, with no child resulting after a sudden trip to New York City. Much later in life, Dietrich would have nothing kind to say about her *Destry* co-star, although they did make another picture together in 1951.

Stewart's friend Burgess Meredith dismissed the notion that an abortion had resulted from the Stewart-Dietrich affair and said, "If you ask me, the person who began those rumors was Dietrich. I think she considered it an unpardonable sin when Jim told her it was over."

But their 1939 feature, *Destry Rides Again*, proved a tremendous hit, revitalizing Dietrich's career and showcasing the fact that the man nicknamed Slats could even play westerns, which no one saw coming.

Jim rolled back through the lion's gates at MGM as a genuine Hollywood star, a talent to be exploited with a real assignment, not middling programmers. This time he was given a romantic A-picture, *The Shop Around the Corner*, about pen pals who unknowingly begin working together at a Budapest leather goods shop and, after many trials and tribulations, fall in love. Sought-after director Ernst Lubitsch, fresh off work with Greta Garbo in *Ninotchka*, also at Metro, led a strong ensemble cast including Stewart and the love of his life to date, Margaret Sullavan. By now Jim had grown accustomed to the exercise of working with Maggie, romancing her and kissing her on soundstages and then sending her home to his Brentwood neighbor, Leland Hayward. If these productions unhinged Jim emotionally, he gave no hint of it on-screen. The smooth, happy, and stage-bound production of *The Shop Around the Corner* wrapped principal photography in six short weeks.

As the holidays approached at the end of 1939, Jim wanted and needed to get away. He headed east, back to New York City, where he met Doddie and Ginny for a reunion, with plans to proceed back home to see his parents for Christmas. The world had reached the end of the 1930s, which for Jim had been a crazy decade that began on the stage playing before dozens and ended on the screen playing before millions. He was thirty-one now as he flew east on DC-3s to reach LaGuardia. Even riding tailwinds it was eighteen hours coast to coast with at least three stops along the way—more if mechanical difficulties arose—offering time to think about the past, present, and future. He felt his life was about to change; he just didn't know how soon. In fact change would come in just days with a new romantic association like none he had had to date.

He had been playing with fire when he got involved with some of the most ego-minded women in Hollywood. Loretta began to scare some sense into him when she came on so very strong and talked marriage. Then, the relationship with Marlene, so sexually sublime and adult minded, had terrified him by the way it ended in high drama. It ended the way it had to end because there could be nothing worse than bringing a movie star home to Indiana, unless it was bringing a pregnant movie star home. That indeed could be worse. So Jim made a rule for himself and he lived by it: He decided he would not marry someone in the business. Period.

Of course, sharing this information on a first date might put a damper on romance, so he continued to play the field. A couple of months earlier, on October 10, he had sat eating dinner at the Cock 'n Bull restaurant at the bottom of Sunset Strip. Across the way, he noticed two very attractive sisters dining together. They were the de Havilland girls, Olivia and her slightly younger sister, Joan, who used the last name Fontaine. Olivia recorded the incident in her journal—she thought it giggle-worthy that James Stewart was so obviously interested in one sister, or both.

Later in the year Jim showed his hand; it had been Olivia, known around town as Livvie, who had drawn his interest. A movie magazine asked Jim to provide his viewpoint as a male in Hollywood to a list of questions. The magazine asked Jim to name an opposite number among actresses to provide the woman's view. He chose Livvie. They had seen each other around town from a distance for years, but on this face-to-face meeting for the magazine piece, she told her diary, "Heavens! I didn't know he was so tall! My gaze traveled up—up—up—and at last I came to the Stewart face." She liked his face; he liked hers.

Up until December 1939 Olivia de Havilland had been known primarily as Errol Flynn's girl in a number of costume pictures at Warner Bros. of Burbank. Rumors around town said Errol and Olivia were on again, off again. Of course, Flynn had been married to French actress Lili Damita since 1935, but that barely seemed to put a dent in his daily consumption of girls anywhere within reach. Errol had already proposed to Livvie, but she told him a relationship was impossible as long as he remained entangled with Lili. Which is not to say Livvie and Errol hadn't gotten physical; after all, he was Errol Flynn and she was only human.

In December *Gone With the Wind* premiered in Atlanta, followed by Hollywood and New York City, and then went into limited release amidst gushing reviews and spectacular word of mouth. Suddenly de Havilland, billed fourth as Melanie Hamilton Wilkes, had become a star of the first magnitude, no longer a damsel in need of rescuing but now a luminary of prestige pictures.

According to the official story, Leland Hayward, now not only Jim's agent but Livvie's as well, called Slats during his stay in New York City with Doddie and Ginny. Was Jim interested in escorting poor dateless Livvie to the New York premiere of *Gone With the Wind*? But Stewart's preexisting interest in Livvie suggests the story of a blind date was a studio invention. Either way, Jim rode a limo onto the LaGuardia tarmac to pick up Livvie, and thus began several days of wining, dining, dancing, and general carrying on.

Jim and Livvie had a lot in common. Underneath, they were a couple of closed books, fierce introverts who were perfectly fine with their own company. Each had grown up with a dictatorial father figure, although hers had been a stepfather. Each thought a lot but said little; each had an internal nervous streak. Each had experienced frustration at a home studio that seemed indifferent or, in Livvie's case, downright hostile. Both placed career ahead of all and refused to rush impetuously into matrimony as so many of their peers seemed to. Yes, Livvie was a movie star, but for the first time since Ginger, Jim wasn't dating a much older, much more famous, sexually experienced movie queen.

Soon, Jim and Livvie were seen at all the hotspots, the Cocoanut Grove, Ciro's, and Café Trocadero being favorite haunts. She even stopped seeing her then-boyfriend, United Artists talent agent Tim Durant, and dated Jim exclusively into the spring of 1940. Marriage rumors abounded, with a different fan magazine taking up the marriage watch each month. For once the tables were turned on Jim—an aloof young woman had managed to capture his imagination because he never quite knew what she was thinking. Was he ready to settle down? He began to wonder, and yet he knew his future was up in the air.

By now the situation in Europe had grown ever more dire. England was tied to Poland by treaty, and when Germany had invaded Poland six months earlier in September 1939, England was obliged to declare war. Now, all that stood between Germany and England was the lush countryside of France. Jim scanned the newspapers daily for changes to the European situation, and nothing kept happening. Sky watchers in London expected German air raids at any moment—hundreds of thousands of wooden coffins had been pre-built and stacked in London in case of the worst. It was the *Sitzkrieg*, the phony war, an oppressive calm before the storm that everyone knew would brew up and everyone was dreading. Jim returned to work on what was, for MGM, an unprecedented production during the quiet time, *The Mortal Storm*, set in Germany and showing how the rise of National Socialism was tearing families and friendships apart. *Confessions of a Nazi Spy*, released by Warner

Bros. a year earlier, had been the first anti-Hitler major production by a Hollywood studio. *The Mortal Storm* would be the second, this time much more personal and upsetting as it depicted corruption of German young people by the Nazi propaganda machine and the removal of Jews from German society. Up to now, the Hollywood studios had been avoiding actions that might alienate their European markets, of which Germany remained a linchpin. But Jack Warner had finally bucked the trend, and now Louis B. Mayer would follow suit.

"The emotional and nervous strain was terrific," said Jim Stewart of the experience of making *The Mortal Storm*, the last of four pictures that would co-star him with the woman he could never have, Maggie Sullavan. As they shot, the British Expeditionary Force of 158,000 troops landed in France in support of French infantry divisions that daily expected to receive a German frontal assault. The free world felt that the combined British and French forces would stabilize the situation. Hitler wouldn't dare attack and suffer the bloody nose the Allies could inflict. But Hitler did the unexpected: The *Sitzkrieg* ended when Germany invaded not France but Norway and Denmark.

Soon after *The Mortal Storm* wrapped, Jim began *No Time for Comedy*, his first picture at Olivia de Havilland's home studio, Warner Bros. In a move not unlike trading big-league ballplayers, David O. Selznick had traded the rights to James Stewart to Jack Warner in exchange for Olivia de Havilland's appearing in *Gone With the Wind*. Warner had done this prior to the release of *Mr. Smith* and *Destry Rides Again* and now in April 1940 when production commenced, he gleefully watched one of the top actors in the world toiling on Warner soundstages. Both Jim and Livvie had told the Warner brass that they would not participate in any PR trumpeting their romance, not for *No Time for Comedy* or for her Warner Bros. vehicle in production, *My Love Came Back*.

Despite the presence of fun and funny Rosalind Russell as his co-star, Jim didn't find anything easy about playing comedy these days. A month into production, news broke that 1,500 German tanks had motored through the Ardennes Forest in front of 1.5 million troops. Supported by Luftwaffe dive bombers, the armor and infantry attacked French cavalry and French infantry, tore through both, threatened Paris, and then made an oblique move northward toward Calais and the English Channel and split Allied forces in two. Far from bloodying Hitler's nose, Allied troops had been driven from the field and just that fast, Europe was about to fall to Nazi Germany.

For what it mattered in a world falling apart, *No Time for Comedy* had been a Broadway hit for Laurence Olivier, and Jim Stewart was no Olivier. A rewrite was in order to pitch the plot toward Jim's unique talents. Instead of portraying an urbane playwright on Broadway contemplating leaving his wife, Jim is a reporter who writes a play in his spare time and meets and falls in love with the actress chosen as the play's star. It was standard boy meets girl, boy loses girl, boy gets girl, with some hints of *Mr. Smith* tossed into the cocktail shaker. The result was an economical Stewart star vehicle that would go on to make money for Warner Bros.

By the time the Warner picture had wrapped, Italy was an Axis participant in the war, Germans had marched into Paris, and, while Jim was on hiatus before starting another picture assignment, France surrendered.

The weight of the world fell upon the shoulders of the cast of his next picture back at MGM, *The Philadelphia Story*. Jim would portray a cynical newspaper reporter who falls in love with a society girl as the second-billed male star to Cary Grant, on loan from Columbia Pictures. The female lead, Katharine Hepburn, had starred in the stage version of *The Philadelphia Story* and rode the Hollywood comeback trail after having been considered box-office poison as recently as 1938. Hepburn believed that this new picture would be her triumph, and the three superstars responded beautifully to George Cukor, one of the most skilled directors in town. The production was efficient but never chummy among Hepburn, Grant, and Stewart as the world spun into fragments in the summer of 1940. During the final weeks of production, the battle for Britain had begun—and Stewart and Hepburn felt great sympathy for Bristol-born Grant. Cast and crew devoured the latest news of German planes pounding British airfields in an attempt to knock the Royal Air Force out of action, while RAF Spitfires scrambled to meet the threat. The German goal of clearing the skies of British fighters would set into motion Operation Sea Lion, the ground invasion of the United Kingdom, and so hundreds of thousands of German troops amassed on the French coastline, waiting. As Jim Stewart followed reports of the action, he confirmed for himself an unassailable fact: This next war would be an air war. The Luftwaffe had used air power as a key component in all its invasions. And now both Germany and England were jockeying for position with, you guessed it, air power. Whoever ruled the skies would rule the world. And this fact meant everything, simply everything, to Jim Stewart.

8
SEEING HISTORY

Gertrud Siepmann began grade school in a two-story brick schoolhouse in Wilhelmshaven. Every morning her class stood facing a larger-than-life-sized portrait of the Führer to recite a pledge of allegiance, the right arm of each child pointed out stiffly in salute. Gertrud's reading books featured stories about the Führer and about what it took to be a good German.

Gertrud was living a happy childhood, but there were exceptions. One November morning in 1938, Riele bundled her daughter up for a trip and said something puzzling: "You are going to see history today." They took a tram downtown where they saw buildings called synagogues that lay in smoking ruins. Entire blocks of storefronts had their windows smashed so that shards of glass covered the pavement. "It was hard to walk," said Gertrud. "My feet slipped on the glass, and the smoke stung my eyes and burned my throat." Terrible things had just happened there. Gertrud's horrified question of her mother was an obvious one, even to a small child. "Why?"

One day not long after *Kristallnacht*, the night of broken glass, Gertrud went to visit her neighbor, Herr Rosenzweig, but he wasn't in his garden and failed to answer the door when she rang the bell. She asked around about the kindly man with the long beard and was told, "He's been taken away to a labor camp where he won't be able to do any more harm." Herr Rosenzweig taken away? He had occupied a warm place in Gertrud's heart, and now that spot darkened with worry. How could he hurt anyone by growing flowers?

At the beginning of spring 1939 came amazing news: The Führer, Adolf Hitler, was going to visit Wilhelmshaven to launch the battleship *Tirpitz*. He arrived April 1, the weather beautiful and great crowds, including the Siepmanns, greeted him. Red banners with swastikas waved in the stiff sea breeze. Then Gertrud saw the Führer in a long green coat adorned with medals. His face was happy as he chatted with other soldiers before standing up at a microphone to speak, his words full of pride for Wilhelmshaven.

Slowly, the Führer's voice changed until he shouted and waved his fists in the air because England was doing awful things to Germany. In a little while Gertrud began to cry. Everyone loved this man, but seeing him in person filled Gertrud with fear and confusion.

War came when Germany went off to teach those "Tommies" a lesson. News reports told of the invasion of England's ally Poland, and then about the Battle of Britain. Late one night, a siren wailed. Hans and Riele hurried the family downstairs to their storage room in the basement. Many families trooped down the stairway in just such a fashion, their faces painted in worry, each to their own storage room.

A low drone and a vibration signaled planes approaching overhead. Anti-aircraft cannons fired, and distant crackles echoed. In a little while came rumbles like thunder. Soon, the roar was constant and frightening. Then it was over. The siren sounded once more, and they returned to their apartment. Out the windows they could see the orange glow of fires burning in the distance that alarmed Pappi as he sent the children back to bed. Not to sleep, exactly, but to bed.

Early in 1941, Hans announced the family must leave and go somewhere safe. All packed their suitcases, and he took them to the Bahnhof and kissed his wife and his four children good-bye and placed them on the train. It was the end of Gertrud's lovely childhood in a home with two parents and three siblings—that day in winter 1941 as the string of passenger cars pulled out of the station in Wilhelmshaven.

9
RESTLESS SPIRIT

Leland Hayward had to fly. Yes, he was one of Hollywood's most charismatic and powerful talent representatives as well as a successful theatrical producer, but first and foremost he was a pilot. Back in 1935 Leland had shown Jim Stewart and Hank Fonda what their newfound motion picture wealth could bring them: Flight was within their reach. Both began lessons at the Bob Blair School at Mines Field on the outskirts of Los Angeles. Jim soloed in twelve hours and flew one hundred hours over the next three years, obtaining his license as a private pilot in August 1938. It was a flying crowd; even Maggie flew. Later when Jim dated Livvie, they went up together, and with Jim's support Livvie later soloed on her way to a pilot's license.

But flying wasn't just fun and games and an escape from terrestrial problems. As the years passed and the world's horizons grew overcast, Jim knew deep down his passion for flight would combine with his family mission, his family responsibility—and most importantly, his obligation to his father, who had drummed it into Jim's head just as old J.M. had once drummed it into Alex—to serve his country in wartime. Jim knew it in his gut and worked in concert with this feeling through the late 1930s, flying out of Clover Field in Santa Monica where Howard Hughes kept his planes. Jim bought a Stinson 105 Voyager, a seventy-five-horsepower high-wing monoplane with a fuel capacity for seven hours of flying. It was painted high-gloss yellow. He picked a Stinson specifically because the Army used that model as trainers, and if he made it into the Army Air Corps—the branch that did most of the flying—he wouldn't need to learn the operation of the Stinson because he already would have logged a substantial number of hours in one.

As soon as his schedule allowed, which was January 1940, he flew his new plane east from Santa Monica to Kansas City to try it out. Relentlessly calm California weather caused him to underestimate the difficulty of the trip there and back. On the way home he flew into a storm and got lost. "I was riding the radio beam into Kingman, Arizona, from about 100 miles away," said Stewart, "when it faded out and I couldn't pick it up again. Below there was nothing but mountains and they all looked alike. I couldn't tell where I was, and I only had a couple more daylight hours to get my bearings. To make matters worse, the storm was tossing the plane around like a cork.... I was worried the buffeting was going to tear the plane apart."

Airsick from the rough ride and running out of daylight, Jim combed his maps and found an east-west railroad line that he figured had to be south—to the left—of his present course, so he banked to port and sank in the sky through the cloud cover to be able to see landmarks. "I turned south," he said, "finally picked up the railroad and followed it into Kingman—with about a half hour of daylight to spare."

The solo voyage showed he was capable of keeping his head and finding a solution while airborne—abilities that would prove critical in years to come. Already, a military future was at the front of his mind. "To get into the Air Corps," he told magazine reporter James Reid toward the end of 1940, "you have to have that kind of training. If we get into the war, I want to get into the Air Corps."

Leland Hayward had dreamed up the idea of creating a school for pilots for the Air Corps, which was as of then a small, undermanned unit. Hayward chose Glendale, Arizona, northwest of Phoenix, for what he dubbed Thunderbird Field, and now he endlessly reviewed blueprints for a set of buildings that would resemble the mythical Anasazi Thunderbird. Ground breaking would start soon, and Jim dreamed of finding his way to Thunderbird when the time came. He enthusiastically invested in the enterprise, as did Fonda and Sullavan. John Swope, veteran of the first FDR administration, had already been designated to manage the field when it began operation. Now Hayward and Swope, along with ex-military pilot Jack Connelly, were also talking about creating a regional airline to connect the cities of California; they intended to call it Southwest Airways.

With the world situation continuing to deteriorate and the logging of flight time imperative, Jim returned to MGM to make a picture with respected director Clarence Brown and Hollywood's most unusual leading lady, Hedy Lamarr. Possessing world-renowned beauty marked her as unusual; as did appearing nude at length in the orgasmic 1933 German picture *Ecstasy*; as did marriage to Austrian munitions magnate Fritz Mandl; as did a bright mind and canny sense of herself and her surroundings; as did a willingness to acknowledge not much in the way of acting talent or sense of camera, lighting, or the business in general. Hedy Lamarr was an international personality, and Jim's new co-star in the MGM romantic picture, *Come Live with Me*. But like many in town these days, she wasn't a classically trained actress, which resulted in many blown takes.

Then the fates stepped in. In September 1940 President Roosevelt signed the Selective Training and Service Act, which required American men aged twenty-one to thirty-six to register for the draft. Jim did, and out of nearly one million men, his lottery number in a drawing held October 29 was 310, which meant he was to report for evaluation before beginning one year of training in the U.S. Army Reserves.

Jim reported immediately, while shooting *Come Live with Me* with Hedy, to enlist in the Army Air Corps. He figured getting in early would enhance his chances of becoming an Army pilot. He had also grown bored with his workload at MGM. The stimulation just wasn't there anymore. The recruiting officer and doctor seemed skeptical when they looked at his paperwork and saw Jim's birth date of May 1908. A thirty-two-year-old pilot? They told him that when war came, pilots would be twenty-one and twenty-two years old, certainly not over thirty. He was urged to reconsider his plan, but Jim looked them in the eye and asked for all due consideration. They assured him they would give it.

So he kept on working and wrapped *Come Live with Me* in time to report for work at United Artists in West Hollywood for a musical picture called *Pot o' Gold* with Paulette Goddard, which he knew was a stinker from day one, and he also started working at MGM as a supporting player in *Ziegfeld Girl*, an all-star extravaganza sequel to the 1936 Academy Award blockbuster, *The Great Ziegfeld*.

At the end of a long day at MGM and a long drive up to Brentwood from Culver City, Jim reached into his mailbox in the quiet winter's darkness of Evanston Drive and pulled out an official-looking letter. He held it in hand and his heart raced at the thought of being called to serve, to being accepted as a man in the real world; to flying not as a hobby but as a living; to wearing an Army uniform and getting everything that went with it. To fulfilling his family mission. Here, inside this envelope, he saw salvation; no, redemption; no, escape. With shaking hands and clumsy fingers, he tore open the envelope there at the side of the street and unfolded a single sheet of paper. He stood there stunned: He held in his hand a six-month deferment from service in the military forces of the United States of America because he was deemed to be underweight for his height and therefore a health risk in the service.

He stayed unmoving in the dark, angling the letter to the

streetlight. He must have read it wrong. But, no, he had been rejected for service despite his cooperation and goodwill at the induction station a month earlier. 1-B. In other words, put on twenty pounds and we'll give you another shot, old-timer. Jim knew that despite milk shakes, potatoes, bananas, and everything else he tried to eat with that stomach of his and that metabolism, he wouldn't gain five pounds let alone twenty.

Jim stormed inside his house and got on the phone. He wondered if the Army's decision was on the level or if Louis B. Mayer was trying to protect his investment in a contract player; if it *was* L.B.'s doing, Jim would put up a fight. He needed verified answers before his father found out the news and assumed that Jim had agreed to a deferment. Then the worst happened: A headline hit the *New York Times* and fanned out across the country. JAMES STEWART IS DEFERRED.

Jim called home as soon as he learned that word had gotten out. The conversation with his father was as unpleasant as Jim reckoned it would be, with Alex reciting verbiage from the newspaper story: "Mr. Stewart's work in motion pictures justifies postponement of his being called into a year of training. The actor is taking a brief vacation between pics...." Alex reminded Jim of his obligation to his country. His obligation to his family. They all were watching from above, not only General Jackson but also J.M. and his brother Archie.

Jim replied that, quite the opposite, he had been counting on a 1-A classification to get him away from Hollywood. He could feel his attention to his work slipping and wanted to break free of Hollywood while good pictures like *The Mortal Storm* and *The Philadelphia Story* remained fresh in people's minds. For a variety of reasons both personal and professional, he assured Alexander Stewart, his mission in life was to be able to serve.

By the end of 1940, Jim had to admit more than boredom with the picture business—his soul was restless. He had reached the heights with *Mr. Smith* and *The Philadelphia Story*, and now here he was, making formula pictures without potential where he was just a face, and not a handsome face at that, and it bored him. Working with Frank Capra, George Cukor, and Katharine Hepburn could change a man, and render working with lesser lights a chore. Yes, Lamarr and Goddard had looks and appeal, but the productions were weak, and only strong performances from the leads might save either. In four short years he had become a veteran of the picture business and was perilously close to losing his way. And after rejection by the Army, even conquest of the top women in Hollywood no longer thrilled him—without half trying, he had managed to reel in new MGM sensation Lana Turner and studio headache Judy Garland.

Then came the ultimate irony: America's Everyman Jim Stewart beat the field on February 21, 1941, to win the Academy Award as Best Actor for *The Philadelphia Story*, topping Laurence Olivier for *Rebecca*, Charlie Chaplin for *The Great Dictator*, and even odds-on favorite Hank Fonda for *The Grapes of Wrath*. Jim wondered if the award was *de facto* recognition that he should have won for *Mr. Smith*, but he was grateful. True to his nature, Fonda steered clear of the ceremony, instead heading off for a fishing trip on John Ford's boat, *Araner*. Hank seemed relieved he didn't win and was "pleased" for his best friend's victory. A couple days after the ceremony, Jim packed up his Oscar and shipped it east to Alex, who placed it on display in the hardware store window.

Jim wasn't distracted from his task at hand for long and began a campaign to get the 1-B draft decision reversed. He did this through the man quoted in newspaper articles about the deferment, Maj. E.J. Plato, the Southern California draft coordinator. Major Plato couldn't tell Jim whether MGM had intervened by asking for a deferment because such a thing would have happened far above his level in direct conversation between MGM and the War Department. But right here at the local draft level, in Plato's office, Stewart used all his Hollywood-earned powers of persuasion to enlist the major's help in circumventing the official reason used to classify him 1-B: the rail-skinny frame staring him in the mirror all his adult life.

Jim went into conference with the doctor at the recruiting station, and Jim's medical file underwent a review. He described the efforts of Don Loomis to pack on weight through proteins in meat, fat in ice cream and whole milk, training with dumbbells, and every other trick employed, all with no effect because Jim was just too high-strung, and his digestion was haywire. He reasoned to the doctor that using standard charts was going to cost the U.S. Army a qualified pilot and a man genetically proven through family history in three wars over eighty years to be a born fighter and natural leader. In the end the doctor agreed to write a letter for Jim pertaining to his unusual physique that stated: "He has maintained this weight without illness for the past nine years while working as an actor. It is a family characteristic. He has a very light frame and slender figure and light musculature of good quality. Thorough physical examination including chest X-ray revealed no pathological cause of light weight."

Jim asked that this statement be placed in his file and that he be reconsidered for classification as 1-A. He couldn't control the machinations of men in the Thalberg Building at Metro-Goldwyn-Mayer, but he sure could take action on his own in a closed recruiting office and hope for the best.

10

THE EAGLE

For studious and overachieving Clem Leone, the years sped by in Baltimore, and in eleventh grade, Clem became a family legend. He walked onto a used car lot and fell in love with an eight-year-old 1933 Chevy Eagle, factory two-tone (green and black), two-door sedan with a spare wheel on each front fender. The price of eighty-five dollars was beyond his reach; he had saved up forty. But it was a man's car and Clem, now spending half his high school days in auto mechanics class, wanted it. Clem had been delivering papers with the understanding that his boss would teach him to drive a car; he had practiced long and hard.

In an unlikely encounter, the undersized high school junior went toe-to-toe with a full-grown car salesman whose credit check revealed Clem to be a highly respected paperboy. An hour later, Clem drove home the Chevy Eagle and parked it at 505 East Randall Street. Mother and Pop stumbled out of the house and stood transfixed at the first automobile in the family, and a sudden wild impulse took the three of them along with sisters Irma and Edith on an inaugural road trip, certainly the farthest Clem had ever been from home, all the way from South Baltimore to the tourist destination of 1941: the Civil War battlefield of Gettysburg, Pennsylvania. President Franklin Roosevelt had dedicated the Eternal Peace Light Memorial there less than three years earlier on the seventy-fifth anniversary of the battle, and Clem's *stepfather had wanted to see it ever since. Suddenly, Clem wielded the power to satisfy such an urge.*

The old Chevy opened up another world for Clem Leone. For a while now he had been intrigued by Sylvia Iafolla, a classmate at Southern High School. Clem would take his violin into the various classrooms and play a tune to entice younger students to sign up for musical instruments, and he would play steadily, flawlessly. Except in Sylvia's classroom. The scrutiny of this little Italian girl three years his junior, mere eye contact and any expression on her pretty face, would confuse Clem's fingers something awful, despite the fact that he was older and more mature. Sylvia confounded Clem. When Clem bought the Chevy, an early thought was to take Sylvia for a ride, but both knew the concept was forbidden by her parents, Alberico—from the Old Country—and Myrtle—one generation removed. Eventually, Clem and Sylvia found a solution: He would pick her up around the corner and take her for a nervous, innocent drive wherever.

Clem lived a studious life in South Baltimore in 1941. But cold winds started to blow across the Inner Harbor, signaling a change of seasons for Clem, Sylvia, and the world.

11
ALIAS JAMES SMITH

In early March 1941 Jim remained on hiatus from his home studio upon completion of the two Metro pictures and one at United Artists, and spent his days at Clover Field in the Stinson working toward a transport license as a commercial pilot. He had gotten close, very close, to the flight time needed to qualify. Arriving home one day he found another government letter in the roadside mailbox. Under the shield of the Selective Service System was printed in capital letters, ORDER TO REPORT FOR INDUCTION as a U.S. Army reservist. Jim stood at the side of Evanston Drive, stunned to silence once again. Chills raked him. He would get away from Hollywood. He would wear the uniform. He would make Dad happy. He might even fly. His greatest relief: L.B. hadn't won. Even if L.B. or Mannix or whoever had worked behind the scenes between Culver City and Washington to keep Jim out, they hadn't succeeded. Now it was official, and he held the precious piece of paper saying he was in. All the way in.

He scanned the page. "You are hereby notified that you have now been selected for training and service in the…" Typed onto the pre-printed solid blank line was the word Army. There. The Army. The Air Corps. Such a relief!

He was to report to draft board No. 245 in West Los Angeles on the twenty-second day of March 1941. Well, there it was. James

Maitland Stewart would follow old J.M. and Union Gen. Sam Jackson and Alex into line to swear the oath. Jim would do what his ancestors always did: feed a restless spirit with conflagration.

He now faced a certain future that would arrive on a certain date. He would later admit, "You have that sick feeling, that pigeon with a wing off, flapping around in your stomach. It's the same feeling you have before a race or before you play in a football game or go in and ask the boss for a raise. It's the same feeling I have when I go to a preview of a picture I'm in."

He returned to Clover Field early and often in March and climbed into the Stinson to log more flight time. He was worried about getting his commercial pilot's rating, as he related to his favorite reporter, James Reid: "You have to pass tests in precision flying. You have to execute a succession of figure eights around two pylons a certain distance apart—which isn't so easy when you have to make your turns in a limited amount of space. You have to be able to come in from a thousand feet and make a full-stop landing within forty feet of a certain white line. You have to know how to go into and come out of tailspins. You have to know how to fly by instruments." He also admitted to Reid he was sweating the four-hour written exam and had enlisted the aid of an Army instructor who stopped by Evanston every night.

Precisely because he arrived prepared and had not only gone by the book but also absorbed it, on Monday, March 10, he earned the coveted rating of commercial pilot that he reasoned would, coupled with his Princeton degree, put him further down the track for consideration as an Air Corps officer and command pilot, offsetting his advanced age of almost thirty-three in a program where ideal pilots were a decade younger than that.

On Sunday, March 16, he took off yet again into the early afternoon sky to log hours, always more hours to impress the Air Corps. He climbed out of Clover Field and banked right, heading north along the coast. Below sprawled Marion Davies' beach house and its outbuildings, bringing to mind the old days of the William Randolph Hearst parties. Days he figured to be done with now. After a while he banked right again and flew over the Warner Ranch at Calabasas, over endless high-rolling hills and tall grass, a beautiful day to fly, but then they all were, days spent powering his plane through the air in utter and total freedom from the cares below. There wasn't room for any thought other than powered flight and the instrument panel. Here he ruled his world, free of the Mayers and any woman who would try to control him.

"There's so much to think about up there," he said, meaning the gauges indicating performance of the ship and the weather outside, "that you forget things down below. Flying is something altogether different from the way I'm earning my living. That's what I like about it.... Flying is sort of a guarantee that life will continue to have variety."

He traced Mulholland Drive, skirting the ridge tops at an altitude of 5,000 and continued east. All of a sudden the engine coughed and the Stinson gave a lurch; coughed again and the nose dropped and he began losing altitude. Where was he, Tarzana? No, no, it was Van Nuys. He spotted the Van Nuys airfield in the distance and headed that way. He put in a call to Van Nuys tower saying he needed to land there, and they gave him a runway assignment. Except he couldn't make it. He muscled the controls and with the engine sputtering kept just enough airspeed to descend with wings level. He heard nothing but the malfunctioning engine and felt its spasmodic coughs and in his ears was the roar of rushing air.

Ahead lay the Van Nuys runways and just then, at 500 feet, the engine quit. Mid-cycle. Quit. And in a power glide he glimpsed a flat farm field and aimed at it. Teeth gritted, gripping the wheel, he maneuvered as best he could into a landing in the field and... smacked into the parched California earth, sending a spray of dirt in all directions. Impact slammed his head off the control panel and he hung there in dust and smoke. Pretty or not, he was down and still alive. He worried how badly he had injured himself; he worried more about his plane.

An ambulance dispatched by the airfield tower came in to scrape Jim Stewart out of the Stinson and hurry him away to a hospital in Van Nuys. Consciousness brought with it worry, no, terror that his Air Corps career had gone down with the Stinson, and what good was a pilot who couldn't keep his ship in the air? His swearing-in was just six days away! He thought as fast as his post-collision brain would go: James Stewart the actor couldn't be admitted to a hospital after a plane crash. No. Impossible. It would be the end of everything. He kept his face down as the attendants pulled the gurney out of the ambulance, and James Stewart admitted himself to the hospital as James Smith.

But even in a town where discretion by the press saved many a star, word about the MGM leading man who cracked up his airplane got out anyway. The story hit the wires as he lay in the hospital with bumps and bruises to his ego and his body.

Buzz Meredith visited him during recovery and said, "He had a bump on his head the size of a baseball and there were cuts on his face, but he was sitting up and smiling. I said, 'Jim, are you sure you can survive a war? You have trouble surviving in your own plane.'"

Three days later L.B. summoned Jim to a private meeting for an inevitable tongue-lashing about the folly of general aviation for movie stars. Jim entered the art deco Thalberg Building and rode the elevator up to three and the great man's office, ready to face the worst. But the fact was that once he entered the service, who was to say he would live to make another picture anyway? He had crashed his plane on friendly territory accumulating flight time to earn his way into the job of Army Air Corps pilot, and sooner or later somebody would be shooting at him from the ground or the air meaning to kill him. Did it really matter what Louis B. Mayer thought anymore?

L.B. started out warmly but cut to the chase. "You're just giving up this wonderful screen career you've made for yourself," he told Jim, "and all you'll be doing is sitting at some clerk's desk on a military base somewhere, and then you'll regret it."

"Mr. Mayer," said Jim, "this country's conscience is bigger than all the studios in Hollywood put together, and the time will come when we'll have to fight."

L.B. changed tactics and asked Jim to consider fulfilling his obligation in the very fine Army Air Corps Motion Picture Unit based at Wright Airfield in Dayton, Ohio, where, Mayer reasoned, Jim would remain just a plane or car ride away from his family. Mayer argued that Jim could do a lot more good for his country as a recruiting tool, urging young men to choose to become pilots or navigators or bombardiers, than he could by serving as one man in one airplane. The boss didn't even ask for an answer. He led Jim out of the office and down the hall and just implored him to keep the idea in mind, to consider it.

Mayer pushed open the door to his private dining room and motioned Jim inside. Voices boomed, "Surprise!" Jim stood in the doorway of a room crammed with more stars seated at the long table than there were in heaven. He looked around to see Clark Gable, Lana Turner, Walter Pidgeon, Judy Garland, Ann Rutherford, Rosalind Russell, Diana Lewis, and Ruth Hussey along with Eddie Mannix, Bill Grady, and the publicity boys, Howard Strickling, Ralph Wheelright, and Otto Winkler. Stewart was shown to a seat next to L.B. at the head of the table and dined there with his MGM family. Afterward, L.B. rose to his feet and talked about Jim's arrival on the lot and ascent to the top pictures in town. He said he realized how seriously Stewart took his work at the studio and appreciated the fact that Jim set such a fine example for other Metro contract players. Then, he looked down at the honored guest and promised that his job would be waiting for him upon completion of the military obligation.

As he settled in his seat, L.B. motioned for Jim to address the gathering. Jim arose much as Jefferson Smith accepting the Senate nomination. Jim said he had asked that nobody at MGM make a fuss about his departure and do something crazy like throw a party. Then he admitted that maybe a party wasn't such a bad idea after all, and his delivery produced chuckles from people who knew of his closed nature and how difficult he found these situations. You could put James Stewart on a soundstage replicating the U.S. Senate in front of 500 actors and extras and he'd be fine, perfectly at home—as long as he portrayed someone other than James Stewart. But ask him to be himself, ask him to let his guard down, and the real Jim Stewart was revealed, the guy with the nervous stomach who had spent years proving his worth through his sex partners.

After dinner with drinks in hand, those in attendance mingled. Stewart said, "Clark Gable came up to me and said, 'You know you're throwing away your career, don't you?'"

"Yep, I know," said Jim.

"You won't catch me doing that," said Gable, "but I wish you Godspeed."

Then every woman made a show of kissing Jim. It started with a peck on the cheek for luck from Rosalind Russell and then one from Judy, then Lana, and then Ann Rutherford. World-class kissers, both Lana and Ann, with neither letting on that they had already bagged Jim. It went with the territory—sooner or later, everyone bagged everyone in the jungle known as Hollywood. Jim seized the moment and approached a woman he hadn't yet bagged, Ruth Hussey, and asked for a date on his first leave, whenever that would be. What was a girl to do but say yes—if he promised to wear his uniform.

Afterward, according to Stewart, Roz Russell wiped the lipstick off Jim's face, and under each stain on the cloth she noted which lipstick belonged to which actress. "I carried that handkerchief with me for the rest of the war," said Jim, "as a good luck token."

The next night Jim was summoned to Franchot Tone's house for a different sort of get-together, a stag party dubbed the Military Ball. Those in attendance, Gable, Fonda, Buzz, Grady, Spencer Tracy, and Robert Taylor, each had trekked to Western Costume for an appropriate military uniform for the evening.

Jim didn't care that he was partying on the eve of induction day because he wouldn't have slept anyhow. At four in the morning, he asked Buzz and Bill to drive him over to Evanston so he could pack. They changed out of their military duds and got him home and then piled into Grady's convertible and raced east on San Vicente over to Brentwood and the intersection of Santa Monica and Westwood Boulevards where Jim and eighteen other inductees had been ordered to rendezvous. Jim and party arrived fifteen minutes late.

Suitcase in hand, wearing a suit and tie, fedora, and raincoat, Jim eased up to a nervous-looking collection of men and their luggage surrounding Army Sgt. James J. Smith. Stewart said to the gathering, "It's a little early in the morning," then, to the sergeant he gave his name. Smith checked Stewart's name off his list on a clipboard. Jim looked around him at the crowded corner and a near riot. He assumed upon arrival that the crowd numbering a couple hundred, all ages and sizes, all manner of dress, were there to see him. He didn't know at the time that the draft board had summoned the press—including newsreel camera crews—to assure adequate coverage of America's most famous draftee, and he never reckoned that the others in his draft group would have entourages larger than that of a Hollywood star.

Jim began to get his bearings. It dawned on him that the crowd included parents of the inductees, sweethearts, and friends. He recognized that the most boisterous members of the crowd were college kids apparently from USC. Lots and lots of them. They didn't have the slightest interest in old fogey Stewart but rather focused attention on two giddy fraternity brothers across the way. Off the sidewalk near the wall of a building, two boys who had been doing some drinking pounded tribal drums while a third played a trumpet and a fourth a trombone. The quartet managed to produce something that vaguely resembled "You're in the Army Now." Kids held signs reading, SO LONG, YARDBIRDS and GOOD-BYE, LITTLE FELLOWS. Jim stood there waiting, hands in pockets, grateful to have others in the spotlight this morning. One of the frat brothers wore an old German trench helmet that put Jim in mind of those sent to him by his dad from Germany, the ones he used as wardrobe in plays produced in his basement. He laughed to himself as photographers pressed in, snapping still photos, and newsreel crews shot motion picture film from vehicles parked at the curb.

Sergeant Smith stood next to Jim and murmured, "We're short one man." He shouted over the cacophony, "Alvin James King! King, are you here? Alvin...James...King!" The sergeant turned to Stewart and said, "He better show or there'll be a warrant issued."

Smith looked at his watch one last time. He shot a glance at the raucous band and shouted, "Cut out that racket!" Word was relayed to the musicians, and the street corner fell silent. To the inductees he said, "We will march down this street to the trolley stop and board the next train downtown! Fall in by twos!" The eighteen men clumsily arranged themselves.

"Move out!" Sergeant Smith ordered, and they ambled down the street in the loosest of assemblages. Jim gave Bill and Buzz a nod. They nodded back to Slats and watched him stride off down the street. He was noticeably taller and more gangling than the men with him, and yet still boyish. They had seen their friend every which way. Sober, drunk, loud, quiet, contemplative, and bemused. Slats was the guy who had somehow put himself in a position where the most famous women in the world were desperate to seduce him, and Meredith and Grady had seen him come home so many times from the hottest nights imaginable.

But they had never seen Jim Stewart look the way he looked now. Jim was gleeful. He might even have been deep-down happy. They didn't understand how this situation would make any man happy, but as he strode down the street and out of sight, on those spindly legs, with that ridiculous gait, *they* were happy because he gave every indication *he* was happy.

Inductee Stewart found himself on West Third Street downtown at Induction Station No. 2. On the second floor, amidst the great clatter of reporters and photographers surrounding him and crowding in, under the glare of lights on stands, he filled out questionnaires. He faced his first fire when a flashbulb exploded as they sometimes did, sending a shower of sizzling glass onto the desk and his papers. He flicked the hot shards onto the floor with the back of his hand and went on grinning.

He was fingerprinted—the press photographed it in multiple takes, from several angles. Eye test? The press was three feet away. A physical behind closed doors revealed that his hearing was 20/20, his visual acuity was 20/20, and he had twenty-eight teeth, normal reflexes, a normal gait, and no hernia, tonsils, hemorrhoids, or venereal diseases. He dressed again and went into another room with other inductees and just as many members of the press corps, raised his right hand, and repeated to an officer facing the group:

"I, James Maitland Stewart, do solemnly swear that I will bear true faith and allegiance to the United States of America and will serve them honestly and faithfully against all their enemies whomsoever. I will obey orders of the President of the United States and the officers appointed over me according to the rules of the articles of war. So help me, God."

The officer said, "Congratulations. You're in the army now." The men were assigned serial numbers and Jim learned his would be 39230721.

From there, he and the others filed onto a bus that drove them south to Fort MacArthur in San Pedro, near Long Beach and the ocean. Stepping off the bus the recruits ran a gauntlet of surrounding soldiers. "Suckers!" they shouted. "Get a load of that one!" somebody said of the skinny man who towered above the others. They were lined up on the parade ground and a drill sergeant taught them to count off. All were assigned barracks and then marched to the Mess Hall for lunch. Jim sat and managed a couple bites of food in a cavernous room full of men and conversation.

After lunch his group marched to the quartermaster depot to be uniformed and equipped. Jim held two pails of sand to force a full load of weight on his size-eleven feet so they would flatten out for fitting with shoes. He was issued a khaki-green uniform. He learned how to stand in formation, open and close ranks, march, and salute. He received a set of dog tags, a regulation haircut, and a Springfield rifle. He slept in bunk beds with all the others—beds spaced five feet apart. He spent the next day on KP, and the day after that scrubbing floors; he was a real soldier now.

On that first trip to the Mess Hall, he realized what an oddball he truly was. Why, these were mostly kids surrounding him, and here he was, more than a decade their senior, the old guy, the tall guy, the quiet guy, and worst of all, the movie star followed around the post by a reporter and photographers. It wasn't easy for Jim Stewart to talk to the other recruits; they had no idea how to approach a motion picture luminary.

He went through a sorting process like all the others, determining what his role would be in the Army, but Jim had programmed his role and now sweated out confirmation of assignment to the Air Corps. He needn't have worried. His military record included a document from the Adjutant General's Office dated March 22, the date of enlistment, indicating that Private Stewart was indeed an Air Corps assignee. That piece of paper meant everything. But there was another piece of paper. Mayer had been in contact with Washington and had gotten his way: After basic training, Stewart would be assigned to the Motion Picture Unit at Headquarters Squadron, 50th Transport Wing, Wright Field, Dayton, Ohio, "for the purpose of making motion picture shorts for the Air Corps. It is believed his services would be particularly effective in securing Flying Cadet candidates." Metro planned to see that its player-soldier kept plenty busy in the service. In the same document, Stewart was named for "the forthcoming School of Aviation Medicine Picture, as well as assisting in directing and as a commentator."

Directing? Was this supposed to be an enticement to Jim? Gosh, everyone wants to direct pictures! Private Stewart looked at the order and saw blood. He wasn't any eighteen-year-old kid staring at orders; he was James Stewart, Academy Award winner and friend of powerful people, and that better goddamned mean something because Jim Stewart was going to war.

He spent five days at Fort MacArthur. On Thursday, March 27, he and several others from his induction class were assigned to Headquarters, Air Corps Basic Flying School at Moffett Federal Airfield in Mountain View, California, outside San Francisco. Jim settled in there and shed himself of that pigeon-with-a-clipped-wing feeling.

He started buzzing about Moffett's runways in an AT-6 Texan trainer, showing potential as a military pilot, and he declared to the press: "I'm feeling swell, getting in good condition, and get along fine with the other draftees. They all treat me very well." He added, speaking now directly to his father, "We enlisted men have come to love the service. Every one of us has turned his face from our normal pursuits and has his eyes lifted to a new ideal. There is a unity of thought and action that can not and will not be broken."

He earned corporal stripes and became a squad leader, his duties including drill instruction for new recruits.

"When you drill, and yell orders all day," said Jim, "going through the manual of arms, by nightfall you're hoarse and ready for bed."

When he had been on station at Moffett for a month, a directive from Washington ordered him to Wright Field, Ohio. Corporal Stewart lost his temper, and because he was James Stewart, secured a meeting unprecedented for a recruit: Jim was welcomed in the office of Col. E.B. Lyon, commanding officer at Moffett Field.

If Jim hadn't been Jim, he would have been cooked now. Since Jim was Jim, he had his flight logs and a photostat of his commercial pilot's license in hand when he walked in to meet with Moffett's C.O. Jim thought it fitting that he was doing battle with MGM in the office of a man named Lyon. Stewart stood at attention before his commanding officer; Colonel Lyon offered him a seat and urged Jim to be comfortable. Jim got right to the point: He had been assigned to the film unit at Wright Field in Ohio and that was the last thing he wanted. He was in the Air Corps and an experienced pilot and his goal was *not* to make movies stateside. He showed his license and his logs. He wanted to be a combat pilot overseas. This had always been his goal.

Lyon was used to hotshot recruits, but not privates as sophisticated, or as unique, as James Stewart.

After the obligatory discussion about Jim's advanced age and how that might make it unlikely he would fly, Lyon provided extraordinary help to a newly minted noncom and air cadet. After reading the Adjutant General's orders and listening to Stewart's story, Lyon sent a request for reconsideration to the Chief of the Air Corps in Washington. He stated that Stewart "does not desire to engage in any phase of Motion Picture activity or publicity while he is in the Army, and he does not desire to be transferred from this station. He has repeatedly, while at this station, shunned publicity. He wants to be treated exactly as any other American boy drafted into the service of his country."

Lyon went on to assert that it was in the Army's best interest to keep Stewart on his current course, that he was only forty hours of flying time in a 200-horsepower aircraft short of qualifying for commission as a second lieutenant. In fact Jim spent his weekends at Palo Alto Airport logging hours at his own expense in a Stinson Reliant and a WACO biplane to boost his flight time in high-performance aircraft. He allocated some of this time to acrobatics, a necessity for Army pilots—anything to stay away from serving as a pretend soldier making pictures for the U.S. government and for an MGM that would force him into the likes of *Come Live with Me* and *Ziegfeld Girl.*

Lyon's request to Washington for reconsideration worked. Stewart remained at Moffett Field and was no longer assailed by orders from Air Corps Headquarters to fly east to Ohio. There at Moffett, far from Culver City, Louis B. Mayer, and the world of Hollywood with its tawdry games and close contact with tortured souls, James Stewart became immersed in the culture of flying.

The army's guidebook for pilots stated, "All pilots must know how to use the Technical Order files," which covered the airplane and its parts as well as its fuel, hangars, flying field, supplies, and other hardware. It also required pilots to have thorough knowledge of the electrical equipment, fuel system, oil system, propellers and accessories, wheels, brakes and struts, air and hydraulic system accessories, ice-eliminating equipment, control units, fire extinguishers, CO_2 inflation equipment, and accessory power plant. In other words, pilot candidates had to be equal parts mechanic, scientist, and mathematician. Jim was no great student, but he had a knack for mechanics in part from spending his early life around handy men at the hardware store.

"He told me that when he was twelve, he made a crystal radio," said Fonda earlier to a reporter. "He said he did it with oatmeal boxes and wires. I didn't believe him, so he made one—and the damn thing worked."

On June 14, 1941, Corporal Stewart made application for promotion to second lieutenant in the Air Corps and that same day wrote his official request to the War Department to be rated a pilot. He was able to document 265 hours of logged flight time piloting an airplane under 200 horsepower, and 102 hours in planes over 200.

Stewart phoned various friends in Hollywood for endorsements for his promotion and began the conversation, "Say listen, I need your help with something...." Leland Hayward responded on Southwest Airways letterhead to the Chief of the Air Corps: "It is a great pleasure to write this letter of recommendation for Stewart. I have known him intimately for many years and have managed his business affairs. I can only state he is a man of high intelligence, integrity, ability, an excellent pilot and an outstanding American in all ways."

Jim's pal Jack Connelly, co-founder with Hayward and Swope of Southwest Airways, affirmed that Jim "is thoroughly capable of fulfilling the duties of an officer in the United States Army."

Wrote Clarence Brown, director of *Come Live with Me*: "His quiet, workmanlike manner and his great sincerity in anything he undertakes should find him a deserving candidate for this commission. I am sure he will prove worthy of any advancement which you see fit to bestow upon him."

Moffett Field Director of Training K.P. McNaughton wrote: "He is a gentleman. He is modest, conscientious, industrious, and intelligent. He is positive without being self-assertive, and a man of few words but a great deal of push. I have flown with him and found him to be a capable pilot. I know that he will bring credit to the Air Corps, and I strongly recommend that he be favorably considered for the commission which he is seeking."

The application crept through channels. On November 13, not quite eight months from his induction, Corporal Stewart made a request to appear before a Board of Officers to determine his eligibility for the military rating of pilot. The next day, he settled into a North American BT-14 trainer and started the single 450-horsepower Wright engine. He demonstrated a series of takeoffs, climbing turns, approaches, stalls, spins, chandelles, steep banks, eights on pylons, and forced landings. He nailed everything and was rated "excellent" by his examiner in a thirty-five-minute flight.

On November 14, a board was convened at the Presidio of San Francisco and determined that Corporal Stewart had received certificates on school courses about organization of the Army and Air Corps, defense against chemical warfare, military law, military discipline, map and aerial photograph reading, military sanitation and first aid, and aerial navigation. Stewart appeared in person at the Presidio, one of many applying for second lieutenant, and was approved by lunchtime when the board adjourned. But his promotion had a catch.

Yes, he would become an Army pilot, effective January 1. But his second assigned priority was "public relations" and his third was "recruiting Air Corps." Said the board, "He is a noted actor and his services could be utilized to marked advantage as public relations and recruiting duties for Air Corps personnel."

On the first Sunday of December, the Japanese launched an attack on the U.S. Navy base at Pearl Harbor, Hawaii, that demonstrated a Japanese commitment to air power in the Pacific, just as the Germans had been using air power to roll over Europe. The looming conflagration would be in large part an air war, bearing out Stewart's earlier belief, and his determination to serve in combat strengthened. But he seemed further away than ever from real service.

12
OVERACHIEVER

Southern High School #70 in the Baltimore City Public School system sat at the intersection of Warren Avenue and William Street in the Federal Hill neighborhood of historic Baltimore. On any given Monday the sturdy brick building bustled with activity inside and out, but not this particular Monday. Today, the regular class schedule was postponed, and all students reported to the auditorium for a special assembly and listened by radio to a joint session of Congress that took place at the U.S. Capitol, just thirty miles away in Washington, D.C.

Seventeen-year-old Clement Leone sat there in fear and rage as President Roosevelt's voice boomed off the walls and ceiling of the auditorium: "Mr. Vice President, Mr. Speaker, members of the Senate, of the House of Representatives... Yesterday, December 7, 1941—a date which will live in infamy—the United States of America was suddenly and deliberately attacked by naval and air forces of the Empire of Japan."

Clem had been at home when the news report crackled on the radio in the middle of the afternoon. He had gravitated to the living room with his parents and brothers and sisters and listened to nonsensical reports of an attack on an American naval base somewhere far off in the Pacific Ocean. To a guy for whom a long trip was a ten-mile bike ride to Dundalk, Hawaii may as well have sat on another planet.

Information had trickled in slowly, and they had sat and listened all

88

afternoon, then all evening. Clem judged his own fear by what he had seen in his stepfather and especially in his mother. And his fierce little mother had been a tight ball of fright up to bedtime.

Now, in the auditorium, Clem hung on the president's every word: "The attack yesterday on the Hawaiian Islands has caused severe damage to American naval and military forces. I regret to tell you that very many American lives have been lost. In addition, American ships have been reported torpedoed on the high seas between San Francisco and Honolulu."

The president told of attacks against Malaya, Hong Kong, Guam, the Philippines, and Wake and Midway Islands. "Japan has, therefore, undertaken a surprise offensive extending throughout the Pacific area. The facts of yesterday and today speak for themselves. The people of the United States have already formed their opinions and well understand the implications to the very life and safety of our nation."

Here Clem sat, half a year from his eighteenth birthday, not fearing that he would soon go off and fight the Japanese, but fearing he would not. He told his mother he wanted to enlist, and informed her that two classmates at Southern High had quit school to enlist in the armed forces. She reminded Clem that he was about to receive the parent-teacher award as top student in his section for the second time, which meant there was no way he could quit school before February graduation.

"Fine," said Clem. "I'll enlist once I graduate."

"No, you will not," said Stella.

Now, Clem had to reveal the worst. "If I don't enlist, if they draft me, I won't get to pick the Air Corps. I want to join the Air Corps."

There was nothing he could say to his mother's response: "I don't want my boys getting shot at." She said it didn't matter anyway. The draft age was twenty-one and he was just a boy with a paper route.

13
STATIC PERSONNEL

On December 11, 1941, Nazi Germany declared war on the United States. Four days later, Cpl. James Stewart appeared on a radio show called *We Hold These Truths* that was broadcast on all four national networks in commemoration of 150 years since ratification of the Bill of Rights. Orson Welles narrated, Leopold Stakowski conducted the National Anthem, an all-star cast participated, and President Roosevelt read a message at the end of the show. Yet Jim had to be *ordered* to appear; he wanted nothing to do with public appearances as a Hollywood star because these trivialities of "public relations" and "recruiting Air Corps" kept him away from his goal of shipping out to fight.

On December 31 Stewart received his pilot rating and promotion from corporal and air cadet to second lieutenant in the Air Corps Reserve, trading in serial number 39230721 for an officer's number, 0-433210. He had won his wings and earned a pay raise to $245 per month. A little more than two weeks later, the war hit home: Fun-loving Carole Lombard, with whom he had worked at Selznick Studios in the 1939 comedy-drama *Made for Each Other*, was killed along with her mother and one of Strickling's press men at MGM, Otto Winkler, while returning home from a trip back east to sell war bonds. Fifteen Army Air Corps fliers from the Ferrying Command had been lost as well when the DC-3 in which all were riding hit a mountain in dark of night not far from McCarran Army Air Field in Las Vegas. Stewart felt gut-punched. Lombard was a dishy dame, loud, talked a mile a minute and cussed a blue streak, but he hadn't met anyone so down to earth in all his Hollywood years. She was one hell of an on-screen kisser, softest lips in the business. And Otto Winkler had died too. Wink was a round little man who worked in the publicity department, worked like the devil in fact. Stewart would see Wink hustling around the lot, usually joined to Clark Gable at the hip. And Wink had attended Jim's going-away party at MGM.

Two days after Lombard died, Jim's status was changed from Air Corps Reserve to active duty in the Air Corps. Twelve days after that he was required to attend a birthday party for FDR (who did not attend) at the Hollywood Roosevelt Hotel in the heart of his old stomping grounds. He appeared in his Air Corps uniform for the sake of reporters and showed off newly earned silver wings.

Late in February he was obligated by Hollywood tradition as the incumbent Best Actor winner to present the Best Actor award for the top performance in 1941, again in uniform, at the Academy Award dinner and ceremonies in downtown Los Angeles. It was a strange night at the Biltmore Hotel on South Grand, strange for so many reasons. First and foremost, the Biltmore Bowl hummed with life but at a lower key, maybe because the war was on everyone's mind, or was it merely the absence of the king and his queen? Gable had always attended these things in general discomfort, as if anchored to a spot of floor, while Lombard would flit about the room dressed to the nines and huddle here with one group, there with another, occasionally pealing with laughter that could be heard across town, it seemed. Now she was dead and Gable was God knew where. Certainly not here.

Lieutenant Stewart stepped back into the world in which he had formerly resided. It already had been a year since he had sat in attendance not thinking he could win for *The Philadelphia Story*.

It was to have been Olivier's award, or Chaplin's, or Fonda's for the best performance of all by far in *The Grapes of Wrath*, yet Jim had won. Now, he stood here at the Biltmore again, tall as always among the people he knew well and knew barely, moguls, directors, writers, producers, and players, with all their quirks and all their drama. Over there, Ginger; over there, Maggie; over there, Norma. Crawford was still Crawford, and Jim saw Hank, aloof as always, and Buzz. Many men present were in uniform—more than Jim expected. John Huston came over and mentioned that he had enlisted in the Army Signal Corps and would soon be inducted. Then Huston started talking about doing a recruiting picture with Jim, nothing big, just a short subject that Huston would direct, and Stewart listened politely. But Jim wasn't really there at all. His head, perched on his lanky frame, looked about, but his brain had remained at Moffett. Moffett was where he wanted to be this night.

Buzz Meredith broke the news prior to dinner and the presentation that he would be inducted into the U.S. Army the next day. Buzz had Olivia de Havilland on his arm; Livvie recently had plunged deep into one of those top-secret affairs with Huston that everybody in town knew about. Such a thing wasn't like Livvie at all, but maybe one had to dive into such situations at least once in life. Jim had done it with Norma, jumped in to find the water icy and uncomfortable, and now dark loner Livvie had leapt, and Jim knew there was no way it was going to end well for anybody, not given this cast of characters. Tonight, Livvie was up for Best Actress against her sister Joan Fontaine. Such a poisonous pair these sisters were, and when Jim and Livvie made eye contact and small talk, each knew the deepest secrets of the other and Jim had never seen her strung so tight.

That evening Jim stood on the dais and presented the Best Actor Oscar to a typically uncomfortable Gary Cooper for his performance in *Sergeant York*. Howard Hawks had directed *York*; Jim knew Hawks from countless interactions at airfields since Hawks was a pilot who had made aviation pictures and liked his planes like he liked his women: fast. So Coop won an Oscar but Livvie did not; Livvie lost to Joanie, and the devastation on Livvie's face was something that no one there that night, at least no one who knew her, could ever forget.

When the evening ended, Jim was grateful to fly north and away from madness, affairs, awards, and petty jealousies. He was in the air, the place where he could be nothing but himself and deal with nothing but a set of controls. Jim was happy to leave that mess back there on the ground far behind. "You're like a bird up there," he said of flying. "It's almost as if you're not part of society any-more. All you can think about is what you're doing and you have a complete escape from your worldly problems."

In April John Huston received his commission in the Signal Corps and Lieutenant Stewart was assigned to the Motion Pic-ture Unit for the short recruiting film that Huston had mentioned at the Academy Awards dinner. Except it wasn't hotshot Huston, fresh off *The Maltese Falcon*, who would head north to meet up with Stewart to make the recruiting tool. It was thirty-eight-year-old Warner Bros. director of short subjects Owen Crump who pulled in to Moffett Field with a caravan of studio grip trucks. Jim was in the air in an AT-6 trainer when they arrived, and he observed the commotion below, unaware until this moment of the intrusion of a movie production unit at his base.

"He landed," said Owen Crump, "taxied up to where we were all waiting, got out. He was furious. 'What the hell do you think you're doing? I'm not going to do a damn thing for this! Not a damn thing!'"

Crump, who had banged out the screenplay in hours and was now on the hot seat to bring home footage featuring Lieutenant Stewart, begged Jim for a few minutes to explain the premise. They went off for coffee. Crump related the recruitment goals for his modest picture—100,000 young men for the Air Corps, including 15,000 captains, 40,000 lieutenants, and 35,000 flying sergeants—not to mention gunners and ground crew. It would be called *Winning Your Wings*, and it was hoped that Stewart would describe the glamorous life of an Air Corps flier.

Jim flipped through the script and grew calmer. "Sorry," he said, "I didn't understand. Sure, I'll do anything you want, whatever."

"The crew was waiting and Jimmy said hello to all of them," said Crump, "then got in his airplane and circled the field again, because that's the way the film started, and he rolled up to the camera into a close shot and he got out and who was it but Jimmy Stewart!"

That morning, Jim quickly studied the script, landed his trainer, and stepped out of the cockpit in uniform and parachute to deliver a forty-five-second introduction to camera. The same morning, Crump directed Jim in short on-camera inserts and voiceover narration. As uncomfortable as Stewart was making this picture, it didn't show. He delivered the line, "Your commission in the air forces is waiting!" with such conviction that men practically vaulted from their theater seats to enlist. He did not mention to these men, or their mothers, fathers, brothers, sisters, and sweethearts, that there would be opposition in those skies, namely Axis air forces, or that flaming death might well result from flying around in the gleaming new planes depicted in aerial beauty shots. He spoke of keeping the war "from our own shores," and espoused the "cause of decency."

Camera negative was trucked back to Hollywood for post-production and insertion of B-roll of recruits, active duty personnel, and heavy aircraft on the assembly line—in this case B-17s.

Winning Your Wings scored big for the U. S. government as a short subject shown in American movie theaters. The abilities of James Stewart the actor masked his reluctance to appear for the Motion Picture Unit, as he seemed confident and dashing and ready to take on the Axis all on his own. The sword had two edges: *Winning Your Wings* proved to be a winner of a recruiting picture and feather in Stewart's cap, but would lead to more requests for public relations work, which would deter him from a path to service in combat.

At Moffett, Jim kept angling to position himself for assignment overseas, which meant he would need to be flying fighters or bombers. He could never become a fighter pilot, not at sixfour and almost thirty-four years of age—fighters required the split-second reflexes of twenty year olds. That left Jim with the bombers. But someone somewhere within Air Corps Headquarters had placed a hold order on Stewart's file that listed him as "branch immaterial" and then as "static personnel," so the only option open for such a pilot was as a flight instructor. He was flying a lot, instrument flying, night flying—was all this flying just meant to keep him busy? Keep him distracted? Then he was ordered to attend instructional courses in how to teach piloting skills, and in April 1942 received a transfer to Mather Army Airfield, east of Sacramento, which for the past eight months had been stamping out navigators for the crews of the four-engine heavy bombers now in production in plants around the United States. There Stewart took more classes in flight training for twin-engine aircraft; once certified as a twin-engine instructor, he would qualify to fly the Mitchell B-25B medium bomber now coming on line—bombers like the sixteen under the command of Lt. Col. James Doolittle that flew off the U.S.S. *Hornet* and dropped bombs on Tokyo, Japan, in a daring April 18 raid. There hadn't been much for the Air Corps to cheer about to this point; now, thanks to the Doolittle raid, energy around Mather spiked.

While Jim had been serving at Moffett Field, Pearl Harbor was bombed. At that time, the U.S. Army operated fewer than 300 bombers divided into fourteen bomb groups. More than fifty other bomb groups existed on paper only. The Army Air Forces organized quickly after Pearl Harbor under Lt. Gen. Henry (Hap) Arnold, who put Maj. Gen. Carl Spaatz in charge, with Brig. Gen. Ira Eaker appointed to run bomber command. These bright, highly experienced Air Corps officers would run something to be called the Eighth Air Force, which commenced operations in January 1942. The next month, General Eaker traveled to England and set up headquarters for the Eighth Bomber Command, but he remained a lonely man until some of his fliers began filtering over in May. All he could do in the meantime was look embarrassed as the RAF bombed Germany nightly with the Americans nowhere to be seen.

Back in California, Lieutenant Stewart became a twin-engine instructor, taking up rookie pilots from the Mather runways six hours a day. It was at Mather he looked in the mirror and noticed some gray hairs mixed in with the brown—the rigors of Army life were showing. He also wore down and at the end of July required a furlough to return home to Vinegar Hill. "The army's fine, but I'm tired out," he told a reporter on landing at the airport in Pittsburgh, where Alex and Bessie greeted him.

A month later he was 3,000 miles away on weekend leave in Hollywood, where he met twenty-six-year-old, brown-haired, brown-eyed singing star Dinah Shore at the home of the Haywards. Shore's soft manner, self-deprecating humor, and Tennessee drawl bowled over the lieutenant and romance took off. For the remainder of 1942, Stewart spent weekends with Dinah in Hollywood, or she traveled to Jim's new base, Kirtland Field, New Mexico, to spend weekends in hotels with him. In between they exchanged letters, and Stewart found an outlet for the sexual frustrations of life on army bases. By now it had become clear that you could take the boy out of Hollywood, but you couldn't quite take Hollywood out of the boy. Not yet, anyway.

14
A GAME OF CHESS

In February 1942 Clem Leone graduated from Southern High School in Baltimore and honored his mother's wishes by not heading for the recruiting station and the Army Air Corps. Instead, he landed a job as an auto mechanic's helper at the local Ford dealership, working five-and-a-half days out of seven for thirteen dollars a week. He arrived early every morning at half past seven to fire up the coal furnace and get things nice and warm for the mechanics when the shop opened at eight o'clock.

Leone's boss treated Clem like a real mechanic and assigned him to real-mechanic work, like complex brake jobs—a process that Clem could easily handle thanks to his vocational training throughout high school. But when Clem approached his boss after a few months and asked for a raise, the response was, "Kid, you don't know enough to be paid more."

Clem pointed out that there were jobs at the big Montgomery Ward building in Southwest Baltimore starting at eighteen dollars a week, and his boss scoffed at this and invited Clem to head on over there and get one. He assured, "You'll be sorry if you go, kid."

Clem wasn't sorry. He found a job repairing toys and small electronics at the eight-story Montgomery Ward Warehouse and Retail Store at 1000 Monroe Street. Now working a shorter, forty-hour week for more money, Clem thrived—as much as any high school graduate could in a world falling apart. Just off the coast not far from Baltimore, German U-boats were sinking American ships on their way to England. Half a world away, American aircraft carriers tangled with their Japanese counterparts at the Coral Sea and then at Midway Island. These carrier-based air battles were proving how important aviation would be in this war.

The months of 1942 crept by and Clem's eighteenth birthday loomed. Stella informed her son that the local copper plant had landed a War Department contract to produce shell casings and was starting new workers at fifty dollars per week. He simply couldn't turn down a sum that would help out the family so much and help the country too.

But turn it down, Clem did. He kept his ears on the news and his eyes on the calendar, fearing some freak collision of his birthday with a decision by Congress to conscript eighteen year olds that would result in Clem serving on a ship somewhere in the Pacific or in a foxhole in Africa instead of where he wanted to be—in the air.

On July 5, 1942, Clem turned eighteen and reported to work at Montgomery Ward as usual. And kept on reporting. Autumn came to the Inner Harbor. Thanksgiving. And then, finally, mercifully, a bulletin reached Clem's ears: Word had it that President Roosevelt was going to lower the draft age.

"They're going to start drafting eighteen year olds, Mother," said Clem.

She looked at him; words failed her.

She sighed. "You aren't going to give me any peace, so go ahead. Join your Army Air Corps." Stella was reduced to one final hope: He's so small. They would never take a boy so small. Would they?

15
DESTINATION: MEAT GRINDER

In August 1942 while at Kirtland Field in Albuquerque, Jim received a promotion to first lieutenant that accompanied his certification as a twin-engine flight instructor. His duties for four months at Kirtland involved taking novice bombardier students up in the air on dry runs. In December he received yet another transfer, this time to Hobbs, New Mexico, to the brand-new Hobbs Army Airfield as one of forty-six pilots to be trained on just-landed B-17 four-engine heavy bombers fresh off the assembly line.

Jim put 100 hours into training on the B-17 at Hobbs and qualified as a four-engine heavy bomber pilot, graduating with his classmates in February 1943. With four-engine certification came a promotion to captain, and Stewart was in the pipeline for assignment to one of the recently formed bomb groups now in training as part of the Eighth Air Force buildup to full operational strength. Jim now saw the path clear and expected to move to an active B-17 bomb group at any time.

Then, word came down: His next assignment would be with the 52nd Squadron, 29th Training Group at Gowen Field in Idaho. Captain Stewart would continue as an instructional pilot and not a combat pilot for inarguable reasons: The Eighth Air Force was just now getting off the ground in England, literally and figuratively. The first mission of the Eighth into Germany had been flown a couple weeks earlier, with fifty-five B-17s and twenty-seven B-24s from the 306th Bomb Group attacking shipyards near the city of Bremen, but bad weather had confused the lead ships and many of the B-24s turned back. The B-17s moved on to their secondary target, the U-boat facilities at Wilhelmshaven, and dropped their loads of 1,000-pound general-purpose bombs. The Germans sat shocked at the audacity of a daylight raid into the Fatherland, and at their own meager fighter response. But the Germans would be surprised only once and quickly learn how to deal with these daylight bomb runs. The Luftwaffe employed a swarming type of attack that became a turkey shoot, with U.S. bombers falling out of German skies at a high rate. This grim big picture even affected Capt. James Stewart, as the Army worried about what a prize Stewart would make if shot down over Europe.

In February 1943 at just about the time Hank Fonda—determined, like Jim, to be in a real war—was enlisting in the Navy and heading to basic training, Stewart reported to Lt. Col. Walter Arnold at Gowen Field, which sat at the southeastern corner of Boise, a city of 28,000 set in high, rolling hills (and challenging flight lanes), with the Sawtooth Mountain Range to the east. It wasn't exactly the middle of nowhere, but it was close. Here Jim felt farther away from the war than ever as he trained B-17 pilots on both daylight and nighttime takeoffs and landings.

Around this time, Jim's relationship with Dinah Shore hit the rocks when she began to find actor George Montgomery more fascinating, not to mention more available. On one of their weekends together, Jim and Dinah had decided to get married and they set out for Las Vegas, but when Jim experienced second thoughts en route, Dinah began to understand that they weren't destined to end up together. Once again alone, which wasn't the worst circumstance, Jim said, "I have no problem being on my own."

His C.O. at Gowen Field, Colonel Arnold, had earned the nickname "Pop" even though at twenty-eight he was more than six years Stewart's junior. Arnold was a career Air Corps man who had earned his wings on bombers at about the time Jim first climbed into a cockpit at Mines Field for flying lessons. Arnold saw frustration eating away at Stewart, who reported day after day and night after night to walk young pilots through their procedures. Jim was serving, no question about it, but both Arnold and Stewart were serving *stateside* while their brother fliers took off daily from bases in England hitting targets in France and Germany, often with little prospect of making it back in one piece. Neither man was willing to spend the war this way without making a stand.

By this time the training routine had become brutal. Beirne Lay, Jr., Air Corps officer and later co-author of *Twelve O'Clock High*, called the pace of training "heartbreaking" as the fledgling Army Air Forces drummed experience into their crews. "Under the relentless pressure being brought to bear by Brig. Gen. R.F. ('Big Bob') Travis, wing commander," said Lay, "crews flew on a twenty-four-hour-a-day schedule during the frigid winter days and nights...." Stewart had landed in the middle of the run-up to European air war and began racking up hours with pilot trainees.

Early on the morning of May 4, 1943, Jim learned that a B-17 training flight out of Gowen had crashed in Mountain Home, fifty miles southeast of Boise. The crash had occurred in the foothills after takeoff with a student at the controls. Among the dead was Jim's bunkmate and copilot on the training crew, Tom Homer, another Pennsylvania boy, from Greencastle—just down the road from Mercersburg, site of Jim's prep school. Stewart rushed to the scene with Arnold for retrieval of bodies of the eight airmen aboard. The experience shook Jim up as he learned firsthand the physics of a heavy bomber crash and what happened to fragile human bodies in such a circumstance.

For three months Arnold had seen Jim as a training pilot and squadron commander in the 29th Training Group; now he saw Stewart as a man facing the responsibility of securing a crash site where his friends lay dead. Jim went about this task by the book, and his sense of personal loss was obvious. Arnold knew Stewart's personnel file had the designation "static" attached to it, but he couldn't let such a man sit out the war stateside. B-17 groups were about ready for deployment, with B-24 groups just forming.

Nick Radosevich, a second lieutenant and one of Stewart's pilot trainees, recalled, "This one day, Captain Stewart told me, 'The 17s are going overseas.' He asked me if I wanted to go with them or stay for the B-24 Liberators. 'What are you going to do?' I asked. 'I'm going to stay for the B-24s,' said Stewart. 'Well,' I said, 'I'll stay, too.' I think he thought the B-24s were bigger, faster, and better than the 17s."

One weekend in June, Jim's sister Ginny married an artist from New York City, twenty-eight-year-old, French-born Alexis Alexander Tiranoff. Although Alexis was a naturalized U.S. citizen and had joined the Army Signal Corps, Alex Stewart didn't approve and said so loudly to Jim on the phone. Jim had never felt close to his sisters and stayed away from the ceremony back in Indiana because he had one leave left and he was devoting that to John Swope, manager of Thunderbird Field. Johnny was getting married in the event of the summer because he had snagged beautiful young stage actress and now-starlet Dorothy McGuire, and Jim was determined to be there. He flew west in time for the July 19 nuptials in the home of Leland and Maggie and stood up for Johnny as best man. Jim said his good-byes to those closest to him because, who knew, with any luck he might be off to war soon.

Fortune finally smiled on Capt. James Stewart. Pop Arnold learned of a new B-24 bomb group, the 445th, that had formed April 1 at Gowen, then had spent a month at Wendover Field, Utah, and since July 3 had been located at Sioux City Army Air Base in Iowa. Word had it that the 445th needed personnel. In retrospect Arnold would say of Jim Stewart, "I felt that if he wanted combat duty, to fight the war, that badly, I'd help him." Arnold called the 445th Bomb Group commander, newly promoted Lt. Col. Robert Terrill, to recommend Stewart.

Arnold used key words in his conversation with Terrill, words that a group commander needed to hear: mature, stable, experienced, by-the-book leader. Yes, Terrill could use such a man as operations officer of one of his four squadrons, the 703rd, even if Stewart *was* a movie actor well up in years at thirty-five and therefore a potential liability to a bomb group in third-stage training before deployment to a combat zone.

Thanks to Pop Arnold—and there was no getting around the fact that Arnold stuck his neck way out to help Stewart—the key moment in Jim's life had arrived. There would never be another like this, not before, not after. On August 3, 1943, he packed his gear and hitched a ride on a B-17 to Sioux City Army Air Base located at Sergeant Bluff, seven miles south of Sioux City, Iowa. There he saluted Colonel Terrill, another stable, commonsense Air Forces officer, a graduate of West Point and veteran of recent combat operations in Egypt, who would be remembered as a "wonderful guy" by his pilots and earn the affectionate nickname "Terrible Terrill" exactly because he wasn't.

Terrill wanted to see how well Stewart could fly in general, and fly a B-24 in particular. Stewart had been checked out in a B-24, but it had been a while. The Boeing B-17 Flying Fortress was a sleek, good-looking aircraft with a rounded fuselage. Its cockpit was cramped for pilot and copilot and its interior confining for crew and bomb load. The Consolidated B-24 offered a far roomier interior and the opportunity for a heavier bomb load, but pilots found the Liberator difficult on the controls, calling for more muscle in operation to offset more sluggishness in response.

Stewart reported to 2nd Lt. Lloyd Sharrard, one of Terrill's best pilots, to be checked out in the operation of a B-24. Sharrard was a lean little guy, nearly a foot shorter than Jim, but he was a dandy with dark hair and dark eyes. He wore his hat at a rakish angle atop his head, and his boots weren't exactly army issue; Sharrard was wearing cowboy boots. Jim was used to pilots still wet behind the ears, and this was a welcome change.

For Jim, despite the changeable winds in unceasingly flat Iowa in summer, months in the left seats of 17s prepared him for the transition to the Liberator. In fact, Sharrard gave him such high marks that Terrill began looking for a squadron leadership assignment for Jim. Stewart joined 703rd Squadron Commander Willis B. Sawyer and Executive Officer M.E. Seymour as operations officer, with the squadron now entering the final phase of preparation for deployment overseas. Daily, the combat crews flew complex formations featuring the combat box, a set of twelve aircraft. They flew practically wingtip to wingtip so that the six machine gun positions of each could protect the guy next door. Then, the combat box joined another and another, until each of four squadrons placed a combat box in a bomb group formation—forty-eight aircraft flying as one entity toward a theoretical target. After landing from their simulated missions, the crews attended ground school.

The 445th Bomb Group did this every day out of Sioux City and sometimes flew night missions. On August 22 Captain Sawyer was transferred to Stewart's old position as a trainer with the 29th in Boise, and Stewart was appointed squadron commander of the 703rd, taking command of fifteen flight crews of ten men each and more than 200 ground personnel who maintained the squadron's B-24s. Any remaining doubt about Stewart's status had been settled, first by Colonel Arnold and then by Colonel Terrill. These men would get Jim Stewart into the fight.

Captain Stewart took his post as new commanding officer of the 703rd Squadron of the 445th Bomb Group of the Second Combat Wing of the Second Bomb Division of the Eighth Air Force. In two-and-a-half years he had risen from private to captain, serving under all manner of leaders. Now, as Squadron Commander Stewart, he drew upon all his knowledge, including years in Hollywood, to ensure that he led a cohesive unit. People had to know how to do their own jobs and have a strong sense of the next guy's job so that everyone knew how all the jobs fit together.

One of the pilots in his squadron, dark-haired and intense 2nd Lt. Victor Smith, hailed from Charlotte, North Carolina, the same hometown as Randolph Scott, and had a stronger Southern drawl than Scott. Stewart learned early on that Smith took an unorthodox approach with the nine men in his flight crew: All of them, commissioned officers and enlisted men alike, met secretly once a week to fraternize. "Rank was not considered and first names were the order of the evening," said copilot Bill Minor. "We could agree, disagree, offer suggestions, etc., without any worry while we ate and had drinks together. Such action was against regulations."

Jim was all about regulations and would never be one to advocate cutting corners or skirting rules. Whatever the regulations were, that's what would be done.

"He went by the book," said Barry Shillito, a copilot in the 703. "I can't stress that enough: *He went by the book*."

Jim learned that a second pilot, George Wright from Baltimore, was keeping things informal with his crew and wasn't interested in his noncoms saluting or calling the officers "sir."

Jim knew that regs stated the four commissioned officers on the crew—pilot, copilot, bombardier, and navigator—were not to fraternize with the six enlisted men. The officers flew in the front of the ship; the enlisted men, mostly sergeants, behind them, which symbolized two distinct strata, and the reason for no fraternizing was simple: The enlisted men were to obey orders without question or argument or a moment's pause.

Right out of the gate, Jim had to determine what to do about Smith and his parties and Wright and his informality—he should speak with both and remind them of regulations. Or should he? Close communication like Smith and Wright were promoting aligned with Stewart's belief that the pilots needed to form bonds with the engineers and others on the crew. To Jim, teamwork and knowing how everyone thought in a crisis meant survival, which trumped even the officer's manual. He decided he would never advocate informality among his crews; neither did he take any action to stop it. Jim was realizing right away that regulations and common sense had to go hand in hand when leading men who were putting their lives on the line every day in service to their country.

Jim met the new operations officer of the 703, twenty-six-year-old 1st Lt. Gilbert Fisher of Leawood, Kansas, who had spent four years as a radioman in the Navy aboard the aircraft carrier U.S.S. *Lexington*. After war had been declared, Fisher joined the Air Corps on a track to become a pilot and now was checked out on both B-17s and B-24s. Fisher moved into quarters with Stewart and joined Jim in training the personnel of the squadron.

But Jim faced a much more serious, potentially disastrous problem than informality in the ranks. Many of his copilots in the 703rd, including Bill Minor, Barry Shillito, Otis Rhoney, and Milt Souza, had started out in P-40 Warhawk fighter planes and moved on to the new and nimble P-51s, but their units in Florida had been disbanded, and the men shipped west to Boise, supposedly for more training. Instead, they were reassigned as copilots in heavy bombers and forwarded to Sioux City, where they landed a few days ahead of Stewart. This was no way for a fighter pilot to contribute to the war effort, muscling the unsightly four-engine bomber already referred to as a "boxcar with wings." The army's decision stuck Stewart with a formidable morale problem. Far worse, none of these men who were in theory entering final-phase training had spent one minute in the cockpit of the complex B-24.

"One of my classmates just flat refused to get into the B-24, and they threatened to court-martial him," said Rhoney. But the adamant stance had worked for the flier in question. "The next time we heard from him, he was in south England flying a P-40." Other hard cases also moved on, but Stewart's presence and leadership style—quiet, patient, understanding—persuaded many of the ex-fighter jocks to at least give Liberators a chance.

Jim knew he was battling an entire mind-set with this group, since fighter pilots tended to be athletic and fearless, not to mention accustomed to controlling a one-man ship. "Single-engine training was to a great extent acrobatics," said Bill Minor. "The best fighter pilots needed to be expert acrobatic pilots because that's how to put the enemy at a disadvantage and make them a target for your fire power. It seemed to me that bomber pilots' training focused mostly on flying straight and level, like commercial airline pilots." Minor wanted bomber pilots to learn evasive tactics, but Stewart's formations went by the book, and evasive maneuvers for a B-24 were not included in that book.

Suddenly, the discontented fighter boys were sent home on leave while Stewart and other squadron commanders in the 445th developed a training program to catch the new copilots up as quickly as possible. Now, a new problem developed as some of Stewart's pilots resented the cocky ex-fighter pilots. But Jim knew it was sink or swim now, or more likely live or die, and his squadron coalesced through all manner of training, such as practice flights, landing on three engines in case one was knocked out, and then on two engines in case two failed. They flew in ever-tighter formations and practiced dropping bombs endlessly. Suddenly the fighter boys were catching up. And as they all flew, and flew and flew, in an exhaustive routine out of Sergeant Bluff, Jim learned all about the officers in his command.

Way back in Boise he had formed a bond with 2nd Lt. Joe Narcovich of Gilberton, Pennsylvania, while coming in on a night training flight. In the pilot's seat with Joe beside him, Stewart brought their Liberator in for a landing in a thunderstorm as lightning struck the aircraft—or came very close. The shock of the flash forced Jim's weight down on the wheel, and the nose hammered into the runway with such force that the front landing gear punched up into the flight deck and nearly killed both men. The bare metal of the nose ground down the pavement to a long, screeching stop. Stewart and Narcovich sat there in shock, Jim murmuring that it was his responsibility, his fault. Neither man would be able to look at the other without remembering that night and that moment.

Jim recognized from day one that some of his pilots were superior aviators with calm confidence far beyond their years. Hotshot Sharrard in the cowboy boots was one of them, former research chemist for Wyandotte Chemicals from Emmet, Michigan, entrusted by Terrill to check out Stewart on 24s. Bill Conley was another, a tall, string bean of twenty-three from Greenville Junction, Maine, who talked of life growing up on Moosehead Lake. Neil Johnson was the third man Jim decided he could count on, a tough-as-nails, movie-star-handsome University of Montana football star from Missoula with a curly head of dark hair that would have made Tyrone Power envious. The fourth was square-jawed Ralph Stimmel from Winchester, Virginia, who once had been voted "most dependable" in his high school class and now was one of the old men of the squadron at twenty-six. The last of Jim's dependable five was William "Mack" Williams, a veteran of the Florida National Guard and at twenty-seven the oldest of the pilots—he had already been married five years to a ballerina from Miami named Catherine.

The remainder of his pilots were all good guys with a world of potential. Leo Cook was a college man from Missouri with a classic profile and an interest in entomology, the study of bugs. His wife, Helen, recently had lost her brother Eldon, who had participated in Operation Vengeance, the successful mission to shoot down the plane of Japanese Admiral Yamamoto. But then Eldon had died in the line of fire of a Japanese Zero four months later.

Bob Kiser, fresh faced and crowned with a mop of dark hair, had been born in Pittsburgh and raised in rural Ohio. At twenty, he was Stewart's youngest pilot and hadn't outgrown all his baby fat.

Bill Kane was twenty-one and hailed from Madison Lake, Minnesota. At the last minute before flying off to England, he had requested leave to rush home and marry his girl, Jean.

Earle Metcalf was twenty-three and the youngest of six children; he had been a stock clerk for Mack Trucks in Terryville, Connecticut, before enlisting in the Air Corps, and like Stewart and Conley, Metcalf was forced to fold his well-over-six-foot frame into the Liberator's cockpit.

Albert Poor was the son of a chicken farmer from Antrim, New Hampshire. He was a quiet country boy with a pronounced New England twang who, when prodded, would provide interesting facts about poultry.

Oliver Saunders, whom everyone called Ollie, was a quiet bookkeeper from Palo Alto, California.

Dave Skjeie, pronounced Shay, was a California kid from Los Angeles of Scandinavian descent whose father had been ground crew in an aero squadron in the Great War.

Charles "Chick" Torpey was twenty-two, from Grand Island, Nebraska, and had just married a girl named Betty who was a dish.

Emmett Watson was an ROTC man from Marquez, Texas, and Texas A&M grad, and possessed a deep-South drawl, as did his copilot from Hickory, North Carolina, Otis Rhoney. Like Jim Stewart, Otis had first gone up in a plane courtesy of a barnstorming pilot, one who had passed through Hickory in 1939 selling rides in a Ford Tri-Motor.

Jim liked these guys, but as their commanding officer and a man ten or fifteen years their senior, he couldn't allow himself to grow close to them. "It's just the practical and proper way to run a command," he explained. "You can't make the men you command into your friends."

The 445th was running up to war and everyone knew it. Jim's family knew it too, and Alex, Bessie, and Doddie traveled west by

109

train for a visit to Sioux City, arriving at a local landmark, the Warrior Hotel, on August 18. Jim traveled up later that day on a pass from Sergeant Bluff to be mobbed by local press. His first and only statement for reporters: "No pictures of me, and no interview. This is the army talking." The proclamation kept reporters away, but the arrival of the Stewarts had already been announced in that day's *Sioux City Journal*. By supper time, denizens were eager to witness the reunion.

"Dolores and I went to have dinner at the Warrior Hotel," said Minor. "Shortly after our arrival, Captain Stewart, his mother, and sister sat down at a table near ours. He introduced us but soon a crowd gathered around his table. Unable to enjoy his family visit, he stood up as tall as possible and explained that this would be his last chance to visit with his family, and he would appreciate some privacy. They left, but soon another crowd swarmed his table. This was too much so they got up and departed the hotel."

The family visit ended at the train station as Jim's usually gregarious father stood with his quiet son. Alex couldn't find a word to say, so he embraced his boy and joined Bessie and Doddie on the train in silence. Later, Jim found that his father had slipped a letter into his pocket, which Jim opened in his quarters that night:

"Dear Jim, after you have read this letter you'll be on your way to danger. I have enclosed a copy of the 91st Psalm and I am staking my faith in these words. I feel sure that God will lead you through danger. I don't know what else to say to you, son, but I continue to pray. God bless you and keep you. I love you more than I can tell you. Good-bye, my dear. Dad."

Love wasn't a word thrown around by Alexander Stewart. Jim could never remember a time Alex had used it with him until this moment. Its use now by a combat veteran brought home for Jim the gravity of what lay ahead.

In September the four squadrons of the 445th Bomb Group scattered for completion of third-phase training. The 700 flew to

Mitchell, South Dakota; the 701 to Scribner, Nebraska; the 702 to Watertown, South Dakota; while Jim and his 703rd stayed put at Sergeant Bluff. The operational practice missions at the squadron and group level became pressure-filled as they practiced forming up on a brightly painted assembly ship nicknamed the Zebra or Judas Goat, practiced heading for the initial point of attack, or I.P., practiced "S"ing (turns to slow down and wait for another group to rendezvous), practiced bomb runs and turns after dropping bombs and reforming the group for the trip home. Stewart had them practicing in ever-tighter formations until they were nearly wingtip to wingtip because tight formations allowed gunners in the front of the ship, in the top turret, in the right and left waist, in the ball turret underneath, and in the tail turret, to protect their own aircraft and the aircraft next door.

On one practice mission, Leo Cook failed to get off the ground at takeoff and damaged his ship. On another, Ralph Stimmel, one of Jim's best men, got so lost that he ran out of fuel and had to land in an Iowa farm field. Stewart sent gasoline to their location, but when Stimmel restarted and ran up the engines, his plane blew down a billboard, injuring some local children who had come out to watch the bomber. Injuring civilians, especially locals, was not the way to win the hearts and minds of superior officers. On another practice mission, Stewart led a night raid by the entire squadron to bomb a target near Mitchell, South Dakota, using sand-filled 100-pound practice bombs, with the 700 as spotters. Due to bomber malfunctions and navigational errors, only three of fifteen planes bombed the target. Stewart's spectacular failure so infuriated Gen. St. Clair Streett, just-appointed commander of the Second Air Force, that he threatened to return the 703rd to Pocatello to repeat their training from scratch. Stewart's pilots saw another side to their commander as Stewart quietly fumed, then unleashed a tirade against his sloppy aviators. General Streett and Colonel Terrill both knew that the outcome had been an anomaly

111

caused by the extreme fast-track training regimen. They also knew that Stewart needed to do better with his command.

Scuttlebutt ran rampant that the 445th was heading for the South Pacific. Many men were adamant in their belief that the Pacific would be their destination; just as many said Europe. Most put their money where their mouths were.

Tensions remained high into October, and by the day all communications were monitored for signs that the move west or east would begin. If it were to be Europe, Eighth Air Force news wasn't exactly promising. Jim had been following the progress of the new air war over there, learning that sixty American bombers had been shot out of the sky by swarming enemy fighters in one day over Germany. On the fourteenth of the month, another seventy-two bombers had been shot down or crashed on landing in one day's missions. Stewart knew the score: His squadron was heading into a meat grinder.

All four squadrons of the 445th Bombardment Group remained at their satellite training bases until receipt of official orders for the overseas movement. Two more weeks passed in painfully slow fashion, with flying kept to a minimum and only a few practice missions. Finally, on October 15 Jim watched 703rd ground personnel and a few aircrews added to the group at the last minute pack up and board trains for Camp Shanks, New York, along with the 445th headquarters staff. Five days later the aircrews assigned to planes received orders to report to their staging area at Lincoln, Nebraska, where the fliers of the 703rd Squadron experienced something akin to Christmas morning and presents under the tree: Factory-fresh B-24H Liberator four-engine bombers painted olive drab awaited them to replace the B-24Ds and B-24Es they had trained on, and each pilot and crew was assigned a ship number. Consolidated plants in San Diego and Fort Worth turned out Liberators, as did the Douglas facility in Tulsa, North American in Dallas, and Ford in Willow Run, Michigan. A new tradition had workers at the manufacturing facilities leaving handwritten notes in the cockpit of each plane for the men who would fly her. It had been reported in *Reader's Digest* that one such note had read, "God bless this plane and crew," a sentiment that had brought the crew of that aircraft good luck in battle. The idea sent the men of the 703rd scurrying onto the flight decks of their new ships looking for similar messages. They shouldn't have been so eager. Bill Minor found a note under a bolt cover in the cockpit of ship number 42-7508 that read, "I hope you don't get killed." And in ship number 42-7508, the message meeting the eyes of Ralph Stimmel's crew was short and to the point. "Fuck you."

Jim knew the B-24 Liberator very well; he had trained new pilots on both the 24 and its older brother, the Boeing B-17 Flying Fortress, and knew all the similarities and differences. They were very much alike in some ways. In both cases the navigator and bombardier sat in the nose of the plane in a glass-encased observatory. In both planes there was a top gun turret behind the cockpit, a ball turret underneath, and a tail turret. But the B-24 featured the top-mounted Davis laminar wing offering more lift and speed and a squared-off fuselage allowing much more headroom from the cockpit on back and a much larger bomb bay that could carry two tons more bombs than the Fortress. Little things made the Liberator superior: Roller-shutter bomb bay doors that slid up into the plane reduced drag and tricycle landing gear offered more stability in takeoffs and landings.

Many aviators in the 703rd Squadron found their new Liberators the devil to fly. "Oh, it was a horrible airplane," said Barry Shillito, Ollie Saunders' copilot. "They called it the 'widow maker' for good reason."

"The two four-engine bombers flew very differently," said Nick Radosevich of the 453rd Bomb Group. "The 17s would almost fly themselves. However, the 24 was a hands-on plane that had to be flown at all times."

The plain-Jane Liberator drew all manner of insults from crews of the sexy-by-comparison B-17s that dominated the American press and newsreels, comments like, "The B-24 is the packing case they send the B-17 to Europe in." Or, as Hal Turell, a navigator in the 703rd described the B-24 Liberator, "On the ground it looks like a slab-sided prehistoric monster wading through swamps."

The air and ground crews assigned to each slab-sided Liberator formed fast attachments to their planes, and all the crews of the 445th championed the superiority of their ships over the flash-and-dash Fortresses.

"We hated the B-17s," said 703 lead bombardier Jim Myers. "We didn't fly with them and they didn't fly with us. One of the things B-24 pilots would do is pull up beside a B-17, feather a prop to slow down his 24, then gun the engines and leave them behind."

"We were now getting used to having 'the lady' around, and we were even falling in love with her," said John Robinson of George Wright's crew about his new airplane, ship number 64439. "We were beginning to feel that we only had her to depend on."

A buzz electrified Lincoln when it was learned that an RAF Spitfire and a Messerschmitt Bf 109e* had been brought to the base for teaching purposes and were parked in a hangar under guard. Jim and the other officers of the 445th got close-up views and a lecture about the features of each aircraft, which brought the war a little closer and made it feel less theoretical.

While still in Lincoln, the crews began to name their planes. Bill Conley's crew dubbed their ship *Lady Shamrock* and Ralph Stimmel's crew went with *Liberty Belle*. The crew of Joe Narcovich dubbed their ship *Big Joe* as opposed to its pilot, little Joe. Earle Metcalf's crew, composed of all northerners and one kid from Arkansas, decided on *Nine Yanks and a Jerk*. Leo Cook's crew named their ship after Leo's baby boy, *Kelly*; Dave Skjeie's crew took the name of Dave's wife, Elizabeth, nicknamed Billie, for *Billie Babe*;

*See Glossary on pages 357–358 for military terms and definitions.

Chick Torpey's crew named their plane for Chick's wife, Betty. Lloyd Sharrard's crew named their ship for themselves, *Tenovus*. Mack Williams and crew named ship 7580 *'Hap' Hazard*. George Wright and crew adapted the popular song "Moonlight Serenade" into *Bullet Serenade* for ship 4439. Al Poor's crew chose a name befitting their New Hampshire farm-boy pilot, *Sunflower Sue*. Southerner Emmett Watson and crew went with *Hell Cat*. Barry Shillito remained infuriated by the double cross that had forced him into the right seat of a Liberator and advocated the name *Pissed Off* for ship 7570, and pilot Ollie Saunders and his crew agreed. The Victor Smith crew couldn't think of a name for plane 7512, but a couple of the gunners went to a local bar called the *Gremlins Roost*, so that's what they named their plane.

A security leak at Lincoln let loose information that the men of the 445th were headed to an air base in England. This breach forced the bombers and crews back to Sioux City for two more weeks of intensive training. Finally, the aircrews flew their planes to Morrison Field in Palm Beach, Florida. By this time the headquarters and ground personnel had boarded the *Queen Mary* bound for that mysterious base "somewhere in England." Orders had the Liberators taking off pointed toward Puerto Rico, and as Jim and his squadron headed southeast and watched the coastline of the United States pass underneath them and out of sight, Stewart unsealed orders that would finally reveal their flight path and destination. He read to Sharrard and the others in *Tenovus* over his throat mic on the interphone: "The 445th Bombardment Group (Heavy) will report to Station 124 located at the village of Tibenham, Norwich, East Anglia, United Kingdom." Then he added, "Wherever the hell that is."

They would learn soon enough. The 703rd wasn't just heading in the general direction of the war in Hitler's Europe; Stewart and his men had been aimed at its very heart.

16
BOY SCOUT

When Clem Leone walked into the recruiting station in South Baltimore on November 30, 1942, U.S. Army personnel advised, "The Boy Scouts are down the street, junior." At eighteen years, four months of age, diminutive in stature, Clem could have passed for an average tenth grader. But he was what he was, an overachiever, and he knew what he wanted: to fly in the Air Corps.

Clem needn't have worried. He was young, fit, bright, disease-free, and cleared the height minimum by more than two inches. He didn't have to be a skyscraper; he just had to stand better than five-two, and he did. Clem was in, and off he went to the booming Camp Pickett in Blackstone, Virginia, for a week of aptitude testing. Clem did well, astonishingly well, and earned himself a ticket to Miami Beach, Florida, along with other cream-of-the-crop recruits fast-tracked to be non-commissioned officers for basic training and another round of tests.

It was now the first week of December 1942, a year out from Pearl Harbor. America was mobilizing like crazy, and demand for beds for recruits far outstripped supply. As a result, Clem reported not to a barrack but to a Miami Beach hotel right on the water where he was to room with two other privates. He began his basic training on the beach stripped to the waist. Learned how to open ranks and close ranks. How to march. Broke for lunch at a cafeteria-turned-mess hall, and received word: He had scored so high on aptitude testing that he would set out at once on a track to become a radio operator. After one hour of basic training, the overachiever earned a stripe and was shipped as a private first class to Sioux Falls Army Air Field in Sioux Falls, South Dakota, for thirteen weeks of radio operator school with a class of three dozen. Graduation earned Clem another stripe, and Corporal Leone earned a third with acceptance to aerial gunnery school. He had risen from civilian to buck sergeant in four months.

In aerial gunnery school at Harlingen Army Airfield in Harlingen, Texas, he studied the .45 automatic pistol, Army carbine, Thompson submachine gun, and .30 and .50 machine guns. He learned to disassemble and reassemble the .50 cal in five minutes, blindfolded. He learned how to operate weapons in every turret of a heavy bomber—upper, tail, nose, and ball turrets—plus hand-held machine gun operation for the waist-gunner position. Then he was up in AT-6 Texans shooting air-to-air and having the time of his life.

Graduation from Harlingen included stripe number four, and Technical Sergeant Leone flew to Gowen Field, where he joined the recently formed 445th Bombardment Group (Heavy). At Gowen, Leone saw his first Consolidated B-24 bomber and fell in love with the ungainly beast at first sight. He was assigned as radio operator to a crew of ten that began training in the B-24. Among his crew were the enlisted men: Dick McCormick, the engineer, a quiet non-drinker like Clem; Ed Cooper, the ball-turret gunner and a ladies man; John Sheppard, the tail gunner from New York; Al Kaufman, curly-headed waist gunner; Lugan Hickey, the other waist gunner, the kid of the bunch from Missouri with buck teeth. The officers were Emery Varga, the navigator; Bill McKee, the bombardier, a little guy like Clem; Don Widmark, the copilot, whose brother was an actor just starting out in Hollywood; and Robert Blomberg, the pilot, a college man and the steady hand any crewman would want in charge.

To an eighteen year old, flying daily in a grand plane with these good guys, war seemed a faraway thing. They took runs into Nevada with 100-pound practice bombs, first flying alone, and then with another plane, then with many others.

Blomberg's crew was assigned to the 700th Squadron of the 445th, and graduated to phase-three B-24 training at Sioux City, where they met up with the rest of the 445th, then on to Mitchell, South Dakota. Months of formations, tactical gunnery training, radio training, familiarization flights, and practice bomb runs. Contingencies of every sort—transferring fuel, cranking up and down the landing gear, sitting in the copilot's seat to learn basic controls. Now these young men began to understand: The war was dead ahead.

Eleven months after he had enlisted, the 445th headed to the United Kingdom, where they would await further orders. Just when Stella Leone back in South Baltimore had begun to relax because her Clem was stateside, the war came calling.

17
DAFT

In autumn 1943 the Royal Air Force remained skeptical about the Americans and their grand schemes regarding aerial warfare against Germany. The RAF, hardened by the Battle of Britain, had gone it alone in a bombing campaign over German cities for the first two years of the war. Indeed, American promises about the arrival of a mighty air armada in England had been empty through the first half of 1942 and beyond. Finally, later in July and into August, the American fliers began to arrive in the United Kingdom. The Americans were, according to the Brits, spoiled, naive, and generally useless, while RAF bombers went into the air every night to "give it back for London" with brutal raids intent on spreading terror and killing as many Germans as possible—military and civilians alike. In the black of night, who knew where those bombs were falling? To the Brits it didn't matter, because you hit either the factory itself or the neighborhood where workers in the factory lived. Either way, factory production would suffer. Either way, the only good German was a dead German.

From the beginning the Americans proposed to wage an air war in Europe by the "precision bombing" of targets in the daylight hours from high altitude, relying on the brilliance of their coveted bombsight that had been invented in 1932 by Swiss engineer Carl L. Norden. At the time of its creation, the Norden bombsight was known as the most complex device in history, with an eyepiece looking through a twenty-power telescope in the middle of a metal housing that was packed with calculation equipment. The device allowed a bombardier to adjust for the speed of the aircraft carrying the bombs as well as air density and wind speed, while, oh, by the way, controlling the flight of the airplane on the bomb run itself.

But for too long the Norden bombsight was nothing more than hot air to Churchill—no big surprise where Americans were concerned. The Brits knew the Yanks were daft for a simple reason. Operating at night, British bombers—Lancasters and Stirlings—could make do without fighter cover. Flying in daylight would make it mandatory for American bombers to operate under an umbrella of fighters, or the Luftwaffe would shoot entire formations out of the sky, just as Spitfires had shot down Heinkel and Junkers bombers in the Battle of Britain. And no American fighter had the range to cover a bombing mission from England into Germany and back again. The result? The American fleet of bombers had been decimated to date, mauled so badly they had stopped flying twice. And Churchill was left to wring his hands and go it alone.

But the Brits didn't count on one thing: Yankee ingenuity. American bombers were developing rapidly on U.S. industrial drawing boards. Engineers were developing more powerful engines and packing each ship with a lethal array of machine guns in turrets in front of, on top of, underneath, and aft of each ship to fend off German fighters. American fighter variants were progressing just as fast.

In America, unseen by the RAF, the buildup of the U.S. Army Air Forces had been going on for a year now. Four-engine-rated pilots like Capt. James Stewart were being minted weekly, and crews of Clement Leones were training in bases across the American heartland.

18
SHAKEDOWN

The 445th Bomb Group was on the move. An advance eche-
lon of staff officers flew from LaGuardia to London via Scotland
on October 15, 1943, reporting first to Eighth Air Force Headquarters and then to Second Bomb Division Headquarters. All
ground personnel, including the ground crews of the planes, arrived in Scotland on the *Queen Mary* November 2. The next day
they reached their final destination, the tiny village of Tibenham,
Norwich, East Anglia, by train to find the new home of the 445th
half finished and mud soaked.

Among Stewart's last actions in the States before heading to
England was to call one of his crews in to rename their plane. Ollie Saunders and Barry Shillito reported to him and he stated the
problem, which had been nagging at him for weeks. "It doesn't
look good for one of our ships to be called *Pissed Off*," Jim told the
pilot and copilot. "Imagine the newsreels shoot pictures and there
you are on the big screen, pissed off. It looks like we have a morale
problem."

"You *do* have a morale problem," said Shillito, who wanted
nothing more than to be back in fighters.

Jim cocked an ear at his second lieutenant as if he hadn't heard
right. "You're not happy in this squadron, Barry?" he asked.

Shillito thought about it. "I'm happy in this squadron. I'm not happy in heavies."

"Well, you're stuck here for the time being," said Jim, "and we need to rename your airplane."

"What do you want us to call her?" asked Ollie Saunders.

"I'm not going to name your plane for you," said Stewart. "She's your baby, not mine."

"Fine, we'll call her *Our Baby*," said Saunders. "Is that all right?"

Jim was taken aback—this was too easy—but he didn't doubt Saunders for a minute because Ollie was a good guy. "Fine," said Jim. "That's fine. I appreciate it."

Then there was the problem of pilots using up their passes to get married prior to shipping out. Otis Rhoney telegrammed his girl, Lea, to meet him in Sioux City to tie the knot, so she did, but they hadn't counted on the waiting period for a license in Iowa. The couple hightailed it into Nebraska with another couple and found a justice of the peace before retiring to civilian quarters for what was left of a wedding night instead of returning to base as required. That's where Stewart tracked them down at 3 a.m. by telephone, but when Rhoney explained the circumstances, Jim didn't get in the way of love. It wasn't easy being C.O. to a group that included ex-fighter jocks who did all manner of flying by the seat of their pants.

The first group of planes of the 703, piloted by Cook, Narcovich, and Saunders and carrying some of the headquarters officers as passengers, including Colonel Terrill, took off November 13 on the southern route to England: Florida to Puerto Rico to British Guiana to Brazil to Ascension Island to Ghana to Senegal to Marrakech to Casablanca to Southampton to Tibenham. Terrill and his group arrived at their new base November 18.

Stewart commanded the second group of Liberators of the 703 from Lloyd Sharrard's ship, *Tenovus*. Sharrard was still wearing his lucky cowboy boots. This group of planes carried most of the crews and some extra base personnel on the same airfield-hopping, continent-hopping route. The first leg from Florida to Puerto Rico was a short one; Jim watched *Tenovus* glide over the peaceful Atlantic, skimming the Bahamas to the accompaniment of the drone of the engines. During the long flight, Jim climbed stiffly into the pilot's seat to spell Sharrard or the copilot, Coleman.

After a stay in San Juan, *Tenovus* lifted off and flew south over Puerto Rico, then over sparkling blue Caribbean waters and into the morning sun heading southeast toward Georgetown, British Guiana. Jim sat in the right seat beside Sharrard, with planes of the 703 taking off every few moments and scattering out in hazy skies. They knew it would be six-plus hours in the air and, because of vertigo, it was demanding flying by instruments over water, so they expected a grueling day.

Suddenly, a Mayday call broke radio silence and Jim shot to alertness. A Mayday? Now, in blue skies over turquoise waters? Jim gathered his thoughts and ordered all ships to report in. One by one they did, except for *Sunflower Sue*. She had sent just one Mayday and then, nothing—a very bad sign. That was the ship of 2nd Lt. Al Poor, the New Hampshire farm boy, who had been flying like the others at 8,000 feet, a crew of ten with four passengers, including Robert O'Hara, the master sergeant of the squadron. But the ships weren't in formation or even in sight of each other while in flight. The other pilots in the vicinity, Wright and Metcalf, weren't even sure where *Sunflower Sue* was, in front of them or behind, and they dropped down to 5,000 for a visual search of the ocean surface.

Jim had been learning that some of the planes were lemons, with fuel leak problems, and there had been rumors that B-24s were blowing up in the air in stateside training; he just didn't know what to make of this.

Sharrard asked Stewart if he wanted to turn back and establish a search pattern. Jim said yes, of course. Then a message came in on the VHF from George Wright's ship that a U-boat had been sighted on the surface of the water and may have picked off *Sunflower Sue* with a well-placed cannon shot. Jim's throat tightened; he couldn't leave those boys back there, but he couldn't risk anybody else if a sharpshooting U-boat was lurking below.

"All right, listen up," he told his pilots. "Remain on course for Georgetown. Any survivors in the water will be picked up by surface ships. There may be a U-boat down there, and nobody's going to make a target flying low in a search. Al's a good pilot and knows what to do; we all had the training for a water landing. Just worry about staying sharp."

Jim led the 703 on, leaving fourteen of their own behind, in the shadow of the United States. Later, Stewart would be informed that an intensive sea search revealed parts of the plane, open parachutes, a life vest, and life rafts. No survivors were found, and no bodies recovered.

The loss of the *Sunflower Sue* fourteen cast a pall on the entire passage to England, which included several exotic stops, including a layover in Marrakech. Finally, the ships of Stewart's group began touching down at Tibenham, Norwich, East Anglia air base on Wednesday, November 24, 1943, the day before Thanksgiving.

Jim tried to survey the terrain as navigator Jim Kidder directed Sharrard in for a landing in light rain on a gray afternoon at the new American air base. They had been flying over bases, bases, and more bases to reach what they figured was their own, a fact confirmed with the tower of Station 124.

Against raindrops Stewart saw three runways sprawling ahead at the place soon to be home, two in an X and a third cutting west to east through the lower portion of the X. Sharrard landed smoothly, then Jim and the others dropped out of the bomb bay and onto the wet pavement of a dead-quiet, flat expanse bordered by trees to the south and farm fields to the west and north. The men huddled against the damp, biting cold. Jim looked all about him; the only distinguishing landmark he could find in the mist was what looked like an ancient church tower in the far distance. Just off the runways and perimeter track, Jim could see mud and puddles all about. He looked down at Sharrard's shiny cowboy boots and smiled at his young lieutenant, who didn't see the humor.

Jim stowed his gear and grabbed a jeep for a spin around the tiny village of Tibenham. Along impossibly narrow country lanes made for ox carts, he saw thatch-roofed cottages and some newer houses, newer as in only a couple hundred years old. There was an old pub called the Greyhound on a lane west of base, and another, the Railway, east of it. Jim needed to know the location of the pubs in case any of his guys turned up missing. Aside from these two watering holes, there was simply no other place for the men of the squadron to get away to. Jim paused before the All Saints Tibenham Church with its 100-foot stone tower and climbed out of his jeep for a look around. The grounds featured an ancient graveyard with weathered headstones at odd angles and weeds throughout. Inside the big old stone building were crypts in the floor dating back to 1688, and a hand-hewn beamed ceiling above. He shivered in the unheated enclosure—at least it was unheated on a Wednesday. On the bright side, he might be attending services here and figured at least they'd be short in wintertime.

The scale of the new 445th Bomb Group air base that Jim continued to circumnavigate by jeep was vast and dwarfed the quaint village around it. Fifty-one giant, paved, "frying-pan" hardstands for parking the bombers sat off the wide beltway perimeter track that circled the runways. Each hardstand was wide enough to easily hold a B-24 with its 106-foot wingspan. West of the runways sat the ammo dump—all the bombs brought in by train and stacked neatly, bombs that soon would rain down on Germany. To the east and north of the runways sprawled facilities for nearly 3,000 men, including the headquarters staff for the 445th and its four squadrons, the 700, 701, 702, and Jim's 703. Each squadron's ships sat in their own cluster of hardstands.

Military structures sprawled a mile this way, to the east, and a mile that way, to the north, reaching across the farm fields of Tibenham village. Quonset huts dominated the landscape east of the runways as far as the eye could see. These half-pipes of corrugated steel sixteen feet wide and thirty-six feet long housed bomber officers or crews, two crews per structure. Quonset huts also made up Operations, Sick Quarters, the Mess Hall, and nearly all other key structures on the base.

The facilities were so spread out that Jim knew he would need to buy a bicycle at once. The other thing he learned right away was that the mud was miserable. Not all the pathways connecting communal sites and facilities had been paved, and the mud was atrocious and stuck to everything.

Jim returned the jeep and hopped a ride up a lane called Plantation Road to his quarters at the northeast corner of the base at Site 7. He saw a group of squat concrete and brick barracks, not Quonset huts but more like deluxe chicken coops. He worried about the low ceilings and, son of a gun, had to duck under the bulkhead of his door and under the I-beams of the ceilings. And it was cold in there, as cold as everywhere else. Lieutenant Fisher arrived with his gear, and he and Jim lit the Franklin stove and threw in some hunks of coal and shivered. They got the feeling they would be doing a lot of both in the weeks to come.

In the evening Jim finally sat down with Albert Poor's personnel file and the Navy report on the sea search for ship and crew. Jim contemplated a letter to Al's adoptive parents, Arthur and Olive Poor of Antrim, New Hampshire.

"Dear Mr. Poor..." he began.

He sat there a long while, staring at the sheet of paper on the desk in front of him. He drew in a deep breath and continued, "I am writing to you to tell you about your son, Lt. Albert Poor, who is missing in the Atlantic after serving his country ferrying his bomber to England."

Jim could barely work the mechanics of a pen on paper—an orderly would type it up for him in the morning; he wondered how many such letters he would be writing home from his new quarters at Station 124.

The next day Jim set to the task at hand, preparing for the action soon to come. He made sure his men had settled in to their Quonset huts, and that they had heat, blankets, equipment, and rations. He drilled them every day—shakedown flights and more shakedown flights for all the crews. He would get them up in the air in the morning and familiarize each man with every other crew member's duties and perspective. He kept stressing: Stay sharp, stay alive. They practiced formation flying, their Liberators roaring over Tibenham. When darkness fell, and it fell very early here, blackouts went into effect as they prepared for nighttime attacks from German fighters and bombers, attacks that kept not coming.

All his men attended "schooling" in the form of lectures on weather, bomber formations, English and European geography, enemy fighters and their tactics, and all aspects of the operation of a B-24.

An important lecture covered the topic of flak, short for *Fliegerabwehrkanone*, which translated to English as "flier defense cannon." Most prevalent of the German anti-aircraft guns was the Flak 41, an 88mm cannon produced by Krupp, with a range up to 37,000 feet. This gun and its earlier models had been observed in operation for months now by the Eighth Air Force over Germany and its occupied territories, and it was a weapon to be feared. Flak, or "ack-ack" as the British called it, could be fired independently or controlled by radar, and either way, its shrapnel could tear apart a fuselage, control surface, or engine, and a direct hit meant trouble and usually failure of the aircraft. Flak was designed to detonate at a certain altitude so it wasn't aimed and fired at a specific ship but rather at the path of an approaching formation. To counter radar-controlled flak, the Tommies had developed "window," strips of aluminum foil like Christmas tree tinsel that were thrown out of the gun ports in the waist of the ship in bundles. Ground radar picked up the echo of window, and fliers noticed that immediately the guns began firing at these imaginary lower-altitude, falling targets. The Eighth Air Force was about to start deploying window, or "chaff" as they called it, in missions coming up.

Jim realized now that they all had so much to learn about survival in the real war, as taught in the daily schooling. They got refreshers on their stateside classroom instruction about bailout procedures and parachute operation. Lectures covered what they should expect if bailing out into Europe. They were reminded not to take personal items on a mission, not photos or love letters or anything of the kind, because these could be used against them or provide information to the enemy. They were told about active partisan groups in France, Holland, and Belgium that helped fliers. If possible, airmen were to evade capture, but if no other options seemed to be available, fliers should surrender in uniform to enemy authorities because at that point protection under the Geneva Convention began, and they should expect the rights of prisoners of war. Interrogation could be harsh and intimidating, but more often German officers with excellent English would attempt to charm information out of prisoners. Fliers were warned that changing into civilian clothes removed the protection of the Geneva Convention and the soldier fell under the classification of "spy" with the possibility of immediate execution. In addition, German civilians had been known to rough up or even kill downed American fliers, so the men were advised to be on guard. If captured, they should reveal nothing beyond name, rank, and serial number. Not the bomb group, squadron, location of base, officers, other fliers—nothing.

Given the intense bombing operations ongoing over Europe, training of the new bomb group remained intense, and crews noticed that a white circle with a black F had been painted on each of the vertical stabilizers on their planes and on the right wing to mark them as the 445th, which had two sister bomb groups always flying with them. These three groups made up the Second Combat Wing—the 389th at Hethel wore a circle C on their tails, and the 453rd at Old Buckenham wore a circle J.

In the 703rd Squadron, Stewart had his pilots log twenty-two hours of flight time in just the first ten days in Tibenham, so much time that the planes of the 703 became living, breathing organisms with the crews their brains and hearts. Stewart welcomed new personnel as they rotated in until soon there were twice as many crews as planes to prepare for upcoming casualties and the illnesses already brewing in the damp farm fields of Tibenham.

On December 12 another Liberator flew in and 2nd Lt. Peter Abell reported to Jim along with copilot 2nd Lt. Bernard Anderson and crew in the ship dubbed *Star Baby*. Abell told Jim they were a B-17 crew that had been switched over to 24s at the last moment and shipped over. He also said that *Star Baby* was something of a mess with a bad fuel tank and faulty hydraulic lines that had made passage over the southern route through Marrakech a weeks-long nightmare.

"Yeah, well, you're not the only one," said Stewart. "A lot of the planes have problems."

He told the men to find their billet and stow gear, then report back to their ship in an hour for a shakedown flight.

"One thing, sir," said Abell. "Our radioman, Don Watts, is down with something. I ordered him to find Sick Quarters."

"Don't worry about that," said Stewart. "At your ship, one hour." Abell's crew saluted; Jim returned it and when they were gone, he hopped in his jeep and went scrounging around base for a radio operator to get *Star Baby* off the ground. He started in the orderly room of the 700th Squadron to see who was around and explained his problem to the duty officer. He asked if any radiomen in the 700 needed flying time. A dark-haired guy was sitting in a chair with its front legs up as he leaned against the wall reading a magazine. The kid's ears perked up; he was a fresh-faced young guy with the hint of a mustache and dark skin.

The legs of the chair crashed forward. "I'm a radio operator, sir," said the kid. "I'll help you out."

Captain Stewart appraised him in an instant. Clear-eyed, lean, maybe a little cocky, and below Jim's shoulders in stature. "What's your name, son?" he said.

"Technical Sergeant Leone, sir."

"Where you from, Leone?" said Stewart, noting the pronunciation of the "e" at the end of the name.

"South Baltimore, sir."

"Well, thanks for offering to help out. I'm Captain Stewart. Go get your gear." Leone hurried out and Stewart called after him, "Jeep's outside!" They drove down the perimeter track to the hardstands of the 703, and Stewart and Leone climbed into the bomb bay of *Star Baby*. Jim was used to the guys recognizing him and staring a little too long at a movie star in the flesh, but there was none of that with Leone, and it was refreshing.

The radioman stowed his gear at the table behind Abell in the copilot's seat as Stewart folded himself into the pilot's chair. Copilot Anderson sat behind Jim. Stewart led Abell through the lengthy checklist—it ought to rattle a pilot to have to see everything from the copilot's perspective, but Abell did all right. The main thing Stewart would watch for: How did his new pilot handle the aircraft? His mastery of the throttles would tell a lot. And his composure.

From the copilot's seat, Abell taxied into position on Runway 0-3 and lifted off. The Liberator smelled of gas, which was a growing source of concern for Jim, and he was impressed that this pilot knew to open the bomb bay doors to increase the circulation of air and bleed off excess fumes. In general, *Star Baby* responded well and Stewart told Abell to head north toward the coast. All the shakedown flights flew north and west to stay away from traffic to and from Europe.

This pilot, like all of them, had already been trained intensively stateside, but that had been on 17s, and the 24 was a different beast. Stewart needed to see for himself the skill of all the men who would be flying behind him, not just Abell but also copilot Anderson and the crew aft. Jim put Abell through a series of turns—level, climbing, gliding, chandelles.

"Hang on, Leone," Stewart said into the interphone with a smile as he ordered Abell into a steep bank and then another one. Stewart watched his pilot's face since they weren't on oxygen; he watched his chest to note rate of breathing and how tense or relaxed the man was. He observed his eyes on the instruments to judge the relationship between man and machine. Stewart was satisfied with the way this pilot responded.

South of the seacoast town of Cromer, with the North Sea visible in the far horizon, Jim ordered one last chandelle and they headed back for base. "Hey, Leone," he said into his throat mic, "any traffic we need to be aware of between here and the station?"

"All clear, sir," came the response.

Jim unhooked, grabbed his clipboard, and stepped off the flight deck as Abell switched over to the pilot's seat and Anderson climbed in beside him. Jim headed back past the top turret and over the catwalk amidships to the waist gun positions. He checked his list and asked who was Alford and who was Reeves. Actually, he yelled it over the roar of the engines. He shouted out questions to each gunner about his position, the operation of his gun, and his other duties—backing up the engineer, transferring fuel, arming the bombs, hand cranking the landing gear, and lowering the ball turret. He met Merriam, the ball turret gunner, asked him a series of questions, and checked out Dougherty in the tail and grilled him as well. On the way forward he pulled down Caton, the engineer, from the top turret. Same routine: series of questions, this time about procedures at start-up and in flight.

So Leone wouldn't feel left out, Stewart ran him through questions about the radio station, channels, frequencies, ship-to-ship and ship-to-tower communications, including how to identify his ship to British or American fighters in an emergency and on what frequency.

Back on the flight deck, standing behind Abell, Stewart could see the familiar steeple of Tibenham All Saints Church in the distance at eleven o'clock. Jim plugged into the interphone system and pointed out the north-south railway line running east of the base and told Abell the church and the train tracks would be his orientation points for Tibenham since all the bases looked alike out here. He ordered a 360-degree landing, which was accomplished nicely. After forty minutes they were back on the ground. Stewart handed Abell a sheet of paper with notes on it relating to specific areas the crew needed work on to better understand the operation of a B-24 since they had come from the 17. The crew jumped out of the plane and into a truck while Stewart drove Leone back up the peri track to the orderly room of the 700th Squadron. On the way he asked the kid from Baltimore how long he had been in the service and what he had done before the war. The answers he received were admirable.

"Thanks for your help, sergeant," said the skipper of the 703 as Leone climbed out. "I appreciate it."

"Any time, sir," said Leone with enthusiasm that seemed genuine. He gave the captain a smart salute, which was returned. Jim liked these boys. He knew he couldn't get attached to any of them, not in this business; Colonel Terrill had reminded him of it, and Jim kept reminding himself. This radioman waddling away under the weight of his flight suit and gear was a pistol—he had to be to earn five stripes while being barely old enough to shave.

Jim found it easy to equate noncoms in the army with the behind-the-scenes people back at MGM, the technical people who seemed to know everything about the science of filmmaking. The director, producer, and camera operator were the officers, and the rest were the enlisted men who made it all happen. Nobody wrote about them for the fan magazines. To audiences sitting in the dark watching silver flickers on the big screen, those people on the film's crew were invisible. But to see them in action was to appreciate them. The lighting men, gaffers, grips, dolly operators, prop and wardrobe specialists all worked at top speed and spoke in short-hand, if they spoke at all, because most of the time the beginning of a sentence spoken by the director would be all the crew needed for communication about what should happen next. They knew the business that well. Jim was starting to see the same phenom-enon here: the sixth sense of a cohesive unit. Difference was, in Hollywood you weren't operating at 20,000 feet and no one was shooting at you. Come to think of it, there was always a Louis B. Mayer or Jack L. Warner or Harry Cohn shooting at you—just not with bullets. Here, some of these great overachieving boys like the gung-ho radioman from South Baltimore would be leaving in the morning and not coming home in the afternoon. Lots of them, Stewart knew. He didn't know how that was going to feel; he wasn't looking forward to finding out.

19
PUSHED BY ANGELS

From the first American air strike into Germany in January 1943, *Luftwaffe General der Jagdflieger* (General of the Fighter Arm) Dolfo Galland had felt deep in his soul that the Americans in their ingenious B-17 and B-24 bombers with their rafts of machine guns would spell the doom of Germany. He began referring to them as the "Four Motors." Dolfo was by now a fighter pilot known and revered throughout Germany, not only for his cigars and devil-may-care personality, but also for the emblem of Mickey Mouse emblazoned across the fuselage of his Bf 109, except this Mickey had a cigar between his lips, a pistol in one hand, and an axe in the other.

Yes, Dolfo knew the threat of the American bombers. He had made his feelings known to *Reichsmarschall* Göring, and Göring dismissed them as unwarranted, saying the soft Americans in their "flying washing machines" were sitting ducks. Göring believed that when Galland's fighters started blowing the Americans out of the skies, they would quickly lose their stomach for a fight. But Galland had seen more and more enemy raids into Germany hitting strategic targets. No matter how many bombers his pilots shot down, more planes kept coming. Far from losing their stomach for a fight, these Americans didn't seem to mind being shot to pieces.

Hitler called in General Galland for a consultation at *Wolfsschanze* to have the American bomber threat explained. The boldness of daylight raids perplexed the Führer, and Galland leveled with him: To combat the Allied air raids into Germany from the Baltic to Italy to Russia, the number of German fighters would have to increase dramatically. Hitler wanted to know how dramatically. Galland said he would need three or four fighters for every American bomber to bring the bombing campaign to a stop. But, said Galland, there was another variable in the equation. If the Four Motors brought fighter escorts with them, he would need even more planes. Many more planes.

Hitler told Galland not to worry, that he would be given more factory-fresh fighters than ever, hundreds more in just a few months, each with more cannons and also air-to-air rockets that could strike from outside the range of the bombers' .50-caliber machine guns. The point was moot, said Hitler, because the Americans didn't have fighters capable of escorting their heavy bombers deep into the Fatherland.

Yet, thought Galland. They didn't have such fighters yet, but soon they would. But Galland also knew of something that could win the war: Herr Messerschmitt's "speed bomber" powered by two jet engines. He had flown the prototype himself, heard the whine of the turbines, and remarked of his moments in the air, "It felt as though angels were pushing." Galland had requested 1,000 of these miracle ships for use defending the Reich. But Hitler believed that the next generation of propeller-driven Messerschmitt fighter, the Me 209, would take care of the situation. The jets would be used for bombing only.

At the end of July 1943, the Tommies and Americans had hit Hamburg hard, which forced Galland and other Luftwaffe leaders to, as he put it, "take stock." The Tommies bombed by night with incendiaries; the Americans followed up by day until a firestorm consumed the city. The result was what Galland referred to as an "extermination raid" that shocked the nation: 40,000 dead, including 5,000 children. "A wave of terror radiated from the suffering city and spread throughout Germany," said Galland.

He made changes to his defense system, and just in time: In August the Americans launched a maximum-effort raid on industrial facilities located in Schweinfurt and Regensburg. On that critical day, his *Jagdgeschwaders*, or JG tactical fighter groups, had intercepted the Four Motors, swarmed, outmaneuvered the enemy, expended all their ammunition and fuel, landed for resupply, and then taken off again to finish the job. Dozens of American bombers had been destroyed; all Galland's pilots needed to do was wait for the American fighter planes to peel away from the bomber stream for refueling, and then the German fighters bounced the American formation.

After a quiet time the Americans returned to Schweinfurt in October, and the same thing happened. Galland's pilots blew them to bits. Finally, the daylight raids stopped. Dead. Finally, the Führer had been proven right about something—the Americans had given up on the crazy notion of daylight bombing. And yet, in Dolfo's heart, he knew better because he was getting to know the Americans and their leader, this Gen. Ira Eaker. They were very good, just as good as Luftwaffe bomber crews, and just as brave. Germany hadn't faced the Americans in the last war until the end, and so who could blame Hitler and Göring for doubting the fighting spirit of these lazy capitalists? No, he couldn't be naive about it. The Americans would be back. Another wave of planes would be coming, and Galland began to plan for that day when the skies over Germany once again grew dark with bomber streams that blotted out the sun. If only he had some of those speed bombers like the one he had flown. But angels were in short supply in Germany as November turned to December 1943.

20
MISSION TODAY

How do you hide out in the middle of a war? That was the question Jim asked himself now, in the far-flung village of Tibenham, East Anglia. He could never find privacy; no, Jim could not. He just wanted to be a soldier; he wanted to serve his time and fulfill his mission because that was what he was supposed to do. But it had been so difficult, really, beginning at Moffett Field. He had expected trouble when he first enlisted, but once he had been transferred north to Moffett in the San Francisco area, he expected the situation to improve. But still reporters had wanted access to him and had called in favors, but Public Affairs had put them off at Jim's request. Over and over and over the reporters had sought him out. Couldn't he just be a soldier? Couldn't he just serve?

He had been ordered to London on December 2 for a press conference—just one and that would be it, he was promised. In the officers' club in Eighth Bomber Command headquarters, he had signed autographs for waitresses and hat-check girls and made a speech for newsreel cameras, blowing his lines on the second take because of nerves. He had been introduced to the press "against a background of deep leather lounge chairs, chefs, ham and roast-beef sandwiches, and double sherries." Then he had sat in one of those leather chairs facing three ladies of the press who had grilled him, including one young reporter who looked uncomfortably like Ann Rutherford and had flirted outrageously throughout the interview. All three had asked ridiculous questions, and Jim had found the exercise embarrassing. He had vowed not to repeat it during his time in England, yet the press and public kept at him.

Wherever he went in the service, whether in the States or in England, people discovered the whereabouts of Jimmy Stewart the movie star—as Bill Minor had witnessed at the Warrior Hotel in Sioux City. But Jim couldn't have it both ways, he knew. He had enjoyed the life of James Stewart, Academy Award-winning MGM star, and now he must pay for that life he had once lived and might live again, for all the wealth he had accumulated, and for all the fame. Even at Site 7 in Tibenham, in the blackness of night, in the damp cold that pierced the marrow of bone, in the mud that everyone scraped from their boots, despite rank, that's who he was, the movie star. He would never achieve the goal of being Ralph Stimmel or Lloyd Sharrard or Bill Conley. He must be Jim Stewart, and he must find a way to fulfill his family obligation despite fame and that other tremendous obstacle, age.

Lying in the pre-dawn darkness on December 13, 1943, Jim heard the doorknob turn and felt cold air streaming into the quarters he shared with Fisher off Wash Lane. "Mission today, Captain Stewart," an operations clerk said gently in the dark.

And so it began. Jim had lain there with the one-winged pigeon in his stomach most of the night, stealing sleep here and there but so little that he couldn't calculate how much he had actually gotten. Occasionally in the night, the noise of the putt-putts, the auxiliary power units aiding the ground crews as they got the planes ready, drifted over the farmlands all the way from the hardstands of the 702nd Squadron, which were nearest to his quarters. Those boys worked all night on the planes to get them ready and would grab sleep during the day while the mission progressed, and then be up and ready when their ships returned in the afternoon. If they returned.

Mission today, sir. Was there an equivalent in the Civil War for Gen. Sam Jackson before Fredericksburg or Gettysburg? He must have known when a fight was coming, and he had seen some doozies. So had Granddad in the Union Signal Corps, following Custer around. And, of course, the German trench helmets proved that Capt. Alex Stewart had been close to the action in the Great War. Now it was the latest Stewart's turn. What would it be like? How would he do? Would the first round of flak get him? How would the squadron commander react when he saw ships go down around him, ships of his squadron, and they must go down sooner or later? Some of his pilots, some of his crews, might not be coming back today. He had to face that possibility.

Captain Stewart had spent a lot of time this night thinking about the beating taken by the Eighth Air Force up to this point. Headquarters kept the facts from the rank and file, but Jim knew the leaders. Hell, the leaders had sought out their Hollywood VIP for companionship, to hear stories of the glamour days and glamour people, and the brass talked a lot more than Jim did, so he knew about Ploesti and Schweinfurt. Knew all about it, and now it was the 445th's turn to be fed into the people mill. It was good that this was a new squadron in a new base and no one had seen the worst, Flying Fortresses and Liberators shot to hell and crew members breathing their last returning to British runways or, worse yet, not returning at all. These boys hadn't seen that. These boys were starting fresh.

Jim angled his watch to see the time: 0505. He rolled off his bunk and up to his height, grabbed his duffel and shaving kit, careful not to bang his head on the I-beams or door frame, and headed outside to the Site 7 showers. Stewart set his shaving kit on a sink and looked at his surroundings reflected in the mirror. The officers flying today were awake, wide-awake; the pilots, navigators, and bombardiers of the squadron. Stewart saw his ship's pilot, Leo Cook, the twenty-two-year-old kid from Sikeston, Missouri, who would fly left seat, with Jim in the right, today in Victor Smith's ship, *Gremlins Roost*. Command wisdom was that a Liberator was a Liberator, so crews were assigned to ships randomly with no thought given to the close bond that had developed between men and planes. It bothered the pilots not to be in their own ships on the first mission, ships they had named and loved. Cook needed to be in *Kelly* for luck and wasn't, and it was eating at him. In Cook's face, in all their faces, Jim saw the same vague frustration at this turn of events.

Not just frustration. "We were all terrified," Jim would remember years later.

There was no forgetting this was December in England. The damp cold knifed in everywhere, including the showers. But he couldn't risk being shot down without one, so under the spray and back out he went. Then he shaved, closely, and the rest of them made fun. He gave it right back—Watch closely, junior. You might be doing this yourself in five or ten years. Later, the men would learn a night's growth of beard would offer a little protection against the rubbing of the oxygen mask; they had been told a close shave would make a better seal of mask on skin.

Jim told his officers to get moving; the truck was waiting. He pulled on long johns, and then struggled into his blue "teddy bear" one-piece electric flying suit. He added socks, then a second pair, and shirt, pants, tie, fur-lined boots, and flight jacket. He tucked Dad's letter and the psalm into his shirt pocket, grabbed his kit and at the door paused, and yelled for them to move it or they'd miss the eggs at breakfast! That kicked the men into gear.

Stewart hustled his men into the Mess Hall, where all the officers of the 445th who were flying today gathered for a breakfast of real eggs, pork, toast, and coffee. Bring on the coffee. The men asked their squadron commander where they were headed.

He smiled the Stewart smile and called over the din of the conversations, "Colonel Terrill will tell us in the briefing." He could see the strain in their faces, in their wide eyes, in their flushed cheeks. Hands shook as they ate. Knees rattled under the table. Coffee spilled over the edges of cups. Jim ate what he could, which as usual wasn't much more than toast and coffee. Many of the men in this room would be his responsibility today since he was flying squadron lead behind Colonel Terrill, the formation leader.

The men moved from the Mess Hall on increasingly unsure legs through the cold, muddy blackness of night with no hint of rising sun. They drove in trucks and jeeps or hopped on bikes from the Mess Hall west to Operations, where they trudged past MPs guarding the doors to connected Nissen huts housing the briefing rooms, one for officers and one for enlisted men. On the concrete floor sat rows of long, backless, spartan benches. Stewart sat squarely in the first row, and the officers filled in around him until the room was packed tight, forcing stragglers to stand at the back. There wasn't much conversation now, just a lot of lumps in a lot of throats. Ahead on the wall was the black curtain, their first black curtain. Behind it, the wall-sized map of Europe they had heard so much about, with the day's target and course marked in red ribbon. The map determined their fate for the day, and the length of the red ribbon gave some clue about the length of their lives.

Would it be a milk run? An easy mission to get the men used to combat operations? Or would it be a rough one into the heart of Germany, the kind that had already cost so many planes and crews?

"Atten–shun!" The men snapped to their feet and Col. Robert Terrill strode in from the back with the intelligence and weather officers. Dressed out for flying, he stepped up onto a platform in the front of the room. From there Terrill looked out at all the young faces.

"Rest!" said a voice, and the men return to their benches.

"Good morning," said Terrill.

The collection of men murmured a "good morning" in reply, with the room so quiet that the putt-putts and the spooling engines of B-24s across the way could plainly be heard. Terrill wore a re-assuring smile for his men. He had been where they were now and knew what they were going through. In fact, he had been out there from the beginning of the Eighth, when each day the planes had been shot up on every mission of every length.

"This is a very exciting day," he said, "the day Station 124 be-comes operational, the day we start giving it back to Mr. Hitler and Mr. Göring. Our target on mission number one of the 445th, will be—"

He turned to the lieutenant holding the pull chain on the black curtain before them, who gave the chain a hand-over-hand yank. The curtain pulled back to reveal a connected set of red ribbons extending from Tibenham across the North Sea east-northeast to the northern tip of Germany, just below Denmark, "—the sub-marine facilities at Kiel, Germany. Ours is one of four missions to be flown today. The first will bomb Bremen with 182 planes; the second will hit Kiel. The 445th is one of five bomb groups of the Second Bomb Division, a total of 113 B-24s that will participate in today's third mission, which will hit Kiel again. Finally, mission four will hit Kiel one last time for the day with 284 bombers." Terrill paused. "It seems that, by nightfall, there won't be much left of Kiel."

A few of the men laughed.

"Let me tell you something about our target," said Terrill. He had their ears, all the men in the room, and the fact that he would personally lead this first mission added to his credibility. "Kiel is the principal base of the German fleet. It's the largest naval arsenal in Germany, and the second-largest U-boat building yard. Right now, as we speak, there are thirty U-boats under construction there." He paced a little. The performer in Stewart recognized a man who knew how to command a stage. Terrill certainly wasn't a Barrymore, this plain-looking man, but he was a command officer and they all could feel the authority in him. "Now, I want you to think about all those American ships that have gone down in the Atlantic. I want you to think about Torpedo Alley off the Carolinas, and about all the troop ships taking our guys over here every day with U-boats ready to strike. A lot of our guys came over on the *Queen Mary*. We were lucky a U-boat didn't hit that. If we knock out Kiel, we save a whole lot of lives."

They had endured months and months of training every day for this moment, for one opportunity to hit into Germany. It would not be a milk run to bomb a French airdrome. Stewart knew by the men's reaction that they were just as happy to get a flight to Germany over with; so was he. His eyes skimmed along the line of the red ribbon: most of the flight would be over water and away from flak. They would hit the target and fly back the same way, over water.

"Your secondary target will be Hamburg," said Terrill, pointing. "A group of P-38s will escort you in. A group of P-51s will escort you out. I want you to stay sharp and keep your formation tight. Keep the ship-to-ship chatter to a minimum because they'll use it to home in on you." He paused and scanned their faces. "Good luck and good hunting, gentlemen."

Terrill stepped aside and Jim got up before a chalkboard showing the formation and position of each pilot and plane. Captain Smith, the intelligence officer, or S-2, briefed on the specifics of the target, the submarine pens, "which are reinforced concrete bunkers that are difficult to knock out. Your ordnance will be ten general-purpose bombs, 500 pounds each. You will be looking for the farthest southwest tip of the harbor at Kiel." He touched a spot on the map with his pointer. "Near that spot is your M.P.I." Stewart committed the mean point of impact to memory.

Captain Smith paused and looked at another sheet of paper. "As you might expect, you will pick up flak at the coastline and it will stay with you all the way to target and back to the coast. Expect it to be accurate. Enemy aircraft will likely be Ju 88s."

The pointer was passed to Lieutenant Curtis, the station weather officer, who said, "Expect ten over ten stratocumulus over the target with tops from 6,000 to 9,000. There should be patches of cirrus above you at 25,000. There will be contrails today. Pay attention to the Pathfinders and bomb on them."

At briefing's end, all bowed heads for a prayer by the chaplain. The men were particularly sober and quiet now. Then they were told to synchronize watches. The lead navigator called, "Hack," and everyone was set to 0905.

Terrill said, "There's every reason to expect mission success." He set down his pointer and smiled again. "Good luck, gentlemen. Let's go flying."

"Atten–shun!" said the voice. The men snapped to. Colonel Terrill and his officers departed.

The officers split up now for briefings by job. Pilots and copilots proceeded to one side of the room; bombardiers to a second; navigators to a third for short, specialized briefings.

In the locker room Jim deposited his effects to ensure that nothing of value—personal or military—would fall into enemy hands if he were shot down, but the letter and psalm stayed in his pocket. Then he stepped into and tightened his parachute harness. Leo Cook said one of them needed to requisition escape kits and purses; Jim said he'd go. He signed for the escape kits for Cook's crew and took his own.

Before handing them out, Jim examined his escape kit. In its waterproof case he found small phrase books in German and Dutch, a compass, a silk map of Europe, a saw blade, rations, and a passport with fake identity along with a photo recently taken showing him in civilian clothes and wearing a three-day growth of beard—he hoped nobody who saw him or his fake passport was a movie fan. He opened a purse containing German and French coins. His kit and the others would be turned in after the mission—if they got back. The U.S. Army Air Forces had thought of everything, but then they had been needing hundreds of these escape kits with the number of bombers falling from European skies each day.

Jim grabbed his duffel containing maps, leather helmet with headset, steel helmet, and .45 automatic and made his way outside to the waiting jeep where the men of the crew, all waddling now under the weight and bulk of their underclothes, heated flight suits, uniforms, and jackets, piled on for a ride out to the hardstand, on which sat B-24 number 512, *Gremlins Roost*. It was a miracle the jeep held them all. After a bumpy ride they found their feet and dropped their bags on the hardstand under their plane to put on Mae Wests, mittens, helmets—whatever would complete their outfits. They filtered toward the plane and bypassed the *Gremlins Roost* nose art. The men of Leo Cook's crew felt it was bad luck to pay attention to someone else's nose art on their first mission. The regular copilot of *Gremlins Roost*, Bill Minor, later explained, "We always preferred to be in our own ship because we knew her, knew how she handled, all her quirks."

Some of the crewmen climbed up into the bomb bay; Stewart, Cook, and the engineer, Moulton, circled the ship, going over the fuselage, wings, vertical and horizontal stabilizers, control surfaces, wheels, tires, engines, and propellers, to assure flight readiness.

Terrill came by in a jeep, and they watched him make a whirring motion with his hands, as in, hurry it up, before proceeding to his plane. The last three crew members sprinted into the opened *Gremlins Roost* bomb bay. Stewart gave a glance to the bomb load: full racks holding 500-pounders that made the ship feel claustrophobic. Nothing announced the closeness of the war like those ten bombs he reached out and touched as he walked by. He leaned low and stepped up to the flight deck, pulled out his checklist, maps, leather flight helmet, and steel pot, and stowed his bag.

He stepped a long leg over the right seat and dropped himself in place behind the wheel. Cook plopped down next to him in the left seat, and both adjusted their seats and pedals, and belted themselves in. Jim checked his oxygen mask. He plugged his headset into the interphone. Moulton climbed out the top hatch and went through the controls check with Cook. Ailerons, check. Elevators, check. Rudders, check.

It was time for chewing gum. Jim unwrapped a stick, popped it in his mouth, and offered some to Cook, who declined.

Jim felt the exuberance rising within him. Since he had first gone up with the intention of earning his pilot's license—war was on the horizon even then—somewhere deep inside he knew he would arrive at this moment. After all the hours piled up to earn a commercial rating; after forced landings and a crack-up; after embracing his low draft number and entering service with a grin; after basic training and struggling to pull his own weight up through the ranks, dodging the press and his old studio all the while; after becoming an instructor of one, two, and four-engine aircraft and teaching dozens of other Army fliers; after fighting the headwinds of Culver City and Washington that would have kept him stateside; after months of Liberator training and the loss of many planes and great crews as they learned the demanding art of combat flying; after all of it, here he sat leading the four assigned planes of his squadron in a fifteen-ship formation of the 445th. Fifteen fully loaded ships minutes from their first mission. He allowed the thrill of it inside him just as he fought back the terror. Cook pulled his checklist and Jim gave it a glance in the pilot's hand. It was a steady hand. Here was this young kid of, what was he, twenty-three? Maybe. But Leo Cook sat there square jawed and riveted on his job, giving every indication he had done this a dozen times already. Gone out to Germany a dozen times, or two dozen. He was that cool a customer. Jim knew his own hands were shaking and hoped Leo wouldn't see.

Cook started down the checklist. "Ignition switches off."

Stewart reached down, and heard his voice respond. "Ignition switches off."

"Master switch off," said Cook.

Jim flipped the master switch down. "Master switch off."

Out on the hardstand, Moulton pulled the propeller through two rotations on each engine.

Cook ordered battery switches on, then ignition switches, then master switch. He reached down with his right hand and pulled up the latch to engage the parking brake. He ordered the power switch set to number one inverter. Jim complied.

Cook reached forward with his right hand to pull the autopilot lever down. "Automatic flight control off," he said, and checked free movement of the wheel. He ordered deicers off, intercoolers open, and cowl flaps open. In their minds' eyes all saw Terrill ordering speed, so they rushed through the checklist. It shouldn't happen this way. They should get things right. After all, this wasn't the usual ship of this crew. It was a blank slug of a B-24 and Stewart didn't know it; the crew didn't know it.

"Propellers set to high rpm," said the pilot, pulling superchargers off and checking mixture controls in idle cutoff. They checked the automatic fire extinguishers.

Stewart shot a glance out his right window and got an all clear from Moulton standing by engine No. 3, and Jim switched on fuel booster pumps so that both pilots could prime No. 3. Engine 3 fired, and Cook switched the mixture control to auto-lean. With No. 3 purring, they started 4, 2, and 1, and the ship sputtered to life. Cook revved engines up to 1,000 rpm and they growled for him. The ship awoke like a prizefighter flexing muscles and ready for the bell. The pilots watched gauges during engine warm-up and all looked A-OK. They checked brake pressure, wing deicers, and propeller anti-icing fluid. Everything must check out; everything must work or disaster would result.

Moulton scampered under the wings, removed wheel blocks, jumped in the plane, and closed the bomb bay. Cook released the parking brakes and the burdened ship struggled forward; she felt pregnant, heavy with child, unlike the flights leading up to this morning. The engines gave a steady, comforting roar when revved to high rpm, and *Gremlins Roost* lumbered into a line of B-24s taxiing down the perimeter track toward Runway 2-1. Stewart knew that little things meant success or failure every moment. They had to keep idling time to a minimum because long idling of a Lib meant engine fouling and a scrubbed mission. Every other pilot knew this—they had better since he reminded them often enough. All had gone through their checklists with cool efficiency and got their planes moving. Just the same, nobody could rush through taxiing because a bomb-laden Liberator had to be steered gently, with minimal application of brakes, or the wheels would fail.

Gremlins Roost was third in line for takeoff. They checked propellers at high pitch and low pitch, and Cook switched the fuel mixture to auto-rich. "Booster pumps on," he said.

"Booster pumps on," answered Stewart.

Cook set flaps and ran up the engines one at a time, 4, 3, 2, then 1.

"Generators on," said Cook on the interphone.

"Generators coming up," answered Moulton. It was no use talking voice to voice now, not with those engines going. Nobody would be able to have a conversation without mics and earphones for many hours.

Navigator Hal Turell of Stimmel's crew vividly described these moments on the Tibenham peri track awaiting the "go" signal:

"Tires squeal as engines rev up to put us into a turn and we take our place in the line of huge gray beasts in the gloom of the morning haze. In front and behind are row after row of Liberators, waiting poised like race horses at the starting gate. The throaty rumble of the engines, the propellers turning and the noses bobbing up and down as the pilots applied their brakes to keep from over running the plane in front. Each time the hydraulic pumps add their high-pitched protests to the cacophony of noise. Nose to tail they wait in a tight line, the end of the queue lost in the mist."

Cook and Stewart watched the tower at two o'clock for the green takeoff flare and there it came. Ships piloted by Second Lieutenant Shurtz of the 702 and then Sharrard poured on the coal, lumbering down the runway and lifting into the air not too long before that runway ran out. Cook got the "clear for takeoff" from the tower. He steered a hard right onto Runway 2-1 and let the outboard engines make the turn at five miles per hour and suddenly *Gremlins Roost* went nose into the wind.

Sure, they had practiced this a hundred times. Literally a hundred, or two hundred, and it was old hat. But the exhibition season was over and now the games counted. Jim felt his heart pounding in his chest and glanced at his watch: 0830. In his ear he heard Cook order him to close cowl flaps. Then Cook pushed the throttles forward all the way so the engines could rev at high rpm. The ship moved forward along the runway, accelerating sluggishly under the bomb load. Jim was used to feeling the ship break into a sprint about now to go airborne at 110 miles per hour, but this morning she kept taxiing. At 125 and with great physical force from the roaring engines of this war beast, Cook pulled back on the wheel and the ship relented and eased into the air. He kept nose down until airspeed reached 135. Stewart raised the landing gear and Cook banked away from Tibenham, heading northeast toward Buncher 5 west of Norwich, where the group would assemble by circling its assigned Buncher beacon in the center of four radio towers that pinpointed the pilot's location. Now, the feeling of a practice mission returned with the plane in the air and responding to controls, with other planes in front of and behind them. Cook reduced power and on they flew up through 5,000 feet to Buncher 5, the racetrack as they called it, where the brightly painted assembly Zebra ship fired rockets to attract its planes and kept them circling until all had arrived to form up and proceed with the mission.

149

The cockpit grew colder but Jim didn't notice; he was marveling at the sight before him. The fifteen planes of the 445th were joined by formations from four other bomb groups, with the 389th off to starboard and high in the lead. Suddenly, he became part of something vital, something like the phalanx of the Greek infantry, a great military force that now aimed itself east-northeast past the English coast and on over water toward the northern tip of Germany. Oh sure, he had been a part of training formations like this, but now each carried two-and-a-half tons of bombs that would soon be armed for delivery and then dropped in Germany.

Then, just as it seemed no more planes could fill the sky, with the Second Bomb Division heading east—there, oh, such a sight. He could see another entire division flying ahead of them, and ahead of that, on the far horizon, still a third division.

The formation shot out past the coastline and over turbulent North Sea waters. They passed through 10,000 feet. "Oxygen masks on," said Cook, and Stewart pulled on his mask and adjusted the straps. He felt the cool, reassuring oxygen meet his nose and mouth and fill his lungs and the lack of sleep last night suddenly meant nothing. Every molecule in his body shot to attention.

Cook was looking down at the surface of the water. "Make a note of that," he said. "Four enemy freighters heading, make it—seventy degrees. I'd say forty miles from the coast. Note also blimps flying over the ships." Stewart made notes as Cook spoke.

"Got it," said Jim, and with a glance down he saw the ships cutting through the water. Would they be warning Germany of imminent danger?

Flying long and high above the North Sea, he stared at the majestic sight of condensation trails forming behind the planes of the giant formations ahead until they were painting the sky in neat rows of white. So beautiful and so contrary to the very idea of where they were going and what they would do there.

Slowly, the extreme cold overwhelmed the adrenalin and Stewart realized he was about frozen. He had forgotten to plug in his electric flying suit. He fumbled to find the receptacle. He hoped for instant relief but it came slowly, oh, so slowly, into his legs, his feet, his hands, as the completed circuit brought warmth everywhere the wires inside the suit contacted. The air temperature had already reached twenty-five degrees below zero as they passed through 17,000 feet. Ice had formed around Cook's mask and ice tinged his clothing all over.

"Test your guns, everyone," said Cook on the interphone. Jim heard and felt short machine gun bursts rattle the ship. The guns were firing in the nose, the top turret just behind his head, the waist guns aft, and the twin tail guns.

In a moment he heard the voice of Myers, the bombardier. "Right-hand gun's out in the nose."

Then Moulton in the top turret. "Right-hand gun out up here too, skipper. Frozen solid."

A third voice, Conwell, said, "Motor's out in the tail turret. I can't move."

"Wonderful," muttered Cook, who was already distracted by the sight ahead. "Mae Wests on, flak vests on, helmets on," he said, a warning that he had spotted the enemy coast. "Get the ball turret down and test the guns," Cook added, sounding very much like a man not on his first mission.

Jim reached for his steel pot helmet and strapped it over his leather helmet and headset.

Ahead in the broken cloud cover, he could see German territory for the first time, the coastline way ahead, forty miles off. It was spectacular, like Hollywood, the lead divisions hitting that coastline and flak exploding around the ships so far off. One moment he could see the panorama and the next moment the clouds obscured, but his mouth got dry in the flow of oxygen and he realized he had stopped chomping on his gum. He was thinking that there it was, dead ahead: the world war.

Leo took one gloved hand off the wheel to break ice away from his mask so it wouldn't clog the discharge vent. As he did it, he kept looking left, ahead, right, ahead, up, ahead—always mindful of where the planes were around him, the formation so tight that wingtips nearly bumped.

Four hours into the flight, with the European coast in sight, Cook said on the interphone, "Hey, Harry, arm the bombs, will you?" Arming wires had to be pulled from each bomb before they would detonate—a job for the waist gunners.

In a moment came the call, "Bombs armed."

The flak at the coastline and inland had grown solid with explosions as gunners on the ground homed in on the first formations flying through. Stewart knew his eyes were wide as they flew straight into their first flak field at 230 miles per hour and hit the turbulence. He reached up and pushed on his chest to feel the letter and psalm and make sure they were there. The smell of cordite, like spent fireworks times a hundred, filled the ship, and he felt his first flak detonation off the starboard cockpit window and then another to port in front of the ship, like a slap in the face.

"Switch to full oxygen," Cook said to the crew, taking them off the demand setting, which was a mixture of oxygen and ambient air.

They climbed through 22,000 feet and now the air temperature reached forty-five below. Everything happened so fast, and there was so much in the control panel for a copilot to concentrate on. Ahead and out the corner of his eye he saw orange explosions and then black puffs of smoke that renewed and deepened the black cloud surrounding them. The plane rattled and shook in the worst turbulence Stewart had ever experienced. His shoulder slammed off the right bulkhead; his head bumped the windscreen. The god-awful smell of that cordite filled his lungs despite the pure oxygen entering his mask. Outside his headset he heard what sounded dimly like hail hitting the ship—shards of shrapnel from the spent anti-aircraft shells.

"They're pretty good," said Stewart of the gunners below. Better to say something, anything, rather than just sit there and take a beating.

The schooling about flak bore no resemblance to the experience of flak. The ship yawed left and right, and pitched up and down, yanking them against their seatbelts, but they flew on over the German coastline just below the border with Denmark, heading due east to the initial point of attack, the I.P., where the bomb run on a straight line to target would begin.

Above in the blue sky four dots appeared. "Fighters, eleven o'clock high," said Moulton in the top turret.

Jim watched the dots grow rapidly as they shot westward. "Hold your fire," he said. "They're P-38s."

"Right," said Moulton as the four fighters zoomed above the formation.

"I.P. ahead," said Leo as the flak continued to jostle the ship.

"We're at the I.P.," said Cook. "Gunther, fire yellow-yellow." Westphal, the radioman, got up from his seat, grabbed his Very pistol and a flare, and shot it out the top port to signal to the group that they'd reached the initial point.

Cook banked right and switched control of the ship over to Jim Myers, the bombardier. It would be Myers steering straight to the target now through his bombsight from the nose of the plane, below the flight deck. The flak had stopped for the moment, and through broken clouds Stewart saw an urban area ahead past farmlands and smoke rising from the edges of the populated areas—Kiel's smoke screen, as per the briefing. Beyond that in the center of the city, he briefly saw vivid orange bomb detonations and smoke rising—a glimpse of the pits of hell as the First and Third Divisions pounded the port of Kiel.

"Bomb bay doors open," ordered Cook, and the rush of air signaling the opening of the doors in the belly bounced off the walls of the fuselage and shot forward into the flight deck.

"Watch for fighters," called Stewart to the formation, but as far as his vision allowed, he could see no enemy aircraft approaching. Suddenly P-51s zoomed over their heads heading east toward the target, four abreast. Jim thought it a lovely sight. Then another group of four fighters, P-38s, cruised past below the formation, also heading east.

Off to the right and ahead the 389th continued to lead, and as Stewart looked at their formation, the flak started to pop around them again and the ship shuddered. Both he and Cook grabbed the wheel on instinct but they didn't have control—Myers did. Out the corner of his eye Jim saw a phosphorous marker drop out of the lead Pathfinder ship of the 389 along with its bomb load.

"Bombs away," said Myers. With one loud click the ten bombs totaling 5,000 pounds salvoed out of the ship, and she lurched upward.

"Bombs clear," came the call from aft.

Leo switched control back to the cockpit and banked right. The cloud cover below was solid now as they came around toward the rally point and rode straight into a storm of flak that rattled the ship and Jim's bones. A direct hit from one of those shells would be the end of their mission and their lives, and it seemed a miracle every second that they continued to survive. The flak had been thicker approaching Kiel, but now as the planes flew over the city's southern sector it grew more accurate. It was predictor control fire—radar-guided guns—that could see the formation even though the formation couldn't see the ground.

In seconds all grew perfectly calm out the windows as they passed the last anti-aircraft battery and headed west over rural countryside. How was it possible, Jim wondered, that they had flown this entire mission, five-plus hours in the air already, without seeing one enemy fighter? Thousands of feet below, the undercast remained ten over ten—completely obscuring views of the ground.

In another forty-five minutes Lieutenant Rayford, the navigator, said, "We should be nearing the coast," and within thirty seconds flak from the coastal guns started to detonate below them by a thousand feet, and they flew west and back over the North Sea. One more flak barrage smacked them around, from the German naval base on the island of Heligoland according to Rayford, and then the flight became routine all the way to the east coast of England. By then the cloud cover had broken up to three over ten, and a setting sun greeted them as they headed inland and circled around to land at Tibenham.

After more than eight hours Stewart stepped off the flight deck and out the bomb bay, and looked at the boxcar with wings that had just taken them all the way to northern Germany. He saw just what flak could do. There were a dozen holes big enough to slide his hand through in the left side of the ship alone, and pockmarks on the bottom of the wing. He dragged his gear behind him and hopped in a truck with the crew for the ride back to the Mess Hall and then barracks. He didn't bother to eat; his stomach wouldn't let him eat anyway. He headed straight for his bunk and a long and deep sleep.

21
A LATE BREAKFAST

The men of Tibenham came to grips with their lives as combat personnel after the Kiel mission and now took comfort in the safety and security of their new home at Station 124. In a physical sense it was anything but comfortable. The pervasive cold called for all the coal they could pour into their free-standing iron stoves, and coal was in short supply. Missions produced nerves and nerves produced diarrhea, but many of the latrines had yet to be completed; instead, buckets were placed in the latrine enclosures. The Mess Hall wasn't calibrated with Operations, so food was running out before all the crews could eat breakfast, and many on the second mission, December 16, flew off to Germany with their stomachs empty.

That second mission of the 445th Bomb Group took twenty-four Liberators to Bremen in northwestern Germany under the command of Maj. Bill Jones, the group operations officer. Twenty-four went out, and twenty-four came back. Some of Stewart's pilots—Wright, Johnson, Narcovich, and Saunders—went out for the first time, and Jim learned what it felt like to brief the group at 0430, then stand at the rail of the control tower and watch the ships power up and take off at 0830. Then came the waiting until they returned after 1600, and there he stood again at the rail to count each ship as it appeared in the eastern sky. It was much easier to fly than to watch, because in flight his mind was occupied every second all day long keeping the ship in the air, minding the formation, and issuing orders.

The 445th attacked alongside the 389th Bomb Group, the "Sky Scorpions" out of Station 114 in Hethel, eight miles north of Tibenham. This sister squadron of the 445th had been in operation since September, so they were old hands and the men of Station 124 were the rookies. Soon, the third and final group of the Second Combat Wing, the 453rd, would go online five miles northwest of Tibenham at Old Buckenham, but scuttlebutt was that they were nowhere near operational.

Jim learned on return of the formation that the day's mission to Bremen, site of Germany's largest shipbuilding yards, had included some action by enemy fighters but not enough to take down any ships in the group. Due to heavy weather, bombardiers in the formation relied on Pathfinders to know when to drop.

The Pathfinder was a wonder of an airplane, a specially equipped B-24 with RAdio Detection And Ranging, or radar, a technology invented by the Brits and improved every month of the war. Now the RAF had found ways to build radar into a bomber, and the American scientists had tweaked the technology until together they arrived at Bombing Through the Overcast, or BTO, to which they gave the code name Mickey. All available technology was loaded into those special Pathfinder B-24s.

The navigator station of each ship was equipped with Gee, a radio navigational aid in operation for the past six months that was based on signals from ground stations shown on a cathode-ray scope. Navigators also had Gee-H, a transmitter that ever so slowly communicated with ground stations to allow for bombing through overcast, but it didn't work consistently. And Pathfinders featured H2X, a radar pulse aimed at the ground that would bounce returns onto a cathode-ray scope to be interpreted as coastlines, cities, or marshalling yards. On days like this when the squadrons bombed Bremen through solid undercast, nobody knew how good the equipment was or where the bombs actually fell. Some of the boys saw black smoke rising up higher than the cloud cover. What was burning? Nobody knew. But then, twelve combat wings had dropped three million pounds of bombs on Bremen in twenty minutes, so smoke was inevitable.

Jim listened in on all the debriefs of his crews and accompanied the men to the Mess Hall to eat and talk about the mission, learn what had gone well, and hear their gripes and concerns. The flak had been intense, much worse than briefing had led them to expect. Machine guns were freezing all over the ships. Many superchargers, which boosted power on the engines, became inoperative at high altitude. The blue heated flying suits were great unless one wire failed, at which point the entire suit failed with it—bad news at 20,000 feet and forty below zero.

Talk soon drifted away from the mission to general grievances. The men had been confined to base since arriving at Tibenham, and they wanted passes to London or at least to nearby Norwich. They were ready to get drunk, and see girls, and, more than anything, get out of the cold. They wanted to go shopping for long johns that the army should have supplied but hadn't. Rumor said the entire ETO was without long johns, and winter was just beginning! They wanted to get away from the mud and couldn't understand why the pathways to important buildings like Operations, Sick Quarters, and the Mess Hall hadn't been paved before the men even arrived. Jim couldn't make promises about changes; he just listened and understood. They wanted to know when they were going up again, and he couldn't answer that one either. They wanted to know why the Mess Hall had shut down so early two days ago on the morning after the first mission when the boys stayed in their bunks to catch up on sleep only to find out they had missed breakfast. Well now, here was something Captain Stewart could actually act upon.

The next morning a master sergeant drove around in a jeep to all the huts of the 445th and made an announcement that affected the lives of all who had flown the previous day, and all who hadn't: "You can have breakfast until ten o'clock by orders of Captain Stewart."

22
TOPAZ BLUE

Three days later on December 20, the morning's briefing replayed in Jim's mind at 26,000 feet:

"Target today: Bremen, the second-largest port in Germany. Bremen has been hit multiple times: November 24, November 26, December 13, December 16. And we will bomb it today. The First Bomb Division will hit it with 225 planes. The Third will hit it with 182. Then we will hit it with 127. That's a total of 534 planes hitting Bremen in thirty minutes. We will look for the marshalling yards in the northern part of the city. We will look for the Deschimag Shipyard, one of the largest shipbuilding yards in Germany. We will look for Deutsche Vacuum Oil refinery. In the southern sector of the city we will look for the Focke-Wulf Aircraft Company."

Jim's second mission was the first for the crew of the *Lady Shamrock*, piloted by Bill Conley, one of the squadron's best fliers. Stewart again sat right seat as the copilot and the mission's group commander, and both Jim and Bill had to fold themselves into the cockpit, Bill as rail thin as Jim if not quite as tall, but both of them knowing they would be sore as hell in eight hours or so. They would fly even higher today than on the first mission, cruising at 26,000, if you could call it cruising. Jim's pilots were returning from missions telling him—and he was learning this himself—that above about 18,000 feet the B-24 became noticeably harder to control, calling for a lot more muscle and exertion from the pilots. And here was *Lady Shamrock* this moment at 26,000 with Conley working like the devil to fly straight and level, and Jim spelling him often.

The air was thin and deadly cold, and the oxygen mask was chafing Stewart's face. Ross Curtis, the Station 124 weather officer, had warned in briefing that at this altitude the air temperature would be minus forty or below and to keep skin covered at all times. Now, ice kept growing around Stewart's mask, and he kept feeling for it and breaking it away. Frost painted the edges of the windows. Conley's eyebrows were white with ice and a white icicle grew down his chest as he sat in the pilot seat and flew the ship. The farther they proceeded into Germany, the more Conley grew tinged in white. Jim looked down; he was frost-covered as well, despite the current flowing inside his flight suit.

As intense as Kiel had been, that mission had also been a cakewalk. But Jim knew that Bremen would be different because of what he had learned after the 445th returned from there days earlier on December 16. Their ships were shot up, their faces frostbitten and shell-shocked. He had watched them retreat silently to their bunks and sleep twelve hours in exhaustion; some hadn't even stopped for the customary shot of whiskey and some chow.

Bremen wasn't far into Germany, but the city was well defended with fighters and anti-aircraft batteries. Battle damage from the sixteenth made that clear. To the south out the starboard window, they could see the smoke screen over the port of Emden, obscuring the city and rising miles into the morning sky. Then flak came up from batteries just east of the Zuiderzee and zipped up to 26,000 feet and cracked and snapped like whips about them, jostling the ship and pinging against the fuselage. The smell of cordite choked Jim and filled his lungs. A hailstorm of metal bits from flak burst as the formation made a sun-drenched target in cloudless skies of gleaming topaz blue as high noon drew near. By now, after two missions, the men knew flak all too well and wore their flak jackets; most wore steel pot helmets, and some sat on spare flak jackets to protect against shrapnel punching up through the fuselage.

Jim grew distracted by a formation of P-47 Thunderbolts gliding past to starboard and another formation to port. The Thunderbolt was a squat, dynamic American fighter bomber affectionately nicknamed the Jug. Four ships stacked together in each formation floated effortlessly past, guarding the B-24 group trudging toward Bremen. He found it deeply comforting to have them on guard, and in fact it was peaceful up here, like Clover Field way back when: peace and the bright sun and topaz blue.

The 445th crossed the Ems River, and in another few minutes the P-47s began to peel off to head back toward home and a fresh batch of fuel. He knew to watch for fighters now; he told the crew to be alert.

In another moment Stewart heard Steinhauer's voice: "We're on the I.P.," said the navigator.

Conley turned over control of the ship to Rankin while Stewart ordered Wilson to fire yellow-yellow flares to signal to the group that they had reached the initial point of the bomb run.

"I can't find any flares, sir," said Wilson, the radioman.

Stewart was about to demand to know why there were no flares on *Lady Shamrock* when Tech. Sgt. Harold "Eck" Eckelberry, the engineer, rushed up behind the pilots on the flight deck. His oxygen mask was plugged into a walking-around bottle. He pulled away his mask long enough to shout to all at the top of his voice above the roar of the engines, "We've got a supercharger out. Frozen. And my interphone mic is dead." With that he hurried back to the top turret.

Flying behind Jim in ship 579, *Paper Doll*, navigator Wright Lee later recounted, "As we passed the I.P. about ten miles from Bremen, the flak barrage peaked, not quite the quantity of the first

Bremen mission, but more accurate and intense. My hands and feet were so cold that at times I could not feel them. My hands warmed up as I rubbed them, but my feet remained lifeless with no feeling whatsoever."

As quickly as the flak barrage began, it ended, and the sky grew clear on a perfect day for flying. Far below, four miles down, western Germany showed lush and green even in December. It didn't look real, all that green below. It looked like a painting.

"Fighters, ten o'clock!" came the call from somewhere aft. Jim strained to look out the window. With his oxygen mask on, goggles pulled down, interphone, and flight suit plugged in, he couldn't move much and he could see nothing. Then he heard, "Fighters all around!"

"Ship going down! Ship going down!" said a frantic voice from another plane.

"I think it's *Good Nuff!*"

Jim tried to think. *Good Nuff*—whose ship was that? Buck Patterson's from the 700? Jim thought back to the chalkboard from briefing. Patterson was in the high squadron behind Jim.

"I see chutes!" called a voice. "Four...five...six. Six chutes." There, survivors. Maybe they could make it back to England somehow, but dropping into Germany was bad business.

More chatter on the radio. "Awalt's ship got it in the cockpit. Still flying." Damn it. Awalt was a good pilot—Jim hoped he could keep his plane in the air. Another ship reported guns frozen and inoperative. Sounded like Chick Torpey reporting; how the hell could the ships cover each other with frozen guns? Ralph Stimmel said they were seeing rockets fired from a German Ju 88. God, the sky was full of bandits. Jim saw Bf 109s and Me 110s swoop past from two o'clock and zip through the formation. Such a powerless feeling all of a sudden.

The running battle between the Liberators and the Luftwaffe continued as the group charged to target, and suddenly the P-47s reappeared in waves of four. Jim heard reports on the interphone; although low on fuel, the Jugs had turned around when they saw the group jumped. Conley and Stewart watched a Thunderbolt streak diagonally down across their line of vision with a Bf 109 on its tail. They had passed from view before Jim could see the outcome but he heard that the P-47 had been hit and was going down.

A moment later the Jugs had swept the sky clear of enemy fighters.

"Bremen smoke screen dead ahead," said Rankin. The vast urban area of Bremen sprawled before Jim with smoke pots dotting the near edges of the city at even points. A little further in were ragged fires from strikes by the First and Third Divisions, with all that black smoke dirtying the air even to 26,000 and obscuring much of the landscape.

The 445th approached the target at 230 miles per hour, with everything happening so fast on the bomb run. Way too fast. Jim couldn't see any enemy fighters, and the chatter on his headset had quieted.

The flak barrage resumed, bursting all about and right at their altitude. The ship would spasm every time a blast came close. Rankin had control through his bombsight; Conley would have done better if he had been able to muscle the controls, but it was Rankin's ship for another couple of minutes.

Lady Shamrock lumbered through the edge of the smoke screen, and the turbulence rocked them. Now and then, Stewart could still see entire blocks burning far below and smell burning wood, even up that high. Conley looked for the lead Pathfinder ships that would be dropping red smoke markers with their load to signal bombs away. No such flares could be seen.

"Can you see flares?" Rankin asked from down below in the nose to the pilot and copilot above him.

"Negative," said Conley.

"I've got a manufacturing plant coming up," said Rankin. The smoke below was thick now; Jim wondered how Rankin could see anything.

"No flares visible," said Conley. "You call the shot."

In a few more seconds Rankin said, "Bombs away."

Jim said into his throat mic, "Wilson, fire red-red to signal bombs away."

"Can't find any red flares either, sir," said Wilson, whom the men called "Pappy." It was a matter to be resolved at another time and place, but Jim already knew that if they made it home, he wouldn't come down too hard on Wilson for forgetting flares on his first mission; he would do better next time.

As Stewart thought this through, the ship resounded with a series of clicks and clacks, very loud, even above the headsets, and the men could feel each bomb letting go by electronic release, entrained over the target, a mixed load of 100-pound incendiaries and 500-pound general-purpose bombs. Click, click, click, click. Every few seconds more bombs let loose, and as each left the ship, she leapt higher in the sky, relieved of all that weight. Jim could feel it, and his urge was to grab the wheel and compensate.

"Bombs clear," said Pappy Wilson.

Conley switched control back from Rankin and banked hard to starboard. With the right side dipped low in hazy skies, Jim could see their bombs hitting the southern portions of Bremen five miles below; bright and violent orange flashes as those big bombs and incendiaries devastated the area near the factory Rankin had spotted.

Conley had just leveled out the ship after completing his turn when Jim heard, "Fighters!"

He could hear and feel the top turret firing four feet above, rattling the entire ship. Then farther back the waist gunners opened up in short spasms. Thank God *Lady Shamrock*'s guns weren't frozen. The gunners had been trained and trained again to fire in short bursts or they'd use up "the whole nine yards" in their belts too soon and overheat the guns for good measure. Jim couldn't see much at first, but then yellow streaks, each an enemy fighter, zipped past from the rear, low to high, and broke left and broke right in front of the formation and were gone from view again.

The chatter continued. "109s, five o'clock." All the action happened behind Conley and Stewart, so it was no use even straining to look. Let the gunners amidships and in the turrets do their jobs.

Conley pointed and Jim could see a yellow 190 at twelve o'clock low and a mile out closing fast, heading straight for their ship. As Conley and Stewart watched, its wing guns started flashing fire, aiming for the flight deck—a new German strategy they had been briefed on. Soon they could hear Steinhauer's machine gun answering from the nose below. Stewart waited for bullets to punch through the windshield and hit him. It was in God's hands now. The German plane zipped past so close over the top of the cockpit that Jim could count the rivets in her belly. He knew the *Lady* had been hit; no way that damn pilot could have missed. A moment later Rankin said the glass in the front turret had been punched through, but he and Steinhauer were all right.

Just in the last few minutes, with distractions constant and everyone breathing hard, ice had encrusted Conley, Stewart, and Wilson, who was sitting behind Stewart at the radio. Jim knocked at the ice grown nearly a foot below his face mask and dropped chunks of ice onto the deck. It was a miracle the guns continued to chatter.

Finally, they passed south of the smoke screen at Emden still flying at 26,000, and more flak burst around them in deadly black puffs. The powder smell filled the ship, and Conley ordered window to be dropped in bundles every few seconds. It was the first time out for the strips of aluminum meant to distract radar, and they all hoped it would do the trick and confuse those guys on the ground. Dead ahead lay the Zuiderzee and the North Sea sprawled beyond it, promising safety in just a few moments more.

The formation droned westward over the coast of Germany

and Holland, then over the Frisian Islands in the North Sea and began a steady descent that had them at 10,000 and off oxygen when they reached the English coast at Cromer. Jim's face stung when he pulled off his mask, and he looked at Conley to see deep red marks where the skin had been exposed under his eyes all those hours in the air.

Soon they were skimming the flat farmlands of East Anglia. They saw the comforting tall tower of Tibenham All Saints Church and circled while ships fired flares if they carried wounded or had been so badly damaged that landing would be a problem. Finally, they touched down on the east-west runway and Jim noted the time: 1450. There was a lot to report, a lot to improve on, and he would listen in on every crew's interrogation by S-2—he always did. He dropped out through the bomb bay and stood to his full height for the first time since 0700 and thought of nothing but the sleep that would come as soon as he could manage it. As he climbed into the back of the truck with the rest of them, it bothered him—he had lost a plane from his formation, and a crew, and some of those boys were likely dead.

There wasn't time to dwell on any of it. The group went up again two days later to bomb marshalling yards at Osnabrück and Münster, Germany, and Luftwaffe fighters shot two ships out of the sky and a third was crippled and crash landed back in England. None of Jim's boys of the 703rd had been lost. Still, the squadron had its closest call yet on that December 22 mission when another Liberator had collided with Earle Metcalf's ship, dug a hole in his wing, and bent a prop. But Earle had kept his head and stayed with the formation to complete the mission despite a gouged wing, flak, and fighters. In just nine days since the group had become operational, a grim sort of mathematics had come into play. Men were being subtracted regularly and, if not subtracted, then shaken so badly they might crack up.

Then came Christmas Eve, a rotten time to fly, and another

mission came down from Division HQ. Never mind that the horrible, dark, wintry dampness of southeastern England had brought with it cold and flu season, which hit the base hard. Never mind it was Christmas Eve. At least today's mission was voluntary for all qualified crews at Station 124.

Jim was restless as he briefed the pilots on a thirty-five-ship sortie to Bonnières, France, on what had been dubbed the "rocket coast" to hit a V-1 launch site. German V-1 rockets were menacing England, London in particular, and killing with random cruelty. In all, 670 B-17s and B-24s would hit twenty-three V-weapon sites on the coast. Jim wanted to fly, but it wasn't his turn in the rotation—it fell to Gil Fisher as group assistant operations officer to serve as air commander for the third section in the formation. Fisher began with a near mutiny after someone failed to alert the Mess Hall that the boys were going up, and many of the crews didn't get to eat at all. Then, Fisher reported to the flight line as copilot and squadron commander on Victor Smith's ship, *Gremlins Roost*, which infuriated the volatile Bill Minor, the regular copilot on Smith's crew who stood there in his flight suit and jacket and holding all his gear. The second lieutenant gave Gil Fisher an earful. After the mission, which was a success except that one ship had crash-landed back in England, Fisher told Stewart about Minor's temper tantrum on the hardstand. "I'll fly every mission my crew flies," Minor had ranted. "If I'm not on the flight deck, I'll fly in the waist as a gunner!" And that's what Minor had done. Minor spent the five-hour mission in the waist keeping the gunners company.

It was a relief for all concerned that the Germans were even more unprepared to receive a Christmas Eve bombing mission than the Eighth Air Force was to launch one. The bad guys had taken the day off and not fired a gun or launched a fighter. If not for two Liberators from the next field over colliding in mid-air killing both crews, the day would have been perfect. Yet Minor's insubordination gave Stewart an issue to deal with—it was laudable that Bill wanted to stick with his crew even when there wasn't a job for him, but one didn't mouth off to a superior officer on the flight line and in front of the crew in question. That must not be tolerated.

As Stewart considered his course of action in the matter, a knock at the door of the Site 7 quarters he shared with Fisher startled them both. It was Second Lieutenant Minor who, hat in hand, requested permission to enter. He edged inside and Fisher closed the door. "I'm sorry for what happened today, sir," he said to Fisher. "I always speak my mind, and sometimes I shouldn't. What I did was wrong." Stewart stood watching; it was a nice moment. Minor glanced at Jim, saluted both officers, and departed.

The men in Stewart's squadron knew their commander wasn't a blood-and-guts leader; neither did they want to give him problems to deal with, so Minor sought approval and Stewart gave it without a word. Jim later said, "I was, in many ways, far happier in the service than I ever was at any time in my life. Closeness and camaraderie with all those wonderful guys. Feeling I was part of a whole, of a divine scheme, with an obligation to do my very best. I wasn't playacting life then; I was living it."

He had been playacting so long, but what choice did he have with a playactor father? He had kept it up until playacting became second nature and made him a natural for the stage and then the picture business. He could look back on highly dramatic roles, playing an army doctor in *Of Human Hearts*, or Jefferson Smith awash in letters on the Senate floor, or Macaulay Connor telling Tracy Lord about moonbeams. Except here he couldn't read any script other than the officer's manual, and often that didn't help at all. Here he was forced away from his natural inclination to be a man alone who found human connections only through playacting. Now it was sink or swim, relating to men to save their lives and his own, and out there on that 20,000-foot limb, Jim found that he loved it.

23
BAILOUT

That week of Christmas 1943 the damp and cold of Tibenham caught up with 2nd Lt. Robert Blomberg, pilot of the crew that included Clem Leone on the plane named after Blomberg's wife, *Shirley Raye*. With their pilot laid up in Sick Quarters, the crew faced the prospect of splitting up for service as replacement personnel on other crews that had lost a navigator, bombardier, gunner, or radioman.

The men of the *Shirley Raye* brightened considerably the morning of December 28 when a pilot ordered the crew out for flight time—2nd Lt. Donald Hansen was the copilot of 2nd Lt. Herbert Planka's crew of the 700 and needed to check out a Liberator that had been serviced and was now airworthy. He was given the *Shirley Raye* crew to do it. All the crews of the 700th Squadron knew each other well by now, and Hansen had flown on the group's inaugural mission as one of five ships of the 700 to go out that day.

"Where ya from, sir?" asked Leone of the tall man with curly hair as the crew jumped off a jeep at the hardstand of the ship they'd be flying.

"Forty-first Avenue, West Seattle, Washington," replied Hansen. "You?"

"South Baltimore," said Leone.

"What was Kiel like, Lieutenant?" asked Al Kaufman, the waist gunner. Kaufman's curly red hair was spilling out from the edges of his helmet like always.

Hansen shrugged. "Long trip, and cold. Lots of flak, but no bandits."

"I hope they'll all be like that when we finally go up," said Kaufman.

"I came in from P-40s," said Hansen. "This four-engine war is hard to get used to." Hansen was staring at the nose art of the B-24H they would be taking up. The name read *Gallant Lady*, with a sexy girl emblazoned underneath. She was already a battle-scarred bird, but the men found such ships comforting because obviously they had been to rough places and made it back. In the silence Clem could see that Lieutenant Hansen was keeping himself from saying more. "How about we go flying?" said Hansen to the crew.

The *Shirley Raye* bunch tossed their gear into *Gallant Lady* for a shakedown flight that began like any other hop in a Liberator. They took off on Runway 0-3 with the smell of gas strong throughout the ship. Hansen asked Dick McCormick, the engineer, to crack open the bomb bay to dissipate the fumes. They headed northeast, and Hansen banked left when he reached the North Sea. The new man was checking out as a pilot, and Clem could imagine this guy taking over for Blomberg on the mission that was surely coming.

High over East Anglia, the edge of Leone's vision caught on something out the radio station window. A puff of smoke on the wing. He fixed his attention on the engines. "Lieutenant, sir," he called into his throat mic. "Smoke on No. 4."

Copilot Widmark looked over his right shoulder out the cockpit window. "Fire on No. 4," he confirmed. A second later Hansen said, "Engineer—transfer fuel from No. 4." Hansen handled the situation beautifully, feathering the engine and banking toward home. The wing extinguisher did its job, and the fire puffed itself out.

The crew counted the seconds and minutes from that instant as the ship headed southwest toward Tibenham. But fifty miles out from Station 124, the fire on *Gallant Lady's* problem engine reignited. Clem looked up at Hansen, and it was clear by the adjustments he was making that he already knew.

"What's our position?" asked Hansen. His voice was up a little now because an engine fire could bring down a Lib fast.

"North of Mundford," reported navigator Varga, "about twenty-five miles west-nor'west of base."

Leone stood from his radio station to peer over the shoulder of the new officer in the pilot's seat. Hansen was straining to see past Widmark out the starboard window as the fire sparked into an inferno that consumed engine No. 4. He could see it was bad, but he kept his cool as Widmark fidgeted in the copilot's seat.

"We can make it," said Hansen into his throat mic. "We'll get home." He steered into a controlled descent with the fire still burning. "Send a Mayday to station," he said to Leone.

Clem sent out the tail number and an SOS to Station 124 and reported their position.

"We need a field of opportunity," said Hansen. "Any field." Clem watched the flying officer wrestle with the controls of the B-24, not an easy thing in calm skies with four working engines; pure hell with an engine on fire affecting flaps and losing altitude.

"Let's shoot for Old Buck," said Widmark. The new base was five miles closer but not yet operational. But Hansen didn't respond; he had his hands full keeping the ship level. "Parachutes on, everybody," said Hansen on the interphone. Behind him, the men snapped chutes into their harnesses.

Hansen gave one last glance at flaming No. 4, and Clem watched his pilot reach for the bailout button. The bell sounded above the roar of the engines. The bomb bay doors slid open. Leone and Engineer McCormick hung there a moment standing behind the pilot's seat and wanting to help. Clem unplugged his headset. Widmark bounced up out of his chair on the flight deck as if guided by a giant spring. He shot between the seats in the cockpit and hit into Leone and McCormick like a football wingback. Leone slammed into his radio table. McCormick, a much bigger man, tumbled the other way. Widmark's eyes were wide as he snapped on his chute.

"You're the copilot," screamed McCormick to Widmark over the roar of the open bomb bay. "You can't leave him alone!" It was too late. Widmark dropped out of the plane and was gone. Leone and McCormick looked forward at the pilot fighting for control of the ship.

Aft, Clem watched Hickey and Kaufman drop out of the plane, and then Cooper went out. Sheppard moved forward from the tail turret and jumped.

"Sir!" yelled Leone, the beginning of a question that couldn't form in his mind. Out the cockpit window he saw countryside coming up fast.

"Get out!" shouted the pilot.

"But Lieutenant!" shouted McCormick.

"Go!" said Hansen.

McCormick and Leone exchanged looks. The engineer forced himself out the bomb bay. Leone gave one last glance at the back of Hansen's head and stepped out of *Gallant Lady*.

Suddenly, Clem was free-falling and lost sight of his plane. This was his first parachute jump after one hour of classroom training, where he had listened intently: Count to ten and pull the ripcord. He counted. Five. Six. Seven. He couldn't breathe. The sky, the earth, a jumbled mess. An eternity with no breath.

Eight. Nine. Ten! He gave the orange metal ring a yank. The chute billowed open and caught the wind, and the sky yanked him up. He heard a grunt punched from his own gut. The harness gripped him tight, too tight at the shoulders and the hips. He struggled for a decent breath or any breath at all.

He came back into focus hanging on his opened chute. He pivoted in the harness and righted himself enough to glimpse McCormick across the way under full canopy. Clem realized in an instant he was much too close to the ground—which he struck like a bag of cement, feet first, and toppled onto his face. In that barest of instants the miscalculation hit him as hard as the ground just had. A classroom jump had little bearing on an actual jump, where altitude dictated how high you counted before pulling the ripcord. A poker-hot sensation shot up his left leg. He writhed in the dirt, gasping for air. But he was alive—very much alive according to his leg. He wanted to stand but knew he couldn't.

He became aware of people rushing to the scene and gathering 'round to see the man who had just fallen out of the sky. He could tell from their intent expressions they felt bad for him. One of these people, a plain-looking woman, inched forward. "Whatcha doin', Yank," she asked in an accent right out of the movies, "practicin' landin' troops?"

An answer gurgled in Leone's throat. It was his first encounter with a member of the British Empire. He made it to a sitting position and felt the pain. In his brain were the moments he had just experienced. The fire. The pilot. Bailing out. Counting. Hanging on a parachute. The ground.

After what seemed an hour sitting there in the company of the locals, an army truck appeared and he was dumped inside it. The truck began to move and knocked him around as he lay on the dark bed. One by one, the other men of the crew joined him—McCormick and then Lieutenant Widmark, Lieutenant Varga, Lieutenant McKee the bombardier, and on and on. The nine of them were scooped up from a wide swath of English countryside and driven to the place where their plane had crashed.

The truck announced its arrival at the crash scene with a squeal of brakes. The men of the crew climbed out, all but Clem with his bad leg, to see the result of *Gallant Lady*'s hard landing. Her nose was caved in, and her left wing had snapped off and burned freely. A few feet away, MPs were talking about the "poor bastard" who hadn't made it out. It was Hansen, the guy from Seattle who had survived a mission to Germany, but not one to Cromer. The *Shirley Raye* crew watched in silence. Widmark turned away from the wreck, and Hickey the waist gunner swiped at his eyes. The wing blazed; the crewmen were immobile and thought about Lieutenant Hansen in there, the man who had

174

gone down with the ship. Later, they would learn he had made it off the flight deck and as far as the radio table in his effort to bail out. But with *Gallant Lady* on her own and nobody at the controls, she must have made a sudden dip and that's where impact got him.

Leone sat back in the truck, leg throbbing, and thought hard about this good man who had kept his wits and saved his crew by punching the bailout button and making sure he kept the plane level while the men jumped. And died for it. "Let's go flying," Hansen the former fighter pilot had said just an hour earlier. Now Hansen was flying with the angels. Life and death came just that fast. Leone felt his comrades around him and knew they were going through the same thing: It all happened so fast.

They had never been this close to death on a plane. Soon they would get much closer.

24
ROMAN CANDLE

By now Jim had settled into a routine, flying as squadron or group commander in the copilot's seat in a rotation that included Colonel Terrill, Group Executive Officer Malcolm Seashore, Group Operations Officer William Jones, and Group Assistant Operations Officer Fisher. Sharing leadership duties had Stewart flying every fifth mission, which seemed fair enough.

Six days after Christmas Eve on the rocket coast, Stewart briefed his pilots on a long and dangerous mission: They would fly due south more than 200 miles over the English mainland and the Channel to the French coast south of Dieppe at Fécamp, then due east more than 400 miles to hit a power plant and marshalling yards at Mannheim, located just across the Rhine from Ludwigshafen in south-central Germany. Stewart sized up the eight crews of the 703 flying today, part of twenty-six ships from the 445th Bomb Group participating. His officers were a quiet bunch when they saw the red ribbon in its long L shape from Tibenham to Mannheim. Weighing on the guys this morning was knowledge of the death of Don Hansen in a B-24 crash two days before while checking out a ship with Bob Blomberg's crew of the 700th Squadron. Hansen was another of the hotshots who had been pulled from the fighters and forced to become copilots in Liberators.

Thank God the rest of the men had managed to bail out, but

176

the crash, due to an engine fire said the survivors, gave new hints to everyone what a dangerous plane the Liberator was. She sported eighteen fuel tanks in that Davis wing with a capacity for 2,750 gallons of fuel, enough for ten hours of flying. But as with any large aircraft, a full load of gasoline made the ship a flying bomb whether it was carrying a bomb load or not. On the Liberator gasoline posed a special problem. There were leaks in the fuel lines of the early models that caused gas fumes to permeate the ship. It was a problem minimized in later models but never fully corrected. Hal Turell, one of Jim's navigators, mentioned in his account of preparation for one mission, "I climbed aboard by going over the nose wheel into the forward compartment. The familiar smell of hydraulic and gasoline filled the compartment."

Copilot Bill Minor said that after takeoff on any B-24 flight, "If all was OK, the pilot generally cracked open the bomb bay doors to exhaust gas fumes—many planes and crews were lost as a result of explosions due to buildup of fumes."

Said Ralph Stimmel, one of Stewart's crack pilots: "The fuel leakage problem, or rather the indication of leakage due to the presence of gasoline odors, was well known on the Liberator. When Liberators were parked on the tarmac, the bomb doors were often left slightly open to allow fuel fumes to be dispersed. The fuel transfer system was mounted on the forward bulkhead of the bomb bay along with the air heating system and main electrical switchgear, which would occasionally spark. It was known that quite a few Liberators just disappeared or blew up in midair."

Stewart wondered if the B-24 might be Germany's secret weapon. Pete Abell's *Star Baby* was one of the more troublesome planes, which is why Abell had been so late reporting to Tibenham. Pete's engineer, Technical Sergeant Alford, had called the ship a "plumber's nightmare," and *Star Baby* decided to give up the ghost on takeoff on a recent mission when she failed to make it into the air, skidded down the end of Runway 0-3 with her full load of bombs and gasoline, and thudded into a ditch. By some miracle she didn't explode, but she was totaled, giving Jim another headache.

And now the group had lost one of its own copilots due to engine fire on a Liberator—betrayed by the plane they wanted to love. It didn't help to stop and consider they would be flying four hours to reach Mannheim loaded with 100-pound incendiary bombs. Jim wondered, and some of the men had hinted at it, if they were really riding around in giant roman candles with one inevitable outcome.

Bill Minor was openly frustrated about the loss of his friend and fellow fighter pilot and pointed to insufficient training and planes that were "poorly designed for the designated missions."

At this morning's Mannheim briefing, Colonel Terrill talked to the assembled men about Hansen and the crash. Terrill said, "Some of you may not be aware that Don was a cousin of General Eisenhower; it's a fact he didn't like to mention because he wanted no special favors. We know that today the thoughts of the general's family are here with us, just as ours are with them." Terrill reminded the group that Hansen gave his life keeping his ship flying straight and level for the duration of an engine fire so every member of the crew could bail out. Aside from one broken bone, said Terrill, they walked away without a scratch. He concluded with, "Don Hansen represented the best that the 445th can be."

The room was perfectly quiet as Jim got up to speak next, briefing the officers on the route to target and the areas of heavy flak and the location of German fighter bases; the war weariness was already evident in their faces after only a few missions. Not so much in Bill Conley and Lloyd Sharrard, because these two were a cut above, too calm for their years, too wise and too competent. But Ollie Saunders and Barry Shillito seemed on edge this morning, Saunders the ex-bookkeeper and Shillito the ornery ex-fighter pilot. They weren't flying in *Our Baby* today; she was out for repairs and they would fly in *Liberty Belle*. Stewart also took note of

Emmett Watson and Otis Rhoney, the Southerners with dueling drawls who had somehow managed to end up pilot and copilot on the same crew. They could have been in pictures, these two, with that pause as they digested information and then a wry comment that would follow like something from the Paramount backlot. But today there was no humor from either, just pale faces and bags under the eyes.

The somber final note from Lt. Jim Paull, the weather officer, predicted temperatures at 20,000 of about thirty below, with good visibility most of the way to target, but overcast at Mannheim. And there would be light vapor trails from the formation to alert flak batteries on the ground.

The men left Ops in jeeps and trucks for the ride over the perimeter track to the hardstands of the 703rd down by Runway 0-3. Jim was flying deputy lead as copilot to Sharrard in his ship, *Tenovus*. Climbing into the Liberator through the bomb bay and wrestling himself into the copilot's seat, Jim knew it was a long, long way to and from Mannheim.

The pilots were finding takeoffs from Tibenham to be an adventure—there were two dozen B-24 bases dotting the landscape of East Anglia around and south of the heavily bombed city of Norwich, roughly one every five or six miles, making the map look like it had developed a case of measles. Each base, whether at Tibenham, or Hardwick, or Seething, or Bungay, or any of the others, held eighteen planes for each of four squadrons, seventy-two per group optimally, and each base would put up twenty or thirty bombers per mission, each taking off every thirty to forty-five seconds until the sky was full of heavily armed, heavily fuel-laden four-engine ships.

In the two working stations of the Second Combat Wing alone—Hethel (389th Bomb Group) and Tibenham (445th Bomb Group)—forty to sixty B-24s took off into an airspace just ten miles in diameter and flew to assembly points that often crossed streams of B-24s or B-17s going in another direction. In another week or two the third station of the wing, Old Buckenham, would become operational, and suddenly the number of planes in this little corner of airspace would jump to eighty or more. The ships would assemble at their usual beacon, Buncher 5. They knew they were at the right place by the radio signal and by spotting their own brightly painted assembly ship.

Often—actually, most of the time—weather in English winter meant takeoff into fog or total cloud cover. It was up to each pilot to know the right heading and speed, as well as the length of each leg before a turn down to the second, because in all that heavy cloud cover, they were totally blind in a sky full of other ships.

In the cloud deck, one miscalculation by pilots flying parallel paths or by the plane ahead or the plane behind, or by a plane from another group wandering through, or a pilot taking off late and trying to find a shortcut to his Buncher beacon, meant two ships brushing against each other and ripping away control surfaces or worse, colliding at 200 miles per hour. Then, nearby ships would see a blinding flash, hear a tremendous explosion, feel a blast concussion that would jostle them and knock over the waist gunners, and twenty crewmen would never be seen or heard from again. It happened regularly to crews that had made it this far through Boise, Pocatello, Sioux City, and the rugged South Atlantic passage, only to die in the friendly air of an English morning, before the Germans had a crack at them. Nothing was more nerve-wracking for the fliers.

"Here and there over this small area in East Anglia," said navigator Wright Lee, "groups are flying at all altitudes from 5,000 to 15,000 feet trying to assemble. Here, one Liberator group slides under a Fortress group and five miles further over there are two Liberator groups heading straight for each other."

After group assembly at their Buncher beacon at 6,000 to 10,000 feet, the formation would climb in altitude as they pro-

ceeded to their "Splasher" beacon near the North Sea for final assembly into the Second Combat Wing prior to heading to targets
in Germany or France.

This morning as they formed up for Mannheim, the 445th
weathered some confusion at Buncher 5 as a formation of B-17s
slowed up the grouping with the 389th taking off from Hethel. Today was one of those sky-full-of-planes days—and the pilots were
learning to keep their heads on swivels looking for ships appearing
unexpectedly, either B-17s or 24s.

Stewart's planes finally got themselves in order and departed the English coastline at the southernmost point on the island,
Beachy Head. Over the Channel the formation was flying crisply,
and Jim began to feel good about their prospects. Sharrard's ship,
Tenovus, was really purring, and all was going well. The gunners
test-fired their weapons and would be donning their flak jackets
and helmets about now.

"No. 3's leaking oil, skipper," said Heck, the engineer, suddenly over the interphone.

"How bad?" asked Sharrard.

"Bad enough," said Heck.

Sharrard looked at Stewart, but as pilot of the ship, Lloyd
would be the one to make a decision. "You call it, Heck. Can we
keep up with the formation to the target and back?"

"If we lose No. 3?" asked Heck, and there was a pause. "No.
No, sir."

Jim could see the French coastline dead ahead, ready to em-
brace the formation—Dieppe far over to port and Fécamp dead
ahead.

Sharrard switched over his radio. "Sharrard to Conley." Bill
Conley was flying group lead today with Major Jones, the exec-
utive officer of the 445th as formation commander and copilot.
"Bill, we're returning to base. Oil leak in No. 3."

"Roger," said Conley. "Good luck." Stewart marveled at these

181

kids every day, pilots in a war who were ten and fifteen years his junior and so incredibly poised.

Sharrard dropped *Tenovus* out of formation in the velvety blue morning sky as the remainder of the group pierced the French coastline. Jim barely caught sight of the flak crackling in orange and black bursts about the ships to the south as Sharrard's B-24 came about and headed north toward home. *Tenovus* felt heavy and lumbering on the flight back until they ditched their incendiaries in the Channel—couldn't risk landing with them aboard—and touched down at Tibenham an hour later, at 1100. Jim climbed out of *Tenovus* knowing he'd have a hellacious time waiting for the group to return near dusk. He rode his bike up to his quarters at Site 7 and tried to read, but all he could do was pace the Quonset hut, his head barely making the space under the I-beams. He went back down to Operations and waited some more, then over to the tower and continued his vigil. He gazed out at the runways and watched seagulls soar about in the fading light of day. Then, finally, the formation made itself known as the faintest of hums on the southern horizon. In five more minutes they roared over the base and Jim felt a wave of relief. There was no point trying to count them; he'd wait until they landed and get their report.

No, dammit, he wouldn't. He grabbed his bike and pedaled to the hardstands of the 703, down in the southwestern corner. His ships began to land, and they taxied ever so slowly over the peri track and parked.

It began to make sense to him slowly, that not enough Liberators had come home to the hardstands. And the ones that arrived were shot up. *Bullet Serenade* pulled up with a big hole in her left vertical stabilizer and flak holes punched in the fuselage. *Lady Shamrock* was shot up. Stewart's crews started to emerge from the bellies of the planes, and they were a sorry-looking lot. One man dropped to all fours and vomited on the hardstand. There was exhaustion and frostbite; it was what he would have felt if he had gone through with the mission himself; guilt washed over him for not completing it.

He trotted over to Bill Conley and Bill Jones just out of *Lady Shamrock*. At that moment Lloyd Sharrard came speeding down the peri track in a jeep, obviously no better at sitting out a mission due to engine trouble than Stewart had been. Sharrard slammed on the brakes, set the parking brake, and jumped out to learn what was going on.

Jim asked Conley how it had gone. Conley was all in—he could barely focus on Stewart. "Lots of fighters near the target. *Liberty Belle* went down. Ollie Saunders. I didn't even get a glimpse, but I heard on the interphone that a 190 got him after the I.P."

"Robbie" Robinson, a gunner on George Wright's *Bullet Serenade*, wandered up. "You talking about *Liberty Belle*? I saw it—saw what happened." Robinson stood there in the dusk, exhausted after the long mission. Even in the thin light Jim could see the ravages of hours in the cold on an oxygen mask carved into Robinson's face. Robbie said five Fw 190s had attacked *Liberty Belle*, and all her guns had answered. Her wing and No. 2 had started burning, and she had fallen to her left, rolled over, and gone down. There had been chutes—three at least.

Conley was looking at Jim. "Ollie had taken your place in the formation, skipper." The implication was clear: If No. 3 on *Tenovus* hadn't been leaking oil, Sharrard and crew, including Stewart, would have gone down over Germany, and if only three out of ten had hit the silk, odds were he wouldn't have survived. Funny how fate was, and how something as simple as an engine leak at 15,000 could save your life.

Bill Jones was the formation commander and looked like hell after eight hours in the air. He came shuffling up as if his parachute harness were too tight. He said, "We lost one over the Channel on the return. Kane's ship *Big Joe* ditched for some reason. I hope they made it out OK."

Jim stood freezing in the damp cold as night descended on East Anglia and the men of the 703rd limped off to waiting trucks. Saunders and Shillito had gone down, the two that had masterminded the naming of their plane, *Pissed Off*. Hadn't he just talked to them about that? Hadn't they just renamed their ship *Our Baby*? They had been awfully quiet at briefing this morning, as if they somehow had sensed what was coming. Now, they were on the run in Germany or captured or dead.

And Bill Kane, the newly married Minnesota kid who had just turned twenty-two a couple months ago, had ditched *Big Joe* in the Channel. Ditching into the choppy North Sea was a worst-case scenario because of the way water could tear up the belly of the plane. They all had learned it in lectures, the physics of a water landing, and it was a last resort because nine out of ten in the crew would likely be killed. My God, twenty men lost to the squadron in a single day. Nobody knew the fate of Kane or his crew or Saunders and his, but what would mess call be like with all those empty seats? Stewart felt the numbness seep into him as he climbed on his bicycle and pedaled up the perimeter track, back toward the control tower and then beyond to his quarters up in Site 7 as cold December darkness settled in.

25
JANUARY ON THE RHINE

It took days for Jim to hear details of Kane's ditching in the North Sea. Copilot Charlie Clemens had died on impact, as had the two waist gunners. The ball turret gunner had drowned, mistaking the top turret for the top escape hatch. Jim learned some of this by visiting navigator Joe Reus in a hospital down in Salisbury where he sat with two broken wrists from impact. But statistics showed that Kane was a hero for setting his plane into the water in such a way that six out of ten survived. What had Jim been doing at twenty-two? Was he a sophomore at Princeton? Or a junior maybe? He certainly wasn't making split-second decisions to save or cost lives as these boys now were doing.

Jim thought it ironic that he heard P-47 Thunderbolts flying over Tibenham as he began another letter to a parent, since said letter concerned Barry Shillito of the ship once named *Pissed Off*. Jim smiled to himself remembering the origin of its replacement name, *Our Baby*. But when they had gone down, Ollie Saunders' crew had been in another ship, *Liberty Belle*, the ship that had slid into Jim's place in the formation on the Mannheim mission after *Tenovus* had developed engine trouble.

Thunderbolts had the habit of buzzing Tibenham's runways and tower later in the day after all the heavies had landed. They would roar past in groups of four just above the deck, their bellies skimming within feet of any Nissen hut sitting out in the open to wake up the dozing bomber boys. The guys at Tibenham loved the show, just as they loved their "little friends" for riding shotgun on the missions into enemy country, and obviously those hotshot pilots had a grand time with their unofficial exercises, and no question it was to razz their friends like Minor, Rhoney, and Shillito.

Nearby, Gil Fisher fed coal to the fire of their stove; Jim had more letters to write. The day before, Wednesday, January 5, Victor Smith's crew of *Gremlins Roost* had been flying in the Tail-end Charlie position of the formation on a mission to Kiel. Tail-end Charlie was a dreaded spot because of the terrible prop wash and because German fighters pounced from the rear, and that's where they got *Gremlins Roost*, firing into the No. 3 engine until the wing caught fire. The bandits always went for No. 3 because this engine controlled the hydraulics of the Liberator, and once the hydraulics were gone deep in enemy territory, as with the *Gremlin*, the ship was all too easy to finish off.

Wednesday the fifth had been a tough day all around. The Eighth Air Force was losing its head of Bomber Command, Gen. Ira Eaker, replaced by Jimmy Doolittle, now a lieutenant general. Nobody knew exactly what the change in leadership would mean in the air, but word was that Gen. Hap Arnold, commander of the Army Air Forces, wanted more action and fewer excuses about weather and mechanical problems from his "Mighty Eighth." To leaders at the hundred bases in England, this potentially meant a more aggressive approach and even more losses in planes and men.

Much later in the evening, Jim wrote: "Dear Mr. Smith: I am writing to tell you about your son...." At least this time Stewart could add, "Parachutes were seen to leave the plane."

Jim thought about Victor Smith's copilot, Bill Minor; it seemed as if just yesterday that Bill had married his girl, Dolores, in the Catholic Church in Lincoln. Jim had loved the idea of the romances deepening between the men of his squadron and their sweethearts as departure day had neared. Back when the B-24s were being ferried to England, Stewart had serenaded the crews by singing on VHF radio, "Oh, how I love the kisses of Dolores. Not Emily, Marie or Doris—just my Dolores." Only Bill Minor and his friends would have known the relevance of the song, but that was enough. No, Jim couldn't get attached to his pilots, but he had gotten attached to them, and now they were falling out of the sky, falling to the fates, and he could only pray for them and hope they had hit terra firma alive.

It was such a lonely life, so cold at times. Jim had become notorious for crankiness and complete lack of cooperation with the press. One report would state, "Many optimistic war correspondents have braved mud and the commanding officer at this base in pursuit of the elusive Jim, but not one so far even has come within sight of him."

Colonel Terrill grew accustomed to making statements like, "Captain Stewart is busy and furthermore he does not want to talk to correspondents because he doesn't want any more publicity. I feel obliged to support him. And I do."

Stewart was also lonely, not for the adulation of female fans, and they were legion, but for the companionship of a woman he could consider an equal, someone who wouldn't compromise his privacy or seek publicity. He would admit later that at times like this he would pay visits to a leading woman citizen in Tibenham with whom he had struck up a friendship. He remained a man who loved women and a man who needed conversation and more when any night might be his last on earth. But it wouldn't be tonight. Even as he finished writing his letters this night, he knew that another mission was coming up, just hours away.

I.G. Farben Industries was a German manufacturing giant employing a quarter million people when the war began. It included Bayer, BASF, and other names known around the world. The massive Farben chemical plant at Ludwigshafen sprawled along a lazy bend in the Rhine River that marked the southeastern border of the city. The Allies wouldn't find out until after the war that among Farben's patents, and one in heavy demand, was Zyklon B, used in death camp gas chambers.

On a frozen Friday, the first of 1944, Captain Stewart found himself in command of sixteen ships of the 445th and sat right seat to Bill Conley, both on oxygen at 21,500 in *Lady Shamrock*, flying lead for the group, with each Liberator carrying ten M1 incendiary cluster bombs of 500 pounds each. The 445th followed the 389th, with the 93rd tagging along to starboard. The bomber stream today training over the German countryside totaled 382 B-17s and 120 B-24s, all headed for I.G. Farben with the intention of blowing it off the map. Overhead and underneath cruised P-47s and P-51s, always a comfort as they zipped past to protect from German fighters.

The formation shot deeper into Germany by the minute. As briefed, Stewart's ships would drop bombs, bank hard right, reduce speed, and descend 1,000 feet to re-form and start for home on a heading of 283 degrees. *Lady Shamrock* arrived at the I.P. at 1125, ten minutes behind schedule owing to the usual difficulties of coordinating a large formation, and saw yellow-yellow flares fired ahead by the lead ship of the 389th confirming that the I.P. had been reached.

"Code word is Match Box," said Sergeant Wilson, the radioman. Stewart ordered Wilson to fire yellow-yellow. Today Wilson was an old hand—today he had flares. They started their bomb run due southeast and soon ran into predictor-controlled flak that began whizzing up and snapping around them. Conley muscled the controls as the ship yawed left and right from flak concussions and bumped up and down. They would be bombing by Pathfinder today, Mickey all the way, bombing through the undercast by radar sets in the Pathfinder B-24s up front. Conley toggled control of the ship over to Rankin, never an easy thing for a pilot to do in a flak field.

The ship's interior air temperature had been at twenty-five below, but the crew stayed plenty warm thinking about where they were, deep enough in enemy territory, and feeling flak bursting all about, peppering the fuselage as if someone were outside throwing gravel by the handful. The bomb bay doors slid open, and Stewart felt the ship suddenly grow quite chilly, down to forty below at least. Welcome to January on the Rhine.

The gauntlet of flak went on through the thirty miles of bomb run from the I.P. One direct hit in the open bomb bay would be instant death, but on they bounced, their muscles cramping by the second in the violent rocking of the ship. So far, luck was with the formation; no ships had fallen, and then the Pathfinder dropped a phosphorous smoke bomb, then its bomb load, and the ships of the 389th let loose their incendiaries, the big boys falling into cotton below and disappearing. It sobered Jim every time, watching the bombs toggle out, about to rain death below. The men in the planes couldn't think about stray bombs and what they might do to civilians. It was a big picture they saw up here, a picture of mighty Germany as far as the eye could see, an enemy that must be brought to its knees.

Stewart watched *Lady Shamrock* fly directly over the falling smoke pot and then heard John Rankin say into the interphone, as if ordering coffee, "Bombs away." Clicking and clacking filled the ship as the bombs toggled out of the machinery holding them. The ship eased higher into the sky without its bombs, and Conley made the hard turn to starboard and throttled back into a controlled descent of 1,000, as briefed, onto a heading of 283 degrees, following the planes of the 389th that already had made the turn.

Conley's eyes riveted on his compass and he gave it a tap. "What are they doing?" he said. Stewart knew what had been briefed—he had been one of the briefers for the 445th this morning. The descent of the 389th was lazy, taking too long, and they weren't throttling back, not near enough. They were pulling far ahead of Stewart's group. Jim looked at his compass. It was as if the 389th was suddenly flying a different mission.

"Uh, skipper?" said a voice on the interphone. Steinhauer, the navigator. "They're not following the course as briefed. They're at 245 degrees, not 283."

"I see it," said Conley. He gave Stewart a glance over his mask. The thoughts cascaded in the group leader's mind. Lone bomb group off course over Germany. Easy pickings for enemy aircraft that would scramble from airdromes for 500 miles. What good did it do for two groups to go off course? He answered his own question—well, if we keep tight we can cover each other. Conley was still looking at him, and then Wilson popped his head over the seat from the radio station and he was looking at Jim as well. The bottom line: The 389th was wing lead today, and the 445th was part of that wing.

The Air Corps paid Stewart—the only captain in the air today—to lead the group, and now he must act.

Stewart switched to ship-to-ship VHF and pressed the button on the interphone. "Winston lead, this is Winston trail. You are at 2-4-5. Briefed turn is to 2-8-3."

The reply came quickly, the tone unmistakable. "We know what we're doing, Winston trail. Get off the air."

"Shit!" said a voice below in the nose, either Rankin or Steinhauer.

"Fuckin' clowns," said the other one.

Just then, Stewart felt a problem with the starboard engines and looked at No. 3. In his ear came Eckelberry, the engineer. "Skipper, supercharger on No. 3 is frozen."

Conley and Stewart discussed whether they should keep the engine running or feather it. They decided to keep it turning to reduce drag on the ship.

But they were down to three good engines and headed in the

wrong direction. Stewart felt himself sweating under his flight suit. Temperature forty below and sweating. He pushed the button again and broadcast out to the other ships in the formation, "F lead to group: All right, listen up. I want this formation as tight as it's ever been. Look sharp. We're covering our wing lead."

"But they're heading for Paris!" said Steinhauer.

"Yeah," said Jim to the navigator. "That means we all are."

Conley said deadpan, under his oxygen mask, "That's not by the book, skipper."

Later they could laugh about it, if there was a later. Meantime, Jim shot Bill a wry look as if to say, just fly the ship, smart guy.

Stewart sent out to the other ships in the formation, "Radio silence, everybody." This exchange was already forty words too many, and the transmissions would be picked up by the bad guys. They'd know there was confusion in the air among the bomb groups returning from Ludwigshafen and prey upon it. But the cloud cover remained solid and maybe that would see the Second Combat Wing through. Jim knew headings and maps well enough to understand that instead of flying west-northwest in the general direction of England, they were flying west-southwest toward Paris, yes, and in the general direction of Spain. That guy up there in the 389th had better be able to explain this when he got back to Hethel, or he'd be busted out. But Jim didn't know what the situation was up there, didn't know what that guy was facing or what he had already faced. Had they all written down the wrong number? How was that even possible? Were they cracking up? Had that pilot gone flak happy? Something else they'd have to figure out later. Hell, it was several snafus a day; this was merely the latest.

Stewart looked off to the right at the ships of the 93rd in an admirable formation and knew they must be wondering what the hell was going on, but they were sticking close too.

Jim unhooked his interphone and flight suit connections, plugged his oxygen into a walk-around bottle, and climbed out of the copilot's seat. He stepped down off the flight deck and folded himself into a six-foot-three midget to slide under the bulkhead and into the nose, then down to Steinhauer's map table to see the formation's present position and where it was headed.

It was a different world down there in the nose, a glass observatory looking ahead and down as opposed to the cockpit above, which looked ahead and up. In the nose there was a sense of vertigo, of falling through that glass front to the earth moving below.

He pulled aside his oxygen mask for a moment. "Where the hell are we?" Stewart shouted into Steinhauer's ear over the roar of the engines.

Steinhauer left his oxygen mask in place and pointed to the pencil line he had just drawn on his map. Apparently they were somewhere in the vicinity of Saarbrücken. Steinhauer ran his finger across the map on this course, which would take them just south of Paris, which was a tremendous waste of fuel not to mention that German fighters would be swarming around Paris and quite likely to knock down some ships of the 445th.

Steinhauer looked at Stewart as if to say, now what? But Stewart had made the decision: We'll look after these idiots because someday maybe the idiots will be us and we'll need another group to return the favor. Jim rapped Steinhauer on the arm and folded himself out of the nose and edged along the catwalk just as flak began to burst around the ship, forcing him to hold onto the bulkhead to keep his feet. He rattled back to the waist gunners to check things out and get their view. It was impossible to tell if these guys were scared—or how scared. They were quiet, efficient veterans now, kids of nineteen or twenty or twenty-one. Their faces were hidden under goggles and oxygen masks, peering out the windows, watching flak bursts, and looking for fighters. At some other time in history, they'd be working at filling stations or farms at this age, sampling their first liquor and their first women instead of flying at 21,000 feet over the middle of Europe, blind, lost, and frozen, with an enemy intent on shooting them down. Every second in the air now, with flak detonations jarring *Lady Shamrock*, Jim felt the pressure of the decision he had made to follow the 389th. He held the future of these boys in his hands.

After five-and-a-half hours in the air, ice hung low beneath their oxygen masks in giant thick icicles, but they didn't bother to knock them off. Stewart peered out the starboard waist window to see a carpet of black smoke and beyond it the 93rd still over there, and then gave the deployed ball turret a glance, and the tail turret. All was shipshape. He made his way forward along the catwalk to the flight deck.

Stewart slid into the copilot's seat, reconnected into the interphone and oxygen system and plugged in his flight suit. The completed circuit sent warmth all the way down to his hands and feet. Boy, did that feel good. He looked all about, scanning every inch of sky visible out the cockpit. The flak had eased and he saw the planes of the 389th ahead but no fighters anywhere at all. He pulled his map for Conley, pointed to their position, and drew a line with his finger showing passage south of Paris.

Jim had so many good pilots in his squadron, and Conley may have been the best. He sat now with his long legs working the pedals, knees almost touching the wheel, showing that pilot's even temperament. He was so painfully young but possessed the wisdom of an old man. Seeing their course didn't cause Conley to curse, or frown, or even laugh. He shrugged. Eh. Shrugged. And kept on flying over unbroken cloud cover below.

"Flak just off the left wing hit the deicer outboard of No. 1," said Conley. "We've got a leak out there. Not sure if the engine was hit; seems to be OK." Stewart knew what the loss of another engine would mean. They would be forced to fall out of formation and hedgehop home as an easy target for the fighters.

In a little while the flak picked up again. They were southwest of Châlons-en-Champagne, France, now, and the radar-guided fire from the ground reached up and smacked them around. In another fifteen minutes, Steinhauer's voice broke the silence. "Coming up on Paris, down there somewhere to the right."

Stewart switched over to address the group. "Winston Group, look sharp. We're going to be visited."

In a moment, Steinhauer said, "Cloud cover's breaking up. Paris visible off to starboard. There's the Eiffel Tower."

"Damn," said a voice, and Jim knew why. Without cloud cover, the Germans would have a clear view of a large formation of American bombers above. Ahead, the 389th was putting distance between itself and the 445th, eager no doubt to get out of the mess they had gotten themselves into, but Jim wasn't making any mistakes. He gave a glance left and right, and his group was as tight as it could be—he loved these guys for going by the book.

Jim looked down and in the northern distance he glimpsed Paris sprawled seemingly forever, the Eiffel Tower prominent in the middle of it, next to the winding Seine. Conley reached over and tapped Stewart's sleeve. He pointed ahead, and they saw fast-moving dots in the sky. Jim figured they were Focke-Wulf 190s but couldn't be certain, couldn't see the distinctive yellow paint on the spinners this far off. All he knew was that German fighters had begun attacking the 389th like a swarm of bees. Jim could see at least six of them without even squinting, and then more dropped in from the 389th's six o'clock. A B-24 up there caught fire almost at once and spun out of formation, spewing flame and smoke as it plummeted to earth. Chutes started to appear. Three, four, five.

Jim watched a German fighter stray too close to a Lib and catch hell. Suddenly, it careened left, spewing smoke, and fell straight toward earth from 20,000, nose first. On went the fray with enemy aircraft all over the 389th. Another B-24 got hit and sank below the others, and from that moment the wounded ship was as good as dead, carrion for the Bf 109s and Fw 190s that buzzed about taking potshots until, to Stewart's horror, the Liberator exploded.

It wasn't all one-sided. Gunners from the formation hit a second German fighter and it blew up into a fireball, and a third broke apart before Jim's eyes. A fourth trailed smoke and veered away. Chutes dotted the sky—German and American.

On they all flew, the formation of the 389th paying for its mistaken compass heading with lives. Jim's eyes darted about, waiting for an attack that still didn't come. Why? he demanded of himself. Why weren't they attacking the 445th? It had to be the tight formation, no other explanation. A third Lib ahead veered right trailing smoke and zoomed off trying to evade pursuing fighters.

"Damn it!" said someone into the interphone watching the panoramic dogfight unfolding before them. It didn't matter that those boys up there had gotten themselves into a mess—they were our guys and they were fighting for their lives. All these miles back the 445th couldn't help.

"Winston Group, watch your formation!" barked Stewart. He knew his guys were good, but now he was learning just how good because the fighters kept staying away. Then Jim heard a shout over VHF from a ship around him; he didn't know which one but it was in his group. He looked up and saw P-47s swoop into view from God knew where and zoom forward to help the 389th. Then another formation, Spitfires, roared past Jim heading forward. A third assemblage of fighters dove in from somewhere off to port, P-51 Mustangs, the new kid on the block and a plane everyone wanted to see in action after glowing reports on its performance in trials.

"Get 'em! Get 'em!" Jim heard in his ear. The vista before them changed at once as the Allied fighters surprised, outnumbered, and punished the Germans in view. It was over that fast, and Jim saw the 389th dogleg right now, heading northwest toward the French coast and in the direction of England.

"We're losing No. 1," said Conley. "Shutting it down."

Below, finally, Stewart could see the French coastline ahead and beyond it the English Channel. The German fighters had melted away by now, and the 445th had held together without drawing any fire at all.

"Listen up," said Conley into the ears of his crew. "We're down to two engines, and we've got to lighten the ship. Toss everything out that isn't nailed down." Once over water, Stewart radioed to Neil Johnson in the deputy lead ship to take over, that they were dropping out and descending on two engines. Johnson asked in that Montana drawl if they'd make it home, and Stewart assured him they would.

Conley took his time over the Channel, and soon the men had jettisoned everything but their parachutes, Mae Wests, and life raft. Thanks to the 389th and their long way around, Conley brought them up to the English coast on a course due north, passing over the Dungeness Lighthouse, then due north over Ipswich. From the radio came a call from up ahead. "Skipper, a ship just went down southeast of Mendlesham."

"Who was it?" asked Stewart.

"Lieutenant Eike, I think," came the response. Eike was a pilot in the 701st Squadron. In another few minutes they flew over the Liberator that had crash-landed in farm fields; Jim could see in an instant that Eike had done a fine job bringing the ship in; he had even avoided a fire.

Lady Shamrock returned to Station 124 after seven hours, sixteen minutes on two engines, the plane shot up by flak. The report would show no combat losses for the 445th on what seemed to be a milk run, but everyone who had participated would know it was anything but.

Stewart had learned a hard lesson about command through living it minute to minute: He really could trust his gut. "I didn't pray for my own life," he remembered. "I prayed that I wouldn't make a mistake." And he hadn't; not this day. He knew he had done the right thing because he had brought his boys, and himself, home.

26
THE DUNGEON OF EPPSTEIN

Riele Siepmann remained in the farmlands of central Germany with her children for two years, until she couldn't stand it any longer. Then she packed everyone up and headed for one of her favorite places in Germany, the *Altstadt* or old town of Frankfurt. The old town was build around the triple-facade, five-story medieval *Römer*, the Frankfurt city hall that stood across the square from Old St. Nicholas Lutheran Church. The people of Frankfurt gravitated here for all their celebrations, particularly the annual *Christkindlmarkt*, with dozens of vendors setting up shop around the beginning of December to offer traditional German bratwurst, pretzels, and beer, all in celebration of the Christ Child and the most magical season of all.

The new home of the Siepmann family was in Eppstein, which sat nestled in rugged hills northwest of Frankfurt, thirty minutes by train. This old-world German town had received its charter in 1318, and here the Siepmanns settled into a plain but sturdy three-story, half-timbered house shared with another family. Eppstein proved a godsend. The three older children had their own mountain to explore and a stream to play in.

The most fascinating spot in town was Castle Eppstein, an elaborate, crumbling bastion begun in the tenth century A.D. and built into a high knoll in the heart of town. Its stout tower rose twenty-five meters from the structures below and dated from the middle of the fourteenth century. Gertrud and her siblings explored what parts of the giant structure they could, although they had been forbidden to do so. Who could resist visiting the open-air dungeon with rusting shackles still hanging from ancient walls?

Gertrud passed her tenth year experiencing the sights and sounds of skies full of big enemy planes moving overhead at high altitude, from west to east, hundreds of planes at a time, so many planes, each leaving a vapor trail, that after they had passed a sunny day suddenly became overcast. The vibration of the planes shook the earth. A little while later she would hear explosions off in the distance, in the direction of Frankfurt. Steady rumbling for minutes and minutes. Sometimes it felt like it would never end, and she could only imagine what was going on there, but she didn't want to imagine it because she had lived it in Wilhelmshaven. She knew those people over the hill in Frankfurt. They were her friends, her family.

Gertrud was playing outside on a Saturday morning, the last Saturday in January 1944, when the enemy planes flew over again. It was a large formation, and it seemed to be heading, as before, for Frankfurt. She tried to continue playing but her heart felt heavy. Gertrud's Onkel Julius, Mutti's brother, and his wife, Tante Julemarie, still lived in the Sachsenhausen section of Frankfurt in the Kottke's family home, a tiny old house that Riele so loved. Gertrud thought of the magnificent *Römer* and the *Christkindlmarkt.* Would Frankfurt be all right? Would all the people there stay safe? Would this nightmare never end?

27
ICEMAN

The highlight of January 1944 was an appearance by Army Air Forces Capt. Glenn Miller and his orchestra in the main hangar near the control tower at Station 124, the twenty-eighth stop in a thirty-seven-date tour of Allied bases in England. The cavernous space was packed to the rafters that night, and Jim couldn't have imagined that the bandleader, not yet forty years old on the evening he spent with the 445th, would be dead in less than a year. Nor could Jim imagine that a decade later he would be portraying Miller on-screen. The event highlighted an otherwise foul weather month over East Anglia, and for that matter, mainland Europe, where the Eighth dearly wished to go. Stewart was able to fly as copilot to Conley in *Lady Shamrock* on a January 14 milk run to the rocket coast to hit Pas de Calais, and another rocket coast mission with Conley to bomb Bonnières on January 21. These productive days interrupted the bad weather streak that had seen four attempts on Frankfurt scrubbed.

The pilots of the 703 had begun to notice a change in Jim after the Ludwigshafen mission and the navigational error of the 389. He had followed his gut and done what he felt was right, and his formation had come through even as the boys from Hethel had not. Beirne Lay, Jr., remarked on what he called a "rising confidence" among Stewart's pilots: "Things seemed to go all right when Stewart was up front. He made free use of the radio, like an aerial quarterback, to advise and encourage the other boys during a mission, and here his experience in films gave him a novel advantage. Because of his precise enunciation, people could understand him. It sounds like a little thing, but clear, quick communication between formations was of extraordinary importance."

Jim had become a self-assured officer, which he proved on January 27 when Terrill passed along word of an imminent promotion for Stewart from captain to major for his combat service to date. Jim asked about promotions for the pilots in his squadron, most of whom were still second lieutenants despite proving themselves through six weeks of tough missions. In fact, they had flown more than Jim had, he pointed out. Terrill said Stewart's was the only promotion at this time, and Jim startled the C.O. by declining it "until my junior officers get promoted." The next day a press release circulated stating that Jim would don the "golden oak leaves" of a major on his shoulders; not coincidentally, Neil Johnson, Leo Cook, and Gil Fisher became captains, and the rest of the pilots of the 703rd moved from second to first lieutenant.

A day later, Saturday, January 29, came a fifth go at Frankfurt as the 445th put up twenty-eight heavies with now 1st Lt. Bill Conley again the pilot and Stewart the group lead in the copilot's seat aboard *Nine Yanks and a Jerk*. The mission started badly when two B-24s, likely from the 392nd Bomb Group, collided southeast of Tibenham's Runway 3-3, causing what John Robinson, just aloft amidships in *Bullet Serenade*, called "a bright flash and then a boom." The planes fell into burning heaps across Tibenham's ancient farmlands. The head of one doomed crew member bounced off the roof of the Railway Tavern, and the rest of him crashed through the roof of Tivetshall Station across Long Row, part of brutal carnage not expected or ordinary in East Anglia, but rather the fortunes of war when 863 heavy bombers formed up in a small stretch of sky for a single mission to a single target. Somehow three of twenty fliers had managed to bail out as the Second Combat Wing went on to assemble with volcanic fuel fires and exploding incendiaries in their wake in the gray morning light.

Overcast had been ten over ten at 5,000, and the group formed up above the weather, or tried to. Once again Jim found the 389th to be trouble, with one of their squadrons causing the wing formation to remain ragged as they set out past Splasher 5 toward the Channel, and ships were scattered all the way to the I.P., with *Nine Yanks* behind sections of the 389th as all barreled toward Frankfurt in clear weather at high levels with no hint of recall. With the crew already on oxygen and the air temperature in the ship at twenty-five below, prop wash from the 389 was playing the devil with control, and the shoulders of both Conley and Stewart ached from keeping their ship flying straight and level in the formation.

Escort fighters, P-47s, had swept above and below the formation all the way into Germany and provided great comfort, those fighter pilots so damned agile in the air. But now those Thunderbolts were turning away to refuel, supposedly to be replaced by Spitfires. Except the Spits were nowhere to be seen, and Stewart knew what that meant. He pressed the button on the interphone and said, "Fighters any second. Look sharp."

Sure enough, against the brilliant blue of the approaching noontime sky he saw dots at one o'clock high. He saw this even before he heard the information shouted into his headset. The enemy planes were some distance ahead and above and made no direct attack. Instead, he watched the fighters drop black objects, first parachute bombs that slowly glided toward the approaching Liberator groups and then, as the single-engine ships flew over Stewart, what looked like lengths of chain let loose. Then Fw 190s buzzed past, firing machine guns, and Jim heard the response of the .50 cals inside *Nine Yanks* and felt the heavy vibration of their action in the ship. More 190s swooped up in front of Conley and Stewart from below and broke right and left.

The formation could do nothing but plow ahead. Steinhauer called out, "I.P. ahead," and Jim looked for yellow-yellow flares from elements of the 389th in front of him, but didn't see any.

Rankin called, "Three minutes to target."

With the initial point already passed, Stewart knew he had to mark it. "Pappy, fire yellow-yellow," he said. "Then send the code word: Cross-eye." As fast as he said the words, radio operator Wilson shot the flares, and now his group had confirmation the I.P. had been reached and the bomb run begun.

He knew the bomb bay doors were sliding open by the blast of cold wind bouncing off every inch of the interior fuselage, sending the temperature yet lower—if that were possible. Far below Jim could make out an ancient castle ruin on a high bluff in the middle of a small German town, a picture postcard moment as machine guns rattled inside the ship and bandits veered this way and that looking for weaknesses in the 445th box.

"I see rockets," one of the gunners said.

"They got somebody!" said another voice on the interphone. "There's a ship going down over there!"

"Chutes? Any chutes?" said an excited voice, and a second later another voice—it was impossible from the front seats of the ship to know who was speaking on the interphone—gave the word, "P-38s!" and Stewart and Conley looked about them. The speedy, twin-fuselage pursuit ships painted dull green swept into view. It was a thing of beauty to see the 190s and 109s turn sharply away and dive toward earth with Lightnings firing machine guns on their tails. In a bare moment the skies were clear of German fighters.

It all happened so fast up there, the painful anticipation in quiet skies and then the sudden deadly action all about, with much depending on a tight formation, quick responses, and a steady hand, but so much more left to chance and whether fate was kind at a given moment.

He scanned the sky and didn't see any fighters at all. "You

know what's next," he said on his throat mic. He braced himself for a sky full of anti-aircraft fire, and the Germans didn't disappoint. In a moment the black detonations appeared in the sky dead ahead, shells zooming up and exploding into burnt popcorn and forming deadly storm clouds, roughly at the altitude of the formation—22,500 feet—but also above and below. Then came a surprise: Rockets fired from the ground and burned hot orange in their ascent up ahead—not accurate, but a potshot would do for the Germans if it took out a ship or caused a couple of ships to knock together.

Jim became aware of interrupted oxygen flow in his mask, looked down, and realized he hadn't been mindful of ice buildup that was now blocking the intake. He had been too preoccupied with the I.P. and the fighters. He took off his mask and the cold got his bare mouth and cheeks at once. He knew if he wanted to make another Hollywood picture, he'd better knock the ice off and replace his mask before he blacked out, and he'd better hurry before his skin started to burn and blister in the deep subzero cold.

As he banged his mask on the interior of the fuselage, *Nine Yanks* rode into the flak and bucked and slammed through the sky. "Target ahead," said a voice.

Jim thought about today's target, aircraft assembly facilities just northeast of the city center of Frankfurt. Stewart's view ahead was of the ships of the 389th as they started to drop their bombs on smoke pots when the Pathfinder dropped. Rankin would be toggling on those planes ahead, and the ships of the 445th flying behind *Nine Yanks* would drop when he did.

"Bombs away," said Rankin, and the forty M47-1A incendiaries, 100 pounds each, began to entrain their way out of the ship with a series of clicks and clacks, in a moment igniting a long swath in Frankfurt. Trouble was, undercast was suddenly solid; they couldn't see what they were aiming at and relied only on Mickey to find the target.

Navigator Wright Lee riding back in the Tail-end Charlie position of the formation watched all the planes ahead dropping bombs on the vast German city of Frankfurt. "You could not but feel a little pity for the people down there.... Enemy or not, as human beings like us with a long history of development and contributions to science, art, medicine and literature, the Germans deserved better, but not under Hitler."

28
BAPTISM

Flying in the high group behind Conley and Stewart was the *Shirley Raye*, with Clem Leone hunkered on his stool at the radio station behind Widmark's copilot's seat. Some first mission, thought Clem. Some baptism of fire. They were over Frankfurt, bouncing through flak bursts and then wading through fighters, and Leone began to wonder if there was any chance he would ever see Tibenham again, let alone South Baltimore.

In his headset he heard that yellow-yellow flares had been fired from the lead ship, which meant they were starting the bomb run. Blomberg's voice was calm, just like it always was in all the months of training, as he switched control over to McKee. Bomb bay doors slid open, three feet from the radio station where Clem sat, to a great roar of rushing air and bursts of flak. The inch of skin on his face between his goggles and oxygen mask felt like it had frozen in an instant. This was it: After almost a year together these ten men had arrived over Germany, a single cog in the angry American war machine.

"Looking good," he heard McKee say. "Looking good." Leone endured a long moment at 22,000 feet, watching the racks of bombs sitting there, hearing the explosions of flak and the howl of the air and the needles of subzero cold as he tried not to look four miles straight down through the bomb bay at Frankfurt.

"Bombs away," called McKee, and Clem watched the racks let

loose to a chorus of metallic chatter. He felt the plane leap higher in the sky. Clem studied all the bomb racks.

"Bombs clear," he told Blomberg over the interphone, and the pilot banked them hard right, away from target. Damn but Blomberg was good. It was clear the brass thought him a talented pilot because they kept using him even as the rest of the crew trained, trained, trained. It was wonderful to have a good man leading the crew, and Clem let out a breath as more than half his first mission had been completed; now they could concentrate on getting home.

Out his observation window he glimpsed a bomb falling from a Liberator directly above. As if from a nightmare, he watched it fall through the frame of the window, five hundred pounds falling to earth. Then he watched it crash through engine No. 3 and hammer the engine—nacelle and all—off the *Shirley Raye.*

He felt his throat tighten. He tried to speak. On the second try, he choked, "No. 3's gone." Clem stared at the gaping hole in the wing. He breathed hard into his mask as he felt the plane lose thrust and sag away from the group toward the earth below. Worst of all, No. 3 controlled the main hydraulic system, which reduced controllability and instantly imperiled everybody aboard.

Blomberg told his crew that he would hold as much altitude as he could and head northwest. He said he was still able to control the ship, and they should be able to make it home without hitting the bailout bell if the fighters would just stay away. He said they were flying above heavy undercast that should conceal them from anti-aircraft batteries.

The crippled Liberator rattled northwest. How fast could you get back to England on three engines instead of four? At lower altitude, flying through choppy air?

"Flak ahead," called Blomberg. "Hold on."

The radar-guided ack-ack had their number all right. Leone held tight as they flew straight into a pothole-strewn highway of detonations. Blomberg and Widmark kept altering course to confuse the batteries. Clem felt each change. But the flak kept finding them.

"Damn!" he heard in his headset. "They got No. 2!" Now they were cooked for sure. He could feel the ship losing altitude, down through 15,000. In his ears he heard communication among the pilots and engineer. Their fast conclusion: Flak had pierced the engine and knocked it out. No restarting.

"Down to two engines," said Blomberg. "We gotta lighten the ship. Save fifty rounds per gun and throw the rest out. Throw out everything you can."

The plane came alive with activity. They ripped away their oxygen masks. Clem looked around his station. He threw the auxiliary power unit out through the bomb bay. All his radio units went except for the base and emergency units. Hickey and Kaufman threw out belts of .50 cal. Hickey grabbed Leone's duffel with all his tools and .45. Before Clem could yell no, it was gone through the bomb bay. The three of them along with Cooper tried to break the ball turret off but failed.

They sank through 10,000 with nothing left to jettison. Cloud cover had increased. They didn't know what was down there.

Leone heard Varga's voice. "Hey, Clem, get me a fix on our position. If we're not over the Channel, we gotta be close."

Leone opened his transmitter and began sending. He could tell the frequency was tied up. He sent again. Nothing. Somewhere over England, a practice mission was tying up the radio frequency. He kept trying. He got nowhere. He ran over the catwalk aft and unreeled his MT-5E antenna, the trailing wire that gave him max signal. Never had he moved so fast. He found his stool again and slammed down on key. He sat there, every muscle tensed. Get off the air. Get off the air.

The frequency cleared. He sent his SOS. Thank God. A base in England understood. Code came back: What is your plane number?

Clem gave the number. We are in trouble. Running on two engines. Can you give us a fix? Clem could barely breathe. He knew he was the life line for all of them.

Code came through. Some GI was out there, sitting at some station in some tower in England. Somebody who probably never had flown a mission but the most important guy in the world right now. Leone got their position and read the numbers to Varga.

"That puts us over Pas-de-Calais," said Varga.

Sun streamed in the windows through breaks in the clouds. They looked out and were shocked at the closeness of the ground. Clem saw villages and lakes.

Flak shook the plane. The moment the clouds parted they were targets. The *Shirley Raye* flew level at 4,000, maybe. They knew the score. They could descend but they couldn't climb. Varga gave Blomberg a heading for Tibenham.

Engineer McCormick slid out of the top turret. "Clem, get up there. I gotta see what I can do."

Leone climbed into the top turret and looked about him. He could see No. 2 dead and No. 3 gone. He could see the ship pockmarked by flak and gunfire. She was flying rough. He had been feeling it, and now he could see it. Wings dipping; some yaw. They had cleared the French coastline and were over the English Channel.

In a moment he heard Sheppard's voice from the tail turret: "Fighters at six o'clock."

Clem swung the turret toward the tail and had guns on his first German fighters of the war, two small dots in the distance that he knew were Bf 109s diving fast on their six o'clock. He cursed himself—when he had requested a fix, the enemy had gotten a fix on *him*.

Wait, fifty rounds per gun? Yes, that was Lieutenant Blomberg's order. Clem sighted up the fighters. What did he have to throw at them, a two-second burst?

He had a 109 in his sights, for what it mattered. The enemy was fifteen or twenty seconds off and closing fast. A two-second burst wouldn't do anything for their chances of reaching home, but he would wait until it was close enough to do damage and he would try.

He heard McKee in the nose. "Fighters at twelve! Fighters at twelve!" More German fighters at twelve o'clock? It was hopeless, Clem realized. To have flown hundreds of miles from Frankfurt after the busted wing, across Germany and France, only to be swarmed by fighters now, over the Channel.

Clem swung the turret around again. Which would he fire on, the two in front or the two on the tail? A grim and rhetorical question. His eyes focused on the two dots approaching from their front. Suddenly he realized: These fighters were green.

"Spitfires!" somebody called. It was like in the movies. Good guys at the last moment.

As fast as he could turn the turret, the Spitfires had zoomed past and engaged the bandits. He watched a Spit drop a 109 in an instant. He watched the other 109 turn and head for the French coastline with that Spitfire on its tail.

In a moment the first Spitfire had pulled up past the right wing of the *Shirley Raye.* "Turn your identification set to position number four," the pilot radioed with a crisp British accent.

Clem dropped out of the turret and raced over the catwalk aft to the tail to switch his crystal set from number eight to number four. He knew what the pilot wanted: His base wasn't sure of this wounded B-24. Who was to say it wasn't full of munitions and under control of German pilots? If the *Shirley Raye* didn't do as instructed, the Spitfire would shoot her down.

The unlikely pair skimmed the Channel at 2,000, and out the window Leone could see another aircraft, a twin-engine Beaufighter, appear off the left wing. Strapped to its belly was a life raft in case the bomber had to ditch. "Mind your altitude," radioed the Spitfire pilot. "Cliffs of Dover ahead on your port side." The little formation headed north by northeast with southern England spread out on their left. Another fifteen miles of water flying put them over land. The Spitfire peeled off as *Shirley Raye* puttered over the rooftops of Woodbridge at 1,500 and continued north to final approach. At last their eyes settled on the glorious tower of Tibenham All Saints.

Clem couldn't see the base ahead, but he heard Blomberg in his ear. "Clem, fire a flare. Let them know we're coming in hot." He grabbed a Very pistol and fired a flare out the upper port. It would be a one-shot landing, and artistry didn't count. Blomberg said to Widmark, "We gotta dive to reach landing speed. Can't afford a stall now. Gear down when I tell you. Let's hope they lock." It was that close—the pilot couldn't put the gear down until the last instant because the drag would retard the speed needed for landing.

The bird seemed to be falling to earth like a bomb, gravity taking over, the roar like a freight train.

"Gear down," said Blomberg. And a second later, bang! They hit and bounced. Another bang and they were down and lumbering along Runway 2-1 toward the tower. They rolled a long way and then stopped. Apparently the landing gear had locked.

Ground crews and some fliers tore out onto the field as emergency equipment rolled in. Leone looked at the ashen faces of his crewmates as they made for the bomb bay and dropped to the pavement below. The leg he had broken was sore from eight hours of flying.

Colonel Terrill walked out to the *Shirley Raye*. With him was Major Stewart, face ruddy from the mission, still in his flight suit and Mae West and wearing a smile straight from the movies.

Terrill was grim-faced and silent as he walked around the ship with its missing engine and a fuselage pockmarked by flak hits, some holes big enough to toss a basketball through. Oil dripped out of No. 2 onto the runway. Then he learned of all the equipment jettisoned. The C.O. turned to Blomberg. "Why didn't you turn this ship around, put it on auto pilot, and let it crash in Germany? We'll never get this thing airworthy again." Terrill stormed off. Stewart smiled into his gloved hand and then gave Blomberg a wink.

"I guess that's sort of like a 'Welcome home,'" said Clem.

"I feel loved," said Cooper as the crew of the soon-to-be-late *Shirley Raye* began the journey to a ceremonial shot of whiskey for a mission barely accomplished.

29
BOYS WILL BE BOYS

"Dear Mr. Metcalf," Jim began. "I am writing to you to tell you about your son, Lt. Earle Metcalf, who is missing in action while serving his country in a bombing raid over France."

Earle Metcalf was a different sort of a guy. It took all kinds to man the 445th, and Metcalf looked like a bookkeeper. Ollie Saunders, who *was* a bookkeeper, had been a pilot in the 703 until he was shot down December 30 and now, according to reports, was a prisoner of the Germans. Well, Metcalf looked more like a bookkeeper than the bookkeeper. He was a fine, quiet kid, and Jim never revealed Earle's secret: This pilot in the Army Air Corps needed corrective lenses. He could do all right without them, but still, he kept them around. It was the sixth mission for Metcalf; he had flown his air-medal mission with Jim to Bonnières on January 21. Now it was nearly two weeks later and Earle was gone, the circumstances of his loss mysterious but leaving no room for hope. The ship he was piloting, *Billie Babe*, had vanished near the assembly point at Splasher 5 in bad weather on what should have been a milk run to the rocket coast; *Billie Babe* hadn't been seen in formation heading over the Channel, the ship hadn't returned to base or landed at any other bases, and no crash debris had been located anywhere around Norwich. She must have blown up in the air—the old Liberator fuel-leak issue—making this a group of ten difficult letters that Jim would write, counting this one to Mr. Metcalf. He couldn't say for sure that these sons and husbands were dead, but it just didn't look good, and he would write and sign each letter because these were his guys of the 703rd.

Jim had just received a letter from Victor Smith's father, Vardry, in Charlotte, North Carolina. Jim's letter and Vardry's apparently had crossed in the mail. In Smith's letter Vardry asked Jim if the other crews had seen what happened to *Gremlins Roost* and if Victor was alive or dead. "My purpose is to try and force his mother to erase from her mind the firm conviction that he has been killed," wrote Mr. Smith. "I want her to realize there is a 50/50 chance he is alive."

Oh, the anguish of the parents, siblings, wives, and girlfriends back home. How this war did hurt, in so many ways. It hurt to fly long missions sitting in your seat for seven and eight hours at a time at twenty and thirty and forty below zero, muscling a ship that seemed to buck like a mule, a ship that seemed to hate you. It hurt to live in the raw cold of Tibenham, a place that was always damp and always chilled, so chilled in his quarters in Site 7 up north of the runways that it clawed its way in the windows of those concrete bunkers and seeped into the marrow of his bones. It hurt when he didn't duck low enough and cracked his head on the bulkhead of the doorway or the I-beam hanging low in the ceiling. It hurt to never see the sun; fog yes, everywhere, every morning it seemed, but what he wouldn't give for a sunny Hollywood day about now. It all hurt; hurt so bad that the men could only come to one conclusion: The weather was on the Germans' side. How could those mired in muddy Station 124, grounded much more than half the time, think anything else? They had landed here nine miserable, soggy weeks earlier and spent every stinking day scraping mud off their boots and cleaning mud off their doorsteps, and when it wasn't mud, it was worse—it was cow manure.

That was life in this merry little corner of England, where the

Clockwise from top left: Union Col. Samuel McCartney Jackson (photo courtesy of the Jay Rubin Collection); Sgt. J.M. Stewart of the U.S. Army Signal Corps; Jim, age three; Jim, age eight; the Stewart family in 1917 before Alex leaves for the Great War. (Photos courtesy of the Margaret Herrick Library, Academy of Motion Picture Arts and Sciences.)

Top: Jim Stewart, Josh Logan, and Marshall Dana perform in the Princeton Triangle Club's first-ever musical comedy presentation, *The Tiger Smiles.* The review premiered Dec. 17, 1930 and toured fifteen major cities. *Time* magazine said of *The Tiger Smiles*, "Its excellence easily equals anything the club has done since it was founded." Left: Margaret Sullavan.

Left: Stewart and Fonda, ladies' men, make the social scene. Below: Jim and the love of his young life, Margaret Sullavan, are photographed with his canary yellow Stinson Voyager. (Photo courtesy of the Jay Rubin Collection.)

Above left: Jim with Norma Shearer in 1938. (Photo courtesy of the Jay Rubin Collection.) Above right: Ginger Rogers and Jim, 1940. (Photo courtesy of the Margaret Herrick Library, Academy of Motion Picture Arts and Sciences.) Below: "Livvie" de Havilland and Jim go out on the town with Burgess "Buzz" Meredith in early 1940. Later, Buzz and Livvie would become an item.

Induction day begins with UCLA frat brothers sending off some of their own with signs and a three-piece band. (Photo courtesy of the UCLA Library Special Collections.) Jim is then fingerprinted, which is covered in multiple takes, both close-up and long shot. The circus atmosphere of this experience will lead him to steer clear of the press for the remainder of the war. (Photos courtesy of the Margaret Herrick Library, Academy of Motion Picture Arts and Sciences.)

Above: Leland Hayward, Margaret Sullavan, First Lieutenant Stewart, and actress Kay Aldridge attend the Hollywood premiere of *Mrs. Miniver* on July 24, 1942. Below: Lieutenant Stewart, meet Lieutenant Gable. Their approaches to Army life, and their goals, would be far different. (Photo courtesy of the Margaret Herrick Library, Academy of Motion Picture Arts and Sciences.)

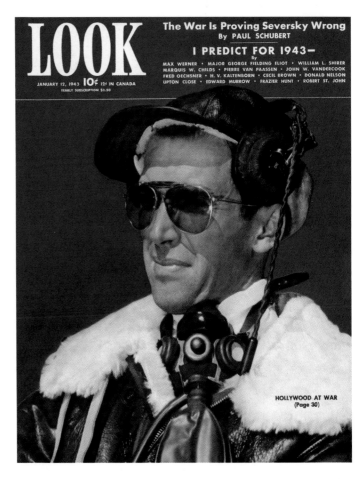

Right: Movie fans get a surprising look at flight instructor Lieutenant Stewart in his January 12, 1943, *Look* magazine cover by Earl Theisen, shot at Kirtland Air Field. (Courtesy of the Michael Mazzone Collection.) Below: At John Swope's July 19, 1943, wedding to actress Dorothy McGuire, Jim chats with matron of honor Frances Starr on the grounds of the Hayward home in Brentwood. Stewart would be transferred to the 445th in just two weeks. (Photo courtesy of the Jay Rubin Collection.)

Above: In this photo from Stewart's collection, some of the boys from *Tenovus* strike a pose in Marrakech. Kneeling: Jim and Lloyd Sharrard, sporting his cowboy boots. Standing: Jim Kidder, navigator; Charlie Wolfe, copilot; Roland Swearingin, 703rd communications officer; and Don Daniel, bombardier. On the back of the photo, Jim is referred to as "a Slim Captain." (Photo courtesy of the Film Stills Collection, L. Tom Perry Special Collections, Brigham Young University.)

Below: B-24Js line up on the Tibenham perimeter track in preparation for takeoff on a mission. (Photo donated to the 445bg.org by Capt. Charles L. Walker, 700th Squadron, 445th Bomb Group, and made available courtesy of Mike Simpson.)

Above: Newly arrived to muddy Tibenham, Captain Stewart walks along the lane near his quarters at Site 7. Below: After their air medal mission to Pas de Calais, the crew of *Lady Shamrock* pose with air commander Stewart. Standing: Jim, Capt. Jerry Steinhauer, 1st Lt. John Rankin, Capt. Bill Conley, Tech. Sgt. Harold Eckelberry, 1st Lt. Gordon Parker. Kneeling: Staff Sgt. Piercel Bordon, Staff Sgt. Kermit Moon, Staff Sgt. Edward Baumgarten, and Tech. Sgt. Francis "Pappy" Wilson. (Photo courtesy of the Eckelberry family.)

Above: An S-2 major shows Captain Stewart maps before he begins a mission as officers of the 445th look on. His flight gear includes a parachute harness, Mae West life preserver, and helmet with built-in headphones. His throat mic plug-in is visible above the Mae West. (Photo courtesy of the Film Stills Collection, L. Tom Perry Special Collections, Brigham Young University.) Below: A B-24 with the circle F denoting the 445th Bomb Group.

Above: Liberators from the 445th Bomb Group return to England after a mission to Germany. Right: Major Stewart is dressed for flight and not looking emaciated due to long johns, blue bunny heated suit, shirt, tie, pants, coveralls, jacket, scarf, and gloves—all for protection from cold that easily will reach forty below zero. (Photo courtesy of the Film Stills Collection, L. Tom Perry Special Collections, Brigham Young University.)

Above and below: Not flying was more difficult than flying for Major Stewart, seen here waiting on the control tower at Station 124 for the group to return from a mission. (Photos courtesy of the Film Stills Collection, L. Tom Perry Special Collections, Brigham Young University.)

Above: The price of service. In the photo top left, Second Lieutenant Stewart poses early in 1942. (Photo courtesy of the Margaret Herrick Library, Academy of Motion Picture Arts and Sciences.) Top right shows Major Stewart two years later, after having flown two months of maximum effort combat missions as a squadron commander. (Photo courtesy of the Film Stills Collection, L. Tom Perry Special Collections, Brigham Young University.) Below: Jim arrives at the St. Regis Hotel in New York City on August 31, 1945, for a reunion with his parents. They're happy to have him back and shocked at his appearance. (Photo courtesy of the Jay Rubin Collection.)

Above: A day after arriving on the *Queen Elizabeth*, Jim meets the press in Brooklyn on September 1, 1945. (Photo courtesy of the Jay Rubin Collection.) Below: "Action!" The tall man runs down a snowy thoroughfare in the desert of Encino, California, in the heat of June for a key shot in Frank Capra's production *It's a Wonderful Life*.

Above: Jim continues to attract the press, this time on his wedding day, August 9, 1949, as he marries Gloria Hatrick McLean at the Brentwood Presbyterian Church. (Photo courtesy of the UCLA Library Special Collections.) Below: In 1976 Jim returns to England. Here he leans on the Operations building at his old base in Tibenham, where he spent four months as a squadron commander in the 445th Bomb Group. (Photo courtesy of the Film Stills Collection, L. Tom Perry Special Collections, Brigham Young University.)

Three shots from 1943. Above left: General Galland (left, with mustache) inspects the situation in Italy. Above right: Clem Leone graduates gunnery school. Below: A snapshot shows the Siepmann family in Eppstein—Gertrud, Anne, Riele, Eva, Hans, Franz, and Christel. (Photo courtesy of Eva Hausch.)

strain of the bad-weather takeoffs and assemblies accumulated in the minds of pilots and copilots because they didn't want to die and they didn't want to kill their crews before the Germans even had a crack at them. It certainly weighed on 703rd Squadron Commander Jim Stewart when he flew in the right seat on missions, and especially when he didn't, when he stood there just a spectator at the railing of the control tower watching the long line of Liberators along the perimeter track with propellers turning, engines revving up, war machines straining at the bit, roaring with such defiance he could feel it rattling his bones and his teeth. He would watch his pilots take off into the pea soup of East Anglia on those raw mornings when damp thirty-five degrees felt like twenty and the cold hit marrow. Sometimes, he didn't even realize how tight he gripped that railing as each Liberator burdened with 5,000 pounds of bombs struggled to get airborne at the end of the gloomy runways.

It was February now, the weather no better and the strain worse. They had lost Metcalf and his crew on the month's very first mission. And here in the middle of nowhere in the English countryside, temperatures remained in the thirties, those damp and unpleasant thirties, and maybe snow would have been better. At least snow would have been different and would have offered a color other than green encrusted in brown, for these were farm pastures after all, and rich ones at that.

"I'd never felt cold like it," said Stewart. "It went right through you. It was a wet kind of cold. The fog was sometimes thick, and freezing, and wet."

No matter what he did, Jim couldn't get warm. He layered on the clothes, fired up the stove, wrapped himself in blankets, or in his flight suit and jacket and blankets, and nothing worked. How long was it since southern California? Months? Years? It felt like forever since he'd had to roll down the windows on his car on Sunset Boulevard or felt the heat of the morning sun in the cockpit of the Stinson. The mind was such a funny thing; he couldn't even imagine those luxuries now.

Jim Stewart was one of 3,900 young men in Tibenham; in fact, he was one of the station's very oldest young men. But all were boys in many ways, and boys were still boys. Any that could play ball, and that was most of them, had stuffed their baseball mitts and favorite bats in their bags for the trip over, and sat staring glumly out fogged windows as the weather forced them always indoors. When they could, they broke out baseballs and mitts and played catch in the hangar behind the control tower. They smoked cigarettes out of boredom and to keep warm. They ate chocolate until there wasn't any more. They passed time more often bundled up with comic books over girlie magazines. King Comics were popular, featuring reprints of Flash Gordon comic strips—Jim's favorite—along with America's Best Comics featuring The Black Terror and Doc Strange. All manner of colorful comics were passed around the Nissen huts until they had become tatters; Action Comics with Superman, Detective Comics and Batman, Marvel Mystery Comics with Sub-Mariner and the Human Torch, Captain Marvel, and the especially intriguing to young men just out of adolescence—or still trapped in it—Wonder Woman. By now a growing roster of superheroes battled the Axis month after month, just like the guys of Tibenham! In a pinch Classic Comics would do, whether Nazis died or not; there was suddenly magic in repackaging a ponderous *Silas Marner* or *Count of Monte Cristo* that had been forced reading in high school into an action-packed half-hour's diversion from the monotony of life at Station 124 on non-flying days.

Capers involved stealing coal from the pile or a keg of beer or sneaking to the Greyhound Pub on Pristow Green, a ten-minute walk west through farm fields or five-minute bike ride past the bomb store. Sneaking down Moulton Road to the Railway Pub produced many giggles and hair-raising adventures—heck, one beer was enough to turn out the lights for some of the boys.

214

Gallows humor reigned, and some of the guys were wickedly funny about the mortal dangers that lay over the horizon. They joked that the breakfasts preceding missions were "fattening them up for the kill," shaved close for the benefit of the fräuleins they might meet, and hoped whoever had packed their parachute wasn't hungover when he did it. Every time they passed the door of Ops for the 703rd, they saw a sign neatly printed in Olde English lettering. It read, "We don't bomb Germany. We shower them with our burning wreckage."

They lived for letters from home but had to be careful about what they said when they wrote back for fear of the censors returning the letter, and they didn't want their loved ones to worry. All anyone in the States could know was that they were "somewhere in England." The letters rolled in from all corners of the family every day, including relatives the men couldn't even remember. Many bored personnel at Station 124 became avid letter writers for the only time in their lives. But it wasn't easy for the fliers among these rookie correspondents because when Jim or any of the aviators wrote home, how could they talk about what it was really like? Should you mention you're so high up that if the oxygen gets shut off you asphyxiate in a couple of minutes? Or tell Mom and Dad the ship's fuselage is so thin that a piece of shrapnel will cut your throat in half a second, and a red-hot tracer from a fighter could split your skull faster than that? Do you mention that on the last mission, poor Sid the other waist gunner had his femoral artery severed by a piece of shell and would have bled to death except the extreme cold had turned his blood to sludge? Or that you were staring at rolled-up bunks on the other side of the hut because the plane the other crew was in took a direct hit over the target and exploded? No, they couldn't say any of those things. They spoke in generalities and said not to worry.

Luckily the men of Tibenham had a number one topic of conversation to capture the imaginations of the folks back home, something none of the other bases could boast: Jimmy Stewart is stationed here at my base. This news produced return letters from family and friends in a deluge. What's he like? Can you send me a picture of you and Jimmy? I would love an autograph, if it's not too much trouble. The men on Sharrard's crew or Johnson's or Conley's could legitimately say, "Major Stewart is way too busy to sign autographs, but when you read in the newspaper that he flew a mission, I was probably flying right there with him in the formation, maybe in the same plane."

Jim's star power wasn't limited to crews and their loved ones back home. Even the command officers wanted to spend all the time they could with him and be seen in candid stills taken by military photographers that might make it back to their local newspapers stateside. This was one thing Jim would just have to grin and bear: exploitation by his superiors. Get a drink or two in him, and Jim might even wander over to the nearest piano and offer up his go-to number, "Ragtime Cowboy Joe." It was a song he had learned to sing and play on the piano long ago, and it came in handy at any and all gatherings of officers now. He had to admit, officers hanging all over him wasn't such a bad thing anyway since he relied on these men for favors—like keeping the press away.

Yes, the man himself had grown more aloof than ever, more buried in his work of keeping the squadron flying and his men in good spirits, those in the air and the crews on the ground. Heck, the boys on the ground worked as hard as anybody to keep the birds in the air, so he made sure to visit them often and keep conversations going, ask questions about the repairs and about tendencies with the Liberators. There were always missions to prep for; every day that the weather held, the group would go up, often with maximum effort.

Yet even the loner grew lonely. He saw what some men of his squadron had at age twenty or twenty-two, a wife and partner who became a lifeline even four miles in the air, or especially that high

216

up. Bob Kiser blushed and smiled his wide innocent smile at the mention of Judy; Neil Johnson had his sweetheart, June; Chick Torpey wasn't only crazy about Betty but had named his plane after her. Bill Minor had eyes only for Dolores. Jim would spend quiet evenings in his quarters revisiting the touchstones of home, the letter from Dad and its copy of the 91st Psalm and the lipstick-smeared handkerchief given to him by Roz Russell. He found them so at odds, one speaking of home and hearth and the other of a man at loose ends, with a hundred conquests and no special woman in Indiana or Hollywood who was waiting for him, worrying for his safety, haunting the mailman for a letter.

He was staying abreast of the news from back home via the *Indiana Evening Gazette*. He read that old Mrs. Gessler, the organist at church, had died after a brief illness; that Pennsylvania was on the verge of an "egg famine" and a coal shortage; that Dad and the fire company had to put out fires at the liquor store on Philadelphia Street on consecutive days that turned out to be the work of an arsonist.

He was forced to read about himself, as with an article titled, STEWART SAID LONELIEST MAN with the subhead, Indiana Captain Too Busy to Talk to News Writers. He knew he was asking a lot, to be a movie star on the one hand and a combat aviator on the other, yet here he was, within a guarded perimeter somewhere in England. Right where he wanted to be.

30
MOTHER NATURE'S A BITCH

The bravest of gunners stowed comic books onto Liberators for the long flight over the Channel and on to Germany, not figuring that they couldn't turn the pages wearing inner gloves surrounded by outer gloves, or see the pages through goggles made necessary at altitude, where the cold hit well below zero.

The problems brought on by weather impressed Major Stewart on Friday, February 4, when he flew second seat to Neil Johnson in *Nine Yanks and a Jerk* on a mission to hit the Adam Opel AG auto manufacturing plant in Rüsselsheim, Germany, that had been converted to the production of aircraft parts. Two Pathfinder B-24s would lead the mission, with Frankfurt the secondary target. Such was the plan, but the Pathfinders aborted early on, leaving several groups of B-24s to improvise. Some tagged onto groups of B-17s that knew where they were going. *Nine Yanks* and the 445th fought high winds, heavy overcast, and malfunctions of the bomb racks and other electrical systems due to the unfortunate combination of high humidity and deep, subzero freezes. From a formation of twenty-two planes, seven dropped out because this or that was frozen. Ultimately, after the primary target became unfeasible, Stewart was about to order an attack on Frankfurt when a group of B-17s passed under the 445th and Jim's group veered off and began looking for targets of opportunity. A break in the clouds revealed a small German town, and Stewart ordered the dropping of 720 incendiary bombs of 100 pounds each, which hit a cow pasture—presumably German cows—southwest of Bonn. So many pastures had been devastated, in fact, that the boys were now referring to themselves as part of the "Eighth Agricultural Air Force," or "Eighth Ag" for short.

How inglorious eight hours in the air could be when nothing worked, and, thanks entirely to weather, nothing at all had worked on Friday, February 4.

Six days later, Maj. Stewart drove over to Hardwick to board an H2X radar-equipped B-24H Pathfinder where he sat right seat as formation commander with Lieutenant Vanderhoek, his pilot. They took off heading east to Buncher 6 to meet up with the 445th, but in the air Stewart learned the Tibenham assembly ship hadn't gotten off the ground and he would have to round up the ships himself in cloud tops up to 18,500 that jostled his ship and everyone else's.

The after-action report hinted at the nightmarish assembly period faced by Stewart and the other pilots: "Adverse weather made assembly difficult. Two collisions involving four B-24s occurred during the assembly period resulting in the Second Division's only major casualties of the day—twenty-eight crew members killed and three B-24s category 'E' battle damage."

Already on oxygen and icing up, Stewart ordered the firing of flares but could only muster six ships out of thirteen scheduled. He made a wide 360-degree swing around Buncher 5 and Splasher 5. This maneuver allowed him to collect ten Libs, and he set out after the 389th almost eight minutes behind schedule, heading northeast over the North Sea on a vector designed to confuse enemy radar. At a point off Amsterdam, the group turned sharply southeast toward the target, Gilze-Rijen Airdrome, one of the oldest in the Netherlands, under Nazi control and used as a base for both fighters and bombers since 1941.

Overcast remained five over ten to the I.P., and this would have been a dream mission to Stewart, with no enemy fighters and no flak, except for a number of unfortunate occurrences. Those ridiculously high cloud tops back over East Anglia; the necessity for Bill Conley to drop out of formation when his superchargers iced up; and the wicked contrails from the 389th ahead that buffeted Stewart's Pathfinder and the ships from Tibenham. And the ice, the goddamn ice that froze the machine guns and the oxygen masks and, potentially, everything but the hot-burning engines. Despite all these problems, in just a few more minutes they would release bombs and head for home.

"Code word is Black Jack," Jim broadcast to the formation.

Just past the I.P. Stewart heard in his ear, "No!" and then a resigned, "Bombs away."

Then he heard Lieutenant Neal's voice in ship 515, *Green Gremlin*. "Rack malfunction, skipper. I think maybe we just bombed a canal."

Jim responded that 6,000 pounds of bombs would tend not to do a canal any good.

A minute later he heard Lieutenant Myers over the interphone. "Uh-oh," said the lead bombardier sitting below Stewart in the nose of the Pathfinder.

"Now what?" said Stewart.

"Ten-ten overcast ahead at target."

"What a bitch," muttered Vanderhoek—at what, the weather? The planes? Mother Nature herself?

Stewart's temper grew short. He reminded Myers that he had Mickey and damn well better use it. In the cockpit they were breaking ice off their oxygen masks; if they didn't, suffocation was next up.

In seconds Myers said calmly, "Bombs away," and dropped a smoke pot with their bomb load for the 445th to release on. The ship jumped as if it had hit a curb.

"Bombs away," Stewart heard in his ear from ships in his formation.

And then, just as quickly, he heard a voice say, "Oh, crap."

A second muttered, "Damn!"

A third said, "Not again!"

Six B-24s had successfully salvoed their loads of twelve bombs, 500 pounds each. But in 619, a ship of the 700th Squadron named *Bunnie*, Lieutenant Blomberg said, "Complete electrical failure, no bombs released."

Lloyd Sharrard in *Nine Yanks and a Jerk* reported the failure of one rack of bombs to let go—nine had released; three had stayed with the ship despite crew members' attempts to kick the bombs out with nothing but air under them at 23,000 feet. Lieutenant Shurtz of the 702nd Squadron in 601, *Sin Ship*, reported the same problem, one rack out of four failing to release.

In the pilot's seat, Vanderhoek had banked hard to starboard, and as Jim thought about the problems of bombing targets in the Low Countries in European winter at high altitude, the Pathfinder ship descended to 22,000 and turned northwest toward home.

To the three pilots with electrical problems he said, "Jettison your bombs in the Channel if you're able. Bring 'em home if you have to."

By now it had become clear that even with a solid briefing and airtight flight plan and all ships returning to base, even when the fighters stayed away and the flak didn't come close, something was going to go wrong. It never failed. And over there in Holland, the barely dented and still operational Luftwaffe runways at Gilze-Rijen proved it.

Would the 445th ever get a break from this damn weather? December had been horrible and January worse. Now this. Skies so frozen that contrails became more dangerous than flak. Skies so frozen that bombs wouldn't release from the racks. And winter 1944 still had six weeks to go.

31
FAT DOGS

Gen. Adolf Galland referred to a large formation of American heavies lumbering over the Channel as "a Fat Dog." He had sensed trouble on January 11 when the Americans had sent more than 600 Four Motors into central Germany to hit aircraft manufacturing facilities. About 240 German fighters had scrambled to meet the Fortresses and Liberators that day. "Over the target areas there were heavy dogfights, " said Galland, "in which we were very successful." More than sixty American bombers had been shot down.

All along, Galland had been adjusting to the tactics of the American Air Forces. From the air war over Italy and the raids of the Four Motors he had learned that the most effective attack on an American heavy bomber was straight on from the front, where the pilots were most vulnerable and the inboard engines were within the field of fire.

He knew these American fliers were worthy opponents, flying as they did in the light of day to attack specific military targets. There was something noble in the way they conducted their business, which is why he recoiled when learning that German civilians were lynching downed American fliers for their "terror bombing" activities. Galland had never heard of such occurrences from the Tommies during the Battle of Britain and believed that Germans were—or should be—better than that. No, the way to defeat the Americans wasn't one at a time on the ground; it was strategically in the air.

On another day when a Fat Dog approached the Dutch coast, Dolfo and one of his officers ran to waiting Fw 190s. They wanted to scout the performance of their own combat formations against the new American fighter, the Mustang. From a respectful distance Galland and his wingman watched "wave upon wave, endless formations of four-engined bombers." They were protected by Mustangs "right and left above them." As the bomber stream passed by, Galland's eye was drawn to a straggling B-17 trying to catch up to the formation. Galland couldn't resist temptation; he dove after the Four Motor and shot her up with his 20mm cannons. He said, "Pieces of metal flew off. Smoke poured from the engines." Soon parachutes from the crippled bird filled the air.

In his ear Galland heard a desperate call from his flying companion. "Achtung, Adolf, Mustangs! I'm beating it—guns jammed!"

Galland learned all he needed to know about the performance of the new, long-nosed Mustang with its Rolls-Royce engine in the next thirty seconds as four Indians dove on his ship firing tracers while he sped east toward Berlin. He used every trick he knew to get away from the swarming fighters and finally succeeded, but the encounter proved sobering. Every day the scales were tipping toward the Americans to an ever-greater degree. More and more bombers were coming over. Better and better fighters were protecting them. And where were they all headed? To the aircraft plants it seemed, to knock out production of new planes, and every time Galland committed fighters to engage the enemy, he lost more experienced pilots that couldn't be replaced.

But Galland still had a formidable air force at his disposal, and he knew how to get the best out of both men and ships. In fact, his Fighter Arm would be unleashing devastation very soon, and in the direct line of fire were the fliers at a base near the quiet East Anglia village called Tibenham.

32
ARGUMENT, PART ONE

At the beginning of 1944, Hap Arnold, commanding general of the Army Air Forces, had issued a directive citing the German Air Force as "an Intermediate objective second to none in priority." Specifically, General Arnold told his commanders, "Destroy the enemy air force wherever you find them, in the air, on the ground, and in the factories." Simply put, the situation in the skies over Europe was grim. Production of enemy aircraft was increasing despite steady bombing day and night, and German fighters continued to knock heavy bombers out of the sky with alarming regularity. Most important in a strategic sense, the Allied invasion of northwestern Europe, code name Overlord, could not begin until the Luftwaffe had been rendered ineffective.

Talk of something called Operation Argument filtered down to Tibenham in January and hung in the air beneath the unrelenting cloud cover of winter in East Anglia. Operation Argument was designed to be a one-week, maximum-effort Eighth Air Force bombing campaign of German aircraft manufacturing and assembly plants. The last such campaign into the heart of Germany to face a gauntlet of flak and Luftwaffe attacks had been labeled afterward as Black Week for the hellacious casualties it produced, so pilots and crews didn't exactly look forward to the launch of Operation Argument, and winter weather over Europe kept delaying the campaign through January and into February 1944.

Major Stewart heard only the vaguest of rumors about some crazy meteorologist who was watching the skies, waiting for weather to be right to unleash the resources of the Eighth Air Force on the birthplaces of the Bf 109s, Fw 190s, and Ju 88s. To make Argument operational, bomber command needed a week of clear weather, which just didn't happen in European winter. Except that in mid-February 1944 it did. Suddenly, the Eighth Air Force consulting meteorologist, thirty-seven-year-old Dr. Irving Krick of the California Institute of Technology, announced that high pressure was building over the Continent and creating what he called "a good-looking sequence." Another in an endless string of Argument alerts went out to all bases, although such alerts were met with open derision because they had all had been false alarms up to then. Besides, the East Anglia bases had been blanketed in snow from a rare storm that had hit the entire island. How could 1,000 bombers take off on ice-coated runways? The men now waged war in snowball firefights that broke out across the sprawling Tibenham base as crews hardened by more than two months of aerial combat sought any hint of home.

Of immediate concern to Jim was the loss of another pilot. Emmett Watson of Texas, one of Jim's most senior pilots at twenty-seven, had crash-landed a couple of days earlier outside Manston in one of the original ships, *Kelly*, and he had come back to Tibenham shaken up physically but his brain had locked up too, and he'd been sent off for evaluation. Stewart responded by giving copilot Otis Rhoney the left seat. Rhoney would take over Watson's crew, but Otis was one of the ex-fighter jocks, and who knew if he could handle the job. Look what had happened to another of the P-40 guys, Don Hansen, when attempting to take the pilot's seat. It was yet another command decision, and they always came with second-guessing, especially for a guy like Jim who worried endlessly about making a wrong move with so much on the line.

As the freezing cold of a Saturday night tightened its grip on the base, the latest Argument go signal sent fuel and bombs into the Libs of the 445th. The ground crews had performed these tasks before only to turn right around and drain the tanks and remove the bombs when weather scrubbed the Argument kickoff mission. Major Stewart went to bed knowing something was up and, like everyone else, believed nothing would come of it and he would arise in six or seven hours not having been nudged awake to fly.

But at Second Bomb Division headquarters, discussion centered around the Second Combat Wing for the first mission of the big week of Operation Argument, which had been dubbed, fittingly enough, Big Week.

General Hodges, Second Division commander, asked General Timberlake, wing commander, "Who've you got leading tomorrow?"

"Stewart," said Timberlake.

"I've got so I don't worry much when Stewart's leading," said Hodges. "We always have a pretty good day."

At 3:00 a.m. the door of Jim's quarters at Site 7 opened and his bed was jostled. "Mission today, sir."

Son of a gun. Stewart jumped to his feet, dressed, and shaved for mission number nine, heart thudding in chest. A few had been true milk runs, but that term implied routine and how could any mission be called routine when it meant responsibility for his squadron, flight at 22,000 and forty below, flak, and the danger of fighters whether they materialized or not? Planes dropped out of the sky every day without a shot being fired because electrical systems went dark, a spark ignited gas fumes, engines conked out, or pilots made errors. "Milk runs" were so dubbed only in hindsight and only because the plane and crew had performed successfully, with the Germans conveniently not showing up.

Before chow, Stewart was summoned for pre-pre-briefing, which meant he was serving as wing or group lead from his co-pilot's seat in *Tenovus*. In the tense briefing room he sat waiting with a little time to think. Too much time to think. He had already passed from rookie formation leader to old hand and now faced demons as he racked up missions. All the flight crews felt it—all the pilots, all the crews. One of these days it would be his turn to go down because quite simply, precious few cockpit personnel made it to twenty-five missions and a trip home. And that's what it took to stop flying: twenty-five successful launches and returns. If he did get shot down and managed to float to earth in one piece, what would Hitler do with an American movie star in captivity—the one who had made *The Mortal Storm* back in 1940, exposing the evil of Nazism to millions of moviegoers? Parade him through the streets of Berlin? Relegate him to a concentration camp? Parole him in exchange for Hess? God only knew.

Jim made it through pre-briefing and then moved on to the pilot briefing. He would have a good group of pilots from the 703 with him in the lead squadron today. Joe Narcovich, Chick Torpey, Ralph Stimmel, and Bob Kiser, who sat in the briefing room reading them a letter from his wife, Judy, about getting a nursery ready for their first child, due in May.

The men bolted to attention by rote when the briefing officer entered the room. Then the black curtain parted and the lead pilots learned the target of the day for the 445th: Braunschweig, better known to the Yanks as Brunswick, which was most of the way to Berlin, about 450 miles from Tibenham. Northwest of the city center of Brunswick sat the Muhlenbau-U Industrie factory, which produced components for the Ju 88 twin-engine fighter bomber. Secondary target for the day would be the Neupetritor factory site.

Deep in thought, staring at the map, charting the course in his mind, Jim already knew the skies and terrain from past missions. They would head due east from Tibenham over the Dutch coast and barrel into Germany. Somewhere near Cloppenburg, he figured, they would bank right to come in over the target before reaching downtown Brunswick. This route might cut down on the flak. It might. In his ear he heard, "We will put up thirty-five ships today. Major Stewart and Lieutenant Conley will be Second Combat Wing lead ship, low. They will be in front of the 445th, 453rd, and 389th. Lead high will be Lieutenant Blomberg in front of Shurtz and Climer. Pathfinders will guide you in, led by Major Jones. Fighter support will be P-47s, P-38s, and P-51s."

Breakfast followed—the traditional real eggs and bacon that signaled the possibility of imminent death. All knew there would be nothing more than canned juice while they were in the air, eight or nine hours. Then Stewart donned his second skin. Gear in hand, he waddled with the others out to the jeep that would take them to the farthest reaches of the base, to the hardstand where *Tenovus* sat, way over near cows that looked on in disdain, no doubt giving sour milk over the fuss.

Up in the bomb bay, he glanced at today's payload: ten general-purpose bombs, 500 pounds each. Conley and Stewart completed the checklist and engines coughed to life at 0835, on schedule. Operation Argument was finally setting into motion. Taxiing on the peri track with outboard engines, he looked skyward at thick cumulus. He could only hope the weather was clear over the target, 450 miles east-southeast. The pilots knew by now: It took time to get all the planes ready for takeoff, and they waited, and waited, for the flare. Finally, at 0908 there it came. Full throttle and they were off, lugging the bomb load to the end of the runway and nudging into the morning air of February in East Anglia.

Conley slugged ship number 132 through the turbulence of cloud cover and broke through into clear blue skies at 4,300 feet. It was a beautiful day for flying. Wind nearly calm, just five miles per hour east-nor'east. At 1028 they had finally assembled, and just then, out the corner of his eye, Jim saw a swarm of B-17s to his left out of position, which forced Conley to bank right to bring his wing to starboard and south of their charted vector. Crap, swinging around to accommodate wayward Forts was going to cost them, and suddenly they were three minutes behind schedule. And schedule meant everything.

To their credit, the Pathfinders adjusted to Conley's maneuver, and no one in the formation felt the need to break radio silence despite the sudden shift. It was the training, Jim knew. The way they trained, the way he taught them to anticipate, to act and react, to hold the formation together come what may; that had saved them on previous missions. It was simple, basic stuff. Stay sharp, keep your eyes open, follow your leader, hold formation.

The wing shot over the North Sea without further incident from those Forts that were now dots on the northern horizon. Ahead of Major Stewart, the vast expanse of water yawned a greeting, and at far left and far right and high overhead, he saw vivid blue giving way to pastel haze. Out the right window of *Tenovus*, he saw the high ships in the combat box to his right spewing broad trails of vapor, one per engine. To his left past Conley flew another grouping of three Liberators, their contrails an unbroken white ribbon trailing behind each ship.

The moments passed. Then, as they blazed at 17,000 over increasingly rugged seas, he spied the coast of the Netherlands. It was just too beautiful, too majestic for wartime.

He knew he was over the shores of the Netherlands because the flak began to snap ahead of him, at first high, then low, then dead ahead. He checked his watch: 1152.

Inland over the frozen, snow-covered Dutch lowlands, he scanned the skies with the sun directly overhead and toyed with the idea of breaking radio silence for just a moment. He groped for his microphone button but stopped himself. They knew what to do without prompting: Watch for fighters coming out of the sun, boys, he said to himself. Wilson reached forward and touched Stewart's arm. Jim turned around and the radioman pointed at his set and then at his headset and made a slashing motion across his throat. Stewart grasped the meaning: The Germans were jamming their frequency. Damn it.

It didn't matter. Hold formation and head east, over the snow-covered patch of land by the Dutch coast, then high above the blue-green expanse of the Zuiderzee that sprawled ahead and to the right and left of the formation. Lectures had covered the situation in Holland in case the fliers were forced to parachute in. The Dutch Resistance was strong but the SS was everywhere and civilians were starving. An American shot down had a better chance of survival in Holland than in Germany, but not much better.

Steinhauer, the navigator, battled through the muck of the interphone and reported winds were pushing them off course to the south, and he was using the Pathfinders and dead reckoning to compensate. He gave them a corrected heading and Wilson shot a message by light to the Pathfinders. In another moment Steinhauer reported they were back on course but had lost one minute.

"Good work, Manny," said Conley.

Major Jones in the lead Pathfinder banked from east to east-southeast south of Bremen and the formation followed suit. There was nothing in the way of firing coming up from the ground, and no fighters presented themselves despite the fact that the formation painted bold streaks of white across the sky. Between the noise of 500 engines of 1800 horsepower each and the vivid contrails, there was no missing the Second Combat Wing from the ground for fifty miles all around. Maybe the Luftwaffe had been drawn to other Eighth Air Force formations streaking toward Halberstadt and Gotha to the south.

At 1304 they turned to port toward the initial point south of Hannover, and at 1310 they reached the I.P. Suddenly, flak hissed up at them and began to detonate ahead. Conley turned over control to Rankin. They flew due east straight into bursting flak that created what felt like potholes in the sky. The ship rocked left and right and left again. Per the plan developed in the briefing, Stewart gave lead bombing position to ship number 306, which was high on their right wing and piloted by Blomberg, with Lieutenant Painter the lead bombardier. Rankin would have the option of toggling on Painter's drop, but weather was clear over the target and Rankin would be able to see what he was aiming at.

"Damn it!" said Conley as flak snapped like lightning outside his window as the ship rocked left, with bits of shrapnel hitting their windows like hailstones.

Conley and Stewart saw red flares dead ahead and a little above their eye line. Parachute flares. "Uh-oh," said Stewart. He had heard about this tactic of signaling ground crews to stop firing by sending up flares so that fighter attacks could commence. Sure enough, immediately the firing stopped.

"I see 'em!" said an excited voice. It was Eckelberry in the top turret. "190s, eleven o'clock high."

Stewart heard Eck firing bursts at the 190s and felt the turret spin as Eck followed the bandit past. He kept hearing play-by-play on the interphone about fighters buzzing around but didn't see them.

"Eight, low, 109s!" came another voice. More machine guns rattled—waist guns maybe, tail guns, Stewart didn't know—and the ship rocked and vibrated from the outbound firing.

Off the right wing he watched bombs away from Blomberg's ship, and the 500-pounders unburdened the Liberator and ship 306 bucked higher in the sky. In a second Rankin said, "Bombs away," and their carton of eggs entrained out and fell free of the ship. Conley toggled control back from Rankin and banked right over downtown Brunswick with fighters buzzing about like hornets from a nest.

"Get 'em, little friends!" they heard a voice say, one of the gunners, and there up high in front of the windscreen Jim saw P-38s streaking into view from above, and it was such a beautiful thing. It was like John Ford's *Stagecoach*, when the cavalry arrived in the nick of time to save George Bancroft and Claire Trevor. Jim would say later that day, "I've never seen so many P-38s. You could see contrails from them and the P-47s for miles."

The German fighters continued to attack. Low attacks, level attacks, in twos, fours; three ships presenting to draw fire, the fourth sneaking in for a strafing run. At the edge of his vision, Stewart saw a Liberator take fire from what must have been incendiary bullets because her wing caught at once and she fell from the sky. It happened too fast to think about, too fast to calculate, how the fighters screamed in at 250 or 300 miles per hour and made their fatal mark and then swerved off in a blur. He felt every bullet, cannon, and rocket hit into his ships. He tried to look for chutes from that burning Lib.

"Who was that?" he asked. "Who got hit?"

"Kiser's ship, I think," said a voice. Yes that felt right, the ship he had seen had been back off the starboard side, and that's where Kiser was in the lead squadron. Dear God, Bob Kiser, Jim's youngest pilot. Pittsburgh kid who had moved to Ohio. Married less than a year to his Texas girl, Judy, the one who looked forward to it being a boy. Maybe he had gotten out. Maybe there had been chutes.

Jim had to hand it to the German fighters—they let the survivors float down. Call it professional courtesy, from air branch to air branch.

Wright Lee in ship 146 would write in his diary, "Another plane, probably from the 453rd Bomb Group...was reported as blowing up by the tail gunner. Meanwhile, the attacks continued with the same fury as when they started, and enemy fighters shot down two from the 389th Bomb Group, a part of our wing. In contrast to the air battle's utter horror, it was a picturesque view as we watched the many descending parachutes blend into the terrain's snow-covered background."

When all remaining ships reached the rally point, and Libs regrouped and offered each other comprehensive covering fire, the 109s and 190s broke off the attacks, but they had exacted a heavy price from Jim's formation. He ordered his ships to tighten up for the flight out. On the hour-plus leg southwest to Cologne and then near two hours northwest over Brussels and Dunkirk, then the Channel and back to Station 124, Stewart had time to think. Big Week, Operation Argument, was something that would be remembered. He had been right there for the first day of it, the bombing, the air battles, the loss of good boys as their planes sank earthward. Sure it was going to cost the Germans, and it might break the Luftwaffe, but the 445th was going to feel this. It was going to hurt; it already hurt.

Back at the hardstand of *Tenovus*, Stewart followed Rankin and Steinhauer out the bomb bay and dropped to concrete as the light of day waned. Conley's ground crew was already going over the ship, and saw by the number of its wounds just how hard the day had been. By No. 2 engine, Jim watched Killer Manning, a staff sergeant in the maintenance crew, put a paw around each of Eckelberry's arms and kiss Eck a hard one on the cheek. All the tension of all the guys seemed to melt away in a gale of laughter.

Eckelberry would remember "a hell of a lot of enemy fighters," while another pilot would call today's air battle over Brunswick, "The roughest ten or fifteen minutes I ever spent." Two other ships had gone down out of the 445th—Lieutenant Neal and crew in *Sky Wolf* and Lieutenant Owen and crew in *Georgia Peach*.

But it wasn't all bad news. Word in Ops was that they had creamed the target in Brunswick, and General Hodges, commanding the Second Division, highly commended the 445th "on its splendid work. This was the most successful mission in bombing to date."

Operation Argument was on; Big Week had begun. How big would it get, and how many ships and crews would it claim? These were the questions to ask, and how it would hurt when they learned the answers.

33
ARGUMENT, PART TWO

Big Week had already been big for Leone. On Tuesday the twenty-second, the crew had been roused at 0330 and listened to the briefing on the target for the day: Gotha and the Messerschmitt assembly plant, Gothaer Waggonfabrik A.G. factory and airfield. This was the essence of Argument, to cripple the Luftwaffe. Leone knew that their skipper, Lieutenant Blomberg, had flown two days earlier in the first mission of Big Week, and it had been a rough one. Now, thirty-six hours after his return, Blomberg would be up in the air again, this time with his own crew.

The long process of saddling up got them into ship 306 at 0815. Weather was hellacious, with low overhead on this week of supposedly clear weather. There was a bad feeling all around about this mission, borne out by talk of high cloud tops with snow squalls and choppy air. As they tried to form up, the 445th could find only one section of the 389th, and the 453rd was missing altogether in clouds and contrails. Finally, they got themselves organized and crossed the Channel, continuing east through choppy air with the formation more or less coming together. Over Münster, the mission was scrubbed because of weather and formation troubles. On the way home, Lieutenant McKee, the bombardier, managed to find a target of opportunity, an airdrome and definitely German. Bombs away.

Back at base they heard that some crews would get credit for the mission but some wouldn't. Blomberg's ship had dropped bombs; Leone and his crewmates would indeed get credit.

Two days later they got their second crack at Gotha, with the air clear and spirits much higher. It was as if they had worked the bad mission out of their system, and with Blomberg a little more rested, the *Shirley Raye* crew could get in, get out, and earn one more credit toward home.

A vast armada would be attacking today—three B-24 wings totaling 238 Liberators hitting Gotha; five B-17 wings totaling 266 Forts attacking the ball-bearing plants at Schweinfurt. The eight bomber wings, 500 planes total, would fly together from East Anglia as if attacking Berlin, then break off for individual runs on Gotha and Schweinfurt. Staying together for part of the run would maximize fighter cover.

Clem's crew had been assigned ship 567, a battle-tested Liberator named *Wacky Donald* with artwork of Donald Duck emblazoned on its nose. It was a renamed ship that once had been *Black Dog*, and never mind that renamed ships were known to be hard luck. Today's mission was playing out beautifully, assembly on schedule in clear weather, and the swing due east over the Channel a magnificent thing to behold with those beautiful Forts high and relentless in the sky to the south, painting the canvas of blue in vivid white contrails and lending a feeling of invincibility to the men in the stubby Libs below. Only one change would have made it better: Major Stewart wasn't leading today; it wasn't his turn on the schedule. Major Evans was formation commander and he was good. All the group air commanders were good, but Stewart was also known to be lucky, and Clem figured they needed all the luck they could get.

At 1140 the mighty force hit the Dutch coast and at 1155 reached the Zuiderzee. Clem looked aft at Hickey and Gunning on the waist guns, wearing goggles and sucking oxygen at 22,000 with ice building downward from the bottom of their masks. M. Sgt. John Gunning was a ground man, the squadron armorer. He had begged to go on a mission, and today he was subbing for Kaufman, who was out sick. If anyone found out that this vital ground crewman was airborne, Blomberg would catch hell. Cooper stood by the rookie crewman watching out the window. Cooper's ball turret sat in the aft section, ready to be lowered when they hit the I.P. Beyond them Sheppard sat sealed in the tail turret manning twin .50 cals, moving back and forth, watching from port to starboard to port again.

They had flown east of the Zuiderzee by now; Leone knew because flak started coming up, detonating in the distance. All at once Gunning grabbed for Cooper and motioned out his gun port. Cooper, now a veteran of these missions, leaned over into the sun and reached for his interphone button. "Bandits, five o'clock high, coming out of the sun." It was the last quiet moment Tech. Sgt. Clement F. Leone would ever know in a B-24 Liberator. Someone in the ship fired a burst, and the battle was on.

"190s! 190s!" A voice; Clem didn't know whose.

He couldn't see as much as one fighter outside his window but knew the sky had come alive with the enemy.

Said Wright Lee, a navigator in the formation, "As we looked out the window, we saw enemy fighters coming up in droves. Bf 109s, Fw 190s, Ju 88s, and Me 110s came zooming into our area, and the individual attacks began."

Leone could feel it in the air and hear it ship to ship as the entire formation was engaged by what seemed to be a hundred fighters, enough that the battle ran on uninterrupted second by second. He hadn't experienced anything like this in his six missions. In his headset he started to hear calls of ships going down and chutes in the air, calls to watch out for pieces of falling planes.

Forward, from the nose, from the top turret, Clem could hear and feel guns firing. In another instant, an explosion hit the tail. *Wacky Donald* rocked right, lurched left. Leone and his stool and equipment flew. "Where's our fighters? Where's our fighters?" shouted McCormick in the top turret. Next thing Clem knew he was flat by the flight deck. In front of him Blomberg and Widmark still had control, but they were frantic.

Aft, the ship blazed. One second it wasn't burning; now it was, hit by what must have been incendiary bullets or rockets. Swirling air streamed in the gun ports and supercharged the sudden inferno. Sheppard back there in the tail turret must be dead. Gunning too, Hickey, Cooper. Flames roared inside the cabin, and Clem reached for a fire extinguisher, careful to keep his oxygen mask in place as he shot a single stream of chemicals into the inferno.

McCormick climbed out of the top turret and grabbed the extinguisher from Clem's hand. Leone went for the lever to the bomb bay door. Must open the bomb bay and get the bombs out of the ship. Failing that, get the men out because the bomb bay was their jump point. He turned the lever. Nothing. Hydraulics out? Switched it again. No good. Without hydraulics in this fight, they were as good as dead.

They felt *Wacky Donald* fall out of formation, descending in the sky, turning back toward home. The flames grew hotter and the wing tanks would go; they had to go, and without the bomb bay open there was no way out. Over his shoulder Leone caught a glimpse of Blomberg fighting with the controls, all taut shoulders doing what he could to keep the ship level so his crew could jump.

Clem saw a figure charge from the tail along the catwalk through the flames. It was Cooper struggling forward past Leone and McCormick, steam rising from his clothes. Fire extinguisher empty, McCormick grabbed a blanket and beat at the flames licking toward the flight deck. Above his radio station, Leone spied Widmark snapping on his chute, and the copilot abandoned the cockpit just as he had in December. He popped the top hatch, shinnied his way up the small opening behind the flight deck, and forced his way out. That little top hatch hadn't occurred to Clem. It was there in case a bomber had to ditch, and the opening was small because in a water event you didn't need a parachute to escape.

Leone had learned on his last bailout that when the officers went, it was every man for himself. Then, as now, the copilot had gone. Clem reached back to his radio station and grabbed his chest chute, snapped it on, and ripped off his oxygen mask. He stepped up to the opened top hatch. The ship was shuddering in death rattles. One hand on either side, he vaulted himself up through the opening, his head now exposed to the frigid air of the slipstream rushing by at 160 miles per hour as *Wacky Donald* flew west into headwinds. He knew he couldn't make it. Such a futile gesture to even try to get his bulky clothing and chest chute through the hatch. He got up so far, head and shoulders out, and was wedged tight with his chute below the hatch, the winds pounding him. He couldn't breathe. He put both gloved hands in front of him on the hatch and pushed until he got his chute over the frame. In the slipstream he had nothing to grab onto but the twin gun barrels of the top turret. He hugged them tight, marveling he had made it this far. His legs dangled out in the open air. Now what? Let go and fly straight back into the twin vertical stabilizers? That would be the end of him, bouncing off those stout columns at such speeds. The boy from Baltimore who wanted to fly was really getting his wish now.

He hung there considering his options, a man alone three miles up, with his buddies below dead or dying, these men he had trained with and grown up with. Then, under him came the answer. Not an option; a certainty. The flames found the wing tanks and the ship exploded. Tech. Sgt. Clement Leone had reached the end of his worries.

34
BLOODBATH

"Dear Mrs. Skjeie," began Jim. "I am writing to you to tell you about your husband...."

Another of his pilots had been lost. Dave Skjeie's father, Endre, was of Scandinavian descent and had served in a U.S. aero squadron in the Great War, inspiring both Dave and his brother to join the Air Corps. Dave had been with Jim since the beginning in Sergeant Bluff and was a fine pilot, but there's just so much you can do when your plane's hit with incendiary bullets, flips over, and explodes, which is what happened to Skjeie's ship yesterday five minutes after bombs away over Gotha. Somehow, two chutes had been seen at the time of the explosion, so Jim's letters to the families of the crew would be vague because the odds were two in ten that their loved one had survived. But Dave himself? It was unlikely he would have had time to untether himself from seat belt, oxygen, heating system, and intercom and climb out of the pilot's seat and off the flight deck to the bomb bay. Jim sat there thinking; Dave had celebrated his birthday at Tibenham on December 6; he had turned twenty-two. And now Jim was writing to Dave's widow, Billie, same age.

The 703rd had also lost Pete Abell and the crew of *Star Baby* above Gotha. Reports said they'd been hit with 20mm incendiary rounds from the cannons of an Me 210 that set the ship ablaze.

239

Chutes were seen before *Star Baby* exploded in the sky. Jim had hopes that Pete had bailed out because once it was clear the plane couldn't limp home, they all would have had time to buckle on chutes and jump, even the pilot, and the plane had indeed remained airworthy for a minute or two, said the reports.

It had been only two months since Jim had checked out Abell and crew after their switch from B-17s and late arrival at Tibenham. Pete was twenty-five and had been born in Oklahoma but lately lived in Saratoga, California, which is where Livvie de Havilland had grown up—outside San Francisco.

The Gotha mission had been a bloodbath for the 445th, and Stewart wondered if Station 124 could ever recover. That morning Jim had watched from the control tower as twenty-eight Liberators from the group set out on the day's mission. Three had turned back and landed after mechanical trouble. Late in the afternoon twelve more limped home. He stood at the railing on the tower and watched them come sputtering in, firing flares to signify wounded aboard or mechanical difficulty. One by one the ships taxied back to their hardstands and shut down engines, and the sky grew still and quiet, so still and so quiet that sea gulls began soaring over the runways in the gloom of afternoon. What a feeling that was, standing there on the upper deck of the control tower staring at empty sky, and at so many empty hardstands.

In all, thirteen planes out of the twenty-five that had flown the mission had been lost. So many brave kids had bought the farm or parachuted into enemy hands, and S-2's interrogations, all of which Jim had sat in on, had revealed the horrors of running air battles over Germany that had taken out some of the finest pilots and airmen in the group. Never had he seen such a day; he had heard about them, days like Black Thursday, but he hadn't been this close. Even the lead ship had gone down, Maj. Jim Evans, squadron commander of the 702nd in the pilot's seat and serving as air commander for the day, with Capt. Henry Bussing his copilot, sitting in the seat so often occupied by Stewart of the 703rd.

Wright Lee of 1st Lt. Norm Menaker's crew in the 702nd Squadron reported of this lead ship and Major Evans: "They were attacked head-on by fighters, the bullets pouring into the nose, where they hit bombardier Cassini a dozen times and ripped the thumb from Lieutenant Massey. The blinding flash, which I saw, was a 20mm shell exploding in the cockpit, injuring Evans, the pilot and our squadron commander, but missing Captain Bussing, the copilot." In desperation Evans had put wheels down to signal surrender, then had fallen out of formation. The Luftwaffe had recognized the signal and backed off, allowing surviving crew members to bail out.

Jim heard that Lt. Robert Blomberg of the 700th also had been lost and was most certainly dead—Blomberg had just flown on Jim's right wing on the Brunswick mission five days earlier, and Stewart believed him to be the most promising pilot in the 700. Damn good flier and quality kid. Now he had likely met his fate, as had that go-getting young radio operator, Leone, who had helped Stewart out on Abell's shakedown flight. Jim's eye had snagged on Leone's name as he ran down Blomberg's crew.

From S-2 reports compiled during the questioning of survivors, Stewart knew that sending the Forts and Libs as one air armada had become problematic at the point when they split and the B-17s headed toward Schweinfurt while the B-24s flew east to Gotha. The Eighth Air Force fighters found themselves with two formations to protect instead of one, leaving the Liberator force vulnerable to attack. The result, as he read from S-2 summaries, was devastating:

"For well over 2.5 hours Nazi fighters, rocket ships and dive bombers poured death and destruction into the formation from every angle. All the latest tactics were used by Hitler's supermen to break up and turn back the attack. They used trailing cables with bombs attached that exploded upon contact. Rockets were going off like the Fourth of July, and parachute bombs were used to some extent. At the coast of Holland flak starts. Waves of Focke-Wulf 190s come in, then queue up and come in one at a time. Other fighters stood off at a distance and shot rockets, then came in close and spewed death-dealing 20mm shells.

"One Bf 109 came firing head-on into a Lib and blew the nose off. As the ship went spinning down, the 109 pulled up into a steep climb. The top turret gunner in the Lib behind cut loose and stopped him in midair. The ship fell off on its back and headed down. Halfway through the formation, it crashed into another Lib in the low element and took her whole tail off. The ship, with its tail off and nose pointing toward the sky, headed into the bomb bay of the Liberator above. The two planes crashed together. Both began to expel men from all sections of the ship. Ten men jumped from the almost stationary planes. The planes broke apart, and the one that crashed into the higher plane started sliding down sideways through the formation. One gunner yelled to his pilot, 'Look out from the right!' and the pilot put the ship into a dive as the pilot just in front pulled up to a steep climb, and the doomed Lib sailed between them with inches to spare.

"When one Lib was hit, the Germans pulled up and waited until the crew bailed out before attacking again. One followed the Lib down, while the others rejoined the attack on the formation.

"One lead ship had a fighter, about the seventh in a long line, come in to about 100 yards, roll and climb and release a parachute bomb that the Lib ran into. The explosion tore the top section off the ship back to the wing edge. The plane burst into flames and went tail first toward the ground.

"Another crew member of a doomed Lib bailed out and was floating to earth when another Lib that was shot down picked up his chute on the jagged edge of one of its torn wings and carried him down out of sight of the formation.

"Frantic attempts by remaining ships to dodge parachutes and parts of aircraft that filled the air. Many men who had bailed out held the pulling of rip cords until they thought they had missed the formation only to find they had opened up right in front of another group of ships."

The ink hadn't yet dried as Stewart read more and more sheets of paper fresh off S-2 typewriters recounting the horrifying Gotha mission, now just hours old.

Navigator Wright Lee said of being in the middle of the day's battle, "There was a temptation to 'chuck it all' and bail out...and live...but you couldn't do that."

Stewart hit the sack with the worst thought of all in the front of his mind: He would be the air commander on tomorrow's Big Week mission if the weather held. He lay there in the blackness with dark visions in his mind, of parachutes caught on jagged metal, of burning Liberators colliding in midair. Of body parts smacking off his windshield.

He got up out of his bunk in the freezing cold darkness. "Walking to the window," he remembered later, "I pulled the blackout curtains and stared into the misty English night. My thoughts raced ahead to morning, all the things I had to do, all the plans I must remember for any emergency. How could I have a clear mind if it were saturated with fear?"

His thoughts drifted back to advice from his father, often-repeated, often-remembered advice about being in a war. Jim had asked his dad if he had been afraid. "Every man is, son," Alex had told him, "but just remember you can't handle fear all by yourself. Give it to God. He'll carry it for you." Jim would have the psalm with him, and his lucky handkerchief. And he would have his wits.

An eternity later, in the pre-dawn morning of Friday, February 25, he heard the door click open in his Quonset hut in Site 7. With an accompanying blast of cold air came words that shot through him like electricity: "Mission today, Major Stewart."

Big Week had reached day five. Jim's brain scraped itself to

243

some semblance of coherence after little or no sleep—he couldn't be sure he had drifted off even once. He needed to be sharp, but how could he be after the horrors of day four and the visions they had produced—all those fine kids that had met their fate.

He followed the routine: shower, breakfast, briefing, suit up, grab gear, hop a ride to the plane. When the truck pulled out, loaded with crewmen, it turned the wrong way and Stewart screamed, "Where the hell are you going, driver?" One of the crew said he had forgotten his charts. "The hell with the charts!" bellowed Stewart and ordered the truck to make for the hardstands. He looked around him and saw faces that had flown yesterday. Just yesterday. And they would fly today because so many men were dead and there weren't enough crews to go around. He felt bad for yelling, but he was the commander, and they would get over it.

The mission today would be one for the books: A total of 754 B-17s and B-24s, escorted by twenty groups of Eighth Air Force fighters and twelve squadrons of RAF Spitfires and Mustangs, would conduct a mass penetration of southern Germany to attack three Messerschmitt aircraft production centers and a ball-bearing plant. A large group would attack Augsburg and Stuttgart, another would hit Regensburg. The Second Combat Division, including the 445th, would go for Bachmann, von Blumenthal & Co., a final assembly plant and airfield for Me 110s and 410s located at Fürth, just northwest of Nuremburg. The briefing had stressed conservation of fuel because they carried ten hours' worth and would be flying nine and a half at least.

Stewart sat as a second copilot and group commander in ship 447, *Dixie Flyer*, piloted by Neil Johnson with Lieutenant Vandagriff as copilot. They carried forty M1 fragmentation bombs. Wheels up was 0931 into heavy overcast. After assembly they flew south through England, passing London to the west and over the Channel, where they donned helmets and flak vests and tested the guns, then continued south. They reached Dieppe on the French coast at 1142, made landfall, and ran the gauntlet of flak.

As the planes headed inland over France, the skies cleared to CAVU (ceiling and visibility unlimited), offering views of rolling French countryside blanketed in snow. The weather was moderate—only twenty below zero at 18,000. On the flight deck, if they were dwelling on the battle of Gotha just yesterday, Stewart saw no indication. But how could they not think about those poor guys yesterday, flying just like this when out of the literal blue all hell broke loose? Would that happen again today, out of the blue?

Flak reached out to them as they flew by, never a surprise yet always a surprise. Their minds were already so focused, and the flak slapped them even more awake.

The earth below them sparkled in fields of brilliant diamonds. Could this really be wartime with the land down there so beautiful, when there was no flak, when there were no fighters?

As they approached the I.P., Jim put on his flak vest and steel pot and spelled Vandagriff in the right seat. By the time they hit the initial point, everyone was alert. The briefing came sharply into focus: assembly plant with an airfield. Surely, there would be finished fighters sitting there, and however many there were, all must be destroyed. Johnson ordered window to be tossed out to confuse the radar, and goddammit they had better toss out more because the flak hit suddenly! They flew straight into a storm of black flak that knocked the ship around. Ahead they could see smoke from the previous attacks rising around Fürth, their target. They flew toward a clot of buildings a little to the north and east of Fürth, buildings already afire. Below, even at this height, Stewart could see an airfield with rows of brand-new fighters on the ground, factory fresh and untouched.

Johnson had turned over control of the ship to bombardier Robinson. They flew a straight, true course in Big Week kind of weather with no obstructions of any kind. The black smoke of the Messerschmitt plant reached almost to their altitude of 18,500 as they passed over it. The energy from the smoke kissed the belly of their plane, and they felt the turbulence.

"Bombs away," said Robinson. The ship lightened of its load of fragmentation bombs, and they got the "bombs clear" from aft.

Johnson switched control back from the nose and banked away. Stewart saw out the right window other bombs falling from their altitude, the bombs of many ships, and then the bombs started to hit, the effect shattering; he could see the concussions of the blasts slamming buildings and the airfield, a whirlwind of destruction that ripped into those new airplanes and blew them to flaming dust.

Flak came up again and boomed to the right and left. All at once a loud bang sounded in the flight deck and rocked them so hard that only their safety harnesses kept them in their seats. Then came an explosion right under them. It lifted the ship, lifted the pilots. Johnson and Stewart took a moment to realize—an .88mm shell had punched up into the bottom of the ship and detonated. They felt frozen air blast straight up into the cockpit from the hole beneath them.

The flight deck cleared of smoke. As it did, Jim looked down to his left and inches from his boot sat a jagged, gaping hole nearly two feet across. He could look down through the fuselage straight to Germany.

"Hydraulics are damaged," said Johnson.

The three punch-drunk men on the flight deck, Johnson, Vandagriff, and Stewart, glanced out the left and right windows to see if propellers continued to spin. All four did, and the ship somehow managed to keep up with those around them.

"Wright to ship 447," they heard in their ears. "Skipper, are you OK?" Wright was just below them in the formation and must have seen what had happened, but radio silence must be maintained and Stewart didn't answer. Just then he realized his map case and parachute were missing; they'd been blown out of the ship and were on their way to Germany. Jim ordered a visual signal to be shot to Wright.

"Fighters, six o'clock high!" Their ship rattled to life with machine guns blazing. Oh no, was this yesterday all over again?

"Where are our damn fighters?" said Johnson into his now-dead oxygen mask. Fighters swarmed about them, Focke-Wulf 190s according to the chatter from the gunners.

The ship convulsed, struck by something, no telling what. "Damn!" said the pilot. "Where are our fighters!"

"Oh, my God!" gasped one of the gunners into the interphone. "Oh, my God." He was watching something out his gun port. "The wing's off that ship! Bail out! Bail out!" Stewart looked; saw the awful sight of a Liberator coming apart. One man had emerged from the crumpling fuselage and his chute opened and caught the air. But one only. How fast they plunged when mortally wounded, these Liberators that had no right to fly in the first place, so ungainly they were.

"No! No!" Another voice. Another 24 hit and careering to earth. Jim didn't see this one, but he knew from the sound of the observer's voice how terrible it was.

Johnson banked hard right again, and the ship responded. They were heading west toward the coast in the frozen air of an open cockpit. Jim glanced out his window and saw a ship right beside him hit—*Nine Yanks and a Jerk*. Jim could have sworn an .88 shell had just gone right through her at the cockpit. But that just couldn't be. *Nine Yanks* pitched and yawed but kept flying; at first Jim thought they were done for. In an instant he no longer worried. That was Mack Williams and he must still be alive.

Below him, Stewart saw the entire target area, buildings aflame with black smoke belching into the sky. To the north, a large building bellowed an angry volcano of smoke thousands of feet in the air. Beyond the buildings sat crumpled, mutilated German fighters that wouldn't fly again. All of a sudden, the airfield's oil tanks caught and erupted in a magnificent explosion so far below Stewart that it might as well have been on a movie screen. A mushroom cloud shot skyward as the target passed out of his view.

The flak kept at them, jostling *Dixie Flyer*. "Crap!" spat Neil Johnson in the pilot's seat. They hung on, hoping for better moments to come.

The fighters never did arrive, but the formation kept together. They flew over what looked to be wintry forest, and then they were shooting west and there wasn't any more flak, and they flew free and clear in the afternoon sky. After yesterday, after taking a flak hit on the flight deck, nobody assumed they would make it home, but minute by minute it seemed they might, their bodies frozen. They reached Pas-de-Calais at 17,000 and more flak, but the Channel beckoned ahead and they shot out over water. The formation continued to hold together as they made land at Beachy Head and followed their flight plan along the coast and then hard left to Tibenham.

The pilots stared at fuel gauges reading near empty. They talked about landing as they descended through 5,000. How were the hydraulics? Nearing Tibenham, the pilots ordered the crew to hand crank the gear down; *Dixie Flyer* remained airborne as the ships with wounded fired flares and landed first. They were running on fumes now. Johnson and Stewart wondered about the structural integrity of a ship hit so squarely by flak? Would she hold together for a landing? They discussed who should sit in the copilot's seat and Stewart said it should be him. As Vandagriff unbuckled and stepped carefully around the hole in the deck, Stewart moved his lanky legs over the seat and settled in beside Johnson. Stewart was the instructor on four-engine bombers after all—the man who had trained many of the pilots in the group.

After the wounded had been landed, Johnson was one of several pilots who ordered a flare fired to say his ship was crippled. When it was 447's turn, Neil aimed for Runway 0-3 with that beautiful base sprawled out beyond. If only they could get down safely, a shot of whiskey, a meal, and a bed awaited. They came in low over the treetops as Johnson told the crew to hold on, and the wheels smacked to earth and she had made it, enjoying the luxury of Tibenham's longest runway. Johnson and Stewart applied the brakes and on she rolled. More brakes, all the muscles they had.

With one final convulsion and physics beyond the capacity of any structure, *Dixie Flyer* came to a scraping stop. Johnson cut the engines and the pilots looked around them. The smell was ungodly. Hot metal and hot rubber. They sat in the open air near the far northern end of the runway with smoke around them and the ship cracked open at the bulkhead behind the cockpit. Muscles ached. The seatbelts had cut into their midsections. But all was still and, after so many hours, quiet. In their ears was the phantom roar of engines and the banshee screech of metal on runway.

As they unbuckled, they knew they didn't have to worry about fire with those empty tanks. So they looked at one another, at faces creased from the rubber edges of oxygen masks and tinged with frostbite, and they slowly made their way off the flight deck and down through the bomb bay as fire crews arrived.

Stewart stood looking at the ship that had gotten them all the way to Nuremburg and all the way back. The flak hadn't just hit under the cockpit. The entire fuselage had been pockmarked by shrapnel, but the crew hadn't said a word into the interphone about it.

The gunners were emerging from the bomb bay now, slowly, full of aches and pains, a group of old men in their twenties.

George Wright landed next and eased his ship around the wounded bird and turned onto the perimeter track before cutting engines. Wright's boys climbed out of their plane and trotted over to see that Stewart and crew were all right, as Liberators still in the air diverted to land on Runway 0-9. As ships continued to touch down, Jim stared at the *Dixie Flyer* lying wounded before him.

"Robbie" Robinson of Wright's crew said, "The tail of the ship was sticking up in the air and the nose was sticking up in the front," with the middle sagging in at the crack in front of the wing.

Said squadron bombardier Jim Myers of Stewart, "He was blue from the cold whistling through the holes in the plane, but he hadn't received a scratch."

Just then Mack Williams managed to land *Nine Yanks and a Jerk* and Stewart rushed over, his legs like soft putty. "Where's Mack?" he asked of the crew emerging from the plane. They pointed him to the far side where Williams stood, face ashen and dragging deeply on a cigarette.

"I thought you were a goner," said Stewart to Williams. They were two men who had survived direct flak hits and somehow still lived and breathed.

A little later, standing in the midst of so many shot-up planes, Jim was heard to murmur, "Somebody sure could get hurt in one of these damned things." But he was down and still in one piece. The Big Week bloodbath that had taken out so many yesterday and again today hadn't claimed James M. Stewart, for whatever reason. This was his tenth completed mission, and meant an Oak Leaf Cluster for his Air Medal. That meant nothing to him; getting his boys back home meant everything. But there were so many gone from his command now, and the strain of today's mission on top of all the others added up. Every time, he felt the weight of leading his squadron and sometimes, like today, his group or even his wing. He felt vulnerable for what the flak and the fighters might do to his body or his plane, sure, but mostly for what they did to his boys. "All I wanted to do was keep them alive and do our job," he said. But in the air he couldn't control who was shot at and hit. He couldn't protect them up there; he could only make the right decisions. But what if he had done better? Would it have saved them? Jim was Jim and that's the way he thought. It was getting to him. All of it. In just eleven weeks, he was ready to unravel.

35
PHYSICS LESSON

Clem Leone sat in the cold, damp dark remembering the day before. He hadn't known right away that *Wacky Donald* had exploded under him. One minute he was hugging machine guns in a 160-mile-per-hour slipstream, and the next he awakened free-falling from 14,000 feet, unable to breathe. He had been here last December 29; he knew the sensation of his dead weight falling to earth, except this time he was tumbling to earth. How long had he been out? He didn't know. How close was the earth? No idea. But he did know where the ripcord was on his chest chute, and he grabbed it and yanked with all his might. The silks spilled out and reached up above him and caught the air. Physics yanked him up so that he no longer tumbled. He hung there on the lines, his head clearing so he could figure out what likely had happened. The swirling fire inside the fuselage must have found the wing tanks, putting *Wacky Donald* out of her misery once and for all. Then he was out in the air like somebody's laundry, the future uncertain under him. His face was wet; from what, he couldn't imagine.

From 10,000 feet, he saw below an expanse of snow-covered ground, some roads, woodlands, and the sharp angles of farm fields. He saw a sizable lake, and he was sinking toward it. Despite being an Inner Harbor boy, he had never learned to swim, so this lake was a problem. He grabbed a handful of lines and gave them a pull. Yes, by pulling with all his weight on one side or the other he could steer the parachute. Good, because he didn't want to survive a bailout only to drown in some German lake.

He drifted earthward for many minutes under that giant white canopy, long enough to signal the entire German army. As the ground approached, he thought of his last parachute landing that hadn't gone so well. He wondered if his leg, still mending, could withstand what was about to happen. He raised himself into a ball and hugged his knees to prepare for impact.

He hit the earth with a thud, tail first. Pain ripped through his core. Above him was clear sky with some blue. There was no sense of an air armada now except for some contrails in various stages of decomposition. There were no other parachutes and no enemy aircraft. Just empty sky.

He couldn't move without pain in his chest. He couldn't draw a decent breathe. He sensed movement about him and struggled to find his feet and shed himself of the lines and silk that now impeded his reactions. As he scrambled up he saw smears of blood in the snow, his own blood, which accounted for his wet face.

Instead of soldiers, he saw civilians, four or five of them, then others, running toward him. He had heard the briefings, that German civilians were capturing and executing "American gangsters" from the sky. He unhooked his chute and tossed it aside, pulled his .45, and waited. In his cloudy mind he believed this was the end. It had to be.

The civilians didn't attack him. They kept their distance, wary of his sidearm. "Hollander! Hollander!" said a man, gesturing to himself. Gesturing to all of them. Again, slowly: "Hollander."

Clem realized: Oh, my God, they're Dutch. It hit him that Blomberg had managed to keep the ship airborne heading west long enough to get them over Holland for bailout. They must be dead: Blomberg, McCormick, and Cooper. He had no idea what had become of McKee and Varga. Maybe they all were dead.

Leone's back hurt like someone had stabbed him there. It hurt like hell, and hot blood still dripped off his chin. He had landed so hard that his just-healed leg pained him, and he wondered if he had rebroken it.

"Bless?" asked the man, pointing at Clem's chest, which he was holding with his arm. Clem didn't understand; he said so with a shake of his head. The stranger said again, "Bless?" And then pointed to Leone's bloody face.

Leone remembered his translation card. Blessed. All he could think to say was, "Protestant."

The man said, "*Kom met ons.*" He motioned toward himself, and he turned and pointed at farm fields and at a hill crowned by a farm house. "*Kom.*" The group shepherded Clem through the fields as fast as he was able. In a few minutes they arrived at the farm on the hill, and Leone was ushered inside to the kitchen, where he sat at a table. A jam sandwich appeared before him with a glass of milk. Then a basin of water and a towel were brought so he could wash his face and hands.

As he consumed the sandwich and drank the milk, he was aware of eyes watching him, a stranger who had participated in the air battle high above and then fell from the sky. He must have made one battle-scorched sight. They didn't know him from Adam, but they wanted to like him, that much was clear.

As he finished his food and toweled off his face and hands, he became aware of commotion outside. Voices were raised in argument, and a man was pushing his way through, rifle in hand. A German soldier entered the kitchen. The barrel of a Mauser stared at Leone. He raised his hands as best he could with the stabbing pains in his body. The soldier reached forward and snatched Clem's Colt from his shoulder holster. There had been briefings about the soldiers that downed fliers could expect to meet. This one didn't look like regular German army. The uniform was nearly right—some sort of militia maybe. He motioned Clem to his feet and outside, down the steps of the house, and then back down the long hill.

By the position of the sun Clem figured he was heading north, past other houses, then onto a road and toward a town. They walked what seemed a long way. He turned to look behind him, and there he saw twenty or more Dutch people trailing behind the soldier.

Clem kept walking along the road. "*Stoppen!*" Clem obeyed automatically. No need for a translator on that one. Ahead and to the right was a field, and some sort of camp strung with wire.

"*Komen! Komen! Op deze wilze!*" The soldier motioned with his rifle for Leone to pass through the gate of the camp. "Inside! Inside!"

Instinct made Leone hesitate. He stood there in a stupor, knowing he could be shot at any second. "Inside!"

A young man in the group of civilians reached out and pulled Leone close. "Run," he said. The young man nodded in encouragement, and smiled. "Run!" And the youth started running toward some trees.

At that instant the crowd descended upon the soldier and tackled him to the ground, almost taking Clem down too. He stood there for a second, stunned at this crazy gesture by people he didn't even know. They were clubbing the soldier with their fists, kicking him; one moment peaceful farmers and the next a mob. He didn't hesitate; he ran.

Through fields and woods he followed the boy to a deep thicket, where he pulled aside some brush. He saw a wooden door flat on the earth. The youth lifted it. "In!" he said and motioned. "In!" Clem did as he was told. Down he went and plopped to the floor of some enclosure, pain shooting through him. He looked up to see a wooden ladder beside him in this frozen gopher hole dug out of the earth. The wooden door closed over him, and he could hear brush being replaced to camouflage the spot.

That was how he had come to be alone in the dark, in the middle of wherever. He kept thinking of Tibenham, that sickly, mud-soaked base now hundreds of miles away. He thought of his dead crew, and of his mother and the telegram she would get, and the grief she would feel. And there was no way he could say, here I am, Mother, in a secret, frozen hole in rural Holland, just west of the German border.

36
THE BIG B

What had the Eighth Air Force accomplished in Operation Argument as its formations were mauled by German fighters over six February days? Had all those boys lost from the 445th died in vain? Hardly. Argument and its Big Week hit aviation facilities all over Germany, true, but the bloodbath over Gotha and other engagements that week had cost Galland's Luftwaffe eighteen percent of its remaining pilots. For the month of February, *Oberkommando der Luftwaffe* noted the loss of 456 fighter planes trying to beat back the American bomber stream. For every American aircraft downed, the Germans lost ten. The manufacture of German fighter aircraft would go on at a record pace, but who would fly them? They were running out of pilots.

On March 8, 1944, the 445th Bomb Group participated in an Eighth Air Force strike against the ball-bearing plant in Erkner, just southeast of Berlin. More than 300 Fortresses and 150 Liberators pounded Erkner while 33 B-24s peeled off and hit Berlin. The next day, the B-17s struck Berlin with purpose, 340 of them at the cost of 39 bombers and 390 fliers killed or missing.

This is what the men of the Eighth Air Force had been waiting for: missions to Berlin itself, "the Big B" as they all called it, because they knew that leveling Berlin gave them the best chance of being done and going home. These were the longest, toughest missions flying the farthest from Tibenham, way over on the eastern side of Germany, behind the best defenses. They welcomed that long red ribbon on the map in morning briefing, yes, and they dreaded it because of the sheer number of hours in the air, coupled with fighters and flak, all of which maximized odds they wouldn't make it back.

Major Stewart had been shaken by the mission to Fürth and didn't fly for more than two weeks. On March 15, nerves fraying, he sat in the copilot's seat to fly a Pathfinder B-24 leading the entire division of 154 aircraft on a strike against Mulenbau-V Industries in Brunswick.

On that mission he became furious with his pilot in ship number 634. He corrected Lt. Kirchenbauer constantly about air speed and rate of climb and would later grumble, "I can't see how precision equipment such as PFF is of any value in the hands of men who are not precision pilots."

Jim's nerves were shot and he was in no mood to be patient. Then, on the bomb run the sensitive Mickey equipment became unstable just as cloud cover obscured the target. Jim had to make an instantaneous decision—bomb blind through the clouds or climb, go around, and come in again hoping the equipment would work on a second try or the cloud cover would clear, yielding better bombing results.

Jim sweated a second and called off the run. The formation circled around, which he knew would expose 154 planes to the dangers of flak and enemy fighters. Sure enough, they saw a fixed barrage of predictor fire ahead and had to fly through it, but they dropped window and the fire became erratic.

Jim turned control of the aircraft over to his lead bombardier at 20,000, who sighted by range and deflection. Bombs away. The others toggled on Jim's ship, and they got out with unobserved results due to ten over ten cover. Despite pilot errors, do-overs, and course corrections mid-flight, it had been a clean mission, with no losses of planes in the 445th, and one in which he had showed mature piloting skills and mature command decisions, even as he knew he was hanging on by his fingernails. As the generals at Division had discussed: Stewart had been key to making the 445th a tightly run, successful outfit. But he didn't know and couldn't predict how long he would be able to hold onto his wits. He wasn't different from any of the others—all the pilots felt the cumulative effects of tough missions. It was just that some, like Neil Johnson and Bill Conley, handled it better. Was Jim's age the difference? Age gave him wisdom for command, but age was his enemy in the air for six or eight hours at a time, with bandits buzzing past his cockpit and through the formation.

One week later on March 22, here he was again, this time sitting left seat and piloting a wing lead Pathfinder toward aircraft manufacturing facilities at Oranienburg and Basdorf, Germany, due north of Berlin. His formation included many pilots who hadn't been the first-teamers of the 703 but now were called on to act like first-teamers. They were replacing guys who had been there from the beginning, like Kiser, Skjeie, and Abell, who had been shot down, and Torpey and Watson, who had gone flak happy. Now, the replacement crews who had been there since the first days in Tibenham stepped up, kids like Gil Schleichkorn from the Bronx. If you had to count on replacements, New York kids were the way to go.

Cloud cover was fierce today, and as the formation neared target, the bombardiers aboard his ship gave Stewart a grim forecast.

"This is pea soup," he heard from Leland Simpson, the lead bombardier. "We can't do anything through this." Yes, they were in a radar-equipped ship and Mickey should work in any undercast, but how do you hit a specific aircraft plant on a specific block from 21,000 feet with a layer of clouds in the way? Do you waste the bombs? Do you kill a bunch of civilians?

With 200 B-24s flying behind him, Jim considered his options.

He knew what the secondary target was: Berlin. He knew he might never get back, and there were 200 crews of ten behind him and some of them might never get back. One last look downward made the decision for him. "Switch to secondary target," he said into his throat mic.

Thinking inside all those planes changed in that instant, and the formation banked right and headed toward Big B. They were so close that in just five minutes Stewart heard in his headset, "Target ahead."

Jim looked out his window and again all was socked in, but Berlin was a general target, not a precision target, and their bomb loads might not take out German industry, but they would demoralize the population and correct Hitler, who had once assured the people of Germany that the Allies could never hit sacred Berlin. Jim knew the load they were carrying this day: incendiaries and high explosives. This mission would be remembered, no question.

Stewart yielded control to Simpson and sat back, and... Bang! Flak jostled the ship as it flew steady and level. Then more bursts and more concussed them over the heart of the city, metal bits rattling off the fuselage. A direct hit here sure would make headlines: Jimmy Stewart dies over German capital!

But here he was; he had made it, he was flying over Big B, and he wasn't a copilot this time. He was in command of his ship and if they got hit right now, he knew he had done his duty. Berlin had already taken a bite out of the 445th. Gil Schleichkorn had crash-landed a ship in England after battle damage flying here on March 9; Norm Menaker and his crew had been shot down here the same day.

"Bombs away," he heard from the nose. With flak bursting all around he felt his plane shudder upward as the bombs entrained out of their shackles in a rhythmic pattern, almost like music.

After a moment, the radioman signaled bombs clear. Jim toggled control back from Simpson and stayed on course, flying straight and level as briefed to allow all the incendiaries to be dropped at proper intervals for maximum effect. Behind his Pathfinder, 6,000 incendiaries let loose over Berlin and fell quietly to earth along with 636 general purpose 500 pounders. All punched through the cottony-gray cloud cover below.

Jim glanced at his watch: 1328. He began a long steady bank to starboard and headed due west. He eased back on the throttles to let the group rally behind him and radioed Simpson to get visual results.

"I see a couple of detonations and some fires burning, but that's all," Jim heard in his ear. "The pictures aren't going to be much help—cloud cover's eight over ten at least."

All the weather was below. Stewart looked about him at a sky clear and vividly blue to the left, the right, and above, with no enemy aircraft anywhere nearby. Finally, they flew beyond the flak of Berlin. He asked his crew if any ships had been hit and they replied negative, the group was intact. Who would have dared to think they could make a milk run to the Big B with barely a scratch to the entire formation?

But the strain continued to mount. Even the stress of switching from a primary to a secondary target was getting to him, and Colonel Terrill could see that Jim needed to miss another few turns as command pilot, maybe more. Stewart kept his thoughts to himself and didn't say he was flak happy; his gray complexion, inability to eat, and shakes said it for him. Terrill had to wonder how much Jim could keep flying at all after what he had been through, but it wasn't Terrill who would bring change into Major Stewart's life; it was another officer in a desperate command situation who would offer Jim a reprieve and keep him out of the flak farm, at least for a time.

37
NO-NONSENSE MEN

The 453rd Bomb Group at Old Buckenham, designated as Station 144, had been operational just six miles up the twisting roads from Tibenham since February 5. The 445th had benefited from luck and some early milk runs, but that same luck had eluded the 453rd. In mid-March, Col. Joe Miller, group commander, was shot down leading a mission to Friedrichshafen, Germany. Said Andy Low, assistant operations officer, "Colonel Miller had been with the group since its inception on June 29, 1943. He had watched and aided its growth from a fledgling organization into a full-grown, hard-hitting bombardment group. This was his fourth mission and his loss was an unexpected and hard blow."

Soon thereafter, Maj. Curtis Cofield, the group operations officer of the 453rd, went down in France. The loss of two air commanders in a month reinforced how dangerous the job was and how much harm to morale could be dealt, because now the 453rd was a ship without a rudder.

The 453rd hadn't been shot up more than the 445th down the road, but they had been shot up worse and lost their commanders. In fact, attrition had caught up fast with the battle-hardened, month-and-a-half surviving veterans of the 453rd; some were flak happy while a few others had run out of steam for a fight. To fill the leadership void, Lt. Col. Ramsay Douglas Potts, Jr., assumed command of the 453rd.

Potts hailed from Memphis, Tennessee, and earned his wings four days after Pearl Harbor at the age of twenty-five. Potts had been in on the ground floor of the Eighth Air Force, with a baptism of fire October 9, 1942, in a raid by his 93rd Bomb Group against the steelworks at Lille, France, that cost Potts his best friend and many other fliers in the group.

He had participated in the top-secret 1943 raid against the Nazi oil fields of Ploesti, Rumania, which resulted in the awarding of five Congressional Medals of Honor. Potts didn't receive one of the medals, but he had been proven to possess exceptional piloting and command skills.

A pilot in the 453rd, Lt. Bob Bieck, assessed the group's new C.O. by saying, "Potts was a no-nonsense man and his presence was felt at once. He was one of the most dynamic officers I have ever known. He was like a caged tiger chafing to be released."

In taking up his new post, Potts requested from headquarters of the Second Combat Wing a group operations officer to replace the late Major Cofield, and by a convergence of circumstances, the man chosen was Maj. James Stewart.

Jim's reputation now preceded him. He didn't always bring everybody home, but his numbers were extraordinarily good in a combat environment where losses were high and morale sometimes wobbled. His "luck" was based on precise flying and on smart decisions large and small, decisions that a man in his mid-thirties made more often than a younger, less-experienced lead pilot. And it didn't hurt that the major had been a success at the business of motion pictures, where he had dealt with executives of the caliber of Louis B. Mayer and Irving Thalberg—two of the major generals of Hollywood.

All that was on the one hand. On the other hand, Major Stewart had flown a dozen missions, most of them rugged, in three-and-a-half months. He took his new assignment to be a mixed blessing.

One of these days, his number would be up, especially when he began to second-guess himself in the air. He couldn't argue with Terrill that he needed to be spelled from duty as air commander. Maybe Jim had accomplished his goals too well. He had arrived in Tibenham as a combat officer, and he had flown his fair share of missions. He had taken on enormous responsibilities, the kind that usually fell on the shoulders of career West Pointers. He was a flier who had led a mission over Berlin, and it was after this one that he learned of his new assignment. But the move wasn't something to accept without some big thinking because he did not come to England to push papers as "Ops." He came to fly bombers in combat. He was an older guy and everyone looked up to him, but he knew his brains were scrambled at least a little bit and that could jeopardize the lives of the men behind him. He had seen too many fliers overextend themselves in his four months at Tibenham, and so after some soul searching, he decided he would go by the book now.

Then, there was the viewpoint of Second Division Bomber Command. If anything, the career of Stewart's MGM stablemate Clark Gable, a captain flying as a waist gunner in B-17s while making a combat documentary for Gen. Hap Arnold, had affected thinking about Stewart. It seemed pretty evident to all that Gable had a death wish ever since the passing of his wife, Carole Lombard, after Pearl Harbor. The army had no use for fliers who wanted to die, but Gable had managed to get in the air with such a publicity flourish that Adolf Hitler had put a bounty on the king's head. The situation gave the Air Corps a headache and got high command thinking about how wise it was for movie stars to fly over enemy territory. Movie stars didn't belong in the ETO—Stewart knew this was the prevailing sentiment and he had battled it all along.

Jim liked Clark Gable—who could do anything but? He was a down-to-earth guy with enormous magnetism. But from Jim's superiors he had learned what a genuine distraction Gable was because Gable knew he was the king of Hollywood and loved to play the part wearing an authentic U.S. Army-issue uniform. He had wined, dined, and led around an entourage of hangers-on, and the army had found it easy to ship him home after five combat missions to finish his documentary. Gable had earned a lot of press and gotten his photo republished many times, but he hadn't made a dent in the fight against fascism. Stewart, on the other hand, damn that Stewart, he possessed command abilities, and his men loved him.

To great heartbreak in the 445th Bomb Group, Major Stewart became the group operations officer of the 453rd at Old Buck. He had lived and died with the boys of the 445th at Tibenham, and they would never forget him.

Stewart reported to Colonel Potts at Station 144 on Friday, March 30, 1944, and settled in for a day before orders came down for the next mission to Ludwigshafen. Stewart spent the night digesting the orders as they came in and all the thousand details, and was able to speak in the morning briefing in his new role as Ops from firsthand knowledge of leading a formation over that particular target in central Germany, south of Frankfurt. Stewart remained on the ground as the 453rd put up a full contingent of ships to Ludwigshafen, and it was a good day: They all came back.

Weather grounded the group for a week, which allowed Potts and Stewart some time to get to know their new bunch. These men weren't hard cases; they had been in business six weeks less than the 445th and had cut their teeth on operations like Argument. The Luftwaffe had shot them up; flak had shot them down. Colonel Miller, their previous C.O., hadn't stressed training in tight formation flying, according to Lt. Ray Sears of the 734th Squadron, and here Jim could contribute right away because he excelled at it. A tight combat box and precision flying meant everything because it offered maximum protection against fighters and gave flak batteries on the ground a smaller target to hit.

At the beginning of April, Potts and Stewart used bad weather days over Europe for practice missions. "I made it my task to fly as soon as possible with the crews from each squadron," said Potts, "in order to assess their proficiency and to compliment them on their skills." Jim couldn't do a lot to tighten up formations in that amount of time, but he could certainly make his pilots aware of the need to keep their grouping tight, to stay sharp, and to follow procedure as briefed.

Around this time, Colonel Potts asked Capt. Starr Smith, S-2 of the 453rd Bomb Group, to serve as Jim's unofficial press officer. "This meant no publicity, no interviews, and no contact whatsoever with the hundreds of war correspondents eagerly seeking feature stories," said Smith. "The only way Jim felt he could continue to be effective as a combat officer was to keep the press completely at bay." It had worked so far; he would keep the streak going.

The second week of April, the war raged back. Stewart prepared the group for Brunswick on April 8, a brutal mission that cost seven ships and crews, and for Tutow and an attack on the Focke-Wulf 190 plant on April 9, which cost two more.

Tours on April 10, Oschersleben on April 11, and Zwickau on April 12 went better. Finally, Stewart flew his first mission as group commander with the 453rd on Friday the fourteenth of April, sitting behind pilot Lt. Orrie Warrington and copilot Maxie Seale as an observer in ship 210, *Heavenly Body*. The plane was the lead of eighteen sent from the 453rd to bomb the Dornier-Werke aircraft parts factory for the twin-engine Dornier Do 217 medium bomber along with a repair depot and airfield above Wessling, just west of Munich and by far the deepest penetration Stewart had made into Germany as a group commander. Background materials labeled the mission as "an aerial show intended for the benefit of Hitler and other German leaders in nearby Munich."

Stewart's 453rd led the Second Combat Wing, which flew with the 20th Wing. Jim had learned that just a day earlier, five ships of his old group, the 445th, had been lost when jumped by German fighters that had pursued them into Belgium. He hadn't seen the list of crews that had failed to return to Tibenham, but he knew it was bad, and he knew it would break his heart when he read the names.

Jim led his wing deep into the German heartland in a long, largely quiet passage with three course changes—all in keeping with the idea of a secret mission to bomb the target near Munich. After rallying south of Friedrichshafen at Lake Constance with the Alps looming high and deeply snow-covered off to starboard, the Second Combat Wing flew due east, south of the Ammersee, a large lake of blue waters. The highway just south of the village of Traubing was the I.P., and there they turned due north for the bomb run with two small lakes to their left and a larger lake and a railroad line to their right. It was beautiful how Intelligence gathered all this info from hundreds of miles off, back in England. The pilots knew just when the flak would kick up—and there it was, right on schedule. They had been briefed to be on the lookout for German fighters painted white and coming out of the formation's white contrails for sneak attacks.

Heavenly Body sailed ahead in skies briefly clear enough that they could see the anti-aircraft batteries firing on the ground below and count their guns by muzzle flash just off the end of the runway at the aircraft repair depot about to be bombed. The flak in front of them lay like a living carpet at about 20,000, just below their flight path, with occasional bursts snapping higher, up toward the formation.

"It wasn't just a small-box barrage like we had seen at other times," said Don Toye of the 445th, flying behind Stewart. "It was spread out in heavy concentration over at least a twenty-mile square," and flak bursts were "so close together it seemed I could step out and walk from one to another."

In the lead, Stewart heard chatter about a Liberator hit amidships by flak off to port and glanced out the window to watch a B-24 with pieces crumbling off just before it began cartwheeling down with fire flaming out of a wing. Another voice reported that the Lib had blown up after it was out of view of the cockpit, sobering for any air commander. Somebody reported seeing chutes, maybe two, maybe three, which was a miracle the way the ship had come apart. Jim touched his chest, as he always did at times like this. Yep, the little bundle was there, the letter and the psalm.

They pressed on, passing the small town of Wessling off to the left. Dead ahead lay the Dornier facility and fifteen miles beyond that, off to the right, Munich.

The flak continued to pound the formation long after Warrington, the pilot, had given the ship to Martin, the bombardier. About to pass under them was the southwest-to-northeast runway of the Dornier factory and aircraft facility. They had been briefed that the assembly building sat just east of the airfield and had dummy trees on the roof. Camouflage nets covered the aircraft shelters. Despite the concealment Jim could see the repair hangar, the designated mean point of impact dead ahead, sitting off the northern end of the field. He could see three dozen Do 217s parked at the northeast corner of the runway. S-2 said more than a hundred Do 217s in newly minted condition were supposed to be hidden in the wooded lands past the northeast corner of the airfield, along with two dozen or more Me 410s.

Stewart knew Martin would drop just short of the M.P.I. It was standard practice for the bombardiers to drop short knowing the few seconds' delay in the formation dropping on the lead plane would put those bombs right down the throat of the building, around the edge of the field where the planes were parked, and into the woods where all the 217s had been hidden.

"Bombs away," said Lt. Martin, and ten general-purpose bombs of 500 pounds each salvoed out of *Heavenly Body* with one loud click, sending it bucking higher in the sky.

"Bombs clear," Stewart heard in his ear, and he watched Warrington rush control of the ship back with a flick of the switch, and he and Seale muscled the yoke and banked right. Stewart grabbed the bulkhead against the Gs of the maneuver. Halfway into the turn he watched the payload plow up the runway in giant explosions before clouds and smoke blocked his view.

"Right down their throat," a voice said on the interphone. And then, "We got those planes by the runway."

Another voice said, "And a hangar."

"Hangar on fire," corrected a third voice.

"Don't get too excited," said an unidentified killjoy. "Some of our guys hit a field a mile off the runway. What the hell were they aiming at?"

"Shit," said someone.

"Eighth Agricultural Air Force," said another wise guy.

Warrington eased back on the throttles at the end of his turn for the wing to rally. They headed west-southwest back toward Lake Constance, and soon calls came in of Fw 190s attacking from five o'clock low. Chatter filled the air. Machine guns rattled the ship and German fighters swarmed through.

"Somebody's hit! Somebody's hit!" said a voice on the interphone. Jim strained to see out to port but couldn't make out anything and had to rely on the radio play-by-play. Where the hell are our fighters? he screamed in his own brain. He heard it was *Tenovus* that had been hit "bad between the waist and the tail," but she still had four engines turning. Then came a report an engine had caught fire and she dropped out of formation, and a few minutes later the tail gunner reported she had exploded. Damn, that had been a fine ship that had always got her crews home safe, Jim included. He allowed himself a quick moment to worry about Jack Farmer and Don Toye, the day's pilots in *Tenovus*, and to hope they got down safely with their crew.

Just then, the fighter screen of P-51s swooped into view and drove off the enemy over the town of Weingarten. Another B-24 was hit and had to peel off and head toward the safety of Switzerland, but other than that, the formation held together. Stewart wanted the ship number or pilot's name, and it was Lieutenant Dooley in 629. Jim had memorized the formation like he used to memorize dialogue at MGM. Dooley, from the triangle off Warrington's right wing in the high squadron. God speed, my friend. There were worse fates than landing a crippled Liberator in neutral Switzerland.

It remained like that through the trip back west, little friends above and around the Second Bomb Division, dogfighting their way through Germany and swatting away the Luftwaffe trying to cause trouble for the Liberators.

Stewart struggled out of the ship late in the day after more than nine hours in the air, feeling the usual frostbite and aches and pains of a long, tense flight and then stepping into the damp cold of East Anglia in what was supposed to be spring. Missions were no different here than in the 445th; yes they were, they were worse because he wasn't even able to sit in the copilot's seat. He was an observer now, with no control other than the issuance of a few orders. He was flying with strangers, men he couldn't yet rely on because he hadn't seen them in the worst of times. Meanwhile, he could only learn from a distance what went on with his boys back at Tibenham. He would reflect later that "all my efforts, all my prayers couldn't stand between them and their fates, and I grieved over them." But he knew they were dying for a cause, just as he was prepared to die for it. He could take hope, though, in what he saw in the air just today, with the Mustangs and Thunderbolts out-fighting those bandits. The Allied buildup in planes and pilots was adding up, and so was the damage to the German aircraft industry and the German flying corps. Success now depended on keeping the survivors focused on their jobs and getting them, and himself, home safe.

38
THE SUMATRAN

As a man on the run with the Dutch Underground, Clem Leone was never safe. He spent his time with various protectors who kept him fed and clothed and maintained his concealment, moving him every so often to a loft here, a basement there, transporting him in the backs of trucks ever south through the heart of Holland. He learned that his ship, *Wacky Donald*, had crashed near the village of Gramsbergen, and two of the crew were captured and taken to the larger town of Hardenberg. Apparently the home guard soldier who had captured Clem, the one jumped by civilians, was never heard from again.

The Dutch were helping other fliers too, Americans and British, along with Dutch military men on the run. Clem roomed in an attic with a Dutch officer who chose a life in hiding over conscription into the *Wehrmacht*, and then with a Tommy named Miller. It was a life adrift with great tension as the fugitives moved from place to place in civilian clothes, which made them eligible to be shot as spies. He never learned the names of the towns where he stopped to live for days or a week or two, and he never learned the identities of the people sheltering him. Or if he did learn names, they were false names in case he was captured and made to talk.

The Underground listened in to the BBC daily, to something called Radio Oranje, named after the Dutch royal family. The Allied broadcasts in Dutch provided news and commentary and an account of the war unavailable in German-occupied territories. After the broadcasts, the spirits of Leone's benefactors would rise, giving him hope.

How the Dutch despised the Germans, referring to them as "Moffen," from "Moffrica," the Dutch nickname for Germany and always spoken with derision. These were not a people who could be conquered, these Dutch. Occupied, perhaps, but not conquered. Some days Clem would stand with his Dutch friends and watch the American bomber stream fly east in the morning toward Germany, formations of hundreds of B-17s and B-24s. Leone would stare up and wonder how many of his friends were up there.

Clem kept moving and found himself in Amsterdam. By now he had acquired a false identity and papers, including a photograph, to account for his dark looks and lack of knowledge of the Dutch or German language. Suddenly, Clement Francis Leone of South Baltimore was portraying a deaf-mute bookkeeper from Sumatra. It was a sedentary existence for the fliers in hiding, yet physical fitness was vital to any plan aimed at returning an American aviator to England. To that end, Leone took walks around Amsterdam in the evenings. A member of the Underground would brief him on the route to travel and then remain a half block back so if one were to be captured, the other could flee. Clem walked right by German soldiers, careful to keep his gaze averted and his stride purposeful. "I walked along as if they weren't there," he said. And if he were stopped, he was prepared: "I had a routine of pointing to my ears and my mouth as if I couldn't speak and couldn't hear, and of course my papers bore this out."

Months passed as the Dutch Underground sought a safe route for downed Allied fliers south through Belgium and France, then across the Pyrenees into Spain. Finally, Leone was on the move, joining five other fliers on a cross-country trek. Mile by mile, they evaded border guards and slipped into Belgium, where waiting cars took the men in groups of two into Antwerp.

Leone was paired with Odell Hooper, Oklahoma native and engineer of the Liberator *Portland Anne* from the 453rd Bomb Group. Hooper's ship had been shot down March 8 on the first Berlin raid, and Odell had been on the run ever since. Now Leone and Hooper were spirited to a one-room, upper-floor apartment in Antwerp where they were cared for by a woman they knew only as Margaret. Then Margaret handed them off on a street corner to a friendly middle-aged man who took them into a dwelling as if to avoid attention. He lit a cigarette, offered them one, and began a conversation in excellent English, wanting to know how they had managed to get this far—where they had come from and who had helped them along the way.

Leone and Hooper stared silently at the stranger.

"Don't you trust me?" the man asked with a smile. "If you trust me, you'll confide in me. How do I know you're not German spies?"

"I trust everyone in the organization," said Leone. "I have to."

"Then tell me. I'm very curious."

Leone met the stranger's gaze. "I never want to know names," he said. "I haven't asked your name. I don't want to know your name or anyone's name. It's been the same everywhere I've been."

Hooper confirmed Leone's policy as the only way to survive in these circumstances.

The man stared at the Americans, threw down his cigarette, and stamped it out. "Come with me," he said and walked into the street. Leone and Hooper followed their new handler to a building with Luftwaffe guards in front. On sight of the man leading Clem and Odell, the guards snapped to attention. What could the fugitives do now? Run? They'd be shot within five steps.

Just inside the door of what turned out to be a busy military office, the suddenly unfriendly man said to a German officer at a desk in English so Leone would be sure to understand and as if also chastising the fools working under him who couldn't even apprehend downed Americans located right under their noses, "Here are two more." And that was that for the escape to Spain.

39
INVASIONITIS

The 453rd Bomb Group at Old Buckenham maintained a brutal schedule of missions through the balance of April, with Stewart endlessly on the ground preparing formations, briefing crews, then waiting out the day to count the returning ships.

He did what he could to get to know his new pilots and crews. One evening, after Jim had spent the late afternoon observing the crews giving their intelligence interrogation reports, he and Colonel Potts were sitting in the officers' club having a drink. In walked 2nd Lt. Matt Williams, looking like hell after a tough mission—a feeling Jim knew too well. Stewart called Williams over.

"You had a tough day?" asked Jim.

"Yes, sir, we did."

Jim motioned to a chair, not usual procedure for the base commanding officer and his group operations officer. "Sit down," said Stewart. "Let me buy you a drink and tell us about it."

The nervous Williams hesitated. "Sir, I've never *had* a drink." He watched the faces of his commanders, who exchanged a quizzical look—and Jim bought a round of Southern Comforts.

Jim realized that he had to bond with four squadrons of pilots more than a drink at a time. In a calculated act of restlessness to cement his place in his new bomb group, and to divert the attention of battle-weary pilots from their grim, nearly suicidal daily task,

Major Stewart and his assistant, Capt. Andy Low, finished their daily after-mission reports one afternoon and Stewart ordered Low to sign out a B-24. There were many ships that had been shot-up and refurbished and needed to be shaken down before returning to operational status. Stewart wanted to get in the air and used as an excuse a need to practice takeoffs and landings. As Low described it, "For staff pilots, who generally flew in the copilot's position of the lead aircraft during combat missions, getting to 'shoot some landings' was a welcome break."

Stewart and Low received from the crew chief a list of systems to check on the Liberator. They took off from the quiet field, remained at low altitude, and Stewart headed for his old station at Tibenham. With what Low described as a "wry smile," Stewart buzzed the tower at Tibenham repeatedly, waking Colonel Terrill from his daily after-mission nap and causing men to scamper out of the tower for the safety of the ground. He then took the ship back to Old Buck and conducted checks of its systems, practiced takeoffs and landings, and awaited the displeasure of Terrill and no doubt also that of Colonel Potts. The commanding officers did not disappoint. Stewart would later describe the incident as a lark, but an officer of his experience and responsibility did not take unnecessary risks that could result in the loss of a ship, either by mechanical failure or by being shot down by a Thunderbolt or Spitfire for unauthorized flight, since the enemy could easily send a Trojan horse B-24 back to England.

Behind closed doors, Jim likely informed Potts of finding a way to bond with his new set of pilots. Method to the madness is proven by the fact that no mention of the incident made his personnel file, although he would never ascribe serious motives to something that "we had thought was a grand idea." In fact, the buzzing of Tibenham tower was the only "war story" Stewart was willing to tell for the remainder of his life.

Maybe it was spring fever, which had broken out with a vengeance in East Anglia after the brutal winter of 1944. Now, more moderate temperatures reached as high as 25,000 feet over western Europe, which the crews of the 453rd Bomb Group learned first-hand as the ambient air in the Liberators no longer dipped to forty and fifty below, freezing the guns and permanently damaging flesh.

Spring brought a fresh decoration for Jim, a Distinguished Flying Cross in recognition of the February 20 mission to Brunswick that had kicked off Big Week. After the brief ceremony at Old Buck, Jim touched the cross-shaped gold propeller fob with its red, white, and blue ribbon and told a *Stars & Stripes* reporter, "I guess I'd best send it home. I'm very proud of it."

Jim still wouldn't work with reporters on personality pieces under any conditions. Those that got within 100 yards described "a dour, almost morose attitude" that accompanied every "no reporters" order he gave at the station. The same reporters noted that his attitude toward filmmaking was one of "divorcement." Said one, "Hollywood seems to have vanished from his consciousness."

The group's pilots had already grown to respect him. Capt. Franklin Webster said of Stewart to a reporter for the London *Daily Express*, "Now there is the hardest working guy on the Station. He sure takes his job seriously. He's at it fifteen hours a day." Webster speculated that Stewart would become a group commander before too long. "He's a good type," he concluded.

By May the missions of the 453rd were all in above-zero-Fahrenheit conditions and after a grim start, May grew into a decent month for the group. On a May 8 mission led by Captain Low to Brunswick, the group was jumped by an estimated 200 fighters and lost eight planes and crews, including two battle-damaged Liberators that collided in mid-air. Three more failed to make Old Buck and crash-landed at other bases. Then the bomb group lost another ship the next day over Belgium. But as the weather continued to improve, so did the mission results, with no more losses of planes or crews for the remainder of the month.

Under Colonel Potts, with an assist from Major Stewart, performance of the 453rd showed a steady improvement. Andy Low was able to report, "The bomb record of this group compares favorably with the efforts of much older and more experienced outfits in this theater. Indeed, at one point during the last two-month period, the 453rd led the entire Eighth Air Force in bomb hits on or near the target."

By now, as the lands became greener and flowers bloomed, everyone in the East Anglia bases focused on one word and one only: invasion—the long-anticipated mass landing of Allied troops on mainland Europe. The psychological condition, dubbed invasionitis, produced symptoms that included oversensitivity to words whispered out of earshot, jumpiness at each announcement on the Tannoy P.A. or each incoming teletype, and speculation about every directive and how it played into the overall plan.

Jim could tell invasion was coming, and soon, because the missions of the 453rd increasingly focused not on the German heartland but on tactical targets in France. The bombs were getting larger, thousand pounders and two-thousand pounders designed to obliterate railroad yards and subterranean rocket and infantry installations near the English Channel.

On May 15 Jim led eleven ships carrying 1,000-pound bombs on a mission to take out the under-construction V-1 rocket coast launch facility in the northern French village of Siracourt. On May 25 he led twenty-six ships toward the primary target of the marshalling yard in the city of Troyes, a mission that quickly went to hell. Instruments in the cockpit didn't match the briefed course, and Jim asked Lieutenant Clatfelter, the navigator, about the discrepancy over the interphone, saying they were ten degrees off course to the right. Clatfelter insisted they weren't, and Mandel, the bombardier down in the nose with Clatfelter, backed him up. Stewart knew they had missed Troyes because he could see it receding out the port window, just as he knew twenty-five planes were flying behind the leader on the wrong course. Ahead lay a town with a railroad yard that had drawn Mandel's attention. "Bombs away," he called, and twelve ships toggled on their leader, raining thirty tons of general-purpose bombs on, as intelligence interrogation reports later stated, the "center of the city" of Tonnerre, France, a civilian target that dated back to the thirteenth century. Horrified, Stewart radioed Captain Low, commanding the second squadron while flying as an observer in a ship piloted by Lieutenant Stokes. Jim asked if Low's navigator had a firm fix on their location. Low answered in the affirmative, and Stewart turned command of the mission over to Low, who had watched the disaster unfold. Low's own bombardier had released on the leader as briefed, even though he knew it to be the wrong target. Now, Low's ship took the lead and turned to starboard to head west, looking for military targets of opportunity over France for the thirteen ships that had not yet dropped bombs. Low settled on the large Luftwaffe airdrome at Brétigny-sur-Orge, just south of Paris.

By this time Stewart, still fuming in the now-trailing squadron, flew into heavy and accurate flak from the guns ringing Paris, and his pilot, Lieutenant Kolb, ordered the dropping of window, which disrupted enemy fire. Bombing on French civilians was a terrible result from what should have been a clean mission in good weather, and it reminded Stewart of the luxuries of life back in the 445th, flying with men he knew so well from all the training and missions that they could read one another's minds.

Back at Station 144 Stewart chastised Clatfelter and Mandel for allowing themselves to be disoriented and more than that, lost, which was inexcusable for the lead crew on a mission with so many others relying on them. But Jim also had to ask himself, should he have been faster to act? More forceful? Gone with his gut over his own navigator? Contacted Low sooner for a navigation check? Should Major Stewart have been a better formation leader on this mission? And the answer, of course, was yes to all. It was his greatest fear, the fear of failure as a commander on a mission.

For the public record, Low would cover for his boss, Major Stewart, when he wrote: "The first squadron flew past Troyes and bombed Tonnerre due to the interference of weather."

In a later meeting among air commanders, according to Beirne Lay, Jr., "Stewart took all the blame for the turkey at Troyes. No mission that Stewart ever flew did more to win the respect of his colleagues than the one mission on which he missed the target and refused to alibi about it."

On May 27 Jim in his role as group Ops prepped his pilots for a bombing mission against the marshalling yards at Saarbrucken, Germany, near the French border. Then, on successive days the 453rd hit German synthetic fuel refinery targets, first at Merseburg and then at Pölitz. By now the Eighth was targeting oil production because a war machine deprived of fuel at critical moments might not be able to move tanks and aircraft to the French beaches receiving the Allied invasion, wherever that might be—and the invasion target was still classified top secret. Imagine a flier being shot down with that information.

On May 30 Jim sent his group off against the Oldenburg Airdrome, an important base for Junkers 88 bombers. The next day they hit rail lines at Lumes, France.

Station 144 waited out June 1 in bad weather, nerves spun tight. June 2 they returned to the air to hit the Normandy shoreline at Saint–Aubin-sur-Mer, with significance that didn't go unnoticed. "For the first time in the history of the 453rd," wrote Captain Low, "the group had as its target, not an airfield, marshalling yard, or manufacturing plant, but a gun position in the Pas-de-Calais area. The four-gun emplacement was situated near Berck-sur-Mer and was the first tactical target the group ever attacked. The fact that it represented a switch from strategic to tactical bombing caused much speculation in the group."

The next day they flew against the airdrome at Berck, a French seaside town 120 miles north of Saint-Aubin-sur-Mer. Would the invasion center there instead? The case for Berck made more sense because the English coast was much closer at Berck than at Saint-Aubin-sur-Mer. The next day, June 4, the 453rd hit an important Luftwaffe airdrome in central France. Invasionitis was reaching a fever pitch, with cash laid down all over the base about where the landings would occur.

In the midst of a hectic schedule of daily operations, a wave of promotions swept through the Eighth as those lucky enough to come home from missions got rewarded. Lieutenant Colonel Potts received a promotion to full colonel on May 27. On June 3, Stewart traded in the gold oak leaves of a major for the silver leaf of a lieutenant colonel. A day later, Captain Low became Major Low. Even the promotions set off a wave of D-Day speculation.

All fell silent for those at Station 144 on June 5, two days into Jim's new rank, with morning weather keeping ships on the ground. Then, around 1300, orders came in to the Old Buckenham base—indeed, to all Eighth Air Force stations in East Anglia: all leaves cancelled. Shortly thereafter, another order: all telephone use suspended. A third order: all bases closed; nobody goes out, nobody comes in. And then, over the P.A. system: "Stand by, everyone alerted!" Adrenalin took invasionitis to new levels.

At 2000—eight at night—the order came down, "All combat crews check with Ops immediately, Waves number 1, 2, 3, 4, 5, and 6 of A Flight, briefing at 2300. B Flight, all waves, briefing at 0300. C Flight, all waves, briefing at 0400." Jim knew—they all knew—this was it, the invasion of Europe.

Coffee started brewing for the all-nighter to come as Potts, Stewart, and the rest of the staff unsealed orders and learned of their target: Normandy. They reviewed formations, crews, and ordnance. Stewart crammed crews, takeoff times, rally points, targets, map coordinates, compass headings, wind speeds, and other critical information into his head.

At 2315, guards locked the doors to the packed briefing room and roll was taken. Colonel Potts stepped up before the men with his jaw set tight. He held telegrams in hand and read a message from General Doolittle that began, "We are summoned to participate in a history-making invasion...."

From General Hodges, commander, Second Bomb Division: "The enemy defenses must be destroyed. The success of all men of all nations participating will be profoundly affected by our efforts. We must not fail them now."

Stewart told them that takeoff of the first wave of six ships would be 0327, and they would carry fifty-two anti-personnel bombs, 100 pounds each. Five waves would follow the first. Zero hour: 0628. Code word: Mairzy Doats. Goal of the 453rd would be complete destruction of the enemy forces' installation north of Saint–Laurent-sur-Mer. He smacked his pointer against a spot on the wall map at the coastline. Secondary target, any railroad, enemy troop concentration, or road junction farther inland. He stressed that precise timing would be of utmost importance.

The target of the first waves was described by Captain Crowley as a defended position 300 yards off shore, about ten miles northwest of Bayeux and one mile north of St. Laurent-sur-Mer. "The complement is probably forty men with machine guns, two-inch or three-inch mortars, and anti-tank guns. It is critical that we knock out this facility in support of the forces that will soon be landing." The crews were told to expect to see the greatest armada ever below them, poised to attack just off the beaches of Normandy.

They did not know as the clock clicked through the end of June 5 and into the beginning of June 6 that the point Crowley had just described, the beach due north of Saint Laurent, would sit in the American invasion sector and carry the code name Omaha.

The first wave lifted off into pea soup at 0327 as briefed, followed by thirty more ships from the 453rd, each carrying 5,200 pounds of anti-personnel bombs. Unrelenting undercast forced the first waves to bomb on instruments; fear of bombing the armada just off the coast made the bombardiers hold onto their loads an extra few seconds.

The crews returned to an interrogation that revealed their frustration. They couldn't see any armada. They couldn't see anything. They had bombed carefully and groped their way back to Old Buck.

As a result of weather, which had been problematic for the invasion all along, and which Eisenhower knew could lead to issues like this, the 453rd missed their target described as critical. Indeed, all the Second Division ships had missed their targets in the weather, setting up a brutal day for the American invasion force that would be pinned down by machine guns, mortars, and anti-tank guns on Omaha Beach.

But the invasion of Europe commenced. All those missions by the Eighth Air Force against military and industrial targets in Germany and its occupied territories, at the cost of hundreds of crews dead or kept as POWs and hundreds of crashed Liberators and Flying Fortresses littering Europe; all those dogfights that had punished the Liberators but had bloodied the bandits again and again had made invasion possible. Now, as troops splashed ashore at Normandy, the war entered a new phase, and Colonel Stewart would face his toughest challenges of all.

40
THEY ARE COMING!

For Riele Siepmann and her family, life went on in Eppstein; life in the middle of the war, in a place on the main air highway one stop before a famous attraction to the American Air Forces: Frankfurt. By now there was nothing left standing in Frankfurt's Old Town; the *Römer* and everything around it had been flattened, and it broke Riele's heart. There would never be happy times at the *Christkindlmarkt* again.

Many days, Riele's oldest, Gertrud, would lie on her back with her brother and sister, mesmerized, horrified, watching dogfights in the sky high above her. "That was always unbearably exciting and sickening," said Gertrud, "because we knew that it was a fight to the death." Some of the little planes had bulls-eyes on them (English), some had stars (American), and some had swastikas (German). She watched planes trail black smoke as they spiraled earthward, planes explode into fireballs, and pilots bail out. "You could see that tiny dark figure, suspended motionless beneath the serene white blossom of his parachute, floating down ever so slowly and gently—so terribly vulnerable!—and you wondered if that man was alive or dead or wounded. It didn't really matter if he was friend or foe; he was a human being in very big trouble."

It wasn't easy growing up in wartime. Noncombatants suffered so—ordinary Germans forced to ration everything. By this point in the war, with so many boys and men away and money so tight, children took on new responsibilities. For Gertrud, now age ten, that meant shopping duties in the tiny stores lining the narrow, cobblestone *Bergstrasse* of Eppstein. Off she would go with her little wooden wagon, a detailed list, a tin can for milk, netted bags for groceries, and the family's ration stamps, to the grocery, the bakery, and the butcher shop, and in each location she stood in a line that moved very slowly, populated by old people or mothers lugging young children.

One day there was a great deal of commotion, marked by motorcycle officials growling into town, the clanging bells of emergency vehicles, and the appearance of German soldiers. Gertrud overheard from townspeople that an American bomber had crash-landed outside Eppstein, and it seemed most of the people in town had gathered along the *Bergstrasse*. "They are coming! They are coming!" Gertrud heard. There was jostling and shouts from the policemen and soldiers. Then through the crowd, Gertrud saw men in brown outfits, cradling wounded arms, limping on wounded legs, staggering along the street. German soldiers with rifles prodded them along. Their faces were so young, so frightened and pale, and the people of Eppstein shouted, "*Terrorkrieger!*" and other hateful things and hurled rocks, and spat at them, and kicked. Nobody was going to split hairs about the Americans hitting strategic targets by day and the Brits fire-bombing to spread terror at night; they were all indiscriminate terrorists who had been victimizing Germany for years.

The dazed young men just kept stumbling up the road. Gertrud couldn't stand it; she ran home and cried her eyes out. It was a scene repeated throughout Germany at this point in the war: American fliers dropping from the sky to be gathered up by officials for questioning before a final stop at Stalag Luft I or Stalag Luft IV. This day alone, the day Gertrud saw the heartbreaking parade on the *Bergstrasse*, eighteen B-17s and two B-24s went down near Frankfurt.

By spring and summer the Eppstein *Bahnhof* attracted the attention of marauding P-47 fighter groups intent on disrupting German rail transport. The fighter pilots would see movement near the train tracks and descend for a look. "We could tell clearly when they started to dive because the pitch of their engines would change," said Gertrud. The first time this happened, the enemy pilots seemed to know they had spotted a group of children because they veered off and flew away toward other targets. The second time the children just had time to dive into the woods when the P-47s opened up with their .50-caliber machine guns and, as Gertrud described it, "stitched the road."

Another P-47 attack on a different day strafed the train carrying Gertrud's mother and brother, Franz, back to Eppstein from a doctor's appointment. Both were wounded in the attack and hospitalized—a piece of shrapnel had struck Franz in the head and penetrated his eardrum, barely missing his brain. Riele came home after a couple of days, Franz in a week. By this time there was talk that Eppstein would need to be defended against a ground assault by enemy troops, talk of a "last stand" at Eppstein. At that point beleaguered Riele Siepmann decided it was time to leave the spacious old house and head for Bavaria, where she hoped her family could find some semblance of peace.

41
GERMANY BURNING

Through the month of June 1944, Colonel Stewart worked within the walls of the Operations Control Room of the 453rd Bomb Group at Old Buckenham to process orders and keep B-24s in the air in daily missions to tactical targets in France, anywhere Allied invasion forces making their way inland from the Normandy beaches were encountering resistance.

By now the Eighth Air Force had reached full operational power, and beyond these tactical missions large strategic missions were aiming vast numbers of bombers at the heart of Germany, like the 1,400 pointed at Hamburg on June 18. With the British bombing civilian populations with incendiaries by night and the Americans following up on strategic targets by day, the results on Germany as a nation were cataclysmic. Bill Eagleson, a bombardier in the 453rd, remembered the view out his window on June 18: "You could see Germany burning. You could look to the south and you saw Brunswick and some of these other big cities were just tall columns of black, black smoke—just like a signal that said, 'Why? Why does this have to happen?'"

Once in a while, the news at Old Buck was good. At mid-month Jim drove a jeep to the hardstand of Nick Radosevich's ship *Lucky Penny* and watched it taxi in from a mission, park, and cut engines. As the crew exited the bomb bay, Stewart said, "This is it for you guys. You're all done." The *Lucky Penny* crew had survived thirty-two missions, two more than the now-required thirty because she had landed for refueling and made a second raid on D-Day and also taken part in a special, Spitfire-escorted lone B-24 raid to bomb a bridge near Paris just days earlier. Stewart and Radosevich went all the way back to Gowen Field together, and Jim found it rewarding that some of the pilots he had trained on heavies were beginning to complete their tours.

Jim continued on at Old Buckenham preparing crews of the 453rd for their missions until July 2, 1944, when he received a transfer "upstairs" to headquarters of the Second Combat Wing at Hethel Airfield, halfway between Old Buck and Norwich. His new assignment: Gen. Ted Timberlake's operations officer for the Second Combat Wing. Here Stewart coordinated the efforts of multiple bomb groups in these ever more complex and destructive missions over Germany.

Jim continued to fly missions himself when he could, his next on July 19 being a maximum-effort attack by more than 1,200 B-17s and B-24s on ten military targets in western and southwestern Germany. Stewart flew with a formation attacking the large Luftwaffe fighter base at Laupheim, resulting in destruction of a hangar and several parked aircraft as well as damage to the runways. By this point in the war, the fighters of Adolf Galland, General of the Fighter Arm, simply couldn't begin to address all the Eighth Air Force strike groups hitting so many targets at once. Post-mission intelligence reports labeled the Luftwaffe response on Stewart's July 19 mission as "extremely moderate," although the flak continued to be accurate and deadly.

More than a month later on September 27, Stewart was at headquarters in Hethel when reports started filtering in about trouble at the 445th involving a raid on a production facility in Kassel, north-central Germany. The Second Combat Wing was going after the fearsome SS weapon, the Tiger tank. It was maximum ef-

fort for the 445th; thirty-nine ships had started the day, which Jim
knew from preparing the paperwork meant that all available crews
had gone up from Tibenham. He gravitated to wing operations to
keep an eye on his old bomb group, and each report grew worse.
The formation had strayed off course in ten over ten undercast
despite being led by Pathfinders. Jim's blood chilled in his veins as
he learned that the formation, lost and without fighter protection,
had missed the mean point of impact by more than twenty miles,
dropped on farm fields, and been jumped by bandits far northeast
of Kassel. He thought about all those boys who had climbed inside
Liberators on the quiet fields of Tibenham that morning, those
runways he knew so well. He sweated out the hours until final reports had four ships making it back to Tibenham to meet four
more that had aborted. Some others had been shot full of holes but
had made it to friendly bases, but twenty-four ships of the 445th
had been shot down. It was a worst-case scenario of what could
occur in the air, and it could happen to anybody on any day, depending on weather, equipment, and human error. You just never
knew. How could a formation leader, as Jim had been and would
be again, not pore over the reports and try to make sense of what
had happened? But he didn't know; nobody at headquarters could
understand it. Jim sat there stunned, accepting the simple, unal-
terable fact that today, in the matter of an hour, the 445th that he
knew, that had been his life at Station 124 Tibenham until just a
few months ago, had ceased to exist.

Galland's fliers, such a menace to the bomber stream, must
be stopped, and in a number of ways: Deny him ships, deny him
pilots, deny him fuel. Stewart didn't fly again until October 15,
three weeks after the Kassel disaster, when he served as commander of seventy-three Liberators of the Second Wing in a raid on the
synthetic oil plant and power station at Reisholz, just southeast
of Dusseldorf. Oil and gasoline had grown so scarce in the Reich
that synthetic oil production had become crucial to the German

286

high command—it was all they had to keep their fighters and tanks operational. So that's what the Mighty Eighth went after, hitting Reisholz hard as part of a larger operation that targeted Cologne, Monheim, Dormagen, and Limburg.

Because of the notoriously deadly anti-aircraft batteries in the Ruhr valley, known for two years now as "Flak Valley," the wing would try a new tactic, attacking in six-ship sections that gave flak batteries dispersed targets to try to hit. "Colonel Arnold stated in the field order that the six-ship sections would fly in a heterogeneous mass," Stewart said in a meeting after the mission, "which is exactly what it was and which I think is good. I felt that the small units were able to avoid prop wash without moving out of the bomber stream or crowding other units near to them."

Stewart then provided a vivid eyewitness description of the bomb run on Reisholz using the wing's new tactic and of the variables at play in any mission:

"At the I.P. the visual code word was given and primary flares were fired. From then on our Mickey set faded and we drifted south of briefed course. By the time the bombardier picked up the target, he had to make a large correction to the left in order to get on it. This trailed out the whole formation, and for that reason I feel that it was not a fair test of the possibilities of bombing from six-ship sections; our bombing was only fair. Several of the sections reported violent prop wash a very short time before bombs away which, of course, is one disadvantage of many small units converging on one M.P.I. to bomb."

Despite the testing of this radical new procedure, results listed for Reisholz in the after-action report showed "hits on factory buildings, railroads and built-up area of target, power station, [and] oil storage tanks."

On November 30 Stewart, flying in a Pathfinder at the front of the 389th Bomb Group, led sixty-six ships in six squadrons of the Second Division on a mission against the marshalling yards at

Homburg in western Germany. All went well generally, although Stewart reported afterward that a formation of B-17s had cut across their path at the I.P., making evasive action necessary. All planes then dropped general-purpose and incendiary bombs on the rail yards at Homburg by Mickey in heavy undercast that made photos and visual observation impossible. Although Stewart saw no enemy fighters through the course of the mission and reported flak as "meager," two ships, both belonging to the reconstituted 445th, failed to return.

The stress of missions continued to accumulate for Jim, his health fragile because of an inability to keep food down. A childhood friend said, "He just couldn't eat he was so upset by everything." She quoted Stewart as saying ice cream and peanut butter were getting him through the war.

Winter again closed its fist on England and Europe, and fliers spent days at a time grounded. The veterans of the Second Combat Wing remembered the previous winter all too well, although not flying now didn't seem to matter quite so much because German ground forces were retreating on all fronts and the Luftwaffe had been pummeled through the course of 1944, with aircraft manufacturing hit hard from Big Week on. During one of those frequent spells of bad weather, with the Eighth Air Force and its fighters grounded, three German armies, including feared SS Panzer divisions, attacked the Allies in the Ardennes Forest of Belgium, punching a hole fifty miles deep through American and British lines. The battle raged for two weeks until fortunes changed thanks to the Eighth Air Force. First, the weather improved, allowing the Thunderbolts to head skyward to harass German columns; second, the concerted effort by the Mighty Eighth to knock out Germany's petroleum industry, including its production of synthetic fuels, had left German tanks abandoned at the side of the road; they had simply run out of gas, as did the entire German offensive known as the Battle of the Bulge. It was the Führer's last major offensive of the war.

That same month Jim Stewart received the silver eagles of a full colonel. He continued to function as chief of staff for the Second Combat Wing and managed to get back in the air February 27, 1945, when he flew in a Pathfinder in front of more than eighty B-24s attacking the marshalling yards at Halle, southwest of Berlin. The mission was flown as briefed, with minimal flak and no enemy fighters.

It seemed as if the Eighth owned the skies as winter was about to yield to spring 1945 with only one wild card left for the Luftwaffe and a lethal one: the Me 262, Hitler's jet airplane that had on notable occasions sliced and diced the bomber stream, zipping past lumbering American four-engine ships and even the fighter escort with such ease that the Allied planes seemed to be standing still. Nobody took a mission over the Fatherland for granted, not even now as the ground forces of Soviet Gen. Georgy Zhukov closed in on Berlin.

42
THE GREAT AVIATION

Dolfo Galland was a military pilot; it was all he had wanted to be since his teenage years. "I had no gift for diplomacy and hiding my true opinion," he reflected later without apology. He knew nothing about politics and scheming and backstabbing, but that's the world he was playing in as he toiled too close to German high command and treachery surrounded him, dangers much worse than anything he faced at 20,000 feet.

Dolfo was also a pragmatist. He knew that the Eighth Air Force was killing Germany. "All Germans had experienced this during the last years of the war," he said, "in the cities, in the factories, on the battlefield, on ships and U-boats: Bombs, Bombs, Bombs!"

Reichsminister Albert Speer, Hitler's chief of armaments and war production, was one like Galland who could see the plain truth: "The real importance of the air war consisted in the fact that it opened a second front long before the invasion of Europe," said Speer. "That front was the skies over Germany. The fleets of bombers might appear at any time over any large German city or important factory. The unpredictability of the attacks made this front gigantic; every square meter of the territory we controlled was a kind of front line."

The only thing that could save Germany was a secret weapon. Rumors flew everywhere of such an invention, although no one knew what it might be. Galland did know. From the first instant he had flown in an Me 262 fighter powered by two turbo-jet engines, he knew, felt in his bones, that this plane would win the war for his native land. With this the Luftwaffe would blow the Americans out of the sky, and no more bombs, bombs, bombs.

But Hitler wouldn't let Galland have his jet planes, even with a strong Allied ground push off the Normandy beaches, even with the daily pounding of Germany's aircraft industry, German airdromes, and the German oil industry by the Eighth Air Force. With targeting by those damned bombers, German oil production that had been at 175,000 tons in April 1944 had been cut to 55,000 tons by June, and 7,000 tons just a few months later. In addition to all the other problems faced by Galland's workhorses, the Bf 109 and Fw 190 fighters, lack of fuel rated among the worst. It was getting so bad that ships ran out of gas and were forced to land in remote strips in France or Belgium and just sit there without any hope of refueling for further action.

So badly had things turned that finally the Führer saw the light and allowed some Me 262s to filter down to Galland, who had recently been forced out of his position as General of the Fighter Arm. Now, he was just what he wanted to be: a jet fighter group commander who could do real damage to the Eighth Air Force.

At Achmer, a spot outside Osnabrück in western Germany near the Dutch border, Galland set up the first airdrome supporting his new jet fighter wing, designated JG 7. Then Galland formed a second active jet fighter group, JV 44, stationed in southern Germany at Munich-Riem and composed of the cream of the crop of German pilots, with Galland himself flying lead. His blood stirred, he said, "The magic word 'jet' had brought us together to experience once more *die grosse Fliegerei*," or the great aviation.

Despite fewer than 200 operational jets at any one time, with numbers dwindling due to bombing raids and fuel shortages, Galland brought his considerable tactical experience to bear against the swarms of Eighth Air Force bombers and their impenetrable fighter screens. Then, on March 18, 1945, wrote Galland, magic happened over Berlin thanks to "the jet fighters of the JG 7.... The Me 262 broke again and again with ease through the American fighter screen and shot down one bomber after the other from the tightly closed formations despite an inferiority of one hundred to one. Besides those shot down by flak, the Americans had to report a loss of twenty-five bombers and five fighter planes."

All across Germany the besieged population had been counting on the rumored "secret weapon" that would save the nation. Gertrud Siepmann's father, Hans, the naval engineer, sat with a group of Luftwaffe officers on a train at this time. "A Luftwaffen lieutenant said that there was indeed a secret weapon, but whether it was ready or not?" wrote Siepmann in his diary. "It must happen very soon or it will be too late."

Said Galland, "Doolittle and Tedder now demanded decisive measures to prevent the operation of German jet fighters." Both Doolittle and Arthur William Tedder, Marshal of the Royal Air Force, understood the threat posed by the Me 262 and would not underestimate it. Another couple of air battles like Berlin could change the war, even at this late hour. So indeed they demanded decisive measures, which put Col. James Stewart back in the air, three days after Galland's jets had sliced through Doolittle's formation with such horrific ease.

43
GROUNDED

On March 21, almost a year to the day since he had flown over
Big B, Colonel Stewart climbed into the bomb bay of a B-24 one
last time, with zero hour at 0800. Did he know it would be his
last mission? Probably he did because of the infrequency of his
own flying and the proximity of the end of the war—Germany was
crumbling figuratively and literally after the total air war waged by
the RAF and the Army Air Forces. On that day Jim served as Second Wing air commander in one of 1,400 Eighth Air Force ships
attacking ten airfields inside Germany.

The target for the Second Wing and the Second Division: a
seemingly nondescript airdrome that had been hit before, next to
the village of Achmer close to Germany's border with Holland. At
Achmer, said Intelligence, the large open grass field was an optical
illusion and really composed of three separate concrete runways
painted green. Under camouflaged shelters next to the runways sat
a full complement of Me 262 jet fighters that had lately been dealing death to flights of the Eighth. The Allies would admit to 200 of
its planes shot down in the latter part of the war by Luftwaffe jets;
the Germans claimed more than 700. Somewhere in between lay
a true number that represented too many dead fliers and too many
lost ships. The only practical way to destroy a 262 was to catch
it on the ground. Stewart's mission was quite simply to lead thir-

ty-one Libs from the 389th, forty from the 445th, and forty-three from the 453rd, covered by two squadrons of P-51s, to clobber the airfield at Achmer with 5,000 fragmentation and general-purpose bombs, rendering it unserviceable. Fragging was aimed at taking out flak batteries to soften up the target for the coup de grâce. Upon completion of the bomb run, Stewart was to give the code word, "Chow's On," at which point the P-51s would swoop in and strafe what remained.

Ironically, Stewart enjoyed his best weather of all on this, the last day of combat leadership in a B-24. Pilots could never even imagine such weather—from the time he went wheels-up at 0620 with the 389th Bomb Group in Hethel to the time he reached the target at 0945 flying at 21,500, he looked at solid CAVU flying conditions, with just a little haze to give the panorama an ethereal glow.

Jim was mindful of the hornet's nest he was after. Stirring it up meant trouble if those 262s got off the ground and swarmed the heavies in his formation. In a matter of five minutes he could be facing a slaughter.

On this fine day for flying, little things were going wrong. Approaching the I.P. they ran into a straggling group of B-24s and had to "S" to stay out of the way, causing Stewart's formation to miss the I.P. by two miles. Flak started coming up, well-aimed flak, and Stewart ordered the formation to try to compensate for missing the I.P.; his code word "Black Sheep" signaled waist gunners to throw out window, four units every ten seconds, to knock enemy radar off-kilter and disrupt the flak. But those two miles caused a problem, which Jim knew from the radio chatter breaking out all around, signaling sudden confusion. He had been careful to keep the formation tight, so what was going wrong?

The 453rd had seen the "S"ing by the 389 and they tried to compensate as well, but they found Stewart's airspeed in the lead too erratic. Now they were too close and got caught in prop wash from the 389 as the 453's planes were overrunning the lead group—on a collision course.

At the front of the 389 in Stewart's Pathfinder, all was well in calm skies. The bombardier called, "Bombs away," and the load of 100-pound general-purpose bombs entrained out.

Up to this moment their bomb run had been clean and the other thirty ships of the 389th had dropped on the lead. But with about two seconds to spare from the last bomb leaving the last ship, Lt. Anderson at the controls increased airspeed and banked right to get the 389th the hell out of the way of the other groups. Behind them, the 445th was running into the 453rd. The bombs of the 389 were smashing the target, but the other two confused groups dropped on roads, woods, and of course, farm fields—an encore for the Eighth Agricultural Air Force. Now 114 B-24s from the three groups tried to restore order all over the sky, overshooting the rally point and straying into Osnabrück airspace seven miles southeast of the airdrome, a flak field they had been briefed to avoid. Flak began crackling around them again, and Jim directed traffic to get the formation in order for the flight home. Thank God these were veteran pilots who had seen it all and knew the definition of snafu and that, even in clear skies with no enemy aircraft attacking, they still faced plenty of danger.

Colonel Stewart returned to Hethel and stepped out of the bomb bay a shaken man. Every plane from all three groups had made it back safely—how, he couldn't imagine. In his time in England, he had witnessed several midair collisions on takeoffs from East Anglia bases. But three bomb groups almost going up in a giant fireball over Achmer, Germany, while Jim was leading? That was too much to contemplate.

Jim had the shakes. It was one mission too many, a failure of a mission in his eyes even though they had smashed the target. Before the end of the day, he and his crew had received a commendation on behalf of the 389th because of the smashing. He wanted nothing to do with this one. It read:

"On this 21st day of March 1945 the members of the following crew of the 389th Bombardment Group, leading the 2nd Combat Wing, are awarded this token for their meritorious achievement in the destruction of the target at Achmer A/F, Germany: Pilot Lt. H.V. Anderson; Copilot Lt. H.D. Benton; Navigator Lt. J.B. Campbell; Bombardier Lt. A.L. Larrance; Radio operator T/Sgt. W.T. Mahoney; Gunner S/Sgt. A.F. Petruccione; Gunner S/Sgt. J.A. Overton; Gunner S/Sgt. F.M. Corbett; Gunner S/Sgt. O. Walls; Pilot Navigator Lt. B.E. Purdom; H2X Navigator Lt. G.P. Rolley; and Command Pilot and Copilot Col. J.M. Stewart."

General Arnold noticed the effect of the mission on Stewart, the cumulative effect of all the missions Stewart had flown or sent others to go fly. "It wasn't ever official," said Arnold, "but I just told him I didn't want him to fly any more combat. He didn't argue about it." Jim went a step further and vowed he would never pilot an airplane again, quite a statement for a man born to do it and evidence of the devastating effects of war on his psyche. He was now an earthbound former Hollywood star, a man wrung out by the rigors of war and a man facing what was, in many ways, a terrifying future.

44
MARCHING TO DEATH

Clem Leone might have died in the plane crash that killed Lieutenant Hansen December 29 of '43. By all rights Leone should have died when he hung in the slipstream at 20,000 feet by holding on to the top turret guns of *Wacky Donald* as she exploded over Gotha on February 24 of '44. He figured he would die when he was turned over to the Luftwaffe in civilian clothes in Antwerp in June. "I don't know why they didn't take me out and shoot me," he said later with a shrug, "but there was a code between the Luftwaffe and the American fliers."

"For you the war is over, my friend," had said the Luftwaffe officer who took Leone and Hooper prisoner. His first night, Clem contracted lice and took them to Stalag Luft IV in German Pomerania on the Baltic Sea. There he joined more than 6,000 other lice-infested American and RAF noncoms who had been shot down over the Continent, including waist gunner Lugan Hickey of the Blomberg crew; Leone was sure Hickey had died aboard *Wacky Donald*, but Hickey told the story of taking a round in his knee, snapping on his chute with fire raging around him, and jumping out the waist gun port.

As summer gave way to autumn and then winter, with the bombing missions continuing, and flak and fighters going up and Allied parachutes coming down, the POW population of Stalag Luft IV swelled to 10,000, almost twice the capacity of the camp.

Everyone knew the Russians were pressing in on the east; they did not know that the Führer had issued an order to the commandants of all the POW camps: Execute the prisoners. Hitler envisioned an army of suddenly liberated Allied POWs picking up arms and joining the Russian attack on the Fatherland. There it was, another death sentence for Technical Sergeant Leone. But the commandants knew better than to leave a trail of thousands of bodies behind them, because Germany was about to lose the war, and the last thing they wanted was capture and execution by the Russians. On February 6, 1945, Oberstleutnant Aribert Bombach, commandant of Stalag Luft IV, took the only course of action open to him. He ordered all prisoners: "Take all you can carry; we are evacuating the camp!"

West they marched, away from the Russians, through deep snow in subzero weather, day after day, the lice thriving on emaciated bodies. Men died by the score. February became March and the death column moved on. Typhus, diphtheria, and pneumonia broke out. Dysentery hit everyone, and the five American doctors on the march fed the men charcoal remnants from their campfires to try to keep the dysentery at bay. It helped a little; mostly the men soiled their clothes and walked on. Frostbite forced the doctors to amputate extremities by night with little in the way of medicine. For food, the POWs scavenged potato piles and robbed henhouses.

When the column found a barn, those lucky enough to be first in would sleep on fresh straw. The majority would settle into old straw and manure. "If you've ever slept in straw with manure," said Leone, "your whole body gets this clammy sweat, and the lice love it. They start running over your stomach, over your body, and you're itching and sweating. It's something you don't want to experience."

Strong prisoners carried the weak. Anything edible was shared. When possible, the Germans provided carts for those too feeble to walk. The commandant had promised that a medical wagon was bringing up the rear to pick up anyone who fell out of line along the way, but prisoners quickly learned the truth: When a POW collapsed, a guard would drop back and, according to a report, "You would hear a shot and the guard would come back into the formation alone."

The German guards, most of them old men not fit for frontline duty, suffered as badly as the POWs, with only one difference—the guards had rations. The column pressed into the heart of Germany. "The war was coming to an end," said Leone. "The people had been bombed pretty bad—I can understand their feelings—but the German guards were so old and so weak that we would carry their weapons in between towns, and then when we approached a town, we'd hand them their weapons so they could protect us from civilians as we marched through the streets."

April arrived. The more enterprising POWs slipped away to join the advancing Allies but most, including Leone, found strength in numbers and marched on, with Oberstleutnant Bombach still in command and dodging the Russians at every turn. The column had started out marching west, then southwest, then south, then jogged east, then doubled back west again—more than 600 miles in three months. By the second week of April they had entered Belgium. No one knew by then how many had died along the way, but it was hundreds. The men were emaciated—Clem's weight had fallen below one hundred pounds.

Winter, one of the coldest in German memory, had just begun to relent. One night the men encamped in a field. They built fires as normal and huddled in groups of three under one blanket for body warmth, as normal. When they awoke the next morning, "No Germans anywhere," said Leone. "We wondered, 'What the heck is going on?'"

Through hazy eyes they watched a British truck drive up with one of the elderly German guards in the passenger seat. "Good morning, chaps," said the driver brightly. "Your guards have all surrendered to Her Majesty's Forces. If you would like to follow along behind, we'll lead you in the proper direction."

For Leone and thousands of his flier comrades, those who had gone off in the morning on missions from East Anglia and other bases across England never to return, the war was finally over.

45
AGED IN EAST ANGLIA

"As the war was winding down," said Capt. Starr Smith of the 453rd Bomb Group, "Col. Jimmy Stewart came more often down to London from Hethel, putting up at the Savoy, going to the theatre, and entertaining friends at the hotel." The Savoy, an Edwardian bastion on the River Thames in the heart of London's cultural district, offered Jim not only luxury accommodations but insulation from the press and public as he began to come to grips with sixteen months of combat.

For those who had not been shot down and become a host for lice, the end of the war brought relief from flying missions and, in Jim's case, the obligations of sending formations into harm's way. But he didn't enjoy real relief from the stress that kept food from digesting while sleep remained elusive; when sleep did come, nightmares came with it. Whether a soldier holed up at the Savoy with plenty of food and fine sheets or pilfered potatoes in rural Germany and slept with lice, the missions remained the missions and there was no escaping those memories.

In March and April, gates had opened in POW camps across all German-held territories, and detainees of Jim's old 445th Bomb Group began filtering back in the direction of Tibenham. Lt. Barry Shillito of *Pissed Off*, one of the disaffected group of former fighter pilots, hopped a ride to Hethel to find Colonel Stewart there;

Shillito was shocked at the change in his old squadron commander. Stewart was gray of face, with bags under his eyes and a furrowed brow. His full head of hair had begun to recede and was half silver. Jim had grown so thin that the skin hung from his neck. It was almost as if Jim Stewart had been imprisoned like the others. "He went flak happy there for a while," said Shillito. "He wasn't flying anymore, and he was quieter than I remembered."

Stewart did not serve as air commander after the Achmer mission of March 21. By the middle of April, spring in England and Europe, the strategic war had been won and the Eighth Air Force ceased all combat operations. There simply weren't any more targets to hit; Germany had been flattened largely by the RAF's indiscriminate carpet-bombing campaign that had grown so brutal even Churchill said toward the end of March: "It seems to me that the moment has come when the question of bombing of German cities simply for the sake of increasing the terror, though under other pretexts, should be reviewed. Otherwise we shall come into control of an utterly ruined land." But it was too late; Marshal of the Royal Air Force Sir Arthur Travers Harris, known as "Bomber" Harris or even within his own hierarchy as "Butcher" Harris, had overseen the annihilation of entire German population centers with years of nighttime incendiary bombings.

With nothing left to bomb, the air war became a ground war, with Allied and Russian armies closing in on Berlin to complete the total destruction of Germany. Hitler committed suicide the last day of April, and on May 7, 1945, the war in Europe ended.

On May 10, General Timberlake became the Second Bomb Division chief of staff, and Colonel Stewart rose to command of the Second Combat Wing. There were no more missions to fly, true enough, but the soldier who had risen through the ranks from that first morning on an L.A. street corner felt enormous pride in beating the odds, making his way to the European Theater of Operations, and completing twenty missions as the grand old man of the 445th and 453rd. This final promotion to wing commander served as recognition of a job well done and of the saving of lives. A commendation recognized Stewart's job through the course of his career in the ETO, from squadron commander to group operations officer to wing executive officer to wing commander:

"Throughout the time you have been associated with this Command you have displayed the most intense loyalty and patriotism as evidenced by your own participation on important combat missions and encounters with the enemy in addition to your staff work. Your initiative, sound judgment, personality, and sincere devotion to duty has contributed immeasurably to the smooth operation of this Headquarters and the morale and efficiency of the men of this entire Command."

In all he received the Air Medal with three oak leaf clusters, plus Distinguished Flying Crosses for the Ludwigshafen mission, when he covered the group on the wrong heading, and the Bremen mission that began Big Week. As with all American fliers participating in the air war over Europe, he received the Croix de Guerre with bronze palm from the French Air Force and a second as an alumnus of the 445th. For Stewart the decorations didn't matter; the experience did. "I met the most wonderful assortment of guys you'd ever want to know during those four years in the service. I came to know what went on in their minds and hearts, I shared their hopes and fears and privations as an enlisted man, and I tried with all my might to lead and protect them when I became an officer."

At the beginning of June 1945, Jim served as presiding officer in the court-martial of a Liberator pilot and copilot who led a mission that involved the inadvertent bombing of Zurich, Switzerland, by six B-24s on March 4, 1945. The circumstances were all too familiar to Jim—bad weather, inoperative Mickey equipment, and misidentification of terrain by the lead navigator who was convinced he was over Freiberg, Germany, as the formation looked

302

for a target of opportunity. The navigator even compared wooded terrain, marshalling yards, and a stream with an aerial photo of Freiberg to confirm he had the right target. The pilot asked him if he was certain; the navigator said he was. The court-martial took place at Second Air Division Headquarters at Horsham St. Faith, just north of Norwich, and on June 2 the jury of twelve officers found both pilots not guilty.

Otherwise, the new Second Combat Wing commander faced only logistical challenges; mainly, how to transition 9,000 men of the 389th, 445th, and 453rd Bomb Groups home. It took him the summer months to do it, and while at Hethel he learned of the dropping of atom bombs on Japan and, on August 14, that Japan had surrendered. The most terrible war in the history of humanity had come to an end.

Finally, on August 27 he boarded the British liner *Queen Elizabeth* with many of his Second Combat Wing comrades as part of a contingent of 14,860 returning servicemen for the five-day trip to New York City.

On Friday, August 31, a great clamor aboard ship announced sighting of the Statue of Liberty from open ocean. The men had seen such hardship, lost so many friends, changed so much inside, that tears flowed freely and splashed into the brine.

Two hours later, the first face Jim beheld on the North American continent, aside from that of Lady Liberty, belonged to forty-three-year-old weather-beaten Leland Hayward: "I'll never forget," said Jim, "he was standing at the bottom of the gangplank with a bunch of red roses. How he got onto the pier, I don't know—absolute top secret, no one was allowed…."

Hayward tried to lead Jim away from the *Queen Elizabeth* as newspaper reporters swarmed them. Stewart ran their gauntlet with many variations of, "I have no plans; I'm just happy to be home." In truth, the passage from England hadn't allowed him room to even sit down a lot of the time, but it gave him room to think about the army he loved and the movie stardom that had given him a comfortable life. Simply put, he couldn't imagine life in a peacetime air force, settling into a routine of drudgery. He was still Jim Stewart, the guy who so easily grew bored; for the past four years he had been flying, teaching, training, planning, fighting, commanding—something different each day, a different mission to prepare for or to lead and different challenges to face. In the North Atlantic he had decided to leave the service; he planned to announce it to his parents that evening. Confetti and silver balloons rained down from the upper decks of the ship, and the bands of Cab Calloway and Sammy Kaye serenaded from the dock. Jim told Leland he wanted to hang around the ship before heading to the St. Regis Hotel where Alex and Bessie anxiously awaited his arrival. "Wait a few minutes," said Jim. "I want to stay until a few of my boys come ashore."

The few minutes turned into hours as he identified men he knew and received their salutes when they stepped off the ship. "I just wanted to savor every moment," said Jim, "so I decided to see everyone else off the ship first.... There's this expression of living in the moment. I didn't want the moment to end."

Jim was staring down the barrel of an uncertain future, and as he looked into each face, so happy and so triumphant now, he had to wonder what lay ahead for these fellas after all they had seen and done, all the friends they had lost, the death they had dealt or witnessed, some of them POWs, and God only knew what they had experienced in captivity. Now, here they were, dispersing into a world without flak or fighters, but full of younger, fresher, better-clothed men who had stepped into their pre-war world and taken their jobs and in some cases their girls. They would be facing families who had become strangers; people who could never relate or understand. And those nightmares and shakes and the need to dull the pain of horrors witnessed or friends lost or simply the accumulation of stress that ground a soul down to nothing—each salute exchanged both ways carried the meaning of all that had come before, and all that lay ahead.

When Jim finally walked away from the *Queen Elizabeth*, he could take satisfaction in having overcome incredible odds to participate in the war effort on his terms, overseas, in combat, not getting a taste of war and then bowing out, but fighting a sustained war on two fronts, against the Axis and against the press, bombing the former and beating away the latter; only on rare occasions did they get nearly as close as they had on induction day and never in such great numbers.

After Stewart reported in at the processing center at Camp Kilmer, New Jersey, to obtain a thirty-day leave, he and Hayward proceeded to the St. Regis, where Alex and Bessie laid eyes on their son for the first time in two years. They were shocked by what they saw—their boy had aged what seemed two decades. He was now a decorated war hero, a full colonel with silver eagles on his shoulders and a command authority that made Alex uneasy. It still meant everything to please Dad, even for a bird colonel weighed down with hardware on his chest, and Dad still wanted to be pleased. He would always want that.

On Saturday, September 1, Jim was required to attend a press conference at the office of Maj. Gen. Clarence Kells in Brooklyn. Questions from reporters focused on the resumption of Stewart's motion-picture career, and Jim said he would like to return to Hollywood and make some comedies. "Why comedy?" he was asked. He replied that the world had seen enough drama and needed some relief from it. One reporter wrote of the eyewitness encounter that Stewart was "a bit gray after four-and-a-half years in the army, and thinner than when he won the Academy Award in 1940."

After the press conference Leland Hayward drove Jim to Connecticut, where Maggie treated her old friend to a fried chicken dinner and all the Hollywood gossip he could handle. He was already thinking about the likelihood of a return to motion picture work and honestly didn't know if he would be welcomed back. It was easy to compare Jim to fellow MGM star and warrior Robert Montgomery, who had been home for nearly a year after joining the navy and serving in Europe. Montgomery had worked immediately upon his return to pictures in John Ford's war picture, *They Were Expendable*, starring John Wayne.

Jim had asked Leland how the landscape looked in Hollywood, and Hayward provided a brutal assessment: Everything was different. For starters, Hayward had just made a deal to sell his agency, Hayward-Deverich, to the new power brokers in town, MCA, which meant Jim was now represented by a young tiger named Lew Wasserman. The biggest nightclubs had been bought and sold and come and gone. Many established male leads were washed up or hanging on at the end of long studio deals. Exclusive contracts were passé; the smart player kept his options open because the industry was experiencing an incredible state of flux. Hayward had gotten his hot new client Greg Peck some one-shot deals at various studios and it was working out—Wasserman would undoubtedly, surmised Hayward, recommend this course for Jim. It was a lot to think about for a man back in the United States for just twenty-four hours.

Jim spent two nights with his parents at the St. Regis Hotel before heading by train to Indiana, Pennsylvania, where Doddie and Ginny had prepared celebrations, such as a parade. When Jim heard about the plans, he cancelled them. "I didn't want to be treated as some kind of hero," he said. "There were plenty of other heroes—real heroes—that earned that honor. For me, going home was a private thing."

Private and yet not private. *Life* magazine sent its premier photographer, Peter Stackpole, to document the homecoming for the September 24 cover story. Stackpole photographed Stewart by the town courthouse as well as in front of the hardware store, behind its counter, out fishing, and at home with his parents and sisters.

"I plan to just loaf while I'm here," said Jim. "And talk. I haven't talked so much in years. It's good to be home with your family." He slept in the same bedroom where he'd spent his teens, the room in which he had followed Lucky Lindy across the Atlantic.

It was almost as if he had never left, that the war was all an imaginary thing. But no, a youth had indeed gone off to war to fulfill a mission, and in a sense the youth had died over there. A battle-scarred, middle-aged man had returned and soon he must take a hard look at sobering facts. He was thirty-seven and looked fifty, and his career as a Hollywood romantic figure was over. He wanted to make a comedy, but that type of picture seemed to be out of fashion. Fox was still making musicals, but who was doing comedy? Detective pictures seemed to be the thing and shadowy melodrama with dames and guns. Murder seemed to be big—but after what he had just seen, the last thing he wanted to make was a picture about death.

"Several of the stars that had been developing nicely came back to find that their momentum was gone," said Hollywood historian John McElwee. "To me, it was all about momentum. If you were out of pictures for two or three years, it wasn't going to help you. You practically had to start over." It wasn't just Jim; many others who had gone off to fight were just returning to Hollywood in the autumn of 1945. Fonda was one, along with Gene Raymond, Tyrone Power, and Warner Bros. stars Ronald Reagan and Wayne Morris.

"Pre-war and post-war are like two different lives," said McElwee. "Everybody was hugely affected by the war. It's like you scooped those years out of people's lives." With the established stars absent, a new crop of male actors had moved into starring roles, including Gregory Peck, Dana Andrews, Cornel Wilde, Paul Henreid, and many others. At MGM, Van Johnson starred in pictures that five years earlier might have gone to Jim. If not Johnson, then John Hodiak. John Wayne had ascended to prominence through constant work during the war years. Burt Lancaster and Kirk Douglas were months away from their first big pictures. It was a crowded field and many stars-turned-soldiers who had been entrenched in Hollywood before the war suddenly had no guarantee of steady work once they hung up their uniforms and returned to the soundstages.

Fonda said, "Some of the fellas who'd been big stars before the war came back looking like hell. That happened to Clark Gable. He looked ten years older. Jim had also aged quite a bit."

But Hollywood had changed in an even more fundamental way. Jim's old flame Olivia de Havilland had stirred the pot when she fought Jack Warner and won release from her studio contract—she claimed that her time spent on suspension for refusing to make what she considered to be inferior pictures counted toward the seven years of service she had agreed to; Warner argued that only the time she actually worked on the lot counted toward the contract. The decision in favor of de Havilland changed the way studios did business—tying themselves to stars for seven years at a time—and now independent production companies were springing up all over town. Did Stewart owe MGM eighteen months on his contract because he had voluntarily entered the service? Or had he been drafted, with the situation out of his control? And did the de Havilland decision mean he was now a free agent in any case? It seemed that MGM should be welcoming its hero back, except...

Stewart had made his position clear about making any war pictures. Imagine *The James Stewart Story* on the big screen, with the man himself in the left seat of a B-24 going head-to-head with the Luftwaffe over Frankfurt. This was Louis B. Mayer's big idea for Stewart's return to filmmaking: a war picture about James Stewart. But Jim had already said no. He had already decided never to use his wartime experiences for publicity purposes; soon this embargo grew to include any conversation about his combat missions. Ever. It was a simple, flat-out no.

On the West Coast, Louis B. Mayer came face-to-face not with the shy and retiring kid he knew but a high-ranking combat officer and a star who had aged out of any youthful roles. Jim himself had quoted a one-liner in his Brooklyn press conference that he'd been using with his officers in England for a couple years: "I'm just not a young fella anymore. I guess I'd only be suitable for playing grandfather to Mickey Rooney."

That left only the war-hero angle for Metro to exploit if they offered Jim a deal, but this upstart clearly wasn't going to play ball with Howard Strickling's publicity department. As a result and amidst a great deal of fatherly fanfare in their face-to-face meeting, L.B. "released" Jim from a contract that had grown as obsolete as the leading man himself, citing the fact that Stewart was a war hero to whom everyone owed a debt of gratitude, and as such, he should be given his freedom to make pictures anywhere he chose. Of course if Jim wanted to return, he could do so on a standard long-term contract. But just as Hayward predicted, Lew Wasserman advised Jim not to return to MGM under such conditions, but to become an independent player instead.

According to a story later told by Jim, the gentle Mayer veneer fell away in a closed-door meeting when Stewart said no to a contract offer. L.B. ranted that Jim was a "son of a bitch," who "would never work in this town again." Somehow, after flying through flak over Bremen and Frankfurt and wiping out jet fighter bases, hearing a Louis B. Mayer diatribe no longer seemed terrifying.

Jim Stewart was a man at sea, untethered by his old employer, yet also away from the regimentation of the service, the adrenalin rush, the striving toward great accomplishments, and the defying of odds with an extraordinary collection of brothers in arms who had become like sons to him. Combat fatigue and shell shock were the terms of the day for what eventually became known as post-traumatic stress disorder, but whatever the name, Stewart suffered along with millions of other combat veterans who had returned to homes the world over, to friends and family who just couldn't understand what they had experienced.

"I saw too much suffering," he confided to a reporter. "It's certainly not something to talk about." He kept it inside from everyone, but then how could anyone who had remained stateside understand what he had gone through, beginning with the men he had lost in training at Boise and then the intensity of the run-up to war? What could he say about seeing B-24s shot to pieces beside him in formation or colliding into a fireball over Tibenham? How could he convey how it felt when so many ships hadn't come home from Gotha? Or to write all those letters home, especially when he knew that the men he was telling mothers and fathers and wives about were dead? Why would he want to talk about his failings as a leader, as when a dozen ships in his formation dropped bombs on an innocent French town? For that matter, how many women and children had died under his bombs? Jim expressed it as: "Sherman said, 'War is hell.' How right he was; how truly he spoke."

At Andrews Field near Washington, D.C., Jim received his discharge from military service, and enlisted in the Officers Reserve Corps because in fact he had been the happiest in his life in the service; he had said so. He didn't want to give that up.

There was only one thing left for him to do now: give Hollywood a shot. When asked about his future he had told a reporter in Indiana, "I hope I get my old job back." But MGM wasn't an option—neither side wanted that. What, make more pictures like *Ziegfeld Girl*? Hell, he might as well retire to the hardware business now and save himself a whole lot of heartache. But he had to give Hollywood a try because acting was the only thing he had ever liked to do, the only thing that could hold his attention. So there he was in mid-September 1945, back in southern California as just another veteran with no guarantees, no place to live, and no prospects that he would ever make a picture again.

46
GOLD LIGHT

It was a ritual; arrive at the Pasadena train station; Fonda there for the pickup. Now they were a couple of veterans, Hank and Jim, and Fonda was another one to gasp at the physical change in his old friend. Presidents of the United States aged this way, not actors gone off to war. Standing there with Fonda was another man, a handsome young guy with a full head of black hair and a terrific presence: Jim's new agent, thirty-two-year-old Lew Wasserman, a young man capable of walking into the office of the formidable Leland Hayward and buying it out in an hour. Of course the press showed up to see Jim into town and wanted to know about his love life, as if he had one, as if it mattered when the weight of the world had been pressing down on his shoulders for two solid years and he was experiencing night sweats and shakes and still couldn't eat. And oh, yes, he hadn't any job prospects—no one had called offering work despite all the press saying James Stewart was coming back to Hollywood a conquering hero in a spiffy uniform and sporting a chest covered with decorations.

Jim was so out of place that he didn't even know where he would live. The ranch house on Evanston in Brentwood had remained in the "family" with Burgess Meredith and John Swope living there until each married, at which point it was rented to others. As a result, Stewart had no place to hang his hat when he arrived back in sunny Southern California.

No problem, Fonda assured him. He could bunk in the "play-house" Fonda had built behind his home in the Hollywood Hills for his kids, Peter and Jane. This was a fully functional, small-scale house, Jim was assured, with a working kitchen, a bar, and two bathrooms, so Jim said an immediate yes and moved in that day.

Jim began reconnecting with his friends around town as scripts continued not to stream in for either veteran. "There was no work," said Fonda. "Only parties and pleasure." Hank had been married to the emotionally fragile Frances Brokaw Fonda for nine years, and after returning from the Pacific had been crammed into close quarters with her, which had been quite a shock. Now Fonda welcomed the renewal of his friendship with Stewart.

"This was our kite-building period," said Jim. "We were like kids. The kites kept getting bigger and bigger." In fact they were navy target kites of the type Fonda had used in the war, so they were man-sized and not kid stuff. The warriors lay about at night listening to music on the hi-fi. It was their way of unwinding from their close relationship to a world war. Soon they were construct-ing and flying gas-powered model airplanes as well.

Jim hit the social scene and felt out of place with his friends. He was used to Hank and Frances, and Leland and Maggie, but now Swope had Dorothy McGuire and Buzz Meredith was mar-ried to Paulette Goddard. Even Josh Logan had taken the plunge and married actress Nedda Harrigan, which threw Jim into crisis, feeling the urge to settle down but not with a Hollywood leading lady. He still believed that would never work; if anything Dad was worse than ever, more set in his ways if that were possible. Just look how much he hated Ginny's husband, Alexis Tiranoff, and made no bones about it. Imagine what Dad's disapproval of Jim's choice of a bride would do to his psyche, not to mention his married life.

Problem was, Jim found himself attracted to strong women, women like Anita Colby, the green-eyed former magazine cover

girl now working for David O. Selznick as a fashion consultant—
the kind of woman Dad would loathe. Jim and Anita had dated,
but then she was dating just about everyone from Errol Flynn on
down, and Jim never figured to have much of a chance. He still
loved women, but the war had wounded him so badly that now he
withdrew, rebelling against his self-indulgent youth spent dashing
about Hollywood, chasing women and being chased by them. It
seemed so long ago, so silly, so senseless. What did it matter now
who laid who? Did he really need to bag Norma Shearer or Marlene Dietrich to prove something to himself? Such a child he had
been back then. Fonda noticed his friend's melancholy, and asked
what the problem was.

"I'm feeling that so much is just so—superficial," was the way
Jim described it.

Fonda said of Stewart, "He...kept on about how all his friends
were married with families, and he was still single. He kept saying
he was getting old, and I said, 'You're not even forty, for Christ's
sake.' He said, 'Yeah, but I feel old.' The war did that to some fellas. So I kept making him build airplanes."

Celebrations ushered in 1946, which felt a lot like the end of
1945, with the Hollywood machinery still turning but bypassing
Stewart and Fonda. Frances Fonda grew desperate with Jim, her
relentlessly present houseguest, and tried to find him a nice girl to
marry, or any girl to marry to get him out of her home.

Finally, the Evanston house became available again. Jim jumped
at the chance to return to his old rental digs in Brentwood, and he
rehired his housekeeper, Daisy Dooley. If only he could move back
into his old workload. If only he could make some money. All Jim's
fretting rolled off the back of wunderkind Lew Wasserman, who
said of Stewart, "He'd been at MGM a long time and it was a different business by then. There were much greater opportunities
on the outside than there were at MGM." Jim saw none; Jim was
staring at a phone that relentlessly failed to ring.

He took a job for Lux Radio Theatre performing *Destry Rides Again* with fading '30s megastar Joan Blondell and stood on the stage bathed in sweat, his hands quaking as he held the script. It wasn't much different than a mission over Achmer: When the confidence is shot, it's shot, and that was the frame of mind of Jim Stewart in early 1946. But he wasn't alone. Many others faced the same problem, among them Hollywood's celebrated Frank Capra. The once-prolific writer/producer/director had spent four years as a colonel in the U.S. Army working directly under Chief of Staff George C. Marshall on a series of documentaries with the title, *Why We Fight*. The immense project didn't involve piloting a B-24 at 20,000 feet in a flak field, but it may as well have for the stress of producing it.

Like Jim Stewart, Colonel Capra was back from four years in the service and terrified of facing the young, sexy, superficial movie capital he had once owned. "It's frightening to go back to Hollywood after four years, wondering whether you've gone rusty or lost touch," said Capra at the dawn of post-war life. "I keep telling myself how wonderful it would be just to sneak out somewhere and make a couple of quickie Westerns first—just to get the feel of things again." Just as Stewart imagined making a couple of Vitaphone shorts to break back in, the kinds of things he had done while a nobody back in New York City, just to get his feet wet.

As with Jim Stewart, no offers were coming Frank Capra's way, which left him with no option but to try his luck as an independent. Capra was a visionary who saw a better world without a studio system that released a studio's product directly into that studio's roster of theaters across the country—the very system that had helped to create Frank Capra.

"I never saw any big change in Capra at all," said cinematographer Joe Walker, "until he came back from the war. He was more anxious." He had good reason to be, as the war had dulled the senses of a public to world events. Suddenly the kind of "everyman" flag-waving that Capra had built his career upon was rendered commonplace. *Meet John Doe* had been a lackluster exit for him, nothing but a reworking of *Mr. Deeds Goes to Town* and *Mr. Smith Goes to Washington*. Since the release of *Mr. Smith*, a half-million American young men had been sacrificed on battlefields around the world, proving that everyman meant every*thing*—nobody needed Frank Capra to tell them any longer. Capra needed something new, he realized, or he was finished.

Said Capra, "People are numb after the catastrophic events of the past ten to fifteen years. I would not attempt to reach them mentally through a picture, only emotionally."

In this frame of mind, Frank Capra called Jim Stewart, who was all too familiar with such thinking. Capra had a project in mind that he felt in his gut could revive his career. It was based on a story called "The Greatest Gift," about a man from a small town who wishes he had never been born. Jim was the only actor in Hollywood whom Capra considered for the role.

They met face-to-face in the presence of Lew Wasserman, and Frank tried to act out the plot for Jim, about this guy who thinks he's a failure and wants to commit suicide, but an angel intervenes. Wait, an angel? Capra noted afterward, "As I tell story it evaporates into thin air. Tell Stewart to forget it. Wasserman dying. Jimmy doesn't want to hear story."

The initial meeting broke up, and Jim remained at loose ends. He hadn't been put off by the supernatural aspects of the plot that Capra had described. After all he had experienced on the broad plain of Tibenham, after so many ships and so many boys had failed to return from missions to Germany, while Jim *had* returned after an anti-aircraft shell had exploded right under him—after all that, Jim understood what Capra was going after.

Calls asking about the availability of Stewart weren't coming in, which prompted Jim to make one of his own, to Capra, who apologized for their earlier meeting by saying, "This story doesn't

315

tell very well, does it?"

The pair reconvened over dinner. Capra asked Jim if he liked the story as told in their previous meeting.

Stewart parried by asking, "Do you like it?"

"Would I be making it otherwise?" said Capra.

Jim paused. "Think I can play it?"

"Don't ask foolish questions," Capra shot back.

Jim thought a second and set down his cutlery. "OK, that's good enough for me."

Capra hesitated. "Yeah, but do you like it?"

Jim leaned back in his chair. "How do I know? I can't make head nor tail of the damn thing!"

But what did it really matter at this point? Nobody seemed to want the director; nobody seemed to want the actor.

Which brought Jim Stewart to the RKO Encino Ranch in the ninety-degree heat of June, after years of flight training and snow and shakes and bombing missions with oxygen deprivation and icicles and death. Jim was back in superficial Hollywood, but he was alive. He was working. He was engaged in something magical again, something to interest people in the art of living, rather than the art of dying.

The sun had slipped below the western horizon, over Calabasas, with the gold light of sunset—every cinematographer's favorite light—transitioning to the purples of dusk, and Capra's moviemakers had gotten into position for the shots to follow. Jim drew in a deep breath. He was looking up a long city thoroughfare. Trees lined the island to the left, buildings to the right. Above, for fifty yards loomed a mechanical assembly that would spew snow at appropriate intervals.

Jim felt relief that the sun was gone because he no longer sweated as if the life were draining from him. He could breathe again; he could relax. He knew this script so well already and laughed because George Bailey was not Jim Stewart. In the script George's brother had gone off to war and George had stayed home. George had been a dreamer who wanted to leave his hometown and see exotic locales; Jim had seen London, Berlin, and the Alps.

"Places!" called Capra through his megaphone. He needed something to project his voice, because this was the San Fernando Valley after all, and sounds tended to disperse in such a wide-open space. The light of day was nearly gone; Jim understood the grand plan and he embraced it.

"Snow!" bellowed Capra, and flakes began to issue from the mechanical assembly to Jim's left.

"And—" said Frank. There was a pause and Jim waited, and a longer pause and Jim felt like a thoroughbred at the gate.

"—Action!" said Capra.

Jim shot into a trot, and just now he understood. Maybe Hollywood wasn't so superficial after all. Maybe Hollywood and his work here was just as important as a mission over Germany. Maybe it was, in its way, more important. He was running forward, toward a future of people and life and a world without bombs. He was back to a make-believe place that created; that didn't destroy. And in make-belief he was beginning a new reality for the ones who had managed to survive to start fresh after the Third Reich, all those men he had saluted coming off the *Queen Elizabeth*, and all the others whose faces he had never seen; men who had fought the war in far-flung corners of the world.

Now he was running for his life, Jim Stewart, former squadron commander of the 703rd. "Merry Christmas, Bedford Falls!" he called into the hot air of Encino. "Merry Christmas, you old Building and Loan!" Suddenly, he wanted to be a part of Hollywood where he felt comfortable and safe.

Jim Stewart had made it back. He had survived, and so would the world.

Epilogue
REACHING BEYOND

"Frank really saved my career," said Jim Stewart of the experience of returning from the war and making *It's a Wonderful Life*.

Capra had provided for Stewart the role of his lifetime in George Bailey, the ambitious, good-hearted, small-town American boy who grows up with such responsibility that he becomes the moral compass of the population and cracks under the pressure. His scenes ranged from comedy to romance and high drama, with the centerpiece of his performance a sequence in the Bailey family living room with wife Mary and their three children. Good-hearted George is at the end of his rope and he snaps, erupting in violence, screaming at his children, flinging objects, and wrecking the room. In acknowledging such a dark place in his soul, this Jimmy Stewart challenged audiences like never before, and, at a deep level, those watching in 1946 understood: This man has just stared into the face of war. It didn't matter that the fictional George Bailey of this picture hadn't served. The man behind the character, James Stewart, had. Across America, across the world, families were seeing this behavior in returning warriors; distance, isolation, and hidden rage always a loud noise or wrong word away. The meltdown in the Bailey living room, with motivation so easily within Stewart's reach, would signal the rise of the curtain on the second act of his Hollywood career. In England and over continental Europe, he had experienced a spectrum of emotions, from the beauty of quiet courage to the corruption of fear, from the horrors of death to the joy of living—whatever any script called for, Jim could play it from life.

At the box office, *It's a Wonderful Life* did well for a sentimental Frank Capra picture released to a cynical, post-war audience. Returns were strong, but not strong enough to overtake the fortune Capra spent on cast, crew, script rewrites, complex special effects, and creation of an upstate New York town at the RKO ranch in Encino, California. A New York town buried in snow, no less. Given these challenges, red ink was all but inevitable.

But Jim was back making viable pictures. By now he was stuck with the simple moniker of "Jimmy," but this man was anything but simple. He couldn't stick by his pledge to give up flying and soon began to go up again, remaining a loner by nature and now a loner haunted by a thousand black memories. "He wasn't hardened by war," said Bill Minor of the 703rd. "He was *saddened* by war and worried about the future of the world."

With the fall of the Third Reich, Jim had been happy to learn how many men of the 703rd Squadron ended up spilling out of POW camps, including pilots Pete Abell of *Star Baby*, Ollie Saunders and Barry Shillito of *Our Baby*, and Victor Smith and Bill Minor of *Gremlins Roost*, along with various crew members from the ships. But some of Stewart's original pilots had indeed died in action along with many of their crew members. Of his pilots of the 703, Bob Kiser and Dave Skjeie died on combat missions to Europe, while Al Poor had been lost on the passage to England, and Earle Metcalf and crew had vanished off the English coast with no trace ever found.

For Jim, life went on. After making magic with Frank Capra, Stewart went back to a Capra-type picture at RKO, *Magic Town*, for Frank's frequent collaborator Robert Riskin. But this time the "fantasy Americana," as Stewart biographer Tony Thomas phrased it, misfired. "*Magic Town* proved that what had been great stuff in the pre-war years was not such good stuff in the post-war years," said Thomas, adding that "its failure caused him to take stock of his movie image and reach beyond it."

But reinvented James Stewart, the one fighting a real war and helping win it—and smashing up the occasional living room—was ready to take off. The picture was *Call Northside 777*, and Twentieth Century Fox producer Darryl Zanuck thought Jim would be perfect for the role of a tough reporter digging into the mystery of a cop killing and winning the release of a man wrongly convicted of the crime. It was shot on location in Chicago and revitalized Stewart's career. Jim now realized how fortunate he had been to ally himself with super-agent Lew Wasserman during this turbulent time in Hollywood when some former favorites were falling off in popularity.

Jim finally settled down in 1949 with a woman who would always outrank him, Gloria Hatrick McLean, a statuesque socialite (not a Hollywood mainstay) with a gregarious personality similar to that of Jim's father. Previously, Gloria had been married to an owner of the Hope Diamond. She brought two sons into the union with Jim and then bore him twin daughters in 1951. She also became his advisor and acting partner in television appearances on *The Jack Benny Show*. In dealing with Alex, tough-minded Gloria hit him head-on, to Jim's horror. Yes, she smoked cigarettes; no, she didn't go to church; get used to it. It worked because she wouldn't take no for an answer. Gloria and Alex got along.

The war had changed Jim down to the molecular level. He could never begin to articulate what those four-and-a-half years, including fifteen months in combat, had done to him. One thing he could do was continue to express a bit of it on-screen. In the dozen years after the war, Jim portrayed many troubled characters with a penchant for violent outbursts that Gloria swore reflected the Jim Stewart she had married. In *Winchester '73* he was a hard, covetous man capable of brutal violence. In *The Greatest Show on Earth*, a circus clown on the run for murder. In *Bend of the River*, a wagon master with a dark past. In *Carbine Williams*, an imprisoned moonshiner turned gun inventor. In *The Naked Spur*, a cowboy full of hate and bent on vengeance. In *Rear Window*, a voyeur. In *The Far Country*, a hard-bitten gunman. In *The Man from Laramie*, an Army officer out to avenge the death of his brother. In *Vertigo*, a neurotic and obsessed ex-cop. In *Two Rode Together*, a coldly pragmatic sheriff rescuing white captives from the Indians for the bounty it will bring him. Sentimental pictures like *The Glenn Miller Story* paid the bills on enormous returns, but the pictures made with noir-ish director Anthony Mann fought off Jim's boredom, the worst enemy of all, and kept his mind engaged as he enacted characters that had been touched and damaged by life's experiences, just as sixteen million veterans of the war had been damaged.

Jim's mother died in 1953; his father remarried in 1954 and passed on in 1961. A year later—after another incendiary performance as a mild-mannered lawyer driven to flashes of rage in John Ford's *The Man Who Shot Liberty Valance*—Jim turned to a succession of family comedies and withdrew behind his image and brand, even adopting an exaggerated version of his halting speech as his own manner of speaking. By this time he had become so hard of hearing, in part from the roar of B-24 engines on long missions, that performing on camera grew ever more difficult; he simply couldn't hear his cues and relied on lip reading to get through. His biggest starring vehicle of the decade, the Civil War picture *Shenandoah*, took a decidedly anti-war turn that seemed out of character for a later James Stewart project. In it he allowed one final scene showing the breaking point for a man pushed too far by the horrors of war. He was by this time a brigadier general in the Air Force Reserve and a hawk on the Vietnam War, who had visited the Asian theater and flown B-52 bombing missions there as an observer. He retired from military service in 1968; a year later,

Jim's stepson Ronald McLean was killed in combat in Vietnam and posthumously awarded the Silver Star. Ronald's loss was a shattering event for Gloria and for Jim.

In 1969 Jim Stewart and Hank Fonda teamed up on a self-styled tribute to their friendship of more than forty years, making the western-comedy, *The Cheyenne Social Club*. In it Fonda's character Harley never shuts up while Stewart's John has little to say. Harley is a Democrat; John a Republican. The characters tolerate each other and, at a deeper level, understand each other and take deep comfort in their association. It became Stewart's last hurrah as a leading man in feature pictures. Next, he tried a homespun sitcom on television, and then played a lawyer in another television series, *Hawkins*, which ran for one season as part of the NBC Mystery Movie. The role of Billy Jim Hawkins earned Stewart a Golden Globe Award in 1974.

The world was changing around Jim. Maggie Sullavan had died of an overdose of barbiturates—either accidental or deliberate—on New Year's Day 1960. Leland Hayward had passed on in 1971, John Swope in 1979. Hardest of all on Jim was the loss of Fonda in August 1982. Toward the end Stewart would visit his friend of fifty years and they would sit together on a park bench, often in silence.

Stewart rarely spoke about his military service and never about combat. He returned to Tibenham and Old Buckenham in 1976 and again in 1983 for commemorations of the war and walked the runways and explored the control towers. But Jim being Jim, the memories remained locked inside. Through the next two decades, acting roles diminished, and as his reflexes declined, Jim gave up flying. When Gloria passed on in 1994 after more than forty-four years of marriage, he lost his fighting spirit and succumbed in 1997 at age eighty-nine.

Jim had remained in touch with a few of his pilots but only from a distance with the occasional card or letter.

Neil Johnson, rugged Montana football star, completed his tour of duty with the 445th and then moved to fighter planes, continuing his career in Korea, where he achieved the rank of major before dying when his F-51D Mustang ran out of fuel and crashed 500 feet short of the runway in December 1950. He was survived by wife June and two children.

Emmett Watson walked away from the February 18, 1944 crash landing of *Kelly*, which shook him up and ended his tour of duty under Stewart. The following January the tough and determined Watson got back in the air but suffered another crash on takeoff. After the war he got into sales, married Ida Jean Winn, had two children, and died in 1987.

William "Mack" Williams, Jim's oldest pilot and one of the most reliable, completed a thirty-year Air Force career and retired in 1972 with the rank of colonel. He was married to Catherine the ballerina for fifty-one years and they had two children. Mack died in 1989.

Bill Kane, who managed to ditch his ship in the Channel and save more than half his crew against overwhelming odds, got back in the air again and retired from the Air Force a major. He and Jean, the girl he rushed off to marry before shipping out, remained together until his death in 1995.

Steady, dependable Ralph Stimmel completed his tour of duty as test pilot for the 445th and also flew missions for the 457th Bomb Group. He married in 1959 and earned his college degree in mechanical engineering in 1961 at age forty-four, raised three children, and died in 1997.

Joe Narcovich, who was sitting right seat when Jim bounced their B-24 nose first into the runway in Boise, finished his service with the 376th Bomb Group, became a businessman after the war, married his sweetheart, Dorothy, and died in Pennsylvania in 2001.

Ollie Saunders of *Our Baby* endured his time at Stalag Luft I to enjoy a long career with Hewlett-Packard and then a long retirement before his death in 2002.

Pete Abell bailed out of the crippled *Star Baby* the same day Clem Leone and crew were shot down, February 24, 1944. Abell was confined at Stalag Luft I until his liberation on June 1, 1945. After the war he married Patricia Farr Pagen, and they raised three sons. Pete retired from a career in insurance sales and died in 2002.

Lloyd Sharrard flew thirty missions in the war (some in cowboy boots), married Betty in 1945, raised four children, and remained in the Air Force, retiring as a lieutenant-colonel in 1965. Lloyd died in 2004 just short of their sixtieth wedding anniversary.

Gil Schleichkorn, the New York City boy, survived the shoot down of *Nine Yanks and a Jerk* in April 1944 and rescue by the Belgian Resistance. After the war he changed his name to Gilbert Shawn and in 1955 married soap star Melba Rae of *Search for Tomorrow* television fame. Melba died of a cerebral hemorrhage in 1971; Gil in 2005. Their son is Fox News reporter Eric Shawn.

Charles "Chick" Torpey flew twenty-two missions and retired a captain in 1945. Chick survived the war and so did his B-24H, which had been dubbed *Betty* for his wife in Lincoln in October 1943. *Betty* the Liberator was declared war weary in May 1945. Betty the wife certainly wasn't war weary and delivered ten children to Chick. After several moves the family settled in Grand Island, Nebraska, where Chick died in 2007 and Betty in 2011.

Victor Smith endured his January 5, 1944 bailout and imprisonment in Stalag Luft I, married Margaret Franklin in 1954, and managed a furniture store. He died in 2008.

The intense and dedicated Leo Cook, who flew as pilot on Jim's first mission, went on to become a squadron commander in the 415th Bomb Group and then enjoyed a long and successful Air Force career, all the while husband to Helen and father to Kelly, for whom he had named his bomber, and also a daughter. He died in 2009.

Bill Conley, Jim's pilot on several missions and one cool customer for his handling of the detour around Paris, survived the war to become the father of four and a pilot for TWA for thirty-five years before retiring to run Conley's Christmas Tree Farm in New Hampshire. He died in 2011 at age ninety.

On the German side, it's possible no military participant fared better after the war than Adolf Galland, General of the Fighter Arm. Galland survived the end of hostilities with JV-44 intact and sought to ally his unit with the Americans in what he believed was a fast-approaching war with the Soviet Union. However, U.S. forces rebuffed his offer, and he ordered his pilots to destroy their jet fighters. Galland was imprisoned until 1947 and over the succeeding decades became a sought-after celebrity who met up with many of his old adversaries of the sky. He died in 1996 a romantic hero for his aerial exploits and defiance of high command, including Hitler himself.

Quiet, thoughtful Hans Siepmann, Gertrud's father, made it a point to voluntarily surrender in uniform, with honor, rather than don civilian clothes to escape the consequences of service to the Reich, as had so many others. Hans went on to spent the spring and summer of 1945 as a prisoner of the Allies. After having been subjected to years of Nazi propaganda about the murderous enemy, his diary entry of May 5, 1945, states, "I must admit that, up to this point, my impression of the English, but especially of the Americans, is a most favorable one." Of the U.S. soldiers, he said, "The guards, the enlisted men as well as their officers, make an excellent impression: slim, athletic figures, open friendly faces, fine postures and good manners." Three days later he wrote, "The English are very hostile towards us, stirred up by reports of unspeakable horrors in the concentration camps where the inmates were apparently slowly starved and tortured to death. If this is really true, the SS has done a horrendous thing." This same day, he added, "There is great anger amongst our people with the German government for having pushed resistance past all limits, for having sacrificed hundreds and thousands of people, and for permitting our cities to be destroyed—in the full knowledge that the situation was hopeless."

Hans was released to return to his family in August 1945. Ultimately, he would begin a new career with the North Atlantic Treaty Organization (NATO), where he worked until his death in 1963.

Gertrud Siepmann fled Eppstein and Frankfurt with her mother and siblings as bombs fell around them and took refuge in Bavaria. Gertrud found employment as a domestic, tended children in an orphanage, and studied costume design. She fell in love from afar with Hollywood star Errol Flynn in the late 1940s, and then, much closer, with an American G.I., Patrick McVicker, who proposed marriage. Gertrud came to America in 1956 and has been known as Trudy McVicker ever since.

After settling in Illinois, Trudy contributed to the family's income by creating collector figurines that she sold exclusively through Marshall Field, the Chicago department store. She presented two of the earliest figurines, depicting Don Juan and Queen Margaret from Errol Flynn's 1949 film, *Adventures of Don Juan*, as a gift to Flynn's daughters—Errol called them "exquisite" in a return letter. Over the years Trudy has been a friend to many notables, including Earl Conrad, who ghostwrote Flynn's multi-million-selling autobiography, *My Wicked, Wicked Ways*. She collaborated with Flynn biographer Thomas McNulty and with James Stewart biographer Tony Thomas on several projects. She also became a translator, converting the diary of her father from German into English, then translating the original notes of cancer researcher Dr. Georg Springer, and printed works for astronomer and UFO investigator J. Allen Hynek, among many other translation projects. After a great deal of coaxing, she agreed to collaborate with Robert Matzen to tell her story in *Mission*, the story of an ordinary German family caught in war.

Clem Leone, the radio operator of Robert Blomberg's *Shir-*

ley Raye crew, returned to the United States after the Stalag Luft IV death march to marry his girl, Sylvia. On their wedding night Clem awoke in a burning Liberator and tried to do what he had been taught: Bail out. Only Sylvia's quick thinking as she threw her arms around his waist kept Clem from jumping out the window of their hotel room to his death. Clem became a schoolteacher and reservist in the Maryland National Guard who rose to the rank of major. Today he lives in retirement in central Pennsylvania and lectures on his experiences with the United States Army Air Forces, the Dutch Underground, and prisoner of war camps. He told a newspaper reporter recently, "In my opinion, there are no real heroes in a war. There's nothing glorious about war. It's mayhem."

ACKNOWLEDGMENTS

James Maitland Stewart didn't fight World War II alone. For generations we've heard "Jimmy" was a real-life American hero, but what does that mean? What did he face? Who did he command and report to? Who were his opponents in the sky, and who did he bomb, and where, and when?

I find "Jimmy" to be a benign red herring of a nickname not suitable for the pre-war ladies' man of Hollywood or the flight instructor, squadron commander, group operations officer, wing commander, and warrior. This is not Jimmy's story. This is the story of the real guy, a quiet, high-strung loner who fought feelings of inadequacy and self-doubt.

Because Stewart didn't fight the war alone, *Mission* includes other fliers in his Bomb Group as well as three full-fledged secondary characters: Clem Leone, an enlisted-man alter ego for Jim who provides a back-of-the-cockpit view of life in a B-24 Liberator; Gertrud Siepmann, a young German civilian who was born in the first year of Hitler's rule; and Adolf Galland, ace fighter pilot who rose to command of the Fighter Arm of the Luftwaffe and faced the might of the Eighth Air Force every day. I believe that seeing the war through the eyes of other characters provides context for Jim Stewart's world and accomplishments.

As always, my first thank you goes to Mary Matzen, who took

my latest good-news, bad-news announcement in typical stride. "The good news is we need to go overseas," I told her. "The bad news is we're going to explore muddy fields, crumbling bunkers, and air bases that aren't there anymore." So off we went. I couldn't have written *Mission* without that trip or without her by my side for two years of intense research and writing.

Next came Dr. Walter Powell, a friend of twenty years who provided expertise about the Eighth Air Force, lent books, magazines, and other historical documents, and offered guidance on my visit to old American air bases in the United Kingdom. Walt's enthusiasm for my project was consistent throughout, with his most appreciated contribution being an introduction to Clem Leone and a personal recommendation to Clem that I was OK. Walt also offered critical feedback to the rough draft that strengthened the final narrative. Truly, without Walt there would be no *Mission*.

Another writer, Michael Bandler, had started a book on Stewart's military career, then donated his research to Brigham Young University, where I reviewed every page. My thanks to Michael for his generosity. Starr Smith wrote a book on the subject of Stewart the bomber pilot, which skimmed over only the highlights. The real chronicle started to emerge from sifting through the Records of the Army Air Forces, World War II Combat Operations Report, 1941–45 for the 445th and 453rd Bomb Groups. The weather report is provided in detail, the initial point is designated, the target defined, and results critiqued. Intelligence interrogation reports for each crew round out the mission experience. And I had it all at my fingertips thanks to Ann Trevor, my crack D.C. researcher.

My thanks go to Mike Simpson for his wonderful, comprehensive, growing website 445bg.org, which I referenced every day of writing about Jim's time at Station 124 Tibenham.

Thank you to the National Personnel Records Center/Military Personnel Records in St. Louis, Missouri, for providing me with the 600-page James M. Stewart military personnel file covering his entire career, from induction in 1941 to retirement in 1968. As with my last book, *Fireball: Carole Lombard and the Mystery of Flight 3*, my secret weapon in terms of research has been Marina Gray, who dug into the life of Jim Stewart and also that of his pilots of the 703rd Squadron of the 445th Bomb Group. She created a dossier on each pilot to help me know these guys and deal with their sudden loss. Marina unearthed so many gems that she nearly earned co-authorship. Readers of *Mission* are experiencing the results of her passionate detective work.

I was privileged to meet and work with people who saw the war firsthand, including Clem Leone, who sat with me for hours of interviews and then reviewed my work with the discerning eye of a scholar. When I veered into anything fanciful, he would wag a finger and say, "That's not history, that's Hollywood!" There was no greater sting than that exclamation coming from Clem, but ultimately, he signed off on this manuscript and attested to its accuracy in capturing life in the Eighth Air Force.

Bill Minor, one of Stewart's copilots in the 703 (and one of the ex-fighter jocks), spent hours answering my questions on the phone and in written communication and introduced me to Barry Shillito, another copilot in the 703, who was also a terrific interview. Thanks also to Harold Eckelberry's wife, Janet, who provided me with Eck's diary of life in Stewart's squadron.

Four books written by fliers of the 703 were of tremendous help. *A Reason to Live* by John Robinson was the go-to source for the experience of flying behind Stewart; *Not as Briefed* by Wright Lee beautifully captured the B-24 experience and also that of being shot down on a mission; *Flight from Munich* by Donald C. Toye and *Kriegsgefangener* by Joseph Reus provided additional vital perspective by those who trained, lived, and flew with Jim.

How could anyone write a book about life in a B-17 or B-24 without flying in them? So, thanks to the Liberty Foundation, off I went for a flight in the cockpit of the B-17 dubbed *Memphis Belle*—

built in 1945 and used in the 1991 motion picture. The B-24 experience came courtesy of the Commemorative Air Force B-24A *Diamond Lil*, a prototype built in 1941 and one of only two remaining Liberators still airworthy.

I spent two days slogging through the mud of Tibenham in the fog and drizzle of November 2015. My thanks go to Eric Ratcliffe for his time and expertise showing me around the one-time base. We rode its runways and explored the surviving structures, including cold concrete barracks identical to the quarters shared by Stewart and Fisher during Jim's four roughest months of combat.

I have known Gertrud Siepmann, known in America as Trudy McVicker, for thirty-five years, but only recently did she share her memories of being a young girl in the middle of the war. Seventy years later it remains painful to be German and to relive the experiences of growing up under Nazi rule. It was a wonderful experience collaborating with Trudy and retracing her steps through Eppstein and Frankfurt in my visits to those places in November 2015. Thanks also go to Eva Hausch, Trudy's sister, for providing the family photo used in this book.

I am grateful to James V. D'Arc, curator of the Brigham Young University Motion Picture Archive, for helping to guide me through the James Stewart Papers MSS 2157 and the Michael Bandler Papers MSS 2210, both part of the L. Tom Perry Special Collections, Brigham Young University. Jim and I shared many hours of thoughtful conversation about Stewart, and Jim also offered critical feedback on the galleys.

Jay Rubin grew up in Indiana, Pennsylvania, and provided insights about both Alex and Jim Stewart. Jay also loaned me materials from his collection and library, and gave me a personal tour of Indiana and the Jimmy Stewart Museum.

My most sincere thanks go to Stacey Behlmer for her support and help with photo research and for pointing me toward gems like the Owen Crump Oral History. Thank you to the staff of the Margaret Herrick Library at the Academy of Motion Picture Arts and Sciences; to Mike Mazzone for encouraging me to write the book; to Sarah Myslis for key communications that affected the finished product and for her proofreading skills; to Carole Sampeck for her friendship, encouragement, and three terrific Jim Stewart wartime candid photos; to Austin and Bonnie Cline for the translation of German correspondence into English; and to my hero Steve Hayes for sharing memories of his friend, Marlene Dietrich.

Thank you to the Academy for access to the Owen Crump Oral History. (Owen Crump interviewed by Douglas Bell, pages 4 through 16 on October 22, 1991, ©1994 Academy Foundation.)

Thank you to the National Museum of the Mighty Eighth Air Force in Savannah, Georgia, and to the Second Air Division Memorial Library in Norwich, Norfolk, United Kingdom.

A big thank you goes to the review team that critiqued the rough draft and provided wonderful ideas for improvement. They are Walt Powell, Rudy Behlmer, Marina Gray, Clem Leone, Mike Mazzone, John McElwee, Bill Minor, and Jim D'Arc.

Thank you to the GoodKnight Books graphics team. Sharon Berk designed the book and created the outstanding dust jacket. Valerie Sloan displayed her photo restoration abilities on the vintage images. Amelia Williams created the frontispiece maps.

Thank you, Leonard Maltin, for writing the foreword for this book. I am among the legion of movie buffs who have been educated and entertained by Leonard's work, and I'm honored to have him join the *Mission* team.

Thank you, John McElwee, idea man, for sending me down the path of writing *Mission*. John knows a good story when he sees one, and this story, of Stewart and the other fliers of the Mighty Eighth, has been tremendously rewarding to explore and to tell.

And thanks to Kelly Stewart Harcourt for approving of this book and its depiction of her dad, an Army flier who wouldn't, or couldn't, open up and talk about the war as he experienced it.

CHAPTER NOTES

Prologue: Unreality

The prologue was written last and drew upon all the research that came before. I interviewed dozens of Armed Services personnel about the experience of coming home from wartime and their feelings of unreality and disconnectedness from friends, family, and co-workers who couldn't possibly understand what had happened overseas. Information about the production of sequences of *It's a Wonderful Life* originated at Wesleyan University. My visits to Encino, California, grounded the narrative in the time and place, and multiple viewings of the motion picture helped as well.

1. High-Strung

Several biographies have been written about James Stewart, and there is little new ground to cover in his years before the war. Research for this chapter involved extensive investigation of the Stewart Papers housed at the Harold B. Lee Library at Brigham Young University, including the Civil War diaries of both Samuel Jackson and James M. Stewart. Jim talked about his love of flying in many interviews, most notably in an article entitled "A Thrill a Minute..." that appeared in *Modern Screen* magazine in February 1941. On *The Tonight Show* with Johnny Carson in 1989, Jim discussed his first flight with the barnstorming pilot.

I visited Indiana, Pennsylvania, to understand the lay of the land, but then I grew up in a small southwestern Pennsylvania town very similar to Indiana. It even had a "normal school" just like Indiana's. The result is an understanding of the largely blue-collar mind-set in a region almost exclusively a mix of white European Protestants and Catholics.

Stewart was and wasn't a "choirboy." Yes, he had a strong Presbyterian upbringing, but when he went off on his own to Princeton and then Broadway, he grew up fast, especially under the influence of cynical and worldly wise Henry Fonda. Brooke Hayward's remarkable *Haywire* provided insight about Fonda, Margaret Sullavan, and Leland Hayward—and Jim's relationship with all of them. Michael Munn's access to Jim and Gloria Stewart as revealed in *Jimmy Stewart: The Truth Behind the Legend* helped in understanding Jim's psychology at this point in his life. More than any other source, magazine interviews conducted with Jim upon his arrival in Hollywood about the days in New York City revealed the Stewart in his mid-twenties. Newspapers of the day provided context for American and European reaction to Hitler's rise to power and what Jim would have been learning about the European situation via headlines and broadcasts. As noted in Stewart biographies, Guthrie McClintic was gay—did "exhaustive rehearsals" with Jim Stewart mean there was a sexual relationship here? I don't believe so, based on evidence and Jim's lack of cold-blooded ambition. Factual information about the Martin Bomber model airplane first appeared in print when Stewart hit Hollywood—both Stewart and Fonda used this story as the one best symbolizing their friendship, and neither felt the need to embellish it because the facts are funny enough on their own.

2. Soaring

Do aviators catch the flying bug or are they born to fly? It seemed that many of the characters in the book were born with aviation in their blood, and since this was universal, the narrative needed a German protagonist who grew up like Stewart—not as a warrior but a red-blooded male interested in sports, cars, girls, and, of course, flying. I chose Adolf Galland because of his love of flight on a human level and because of his rise through the ranks of German military aviation to a point at which he was in direct opposition to the Eighth Air Force bomber stream that included Jim Stewart in front of numerous formations. The voluminous writings of Galland served as a foundation for understanding his character, and *Fighter General: The Life of Adolf Galland* by Toliver and Constable provided additional background. Galland's introductory chapter also helps to flesh out post-World War I Germany and hints at the sinister master plan that began to manipulate young men like Galland while providing them with the outlet they needed to get up in the air and fly.

3. Factory Work

My visits to MGM studios and the Los Angeles area in general, including Evanston Drive, established the otherworldly place that Jim first saw in 1935. Articles from 1936 detailed Fonda's early days in Hollywood, as did his autobiography, *Fonda: My Life*. Scott Eyman's excellent *Lion of Hollywood* provided grounding in the kingdom of Louis B. Mayer and the power struggle with Irving Thalberg. Magazine articles began appearing about Stewart in the second half of 1936 as the MGM publicity machine sought to establish the studio's new and unusual contract player. In these pieces Jim discussed his experiences to date as a studio player. For example, the December 1936 issue of *Hollywood* magazine ran the feature "He's Unmarried but Willin'" to coincide with Stewart's first starring role in the B-picture *Speed*. In it he compares and contrasts New York stage acting with his past year's work on the screen. He also discusses life in Brentwood with his cronies and the ubiquitous cats.

4. Silver Birds

Mission called for a number of different perspectives, including those of the enlisted men who flew behind the pilots in the bombers. The officers on the flight deck literally turned their backs on the men of the flight crews and yet relied on them for survival on every combat mission. So, who were these guys aft of the cockpit? Well, they were ordinary young men like Clem Leone, and many sought out the Army Air Corps because of a fascination with flight that began in childhood. Leone becomes the flip side of Stewart—someone whose luck ran out, resulting in a shoot-down and time in a POW camp. In-person and telephone interviews with Clem in 2014 and 2015 revealed details about his incredible life and wartime experiences, and since he's an authority on the Eighth Air Force and Stalag Luft IV who continues to lecture on these subjects, he provided a wealth of documentation to verify his wartime story. Seeing the world through Clem's eyes also reveals the state of commercial aviation in the United States during the 1930s when passenger service was just being established and bi-planes were still a common sight flying over the American landscape.

5. Reliable Girls

James Stewart became a ladies' man in Hollywood, and by accounts Ginger Rogers was his first girlfriend and among his most serious. One biography claims that Jim lost his virginity to Ginger, but evidence goes in another direction. Walter Pidgeon's observations were made to Stewart biographer Lawrence Quirk. Ross Alexander's death by suicide was reported in newspapers of the day, and Henry Fonda detailed the friendship of Hank and Jim with Alexander in *Fonda: My Life*. Jim confided to one officer with whom he served at Tibenham that his relationship with Jean Harlow had been intimate—Jim was tight-lipped until he had downed a couple of drinks, at which point he would open up a little. He also mentioned Lana Turner as a hot number.

6. A Storybook Life

The story of Franz Siepmann going down with the *Cöln* was reported in *Auf See Unbesiegt* (*Unconquered At Sea: 30 Individual Depictions from the War at Sea*), published in Munich in 1921. Gertrud Siepmann—known in America as Trudy McVicker—was interviewed at length about her experiences in Germany before and during the war. She had chronicled her life in a series of short written pieces that she provided along with a diary kept by her father, Hans Siepmann, detailing his life at the end of World War II. German history is so tainted by the evils of the Nazi regime that the nation at peace in the mid-1930s is difficult to imagine.

7. Mr. Smith Goes Hollywood

James Reid became one of Stewart's favorite reporters and generated some of the most insightful articles of this period. By mid-1938 Jim was growing weary of constant questions about his romantic entanglements, and no wonder: He was embroiled in a tempestuous affair with Norma Shearer that had become uncomfortable for him, and he remained in love with Margaret Sullavan, even mentioning her to Reid as the perfect girl. Various articles of the time and retrospective biographies yielded tidbits about his romantic escapades, and the near-casting of Gary Cooper in *Mr. Smith Goes to Washington* was recounted in the Arthur Marx biography, *Goldwyn*. Did Stewart "go Hollywood" with a suitably swelled head at this period? Even Henry Fonda thought he did. But when his girlfriends are, in order, Ginger Rogers, Norma Shearer, Loretta Young, and Marlene Dietrich, a superiority complex might result. Insight into Dietrich was provided by Hollywood writer and actor Steve Hayes, who knew Marlene in the 1940s and '50s.

Stewart and de Havilland became quite the couple in 1940—to fan magazines the perfect couple with marriage inevitable. My previous work, *Errol & Olivia*, provided ample background material on what made de Havilland tick; in fact, she and Jim were a lot alike, and this one could have won over Alex and Bessie back home except for one fact: Olivia's career was her life at this time and she was even less matrimonially minded than Stewart.

These days, more than seventy-five years past the outbreak of World War II, global history has been disconnected from the making of classic pictures like *The Philadelphia Story*, but the shadows cast by world events were giant—especially for Bristol-born Cary Grant and for Jim Stewart, who had already made it his personal goal to join the Army Air Corps.

8. Seeing History

I only recently discovered that my friend Trudy had been an eyewitness to the aftermath of *Kristallnacht* and had seen Hitler speak and had lived through RAF bombings at the beginning of the war. These experiences plus her later intersection with the Eighth Air Force in the Frankfurt area made her viewpoint critically important to the narrative. Gertrud was only five years old when she saw the Führer, so she remembers being frightened by Hitler but not details of the day. The account of what he said was drawn from various repositories of his major speeches and color newsreels documenting the launching of the *Tirpitz*. Among the items left on the "cutting room floor" were stories about Gertrud's visits to the farm of Antje, her nanny, across the Dutch border, with Holland already under German occupation. When the Siepmanns fled from Wilhelmshaven, their first stop was that farm in Holland before they moved on to various places and finally arrived in remote Ottmannsdorf.

9. Restless Spirit

Jim's was indeed a restless spirit from childhood on when he would grow bored with any routine. Acting gave him new people to become in a new setting and facing new challenges every couple of months. But by the second half of 1940, he could feel himself growing bored with vehicles like *Pot O' Gold*, which he refused to see on first run and came face-to-face with only when it appeared on television a decade later. He called it "awful." Military service began to look better and better, and he actually felt relief when he "won the lottery" and was drafted. His recounting of the solo flight from Kansas City back to Hollywood came from the James Reid *Modern Screen* piece of February 1941, in which Jim also plainly stated that he wanted to join the Air Corps. The Michael Bandler Papers at Brigham Young University proved extremely valuable in telling the story of Jim's deferment, his father's reaction, and the events that ensued. The official doctor's statement about the biology of Jim Stewart was found in his personnel file.

10. The Eagle

Clem Leone provided remarkably accurate memories of life in South Baltimore in 1941 at a time when America remained isolationist even as the Japanese and Nazi empires were gobbling up territory around the world.

11. Alias James Smith

The Bandler Papers contained an account of Stewart's "crack-up" in his Stinson 105 just days before he was to report for induction into the Army Reserve and detailed accounts of the crazy morning he reported to a street corner and was marched off to the induction station. Evidence that Louis B. Mayer and the War Department were working together to keep Stewart stateside can be found when coupling Jim's memory of his conversation with Mayer and documents in his personnel files that state Jim was to report to Wright Field to make recruitment films for the Air Corps. From his earliest days at Fort MacArthur, it's clear that Stewart would fight stridently to be allowed to serve on the front lines of Europe. Stewart's Army personnel file runs hundreds of pages and provides details about his progression through the ranks and his battles to see active service in the war. The files also contain the endorsement letters written by his friends as Jim sought to earn his wings as a military pilot.

12. Overachiever

Clem described the experience of sitting in the high school auditorium listening to FDR's December 8, 1941 speech, and the sudden shift in sentiment in America from isolationism to revenge. Even an A student two months from graduation was ready to run off and enlist, and only his mother's insistence that he finish school kept him at home.

13. Static Personnel

The story of Stewart caught between the worlds of the Army and Hollywood is hinted at in his personnel file and has been told in biographies. *Winning Your Wings*, one of the most successful recruiting films of World War II, is available for review. Owen Crump's Oral History at the Academy of Motion Picture Arts and Sciences was a key document to help tell the story of *Winning Your Wings* production. (Owen Crump interviewed by Douglas Bell, pages 4 through 16 on October 22, 1991, ©1994 Academy Foundation.) My site visits to Moffett Field while a contractor for NASA provided insights into the place where Stewart spent his early military career. Research into the Academy Awards ceremony of 1942 was conducted at the Academy's Margaret Herrick Library. Information about Stewart's relationship with Dinah Shore was found in gossip columns of the day and in Stewart biographies.

14. A Game of Chess

Interviews with Clem Leone revealed his desire to volunteer for service to ensure he could choose the Air Corps. Research into changes to draft laws after the outbreak of war completed the story.

15. Destination: Meat Grinder

Stewart's personnel file includes information on his transfers and responsibilities at each airfield. While his fame proved to be a hindrance in landing a combat assignment, his age was even more of a deterrent. He was much too old and much too tall to be fighter pilot material, and under normal circumstances all he could have or should have expected as a flying officer above thirty years of age was a series of assignments as a multi-engine instructor stateside training young pilots and copilots. Starr Smith's book *Jimmy Stewart: Bomber Pilot* provided some nice detail on Stewart's time at Gowen, and military records filled in some blanks on the crashes of training flights. The two-part, in-depth article "Jimmy Stewart's Finest Performance" that Beirne Lay, Jr., wrote for the *Saturday Evening Post* detailed the dangerous pace of training at this time. Nick Radosevich was quoted in a *Charlotte Sun* article by Don Moore dated October 22, 2006. Information about the formation of the 445th Bomb Group (Heavy) and Jim's appointment as squadron commander of the 703 was found in the Records of the Army Air Forces volume, "History of the 445th," a record compiled during the war by R.A. Kidwell, and a second, "History of the 445th Bombardment Group (Heavy)," compiled by Rudolph J. Birsic in 1947. Marina Gray, one of my researchers, created dossiers on each pilot under Stewart's command.

Insights on the 703rd Squadron were provided by Bill Minor, copilot of *Gremlins Roost*, and Barry Shillito, copilot of *Pissed Off/ Our Baby*. Minor's account of the Warrior Hotel incident was told to me in my interviews with him. Also, Minor forwarded documents pertaining to the copilots of the 445th who had formerly been fighter pilots. Otis Rhoney was quoted speaking about the fighter pilot conflict in the article "From Hickory to Normandy" in the *Hickory Daily Record*, September 27, 2010. Information about the B-24 was provided by Minor and Shillito, two men who flew the Libs, with corroboration by Ralph Stimmel as quoted in the online piece "Liberator Explosion" by Colin Schroeder (http:// www.39-45war.com/liberator.html). Martin W. Bowman's book *B-24 Combat Missions* is one of the best sources for understanding the Liberator and the men who flew them. The incident with the failed practice bombing mission and Gen. Streett's reaction was related by Barry Shillito. Jim Myers' feelings about the B-17 were made known in the article "He Flew with Jimmy," published online by Don Moore.

My flights in the cockpits of both the B-17 and the B-24 and in-air exploration of the forward navigator and bombardier positions, catwalk and bomb bay, waist guns, and tail turret positions of both ships provided helpful background regarding the feel of the planes on the ground and in the air. Information about the 703rd Squadron was found in the Records of the Army Air Forces set of documents entitled "Individual History of the 703rd Bombardment Squadron."

16. Boy Scout

My interviews with Clem Leone provided detail about his grueling half day of basic training on the beach in Miami and then his meteoric rise to technical sergeant. Key events in Leone's military career were related in the *Baltimore Sun*. Leone's experience mirrored that of the many thousands of men selected for service on heavy bombers.

17. Daft

Information on the Norden bombsight was found in multiple sources, including *B-24 Bombing Missions* by Bowman and *Consolidated B-24 Liberator* by Graham M. Simons. The early history of the Eighth Air Force, including Ploesti, was detailed in *Army Air Forces in World War II*, published by the Office of the Air Force. Information also was drawn from *The Mighty Eighth* by Gerald Astor, who covered the diverging strategies of the RAF (carpet bombing

German cities and killing indiscriminately by night) and United States Army Air Forces (bombing strategic targets by day).

18. Shakedown

The passage of the 445th to the United Kingdom was detailed in the "History of the 445th" by Kidwell and "History of the 445th Bomb Group" by Birsic. The loss of Albert Poor's ship, *Sunflower Sue*, was mentioned in Kidwell, but details appeared in John Harold Robinson's *A Reason to Live*. Robinson also provided additional details in correspondence with Bill Minor. Barry Shillito described the renaming of *Pissed Off* in an August 2015 interview. Descriptions of Tibenham and Station 124 were based on my visits conducted in late November in damp, cold, rainy weather identical to that first experienced by the men of the 445th in November 1943. Supplemental facts about Station 124 and surrounding bases were found in Roger A. Freeman's *Airfields of the Eighth: Then and Now*. Information about the "schooling" of bomb group personnel was related by the interview subjects and supplemented by *B-24 Combat Missions*. Pete Abell's shakedown flight with Stewart and Leone was described by Clem Leone, with additional details about the Abell crew found in *The Erwin Nine* by Hilda Padgett.

19. Pushed by Angels

Galland's own writings detail his rise to prominence among German fighter aces and his conviction that the Me 262 could win the war for Germany. *Fighter General* provided additional insights, as did *Fighting the Bombers*, edited by David C. Isby. Statistics about the number of German fighters in production in 1943 were found in *Death from the Heavens* by Kenneth P. Werrell.

20. Mission Today

Details of the December 2, 1943, London press conference were found in the Michael Bandler Papers at Brigham Young University. The best-detailed look at a mission briefing was found in the November 29, 1943, issue of *Life* magazine in an article entitled "Target: Germany." Details of mission number one of the 445th Bomb Group to Kiel, Germany, were found in World War II Combat Operation Reports 1941–1945, 445th Bomb Group, Box 2229. These reports on each mission detail the personnel on the planes, the position of the planes in the formation, the ordnance dropped, weather reports, the route to and from target, summaries of flak and enemy aircraft encountered, and intelligence interrogation reports compiled with each crew during post-mission debrief.

The pilot's checklist was covered in the War Department training film *Flying the B-24D 4-Engine Land Bomber*. Hal Turell's account of B-24 takeoffs was found on the 445th Bomb Group web site at 445bg.org. Of historical note, the December 20 mission to Bremen resulted in the incident detailed in *A Higher Call* by Adam Makos and Larry Alexander, in which the B-17 *Ye Olde Pub* was shot to pieces and barely able to stay in the air; the crippled bird was escorted over flak batteries and back to the safety of the North Sea by German fighter ace Franz Stigler in one of the most compassionate incidents of World War II.

21. A Late Breakfast

The "History of the 703rd Bombardment Squadron" contains details about life at Tibenham. Combat Mission Reports provided detail on the December 16 mission to Bremen. Robinson's *A Reason to Live* described Stewart's order to provide a late breakfast for the fliers of the Bremen mission.

22. Topaz Blue

The combat mission report for Bremen provided all necessary details and was supplemented by Robinson's account in *A Reason to Live*. This was the first mission for Harold Eckelberry, waist gunner of *Lady Shamrock*, who wrote a diary entry for each mission, and for December 20 he mentioned Captain Stewart by name as his copilot. Bill Minor's temper tantrum on the Christmas Eve mission was related by Minor along with the story of his apology to Gil Fisher. Stewart's quote about being happy in the service was found in Quirk's *James Stewart: Behind the Scenes of a Wonderful Life*.

23. Bailout

Clem Leone recounted the story of the Hansen flight in a 2014 interview, and a year later I learned from Bill Minor that Hansen had been one of the P-40 fighter jocks reassigned to copilot status aboard Liberators. Minor called the death of Hansen "an emotional ordeal" made all the more frustrating by B-24 aircraft that weren't up to the rigors of daily operation. Said Minor, "Our single-engine training was better suited to the fighter pilot's job than the multi-engine training had been for bomber multi-engine pilots."

24. Roman Candle

Details of the December 30 mission were found in the Combat Mission Reports, and Barry Shillito recounted for me the fact—not documented elsewhere—that when Sharrard and Stewart pulled *Tenovus* out of formation and returned to base, Saunders and Shillito in *Liberty Belle* took that spot, and shortly thereafter were shot down. Robinson saw *Liberty Belle* go down as related in *A Reason to Live*. After two-and-a-half weeks of combat operations, the stress on Stewart was beginning to mount, whether he flew on a particular day or not. Examples of Stewart's letters home to relatives of downed fliers from the 703 survive and reveal the pressure on a leader in these circumstances. The buzzing of Tibenham by buddies of the waylaid fighter pilots was chronicled in the "History of the 703rd Bombardment Squadron" in the Air Force archives. Details of Jim's relationship with Bill Minor were related by Minor in interviews. Information about Stewart's liaison with a woman in

Tibenham was revealed by Gloria Stewart to Michael Munn and appeared in Munn's Stewart bio.

25. January on the Rhine

Details on the January 7 mission to Ludwigshafen were found in the Combat Mission Reports, with additional descriptions by Robinson in his book and Eckelberry in his diary. The erroneous compass heading of the 389th was covered in Starr Smith's book and mentioned in intelligence interrogation reports. It was also described in the commendation Stewart received for his conduct that day.

26. The Dungeon of Eppstein

Gertrud Siepmann wrote about the move to Eppstein and its close proximity to Frankfurt, where she would soon intersect with the Eighth Air Force as she watched the massive bomber stream fly overhead. An understanding of Eppstein with its ancient castle resulted from my site visit in November 2015. Old Town Frankfurt has been reconstructed to its pre-war appearance. I spent two days at the 2015 *Christkindlmarkt* celebration of German food, music, and Christmas that reaches back a couple of centuries. This close-up experience with German culture reminded me that most of these people were descendants of combatants and civilians of World War II, and that many citizens of Frankfurt and of Germany as a whole were caught in the crossfire of the war and just wanted it to end.

27. Iceman

The Glenn Miller visit to Tibenham was mentioned in *Airfields of the Eighth* and also by my on-site guide in explorations of the lands comprising the old base, Eric Ratcliffe, 445th Bomb Group historian. Details of the January 21 mission to Bonnières and the January 29 mission to Frankfurt were obtained from the Combat Mission Reports. The Beirne Lay, Jr., quote was found in his *Saturday Evening Post* two-part article about Stewart's war service. The collision of B-24s near Tibenham's runways was mentioned in "History of the 445th" by Kidwell and in Robinson's *A Reason to Live*. Additional details were provided by Eric Ratcliffe. Wright Lee's quote was taken from his excellent book, *Not As Briefed*.

28. Baptism

The Frankfurt mission of January 29 provided an intersection of three characters, Stewart, Leone, and Siepmann. It was a memorable first mission for Clem, who watched a falling bomb shear off engine No. 3. My interviews with Leone provided details about the Frankfurt mission, which were corroborated by the official records. The bomb group's public affairs officer wrote a feature story on the last flight of the *Shirley Raye* from the perspective of the Blomberg crew's engineer, Richard McCormick. This document was found in the "History of the 445th." I had hoped to develop the character of Princess Marie Alexandra of Baden, a granddaughter of Tsar Nicholas I, who was working as a volunteer aid worker in Frankfurt and was killed at the age of forty-one in the bombing that day, but felt I had to let her go because of the other German characters that had emerged.

29. Boys Will Be Boys

Accounts of life at Tibenham were drawn from all the men I interviewed as well as from "History of the 445th," and from letters from Tech. Sgt. Bob Springer, a radio operator in the 702nd Squadron. My understanding of the village of Tibenham and the layout of the base, including Site 7 and Stewart's quarters, were the result of onsite visits in 2015. Jim's disdain for the press was noted throughout the war and cited specifically in the article "Stewart Said Loneliest Man," which appeared in his hometown newspaper, the *Indiana Evening Gazette*, on Monday January 10, 1944.

30. Mother Nature's a Bitch

No trace of Earle Metcalf, his crew, or *Billie Babe* was ever found. The New Testament that Metcalf had carried to Tibenham from the States turned up in 2015; apparently he had loaned it to a crew member grounded by frostbite. Somehow the Bible ended up as a listing on eBay, where it was purchased by a World War II buff and returned to the family. The Rüsselsheim mission was documented in the Combat Mission Reports, as was the mission to Gilze-Rijen six days later. Winter was proving to be relentless, especially four miles up, and causing all manner of malfunctions in the planes and frostbite in the men.

31. Fat Dogs

Galland wrote about his day chasing the bomber formation, shooting down a B-17, and then learning firsthand the danger of the new American P-51 Mustang and barely escaping with his life. "I simply fled," was the way Galland phrased it.

32. Argument, Part One

Volume three of the *Army Air Forces in World War II, Europe: Argument to V-E Day*, published by the Office of the Air Force, provided perspective on the Pointblank Directive and Operation Argument (although I avoided direct use of Pointblank because I didn't want to overwhelm the reader with code names.) Gerald Astor's *The Mighty Eighth* and Bill Yenne's *Big Week* were instrumental in gaining perspective on Operation Argument, and Astor documented the predictions of meteorologist Irving Krick that proved accurate enough to allow Argument to commence. The exchange between Hodges and Timberlake was recounted in part two of Beirne Lay's *Saturday Evening Post* series on Stewart. Combat Mission Reports provided the detail on Brunswick, with support from Eckelberry's diary—including the kiss Eck received from Killer Manning when Conley's crew arrived back at Tibenham.

33. Argument, Part Two

Combat Mission Reports provided details on the scrubbed February 22 mission to Gotha and the redo two days later. Interviews with Clem Leone brought to light the sudden chaos when an Fw 190 hit *Wacky Donald* with incendiaries as she approached the target, part of the giant running air battle that ensued when Galland's fighters jumped the Second Combat Wing formation in repeated attacks.

In September 1979 during the construction of new housing near the city of Hardenberg, Holland, the nose turret of *Wacky Donald* was unearthed. When the plane had crashed, killing Blomberg, McCormick, and Cooper (with Sheppard and Gunning already dead), she had destroyed the home of a farmer named Reinders, and the nose had bored into the earth. Located in 1979 with the twin .50 caliber machine guns was an unopened aluminum box containing belts of ammunition. The Explosive Clearance Service of Culemborg was called to secure the scene.

34. Bloodbath

The loss of the ships of Skjeie and Abell was documented in the Combat Mission Reports, with additional information on the Abell crew contained in *The Erwin Nine*. Wright Lee described his experiences on the Gotha mission in his book, *Not As Briefed*. The battle over Gotha was so bloody that a special narrative was created by the 445th to help explain what had happened, portions of which were reprinted in this chapter. Jim's sleepless night prior to the February 25 mission and his quotes were taken from Starr Smith. Combat Mission Reports detailed the mission to Fürth, which was also flown by Robinson of the Wright Crew and described in *A Reason to Live*, and by Eckelberry on the Conley crew and captured in his diary. Robinson described the anti-aircraft hit to *Dixie Flyer* that almost knocked Stewart out of the ship. The direct flak hit to *Nine Yanks and a Jerk* was covered in Scott E.

Culver's book of the same name. It was a miracle that both planes and crews made it home under those conditions. Jim Myers described Stewart's post-mission condition in the newspaper article "He Flew with Jimmy Stewart."

35. Physics Lesson

Fliers sometimes awakened in a free-fall after being concussed by an exploding plane. Wright Lee described a similar experience in *Not As Briefed*. Interviews with Clem Leone brought to light the moments after *Wacky Donald* exploded under him. He parachuted to earth far enough south of Hardenberg that German authorities didn't spot him. But then they had their hands full with Varga and McKee from the Blomberg crew, both of whom had come down in the village of Gramsbergen. I visited all these sites to understand the terrain where Leone landed to begin his months on the run.

36. The Big B

Stewart's displeasure over the performance of his pilot on the March 15 mission was recorded in the Combat Mission Reports. His temper was growing short now after becoming a little "flak happy" with the February 25 direct hit. Reports for the March 22 mission detailed the primary and secondary targets and decision to bomb Berlin as a general target. A character that appeared in rough drafts of *Mission* was Selma Lesser, a German Jew who spent the war hidden in a basement in Berlin. After she had lost everything, Allied bombing even destroyed the building in which she was hiding. Selma's diary touched me, but I felt that the story of the Siepmanns was as far as I could delve into the German civilian viewpoint without too much disruption to the Stewart storyline.

37. No-Nonsense Men

Biographical information for Ramsey Potts was found in his *Washington Post* obituary and in *The Mighty Eighth*, among other sources. Stewart's transition to the 453rd was detailed in Starr Smith's book and in *An Emotional Gauntlet* by Stuart J. Wright. I consulted Combat Mission Reports for Stewart's early work with the 453rd and especially for his first mission flying to Wessling and the Dornier factory. Supplementary information was found in the online article "Short Snorter Linked to Movie Star," by Kerry Rodgers at numismaster.com.

38. The Sumatran

Clem Leone detailed his life on the lam in Holland to me in a series of interviews. His collection includes many photos and letters from people who helped him elude German authorities along the way. His false identify as a "deaf and dumb Sumatran" got him through close scrapes until his luck finally ran out in Antwerp. Leone's experiences are intended to remind the reader just how close Jim Stewart was to a similar life on the run or to death like Blomberg or Skjeie in a flaming Liberator.

39. Invasionitis

The "History of the 453rd Bombardment Group" found in Air Force records provided a running narrative about the days preceding invasion and conveys the excitement men like Stewart felt as D-Day was at hand. The East Anglia bomb groups might have played a prominent role in the success of the landings had it not been for the weather. The May 25 mission had been a near disaster and revealed an air commander coming apart at the seams. He didn't fly for the next fifty-six days. Beirne Lay's assessment of that mission was found in part two of the *Saturday Evening Post* series.

40. They Are Coming!

Gertrud described the dogfights she witnessed in autobiographical pieces written in the 1990s. Interviews with me shook loose her dark memory of seeing the American aircrew paraded through Eppstein and assailed by her neighbors. She vividly recalled the strafing attacks by groups of P-47s.

41. Germany Burning

Wright's *An Emotional Gauntlet* contained the Eagleson quote. The Radosevich episode was found in a 2006 *Charlotte Sun* article by Don Moore. The Kassel raid that decimated the bomb group at Tibenham was described by Kidwell in the "History of the 445th." Combat Mission Reports provided detail about the Reisholz raid and included many quotes by Stewart about the effectiveness of the six-ship sections. Combat Mission Reports also were consulted for the raids on Homburg and Halle.

42. The Great Aviation

Galland's writings were an invaluable reference for the German perspective on the relentless American bombing campaign, with supporting information found in *Fighter General, Fighting the Bombers,* and *Hitler's Eagles: The Luftwaffe 1933–45*. Hans Siepmann's diary spoke numerous times of the "secret weapon" that would save the day for Germany; indeed, if Galland had been able to use twin-engine jet aircraft as fighters in 1944 when German industrial production was still formidable, the course of the war would have been changed. But his two jet fighter groups were formed much too late to stem the tide.

43. Grounded

Combat Mission Reports chronicled Stewart's last mission to Achmer. As had happened on the way to Troyes, Jim no longer had the confidence and quick decision-making skills that had made him a success in his first two-plus months leading attacks. Starr Smith touched on the circumstances that led to Stewart's grounding, and Barry Shillito had heard anecdotal information about it. By then, Stewart didn't have any reason to fly; the war had been won.

44. Marching to Death

Multiple interviews with Clem Leone provided the basis for this chapter, supported by his own files collected in an attempt to understand what he had endured. Government records described conditions at Stalag Luft IV; a government investigation was conducted about the death march, and testimony of survivors found in those hearings was used to supplement descriptions of the experiences of Leone and the others. Information about the march is easily obtained on the Internet and makes for compelling reading.

45. Aged in East Anglia

It was quite a juxtaposition, writing the chapter about Leone and his lice one day, and then transitioning to Stewart at the Savoy the next. Such were the fates for fliers on the same mission—most made it home and lived one life; some didn't and lived another, if they lived at all. My interviews with Barry Shillito included his description of returning to Hethel and meeting up with a greatly changed Jim Stewart. Starr Smith discussed Jim's last days of active service, as did Quirk and Munn. Jim provided his own eyewitness account in *Haywire* of seeing Leland Hayward at the bottom of the gangplank. In particular, Munn quoted Jim in nice detail about the afternoon spent at the *Queen Elizabeth*. Newspaper accounts described Stewart's appearance and demeanor as he returned home, and *Life* did the cover story and photo essay in which Jim represented the millions returning home from the war. The September 4 issue of the *Indiana Evening Gazette* covered Jim's homecoming; another article in the *Chester Times* mentioned Jim's intention to "loaf" in Indiana for a while. John McElwee, always a go-to source for perspective on cinema history, provided context for the Hollywood to which Stewart returned, with supporting quotes supplied by Hank in *Fonda: My Life*. Various news articles quoted Jim on his frame of mind and doubts that there was still a place for him in Hollywood as a leading man.

46. Gold Light

The Last Mogul by Dennis McDougal proved to be an excellent source for background on Lew Wasserman, with support from *When Hollywood Had a King* by Connie Bruck. *Fonda: My Life* described Stewart's habitation of Peter and Jane's "playhouse." The emergence of *It's a Wonderful Life* as the first Stewart post-war picture was covered in various Capra biographies and documented in the Frank Capra Archives at Wesleyan University. The conversation about Stewart accepting the role became a favorite story for both men and grew in scope over the years. This version was recorded soon after it had taken place and published in *Motion Picture* magazine in conjunction with the release of *It's a Wonderful Life* at Christmas 1946. Visits to the Margaret Herrick Library unearthed details about the film's production. My understanding of movie sets results from a quarter-century in film production and many visits to Hollywood studios and movie locations, including Encino.

Epilogue: Reaching Beyond

It's always a challenge to take characters to their twilight years and death. I was aided in this task by Marina Gray, whose research on the pilots proved invaluable throughout the project. The Stewart Papers at BYU shed light on hidden aspects of Jim's post-war acting career. The reminiscences of Clem Leone and Trudy McVicker detailed their lives up to today, and Hans Siepmann's unpublished diary, provided by Trudy, offered a fascinating look at the fall of the Reich as seen by a German officer. One story I decided not to tell in the epilogue involved Robert Terrill, Jim's group commander at Tibenham. At ninety-two, Terrill committed suicide at the grave of his late wife at Arlington National Cemetery in 2014, a tragic end to the life of someone critical to this story. I didn't have the opportunity to meet Colonel Terrill, and how I wish I could have involved him in the development of *Mission* for so many reasons.

GLOSSARY

Bandits—American pilots' nickname for German fighters.

Bf 109—a long, slender single-engine German fighter aircraft produced by Messerschmitt.

BTO—"bombing through the overcast" via early radar technology built into special Pathfinder B-24s.

Buncher beacon—a radio tower that attracts planes for assembly prior to a mission.

CAVU—pilot reference to Ceiling And Visibility Unlimited, or perfectly clear flying weather.

Combat box—a set formation of heavy bombers deployed in triangles of three each, offering maximum defensive protection from the machine gun positions on each plane.

Entrain—dropping of bombs one at a time.

ETO—European Theater of Operations.

Feathering a prop—shutting down a damaged engine so the propeller no longer spins.

Flak—German anti-aircraft fire; known as "ack-ack" to the British.

Fw 190—dangerous German fighter produced by Focke-Wulf.

Gee, Gee-H, H2X—various radar technologies built into Pathfinder B-24s for the purposes of "bombing through the overcast."

Hardstand—paved pad big enough to hold a bomber and the place where it was serviced; also known as a "frying pan" for its round shape.

Indians—German pilot nickname for Allied fighters.

I.P.—initial point of the bomb run; from there a straight line to target.

Ju 88—maneuverable twin-engine German bomber produced by Junkers.

Jug—nickname of the P-47 Thunderbolt American fighter-bomber.

Lightning—the P-38 twin-engine, twin-fuselage American pursuit plane.

Mae West—life preserver worn over the flight suit in case of a water landing.

Me 262—twin-engine jet fighter-bomber produced by Messerschmitt; the world's first jet aircraft.

Mickey—nickname for H2X "bombing through the overcast" technology loaded on Pathfinder aircraft.

M.P.I.—mean point of impact, the spot just short of the target where the lead bombardier aims his bombs.

Mustang—the P-51 advanced American single-engine fighter that entered use at the end of 1943.

Pathfinders—B-24s loaded with special technology that helped the formations find targets through heavy overcast. Pathfinder or H2X aircraft led most formations.

Perimeter or peri track—the paved road circling the runways; used for Liberators to taxi into position and as an access road for vehicles.

"S"—in-flight series of maneuvers to slow down a formation.

Salvo—dropping of a bomb load all at once.

Spitfire—the British single-engine fighter in heavy use in the war.

Splasher beacon—a permanent radio beacon in England used for large formations of bombers to gather prior to a mission.

Thunderbolt—versatile American P-47 single-engine fighter-bomber.

Toggling—the act by a bombardier of flipping his bomb switch when he sees the lead bomber drop; also refers to the act of a pilot turning over control of the plane to his bombardier.

Undercast—the cloud layer beneath an aircraft, expressed as a percentage; 5/10 represents partly cloudy; 10/10 equals solid cloud cover.

USAAF—U.S. Army Air Forces.

Walk-around bottle—a portable oxygen tank that a flier plugs into to allow freedom of movement in a bomber at high altitude.

Warhawk—the P-40 single-engine American fighter.

Window or chaff—strips of aluminum foil thrown out the waist windows of the plane to confuse enemy radar.

Zebra—garishly painted B-24s used to assemble aircraft after takeoff.

SELECTED BIBLIOGRAPHY

Astor, Gerald. *The Mighty Eighth: The Air War in Europe as Told by the Men Who Fought It*. New York: Donald I. Fine Books, 1997.

Basinger, Jeanine. *The It's a Wonderful Life Book*. New York: Alfred A. Knopf, 1986.

Bowman, Martin W. *B-24 Combat Missions*. New York: Metro Books, 2009.

Carigan, William. *AD LIB: Flying the B-24 LIBERATOR in World War II*. Manhattan, Kansas: Sunflower University Press, 1988.

Childers, Thomas. *Soldier from the War Returning: The Greatest Generation's Troubled Homecoming from World War II*. New York: Houghton Mifflin Harcourt, 2009.

Craven, Wesley, and James Lea Gate, Editors. *The Army Air Forces in World War II*. Washington: Office of Air Force History, 1983.

Culver, Scott E. *Nine Yanks and a Jerk*. Lexington, Kentucky, 2016.

Enloe, Cortez F., Editor. *The Effect of Bombing on Health and Medical Care in Germany*. Washington: War Department, 1945.

Fishgall, Gary. *Pieces of Time: The Life of James Stewart*. New York: Scribner, 1997.

Fonda, Henry as told to Howard Teichmann. *Fonda: My Life*. New York: New American Library, 1981.

Fonda, Jane. *My Life So Far*. New York: Random House, 2005.

Freeman, Roger A. *Airfields of the Eighth: Then and Now*. London: After the Battle Publications, 1978.

Galland, Adolf. *The First and the Last*. San Bernardino: Popular Classics Publishing, 2015.

Hayward, Brooke. *Haywire*. New York: Alfred A. Knopf, 1977.

Isby, David C., Editor. *Fighting the Bombers: The Luftwaffe's Struggle Against the Allied Bomber Offensive*. London: Greenhill, 2003.

Jablonski, Edward. *Airwar: An Illustrated History of Air Power in the Second World War*. Garden City, New Jersey: Doubleday, 1971.

Keeney, L. Douglas. *The Pointblank Directive*. Oxford: Osprey Publishing, 2012.

Kershaw, Robert. *A Street in Arnhem: The Agony of Occupation and Liberation*. Philadelphia: Casemate, 2014.

Lee, Wright. *Not As Briefed: Memoirs of a B-24 Navigator/Prisoner of War 1943-1945*. Spartanburg, South Carolina: Honoribus Press, 1995.

Makos, Adam with Larry Alexander. *A Higher Call*. New York: Berkley Caliber, 2012.

McNab, Chris. *Hitler's Eagles: The Luftwaffe 1933-45*. Oxford: Osprey Publishing, 2012.

Meredith, Burgess. *So Far, So Good: A Memoir*. New York: Little, Brown, 1994.

Munn, Michael. *Jimmy Stewart: The Truth Behind the Legend*. New York: Skyhorse Publishing, 2006.

Overy, Richard. *The Bombers and the Bombed: Allied Air War over Europe, 1940-1945*. New York: Penguin Books, 2013.

Padgett, Hilda Britt. *The Erwin Nine*. Johnson City, Tennessee: The Overmountain Press, 1993.

Pilots' Information File 1944: The Authentic World War II Guidebook for Pilots and Flight Engineers. Atglen, Pennsylvania: Schiffer Military/Aviation History, 1995.

Quirk, Lawrence J. *James Stewart: Behind the Scenes of a Wonderful Life*. New York: Applause Books, 1997.

Rauscher, William V. *Pleasant Nightmares: Dr. Neff and His Madhouse of Mystery*. Neptune, New Jersey: S.S. Adams, 2008.

Reus, Joseph H. *Kriegsgefangener: War Prisoner*. Edgewater, Florida: Atlantis Productions, 2011.

Robbins, Jhan. *Everybody's Man: A Biography of Jimmy Stewart.* New York: G.P. Putnam's Sons, 1985.

Robinson, John Harold. *A Reason to Live.* Memphis: Castle Books, 1988.

Simons, Graham M. *Consolidated B-24 Liberator.* South Yorkshire, United Kingdom: Pen & Sword Aviation, 2012.

Smith, Starr. *Jimmy Stewart: Bomber Pilot.* Minneapolis: Zenith Press, 2005.

Thomas, Tony. *A Wonderful Life: The Films and Career of James Stewart.* Secaucus, New Jersey: Citadel Press, 1988.

Toliver, Raymond F., and Trevor J. Constable. *Fighter General: The Life of Adolf Galland.* Zephyr Cove, Nevada: AmPress Publishing, 1990.

Toye, Donald C. *Flight from Munich.* Salt Lake City: Northwest Publishing, 1993.

Werrell, Kenneth P. *Death from the Heavens: A History of Strategic Bombing.* Annapolis: Naval Institute Press, 2009.

Wright, Stuart J. *An Emotional Gauntlet: From Life in Peacetime America to the War in European Skies.* Madison, Wisconsin: Terrace Books, 2004.

Yenne, Bill. *Big Week: Six Days That Changed the Course of World War II.* New York: Berkley Caliber, 2012.

INDEX

Abell, Peter 129, 130, 131, 132, 177, 239, 240, 241, 258, 319, 323
Achmer mission (3/21/45) 293–296
After the Thin Man 38
Alexander, Ross 21–22, 27, 41–42
Alford, Allen 177
All Quiet on the Western Front 37
Anderson, Maxwell 19
Andrews, Dana 307
Anna Karenina 29
Arnold, Henry ("Hap") 96, 186, 224, 262, 296
Arnold, Walter ("Pop") 100, 101, 102–103
Art Trouble 21
Arthur, Jean 53
Astaire, Fred 37, 45
Ayres, Lew 37
Barrie, Wendy 39, 48
Beau Geste 51
Bend of the River 321
Bennett, Constance 54
Berlin mission (3/22/44) 257–259
Betty 115, 324
Bieck, Bob 261
Big Joe 114, 183, 184
Billie Babe 114, 211
Bismarck, Otto von 20
Black Dog 235

Blair, D. Hall 7
Blomberg, Robert 117, 118, 170, 176, 205–210, 221, 231, 234, 236, 237, 241, 252, 326
Blondell, Joan 314
Blue Angel, The 54
Bob Blair School 64
Boles, John 40
Bombach, Aribert 298, 299
Bonnières mission (1/21/44) 199
Born to Dance 39, 41
Brackett, Charles 48
Brand, Max 53
Bremen mission (12/20/43) 160–167
Brent, George 40
Brown, Clarence 66, 86
Brunswick mission (2/20/44) 227–233, 241
Brunswick mission (3/15/44) 256–257
Bullet Serenade 115, 182, 200
Bunnie 221
Bussing, Henry 240
Call Northside 777 320
Calloway, Cab 304
Capra, Frank 46, 50, 51–52, 69, 314–315, 316, 317, 318, 319
Captain Blood 41
Carbine Williams 321
Carradine, John 42

Carry Nation 17
Chamberlain, Joshua 10
Chaney, Lon 47
Chaplin, Charlie 69, 92
Cheyenne Social Club, The 322
China Clipper 34
Churchill, Winston 120, 301
Clatfelter, Ken 275, 276
Clemens, Charlie 185
Climer, Ted 228
Clover Field 64, 73, 74
Cofield, Curtis 260, 261
Colbert, Claudette 51
Colby, Anita 312–313
Colman, Ronald 29
Cöln 43
Columbia Pictures 50, 51
Come Live with Me 66, 67, 85, 86
Confessions of a Nazi Spy 58–59
Conley, Bill 108, 114, 138, 160, 161, 164, 165, 166, 167, 178, 181, 182, 188, 189, 190, 191, 193–196, 199, 200, 201, 205, 216, 220, 228, 229, 231, 257, 324
Connelly, Jack 66, 86
Conrad, Earl 325
Cook, Leo 108, 111, 114, 122, 139–140, 144, 145, 146–149, 150, 151–152, 153, 154, 200, 324
Cooper, Ed 117, 207, 210, 236, 237, 252
Cooper, Gary 51, 92, 93
Crawford, Joan 39, 45, 51, 54, 92
Crump, Owen 93–94
Cukor, George 61, 69
Curtis, Ross 161
Custer, George Armstrong 8, 9
de Havilland, Olivia 56–58, 59, 64, 92, 93, 240, 308
Destry 53
Destry Rides Again 53, 54, 55, 59, 314
Diamond, Legs 19
Dietrich, Marlene 53–55, 56, 313

Divided by Three 22–23
Dixie Flyer 244, 248, 249
Dooley, Daisy 313
Doolittle, James 95, 186, 279, 292
Douglas, Kirk 308
Durant, Tim 58
Eaker, Ira 96, 136, 186
Eckelberry, Harold 162, 231, 233
Ecstasy 66
Eddy, Nelson 29, 38
Eike, Lester 196
Eisenhower, Dwight 178, 280
Evans, Jim 235, 240, 241
Far Country, The 321
Farmer, Jack 267
Farmer Takes a Wife, The 28
Fisher, Gilbert 106, 168, 169, 176, 186, 200,
Fleming, Victor 28
Flying Down to Rio 37
Flynn, Errol 57, 313, 324, 326
Fonda, Frances 312, 313
Fonda, Henry 17–18, 19, 20, 22, 23, 27–28, 29, 32, 36, 38, 39, 40, 41, 42, 47, 64, 66, 69, 79, 85, 92, 100, 307, 308, 311–312, 313, 322
Fonda, Jane 312
Fonda, Peter 312
Fontaine, Joan 56, 92, 93
Foran, Dick 21
Ford, John 69, 306, 321
Fort MacArthur 82
Fox Studios 21, 22, 41, 49
Frankfurt mission (1/29/44) 200–210
Free Soul, A 46
Friele, Aleta 21, 27, 41
Fürth mission (2/25/44) 244–250, 256
Gable, Clark 1–2, 29, 30, 37, 46, 50, 77, 78, 79, 91, 262–263, 308
Galland, Adolf 24–26, 134–136, 222–223, 285, 286, 290–292, 325
Gallant Lady 171, 174, 175
Garbo, Greta 28, 29, 32, 37, 48, 55

Garden of Allah, The 53
Garland, Judy 69, 77, 78
Gay Divorcee, The 37
Geneva Convention 128
Georgia Peach 233
Gilze-Rijen mission (2/10/44) 219–221
Glenn Miller Story, The 321
Goddard, Paulette 67, 69, 312
Golden Dog, The 16
Goldwyn, Samuel 51
Gone With the Wind 50, 57, 59,
Good Nuff 163
Goodbye Again 17, 20
Gorgeous Hussy, The 39
Göring, Hermann 134, 142,
Gowen Field 99, 100, 101, 102, 117,
    285
Grady, William 23, 28, 31, 39, 77,
    79, 80–81
Grant, Cary 60, 61
Grapes of Wrath, The 69, 92
Great Dictator, The 69
Great Ziegfeld, The 67
Greatest Show on Earth, The 321
Green Gremlin 220
Gremlins Roost 115, 140, 145, 148,
    149, 168, 186, 212, 319
Grosz, George 25
Gunning, John 235, 237
Halle mission (2/27/45) 289
Hansen, Donald 170–175, 176–177,
    178, 225
'Hap' Hazard 115
Harlingen Field 117
Harlow, Jean 38, 42
Harrigan, Nedda 312
Harris, Arthur Travis 301
Hawkins 322
Hawks, Howard 92–93
Hayes, Steve 54
Hayward, Leland 28, 40–41, 46, 55,
    57, 64, 65–66, 86, 102, 303, 304,
    305, 306, 309, 311, 312, 322

He Who Gets Slapped 47
Healy, Ted 39, 42
Hearst, William Randolph 47, 75
Heavenly Body 264, 265, 266
Heck, John 181
Hell Cat 115
Henie, Sonja 54
Henreid, Paul 307
Hepburn, Katharine 60–61, 69
Hickey, Lugan 117, 173, 207, 235,
    237, 297
Hitler, Adolf 20, 63, 115, 134–135,
    142, 227, 241, 258, 262, 264,
    288, 289, 291, 301, 324
Hobbs Field 99
Hodges, James 226, 233, 279
Hodiak, John 307
Homburg mission (11/30/44) 287–288
Homer, Tom 101
Hooper, Odell 270–271, 297
Howard, Shemp 21
Hughes, Howard 64
Hussey, Ruth 77
Huston, John 92, 93
Hynek, J. Allen 326
Iafolla, Sylvia 72, 326
Ice Follies of 1939 51
It Happened One Night 50
It's a Wonderful Life 315–317, 318–
    319
It's a Wonderful World 51
Jack Benny Show, The 320
Jackson, Samuel McCartney 10, 30,
    68, 74, 139,
Johnson, Neil 107, 156, 196, 200,
    216, 217, 218, 244, 245, 246,
    247, 248, 249, 257, 322
Johnson, Van 307
Jones, Bill 156, 176, 181, 182, 183, 228
Kane, Bill 109, 183, 184, 185, 323
Kassel raid 285–286
Kaufman, Al 117, 170–171, 173, 207,
    235

Kaye, Sammy 304
Kells, Clarence 305
Kelly 114, 140, 225, 323, 324
Kidder, Jim 124
Kiel mission (12/13/43) 138–155
Kirchenbauer, Al 256
Kirtland Field 96, 99
Kiser, Bob 108–109, 217, 227, 232, 258, 319
Kolb, Don 276
Krick, Irving 225
Lady Shamrock 114, 160, 161, 162, 164, 165, 166, 182, 183, 188, 193, 196, 199
Lamarr, Hedy 66, 69
Lancaster, Burt 308
Last Gangster, The 41
Laupheim mission (7/19/44) 285
Law, Jack 12–13
Lay, Beirne, Jr. 101, 199–200
Lee, Wright 162, 180, 204, 232, 236, 241, 243
Le Gallienne, Eva 19, 21
Leone, Clement 34–35, 71–72, 88–89, 97–98, 116–118, 130, 131, 132, 133, 170–175, 205–210, 234–238, 241, 251–254, 269–271, 297–299, 326–327
Leone, Stella 34–35, 71, 88–89, 98, 118
Lewis, Diana 77
Liberty Belle 114, 178, 183, 185
Life 51, 306
Lindbergh, Charles 15, 307
Lloyd, Harold 31
Logan, Joshua 16, 17, 18, 19, 21, 47, 48, 312
Lombard, Carole 1, 28, 51, 90, 91, 262
Loomis, Don 31, 70
Lost Horizon 50
Low, Andy 273, 274, 275, 276, 277, 278
Löwenhardt, Erich 24

Loy, Myrna 38
Lubitsch, Ernst 55
Lucky Penny 284, 285
Ludwigshafen mission (1/7/44) 187–196, 302
Lux Radio Theatre 314
Lyon, E.B. 84, 85
MacDonald, Jeanette 29, 38
Made for Each Other 51, 90
Magic Town 319–320
Maltese Falcon, The 93
Man from Laramie, The 321
Man Who Shot Libery Valance, The 321
Mandl, Fritz 66
Mannheim mission (12/30/43) 176–184
Mann, Anthony 321
Manning, Killer 233
Mannix, Eddie 30, 73, 77
Marie Antoinette 47
Marshall, George C. 314
Marx Brothers 29
Mather Field 95
Mayer, Louis B. 30, 39, 59, 68, 73, 76–78, 82–83, 85, 261, 308, 309
McCarran Field 91
McClintic, Guthrie 22, 23
McCormick, Myron 16, 19
McCormick, Richard 117, 171, 172–173, 174, 208, 236, 237, 252
McElwee, John 307
McGuire, Dorothy 102, 312
McKee, Bill 117, 174, 205, 208, 234, 252
McLean, Ronald 321
McNaughton, K.P. 86
McNulty, Thomas 326
McVicker, Trudy 326
Meet John Doe 315
Menaker, Norm 241, 258
Mercersburg Academy 14, 15
Meredith, Burgess 19, 21, 55, 75, 79, 80–81, 92, 311, 312
Metcalf, Earle 109, 114, 123, 167, 211, 213, 319

Metro-Goldwyn-Mayer 23, 27, 28–32, 38, 39, 40, 45, 47, 48, 50, 51, 53, 55, 60, 66, 67, 69, 70, 73, 75, 77, 78, 91, 307, 308, 309, 310, 313
"Mickey" (Bombing Through the Overcast) 157, 188, 203, 220, 256, 257, 287, 302
Midsummer Night's Dream, A 41
Miller, Glen 199
Miller, Joe 260, 263
Mines Field 64, 101
Minor, Bill 105, 106, 107, 110, 113, 138, 168–169, 177, 178, 186, 187, 217, 319
Mix, Tom 53
Modern Screen 46
Moffett Field 83, 84, 85, 86, 92, 93, 95, 105
Montgomery, Robert 30, 306
Moorhead, Fergus 8
Morocco 54
Morris, Wayne 307
Morrison Field 115
Mortal Storm, The 58–59, 68, 227
Moulton, Robert 145, 147, 148, 151, 153
Mr. Deeds Goes to Town 50, 315
Mr. Smith Goes to Washington 51–53, 59, 69, 315
Munn, Michael 18
Murder Man, The 31
Mutiny on the Bounty 29
My Love Came Back 59
My Wicked, Wicked Ways 326
Myers, Jim 114, 151, 153, 154, 220, 250
Nagel, Anne 41
Naked Spur, The 321
Narcovich, Joe 107–108, 114, 122, 156, 227, 323
Natwick, Mildred 21
Naughty Marietta 29
Navy Blue and Gold 41

Neal, Stanley 220, 233
Neff, William 7, 14, 15,
Next Time We Love 40, 41
Night at the Opera, A 29
Nine Yanks and a Jerk 114, 200, 201, 203, 218, 221, 247, 250, 323
Ninotchka 48, 55
No Time for Comedy 59–60
Norden, Carl L. 119–120
Normandie 54
O'Brien, Pat 34
Of Human Hearts 42, 169
Olivier, Laurence 60, 69, 92
Our Baby 122, 178, 184, 185, 319, 323
Owen, Alvin 233
Pan American Airways 34
Paper Doll 162
Paramount Pictures 22, 51
Pas de Calais mission (1/14/44) 199
Pasternak, Joe 53, 54,
Pathfinders 157–158, 188, 203, 218, 219, 220, 221, 228, 229, 230, 255–256, 258, 259, 286, 295
Paull, Jim 179
Peck, Gregory 306, 307
Philadelphia Story, The 60–61, 68, 69, 91
Pidgeon, Walter 40, 77
Pissed Off 115, 121, 184, 185, 300, 318
Plato, E.J. 69
Poor, Albert 109, 115, 123, 124, 126–127, 319
Porter, Cole 39, 50
Pot o' Gold 67
Potts, Ramsay, Jr. 260–261, 263–264, 272, 273, 275, 278, 279
Powell, Eleanor 39
Power, Tyrone 307
Queen Elizabeth 303, 305, 317
Queen Mary 115, 121, 143
Quillan, Eddie 31
Radosevich, Nick 102, 113, 284–285
Rae, Melba 324

Raft, George 54
Rankin, John 162, 164–165, 166, 188, 189, 190, 202, 203, 230, 231, 233
Rayford, Marshall 154–155
Raymond, Gene 307
Readers Digest 113
Reagan, Ronald 307
Real Glory, The 51
Rear Window 321
Rebecca 69
Reid, James 46, 47, 48, 65, 74
Reisholz raid (10/15/44) 286–287
Remarque, Erich Maria 54
Reus, Joe 185
Rhoney, Otis 106, 109, 122, 179, 225
Riskin, Robert 319
RKO Radio Pictures 37, 42, 316, 319
Roberta 37
Robinson, Edward G. 41
Robinson, John ("Robbie") 114, 183, 200, 250
Rogers, Ginger 37–38, 42, 45, 48, 50, 58, 92
Roland, Ruth 15
Rooney, Mickey 309
Roosevelt, Franklin Delano 66, 71, 88, 89, 90, 91, 98
Rose-Marie 38
Russell, Rosalind 59–60, 77, 78, 217
Rüsselsheim mission (2/4/44) 218–219
Rutherford, Ann 77, 78
Saunders, Oliver 109, 113, 115, 121–122, 156, 178, 183, 184, 185, 211, 319, 323
Sawyer, Willis 104
Schleichkorn, Gil 257, 258, 324
Seale, Maxie 264, 267
Sears, Ray 263
Seashore, Malcolm 176
Selznick, David O. 50–51, 59, 313
Selznick Studios 90
Sergeant York 92

Seventh Heaven 41
Seymour, M.E. 104
Sharrard, Lloyd 103–104, 108, 115, 122, 123, 124, 138, 149, 173, 178, 179, 181, 182, 183, 216, 221, 324
Shawn, Eric 324
Shawn, Gilbert 324
Shearer, Norma 46–47, 48–49, 54, 92, 313
Shenandoah 321
Sheppard, John 117, 208, 237
Sheridan, Philip 8
Sherman, William T. 8–9
Shillito, Barry 105, 106, 109, 113, 115, 121, 178, 184, 185, 300, 319
Shirley Raye 170, 174, 205, 206, 208, 209, 235, 326
Shop Around the Corner, The 55
Shopworn Angel, The 45
Shore, Dinah 96, 100
Shurtz, William 221, 228
Siepmann, Franz 43
Siepmann, Gertrud 43–44, 62–63, 198, 281–283, 292, 326
Siepmann, Hans 43–44, 63, 292, 325–326
Siepmann, Mariele 43–44, 62, 63, 197, 198, 281, 283
Simon, Simone 41
Simpson, Leland 257, 258, 259
Sin Ship 221
Sioux City Army Air Field 103, 104
Sioux City Journal 110
Siracourt mission (5/15/44) 275
Skjeie, Dave 109, 114, 239, 258, 319
Sky Wolf 233
Small Town Girl 39
Smith, Kent 21
Smith, Starr 264, 300
Smith, Victor 105, 106, 113, 115, 140, 168, 186, 212, 318, 324
Southwest Airways 64, 66, 86
Souza, Milt 106, 109

Spaatz, Carl 96
Speed 39, 42, 48
Speer, Albert 290
St. Johns, Adela Rogers 49
Stackpole, Peter 306
Stakowski, Leopold 90
Star Baby 129, 130, 177, 239–240, 319, 323
Stars in Your Eyes 48
Steinhauer, Jerry 162, 190, 191, 192, 194, 202, 230, 233
Stewart, Alexander Meade 6, 69, 96
death 320
influence on Jim 12, 15, 18, 42, 64, 68, 73, 109–110, 243
military service 8, 10–11, 30, 74, 110, 139
personality 7, 12, 13, 102, 305, 312, 313, 320, 321
views on sex and women 12, 36
Stewart, Archibald 8, 10, 68
Stewart, Elizabeth Jackson 6, 7, 18, 96, 109–110, 305, 321
Stewart, Gloria Hatrick McLean 320, 321, 322
Stewart, James Maitland (1839–1932) 8, 9, 10, 13–14, 16–17, 30, 42, 64, 68, 74, 139
Stewart, James Maitland
acting 11, 16, 17, 18, 19, 20, 21, 22, 30–31, 32–33, 38, 52, 319, 320
ambition to serve 64, 65, 66–67, 68, 69, 73, 83, 84, 87, 305
aviation accidents 75, 106–107, 249–250, 322–323
avoiding press attention in the service 93, 110, 137, 138, 187, 217, 274, 305
B-17 pilot 99, 102, 103, 104, 112
B-24 pilot 102, 103, 112
Best Actor Academy Award 69, 91–92
civilian aviation 13, 22, 64–65, 73–75, 83, 93, 296, 318, 321

commendations/decorations 250, 274, 295–296, 302
court-martial presiding officer 302–303
death of comrades in arms 101–102, 124, 126–127, 183–184, 185–186, 211–212, 268, 310
easily bored 12, 32, 68, 69, 304, 320
education 12, 14, 15–16, 18,
Europe before the war 53–54, 58–59
family mission 6, 8, 9–10, 15, 16, 64, 67, 68, 73
flight instructor 95, 96, 99, 100, 113
home life 6–7, 12, 13, 14, 27, 306–307
in Hollywood 27–33, 36–42, 45–51, 55–60, 66–69, 76–79, 91–93, 305–306, 307–308, 309, 310, 311–312, 316–317
induction and basic training 79–83
introvert 7, 12, 13, 15, 48, 49, 57–58, 78, 100, 187, 216–217, 318
leadership style 103, 105–106, 109, 111, 121–122, 127, 131–132, 158–159, 168–169, 190–195, 199–200, 225, 256, 257, 261, 272–273
music 7, 13, 14, 16, 216
perfectionist 13–14, 276–277, 310
promotions 83, 99, 105, 200, 278, 285, 289, 301–302
refusal to discuss war 308, 310, 322
relationships and sex 12, 15, 18, 36, 37–38, 39–40, 46–50, 54–55, 56–58, 69, 78, 96, 100, 187, 312–313, 319–320
religion 6, 110, 140, 144, 217, 243
stress of combat 138–139, 243–244, 250, 259, 276–277, 288, 295–296, 301, 307, 309–310, 320

weight issues 7, 31, 32–33, 49, 67–68, 70, 288

winning wings 84–87, 90

Stewart, Mary ("Doddie") 12, 55, 57, 109–110, 306

Stewart, Virginia ("Ginny") 12, 55, 57, 102, 306, 312

Stimmel, Ralph 107, 111, 113, 138, 148, 163, 177, 227, 323

Streett, St. Clair 111–112

Strickling, Howard 39, 47, 77, 90, 309

Sullavan, Margaret 17–18, 19, 21, 28, 40, 41, 45, 46, 48, 55, 59, 64, 66, 92, 102, 305, 312, 322

Sunflower Sue 115, 123, 124

Sunset Boulevard 48

Swope, John 17, 36–37, 39, 47, 49, 66, 102, 311, 312, 322

Tale of Two Cities, A 29

Taylor, Robert 30, 40, 79

Tedder, Arthur William 292

Tenovus 115, 122, 123, 179, 181, 182, 183, 185, 226, 228, 233, 267

Terrill, Robert 103, 104, 111–112, 122, 132, 140, 141–142, 143, 144, 145, 176, 178, 187, 200, 210, 259, 262, 273

Thalberg, Irving 30, 47, 261

They Were Expendable 306

Thin Man, The 38

Thomas, Tony 319–320, 326

Three Stooges, The 39

Thunderbird Field 66, 102

Timberlake, Ted 226, 285, 301

Tiranoff, Alexis 102, 312

Tone, Franchot 30, 79

Top Hat 37

Torpey, Charles ("Chick") 109, 115, 163, 217, 227, 258, 324

Toye, Don 265, 267

Tracy, Spencer 31, 32, 38, 79

Travis, R.F. 101

Triangle Players 16

Trippe, Juan 34

Troyes mission (5/25/44) 275–277

Turell, Hal 114, 148, 177

Turner, Lana 69, 77, 78

Twelve O'Clock High 101

Twentieth Century Fox 320

Two Rode Together 321

Udet, Ernst 24

United Artists 67

Universal Pictures 21, 40, 53, 54

University Players 17, 21,

Van Dyke, W.S. ("Woody") 38

Vandagriff, William 244, 245, 246, 248

Vanderhoek, Paul 219, 220, 221

Varga, Emery 117, 172, 174, 207, 208, 252

Vertigo 321

Vitaphone Pictures 21

Vivacious Lady 45, 50

von Richtofen, Manfred 24

von Sternberg, Josef 54

Wacky Donald 235, 236, 237, 238, 251, 269, 297, 325

Walker, Joe 314

Walsh, Raoul 1

Warner Bros. 34, 41, 59, 60, 93

Warner, Jack L. 59, 308

Warrington, Orrie 264, 266–267, 268

Warrior Hotel 110, 138

Wasserman, Lew 306, 309, 311, 313, 315, 320

Watson, Emmett 109, 115, 179, 225, 258, 323

Wayne, John 306, 307–308

We Hold These Truths 90

Webster, Franklin 274

Welles, Orson 90

Wessling mission (4/13/44) 264–268

Westerner, The 51

Wheelright, Ralph 77

Whelan, Tim 31

Why We Fight 314

Widmark, Don 117, 171, 172–173, 174, 206, 210, 236, 237
Wife vs. Secretary 38
Wilde, Cornell 307
Wilder, Billy 48
Wilkerson, Billy 40
Williams, Matt 272
Williams, William ("Mack") 108, 115, 247, 250, 323
Wilson, Francis ("Pappy") 165, 166, 188, 190, 202, 229, 230
Wilson, Woodrow 8
Winchester '73 320–321
Winkler, Otto 77, 90, 91
Winning Your Wings 93–95
Wright Field 77, 83, 84
Wright, George 105, 106, 114, 115, 123, 124, 183, 246, 249
Yamamoto, Isoroku 108
Yellow Jack 22
You Can't Take It with You 46, 50
Young, Loretta 49–50, 56
Young, Robert 41
Zanuck, Darryl 320
Zhukov, Georgy 289
Ziegfeld Girl 67, 85, 310